The Progressive Revolution in Politics and Political Science:
Transforming the American Regime

The Progressive Revolution in Politics and Political Science:
Transforming the American Regime

Edited by

John Marini and Ken Masugi

THE CLAREMONT INSTITUTE
FOR THE STUDY OF STATESMANSHIP AND POLITICAL PHILOSOPHY

ROWMAN & LITTLEFIELD PUBLISHERS, INC.
Lanham • Boulder • New York • Oxford

ROWMAN & LITTLEFIELD PUBLISHERS, INC.

Published in the United States of America
by Rowman & Littlefield Publishers, Inc.
A wholly owned subsidiary of The Rowman & Littlefield Publishing Group, Inc.
4501 Forbes Boulevard, Suite 200, Lanham, Maryland 20706
www.rowmanlittlefield.com

PO Box 317
Oxford
OX2 9RU, UK

British Library Cataloguing in Publication Information Available

Library of Congress Cataloging-in-Publication Data

The progressive revolution in politics and political science : transforming the American
regime / edited by John Marini and Ken Masugi.
   p. cm.
 Includes bibliographical references and index.
 ISBN 0-7425-4973-9 (cloth : alk. paper)—ISBN 0-7425-4974-7 (pbk. : alk. paper)
 1. Political science—United States. 2. Progressivism (United States politics) I. Marini,
John A. II. Masugi, Ken.
 JA84.U5P75 2005
 324.2732'7—dc22   2005008646

Printed in the United States of America

♾™ The paper used in this publication meets the minimum requirements of American
National Standard for Information Sciences—Permanence of Paper for Printed Library
Materials, ANSI/NISO Z39.48-1992.

Contents

PART II: THE PROGRESSIVE PERSUASION IN PRACTICE AND THEORY

Preface

The Progressive Revolution in Politics and Political Science: Transforming the American Regime is the first volume in the Studies in Statesmanship and Political Philosophy series of the Claremont Institute. Future volumes will explore various policy issues and the abiding themes of statesmanship and political philosophy as they illuminate the principles of the American founding. These works will seek to demonstrate the continuing vitality of America's founding principles and the necessity of a resort to first principles on matters of policy and statesmanship. The essays published in the present volume explore the Progressive attempt to undermine the principles of the American founding as the prelude to radical reform based on novel and alien principles. The Progressives were phenomenally successful in this revolutionary endeavor. Subsequent volumes will explore the possibility of reversing the tide of Progressivism that dominated political thought and practice in the twentieth century and restoring the principles of the American founding as the rightful principles of constitutional democracy.
Edward J. Erler
Series Editor

Introduction

John Marini and Ken Masugi

The Progressive Revolution in Politics and Political Science: Transforming the American Regime attempts to elucidate the profound transformation in the theory and practice of American government that occurred throughout the twentieth century. That transformation, the legacy of Progressivism, is impossible to understand without some awareness of the political and intellectual tradition it sought to replace. Whatever diversity existed in their ranks, Progressive reformers were united in their opposition to the political theory of the American founding. That opposition entailed a rejection of the philosophic tradition of natural right and limited government. The natural right tradition was fundamentally transformed by the acceptance of a Philosophy of History that culminated in a fusion of theory and practice made tangible in the Hegelian idea of the state. The state was meant to re-establish a political whole that would reunite the social and political, the public and private, and make citizenship the ground of freedom and virtue.

Progressive theorists sought to recreate various features of the classical city, long since superseded by Christianity and modern political philosophy. Progressivism demanded nothing less than a political solution to the human problem in which the self-evident superiority of science would dispense with the necessity of metaphysics and religion.[1] Consequently, it was the purpose of the state, and its rational

1

bureaucracy, to solve every economic, social, and political problem. It followed that the power of government must be unlimited. In the American Founders' view, it was nature itself which imposed limitations upon the power that could be safely entrusted to human beings: Men are not angels; they are rather "created equal." Consequently, the power and scope of government must be limited, and its fundamental purpose must be to protect the rights of individuals.

On the other hand, the Progressives, by denying those permanent characteristics of human nature, insisted that the transformation of society would result in the alteration of man himself. In their view, at the end of history, or when a democratic society has been achieved, there can be no limitation upon the power of government. Indeed, the purpose of government in the rational, or administrative, state is to solve every human problem through government and its bureaucracy. Moreover, the kind of organized intelligence necessary to solve the political, social, and economic problems of society would be created in the newly established social science disciplines within the research university.

It is not surprising, therefore, that the modern discipline of American political science was created for the specific purpose of becoming the "applied science" of the modern, administrative, state. However, like the other social sciences, its theoretical foundation was derived from an intellectual revolution that occurred in Europe, primarily Germany, at the end of the eighteenth century. It was dependent upon the acceptance of a Philosophy of History that grew out of the political thought of Rousseau, Kant, and Hegel. Their critique of the modern doctrine of natural right in Locke, Sidney, Montesquieu, and Blackstone had the practical effect of destroying the theoretical ground of limited, or constitutional, government. It served also to undermine the older philosophic tradition that had provided the rational ground of modern natural right. Subsequently, the Philosophy of History, which had been established first upon a metaphysical foundation, became authoritative intellectually throughout the scientific community in the biological theories of Charles Darwin. The theory of evolution, a scientific vindication of historicism or the belief that "history shows us that all principles of justice are mutable,"[2] had a great impact upon American Progressive intellectuals in the post-Civil War era. The Progressives attempted not only the redirection of the scope and purpose of government, but the establishment of an empirical science of politics that reflected the new understanding of man as a historical, or evolving, being.

The Hegelian doctrine of the rationality of History together with his concept of the state provided the theoretical ground of Progressivism. By the end of the nineteenth century, the newly trained university intellectuals, and many politicians, had accepted the view that a divinized History, not "the Laws of Nature and of Nature's God," provided the ground of meaningful social and political knowledge. If man makes himself human by his own production, it is not surprising that Progressive intellectuals came to view the economy as the driving force of history. Consider here Charles Beard's *An Economic Interpretation of the Constitution of the United States.*[3] Subsequently, by expanding government's role in the economy and society, the politicized academics hoped to facilitate the transformation of the regime from a constitutional, or limited, government into a modern rational, or administrative, state. It was recognition of the view that the historical process is rational, which made possible the understanding of the meaning of the end of history. In practice, it meant that the universal, and final, principles of politics have made their appearance on the world stage. Once mankind recognizes and accepts that view, there will no longer be partisan quarrels over political principles. Therefore the problems of human life can be solved in a nonpartisan or neutral manner. Politics will be replaced by administration. Furthermore, once a democratic society has been achieved, a technically rational government poses no threat to the liberties of the people. Indeed, freedom itself is redefined in terms of social, rather than individual, purpose. Government is therefore understood to be an ethical organization, an engine of compassion, which establishes a common ground of freedom by progressively redefining and securing rights, now understood as satisfaction of need or desire. Control of the economy was to be a central obligation of government. As Franklin Delano Roosevelt made clear before his election, "I have described the spirit of my programs 'a new deal' which is plain English for a changed *concept* of the duty and responsibility toward *economic* life."[4] In order for men to be free, government must assure that they are no longer necessitous.

The American Constitution, on the other hand, was the product of a tradition of political thought that stretched from Aristotle and Cicero to Locke and Sidney.[5] Although *The Federalist* had touted the "new science of politics" as fundamental to the practical success of good government in the United States, the political science of the Constitution was not an achievement of social science but of traditional political philosophy. It rested upon ancient and modern conceptions of justice, nature, and reason. In its origin, political science—that is, political philosophy—was intended to be a comprehensive reflection on the meaning of justice, or the common good. Such a reflection was possible because of the nature of man, his capacity for reason and choice. The alternative is government by accident and force. *The Federalist's* political science, a "new science of politics" that nonetheless preserved the natural or pre-scientific understanding of the political, rested upon the necessity of a social contract, as the ground of political right. The rational defense of individual rights required the creation of a constitutional government. It was of necessity, limited government, because it was established in recognition of man's nature, his imperfectability, of his unchanging capacity for evil, as well as good. If "the latent causes of faction are sown into the nature of man," as Madison insisted, then tyranny is a problem coeval with political life. Although the end of government is justice, human nature required that the institutions of government must be structured in such a way as to prevent tyranny by making ambition counteract ambition. In short, the political science of the American Founders was inextricably linked to the idea of constitutionalism, which came to be understood as partisan attachment to the Constitution itself.

The American Founders, unlike the Progressives, understood political phenomena directly, as a matter of reflection and choice, unmediated by a Philosophy of History. Theory and practice, or ends and means, were thought to be intelligible and separable. Theory, or understanding, provided the basis for discerning the principles of government. Practice was subordinate to theory and was to be regulated by prudent necessity. It required a reasonable and realistic understanding of the relationship of theory and practice, of ends and means. Consequently, prudence, not science, was the virtue thought to be paramount in terms of understanding political practice. But prudence is necessarily concerned with means; it presupposes the possibility of moral virtue, to direct men to the right—or good—ends. In America, those ends were thought to be good because they are in accordance with the "Laws of Nature and Nature's God." It was the public philosophy embodied in the idea of the social compact which provided the rational and theoretical justification for the Constitution, its institutions of government, and the consensus on the goodness, or justice, of limited government.

The Progressive rejection of the Constitution was a practical necessity once the principles inherent in the idea of natural right and the social compact were denied. The triumph of Progressive thought, which had incorporated the Philosophy of History, and the idea of the state as the ground of social justice, destroyed the theoretical foundation of American constitutionalism. In attempting to establish the new social sciences, and political science as a discipline, Progressivism claimed the authority of the natural sciences, and positivism and empiricism, not philosophy or metaphysics, as the means to attain meaningful knowledge. It was able to do so, by accepting the idea of the state as a normative foundation, and social justice as the goal that could be measured empirically. Thus, it would become possible for the social sciences to separate facts and values, or the empirical and normative. Subsequently, the discipline of political science would become the practical science of the state. It could utilize the empirical method as the means to develop useful knowledge on behalf of the administrative state. At the same time, political science, as a discipline, could no longer make value judgments or speak authoritatively about politics.

The Constitution still animates the institutional structure of the American government through the separation of powers, and many political quarrels are debated on constitutional grounds. But, the political philosophy that provided the *raison d'etre* of constitutionalism is little more than a memory. In the twentieth century, Progressive thought would become dominant in the disciplines of the social sciences and history. It was established as the legal orthodoxy in the acceptance of positivism in the law schools. In short, the political thought that legitimized constitutional government, long under attack in those strongholds of Progressivism, has no institutional support, outside of the apparatus of government itself, which is a creation of the Constitution. The abandonment of the political philosophy upon which constitutionalism rested, could not have but a profound effect upon the structure and functioning of the institutions in a regime which is derived from it. The political branches of government lack any comprehension of their constitutional role, or the necessity of defending it.

Thus, constitutional questions are thought to be the exclusive province of the judiciary. As a result, the Constitution itself has become a part of the agenda of Progressivism. The courts have gradually adopted the Progressive view that the Constitution must be interpreted as a "living" or "evolving" document. The natural right foundation of the social compact, which necessitated distinguishing statutory law from the fundamental (or constitutional) law of the compact, has almost no defenders.

The profound political revolution brought about by Progressivism, combined with the intellectual transformation in the theory of politics, has made it difficult to understand the theory and practice of the original American constitutionalism. As a result, the defense of limited government, the product of the American founding, has become exceedingly difficult. This book is an attempt to lay the foundations for the recovery of an understanding of the difference between Progressivism and constitutionalism. In original essays, the eleven contributors to this volume specify the changes in the new world Progressivism brought into being. As each argues, the Progressive revolution strove to bring about regime change for America. The essays in Part I contrast the views of the American founding with various Progressives on the major political institutions and practices. The authors emphasize the revolutionary differences in the politics of each world-view.

In Part II the contributors characterize the radical nature of Progressivism. They make clear the power of the Progressive persuasion in a variety of contemporary political issues and in the self-understanding of the American mind, in particular that of the profession of political science.

Together, the eleven essays in this book bring to life the power and ambition of the Progressive movement. Moreover, they illuminate the questionable paths down which Progressives and their progeny have taken this country. The essays have a political but nonpartisan purpose—the restoration of constitutional government. Whether liberal or conservative, current policy owes the core of its thinking to the Progressive revolution of a century ago. Though their names lack the renown of a Washington, these revolutionaries saw themselves as transcending the Founding Fathers' colonial shortcomings.

In the first section, six essays note the distance the Progressive revolution has taken us from the Founders' natural rights understanding of American politics and the limited government this necessitates. Thomas G. West makes evident the distance the Progressives have taken us from the views of the Founders on issues such as the rule of law, federalism, and the separation of powers. While the original Constitution has not been entirely replaced, West maintains that the principles on which it was grounded were repudiated by Progressivism; consequently, the institutional structure that the Constitution was intended to establish has been greatly modified.

Four essays contrast the spirit of the founding versus that of the Progressives. By focusing on the conception of self-government espoused by two highly regarded presidents, Will Morrisey notes distinctions rarely even considered between Washington the Founding Father and Theodore Roosevelt, the first Progressive president. Thus, Morrisey's scholarship transcends the current scholarly focus on "leadership" and focuses instead on the fundamental principle of self-government central to the notions of citizenship and statesmanship. The implications of a Progressive versus a constitutionalist approach to the great American dilemma of equality are established by Peter C. Myers in his study of Frederick Douglass. Douglass provides a powerful natural rights argument for the success of a limited Constitution that included black Americans as full citizens. By contrasting James Madison and Woodrow Wilson, Scot J. Zentner provides an alternative explanation of the development of American political parties. Wilson's understanding of democracy and parties is at fundamental odds with Madison's conception of party and of Congress's place in constitutional government. Wilson's radical expansion of rights, argues Paul Carrese, contrasts with the sobriety of Montesquieu, Blackstone, and other philosophic influences on the Founders.

Edward J. Erler concludes the first section in a monograph that reflects on the transformation of the Constitution from a document of organic law to one of organic will. Hence, the entire structure of constitutional government and the appropriate rhetoric of constitutionalism must be reconsidered in any statesmanship that would return us to the principles of the founding.

In Part II, five essays consider the effects of the Progressive revolution on a host of key policy and academic issues—the welfare state, property rights, free speech, and the very self-understanding Americans have of the way they study their history, their political science, and their place in Western civilization. The first two essays note the theoretical bases of the Progressive transformation of social science and politics. John Marini's essay surveys the common themes behind all these developments. From Rousseau to Hegel, Progressivism's political philosophy uprooted the notion that nature provided a standard for political life. The new political science lacked any such moorings and thus could reconstruct itself and the polity at will. John G. West shows the role that Darwinism played in assailing natural rights and religion within the American political tradition. Moreover, he notes the extent to which Darwinism informed the Progressive revolution and its conception of the new welfare state.

At the same time, the Progressive state denigrated the importance of property rights in limiting the political power and enhancing individual virtue. Eric R. Claeys shows how zoning fulfilled the Progressive agenda by allowing local governments to have greater control of how and where their citizens work and live. The crucial political freedom, that of speech, also underwent a transformation in the Progressive era, as can be seen in a careful examination of John Dewey and other Progressive thinkers and their contemporary followers. Thus as Tiffany R. Jones argues, by using the characteristic Progressive notion of reform, government can regulate speech under the guise of campaign finance reform.

Finally, Larry Peterman puts American political science in the greater context of Western civilization itself. He contrasts the contemporary heirs of Progressive political science, in particular economist Anthony Downs, with the founder of political science, Aristotle. In doing so, he shows that the contemporary crisis of American politics, and Western civilization itself, is attributable in part to the rejection of the philosophic tradition of natural right, and its replacement by a Philosophy of History, and the scientific study of politics.

The discovery of the rationality of history transformed the study of politics in the nineteenth century. The attack on constitutionalism by the Progressive intellectuals was animated by a theory of government radically at odds with the view of the American Founders. It is rooted in the theoretical assumptions born of a rejection of the philosophic tradition and the idea of natural right. Most importantly, it entailed the rejection of the principle of limited government, which led to the abandonment of prudence as the fundamental political virtue.

By the end of the twentieth century, the assumption that the unlimited power of government would be used only for benevolent purposes was shattered. Tyranny was not a thing of the past. Moreover, it had become clear that the political moderation of those constitutional democracies opposed to tyranny had been dependent upon a philosophy of government that was rooted in the principles of natural right. It was the people of those regimes that embraced the most radical of the ideas of Progressivism who suffered the greatest tragedies. Though varied in approach and focus, all the articles affirm the central thesis of this book: That the Progressive intellectuals and politicians consciously sought to change the fundamental principles on which this country had been based, and that they succeeded remarkably well in that ambitious endeavor. Although elements of the old regime remain, it remains to be seen whether the political moderation of the governing institutions can long endure in the absence of an understanding of the principles that brought them into being.

Endnotes

1. Indeed, within the state, it is the objectivity of science, which makes it possible for those who seek knowledge to be neutral and nonpartisan. It also necessitates the separation of politics and administration. The rational bureaucracy can exercise unlimited power because it seeks only knowledge, which is to be used on behalf of the common good. Consequently, in Hegel's view, the state provides a haven for science because its goals are compatible: knowledge of "objective truth." As Hegel noted: "the state is universal in form, a form whose essential principle is thought. This explains why it was in the state that freedom of thought and science had their origin ... Science too, therefore, has its place on the side of the state since it has one element, its form, in common with the state, and its aim is knowledge, knowledge of objective truth and rationality in terms of thought." G. W. F. Hegel, *Philosophy of Right*, trans. T. M. Knox (New York: Oxford University Press, 1967), 172-73.

2. Leo Strauss, *Natural Right and History* (Chicago: University of Chicago Press, 1953), 9.

3. Charles Beard, *An Economic Interpretation of the Constitution of the United States* (New York: Free Press, 1941 [originally published in 1913]).

4. Franklin Delano Roosevelt, "Acceptance Speech," Democratic National Convention, July 2, 1932, in *The Public Papers and Addresses of Franklin D. Roosevelt,* Samuel I. Rosenman, ed. (New York: Random House, 1938), 1:659.

5. See Thomas Jefferson, letter to Henry Lee, May 8, 1825, in *Jefferson,* Merrill Peterson, ed. (New York: Library of America, 1984), 1501.

·⁓Part I⁓·

The Progressive Critique of Constitutionalism

·⁓Chapter 1⌣·

Progressivism and the Transformation of American Government

Thomas G. West

Since 1900, but especially since the mid-1960s, American government has been changing into a new form that has been called the administrative state. This revolution—which we will call liberalism, as it calls itself—is as radical as was the American Revolution in 1776. It began with a new theory of justice and of government.

What happened over the last hundred years was, first, a vigorous theoretical attack on the founding principles, followed by a series of practical victories for the new approach to government. Charles Kesler has labeled the key moments in these victories "the three waves of liberalism," corresponding to the three most productive liberal presidents: Woodrow Wilson, Franklin Roosevelt, and Lyndon Johnson. This long battle has also seen liberal retreats and occasionally outright defeats, as the epic struggle between liberalism and the older constitutionalism continues.

We can now look back on the twentieth century as a time of a great contest for the American soul between two strongly opposed conceptions of justice, with the liberal view winning out, but only incompletely. The contest continues in the new century. Meanwhile, the American people remain deeply divided, not just *among* themselves but also *within* themselves, over which of the two fundamentally opposed conceptions of justice is right.

13

MODERN LIBERALISM AND THE REJECTION OF NATURAL RIGHTS

Enlightenment thinkers like John Locke, William Blackstone, and Montesquieu were the three most cited European philosophers in the political writing of the founding era. Following the lead of Rousseau, later writers, many of them Germans, developed an approach to politics that turned against the Enlightenment and the American founding. Thinkers like Hegel and Marx and their students became the teachers of the founders of modern American liberalism.

In the late nineteenth century, educated Americans began to turn away from the natural rights theory of the founding. Their doctrines of relativism and historicism—the denial of objective truth and the claim that "values" change over time—took its place. Relativism is the view that there is objective knowledge only of facts, but not values. Science can know the truth about the material world, but it cannot tell us how to live. Historicism claims that all human thought is rooted in a particular historical time and place, so that the human mind can never escape the historical limitations of its own time. These two doctrines led men like Henry Adams to dismay and despair over a universe ultimately devoid of meaning.[1] But relativism and historicism were combined by other men (somewhat inconsistently) with an enthusiastic faith in Science and Progress. This rejection of the founding principles occurred on both the right and the left of the political spectrum.

On the right, for example, Progressive era sociologist William Graham Sumner wrote: "There are no dogmatic propositions of political philosophy which are universally and always true; there are views which prevail, at a time, for a while, and then fade away and give place to other views."[2] On the left, Woodrow Wilson openly criticized the founding principles as obsolete. In *The State*, Wilson dismissed with scorn the Founders' theory that government is grounded on a social compact and a law of nature. Progressive era liberals like Edward Bellamy, Herbert Croly, and John Dewey were equally hostile to the Founders' approach.[3]

Just as the ground of the Founders' natural rights theory was human nature as a permanent reality, the ground of the modern rejection of natural rights was a denial of human nature. Historian Richard Hofstadter's casual dismissal of the Founders' view in the 1940s was typical among liberal intellectuals throughout the twentieth century, for whom a Darwinian view of human nature was unquestioned orthodoxy: "But no man who is as well abreast of modern science as the Fathers were of eighteenth century science believes any longer in unchanging human nature."[4]

John Dewey, the most influential founder of modern liberal theory, began writing during the Progressive era but continued to influence the development of modern liberalism over the course of the entire first half of the twentieth century. Dewey expands on the idea that human beings have no nature: they are born as empty vessels, as nothing in themselves. As such, the individual becomes a product of a historical context: "social arrangements, laws, institutions ... are means of *creating* individuals.... Individuality in a social and moral sense is something to be wrought out."[5] There can be no natural rights because there is nothing of any value that human beings possess by nature that they could be said to have a right to. "Natural rights and natural liberties," Dewey insists, "exist only in the kingdom of mythological social zoology."[6] The Founders thought that intelligence was and should be uniquely one's own. Jefferson for example famously argued that "Almighty God hath created the mind free."[7] For Dewey, on the other hand, intelligence is "a social asset," "clothed with a function as public as its origin." That is because society, not the individual, makes the mind. Therefore society, not the individual, is the rightful owner of the human intellect.[8]

Dewey's rejection of human nature was also a rejection of the divine. In the Bible, Paul says that it is in God that "we live and move and have our being." Dewey writes that it is "in the social conditions in which he [man] lives, moves, and has his being."[9] For Dewey, neither nature nor God makes man. Man makes himself, collectively, through "social conditions." Reality is socially constructed.

Most Americans in the founding era were religious believers. Others at that time, whether believers or not, held that reason is capable by itself of discovering the same timeless truths. It does not matter to Dewey whether they were followers of Reason or of Revelation. They were wrong in either case. "They put forward their ideas as immutable truths good at all times and places; they had no idea of historic relativity."[10]

The repudiation of the idea of natural law and natural rights requires a new understanding of the purpose of government and its relationship with the people; in short, it requires a new definition of democracy. Dewey argues that human beings *are* "nothing in themselves"; it follows that they can *do* nothing on their own. According to Dewey, intelligence, talents, and virtues, as well as rights—all the things the Founders said humans were born with or acquired through the exercise of their natural talents—are produced by the social order: "The state has the responsibility for creating institutions under which individuals can effectively realize the potentialities that are theirs."[11] In Dewey's view, it is a mistake for government merely to protect people from injuring each other and otherwise to leave them alone. Government must take in hand the actual direction of people's lives.

For Dewey, the old definition of democracy as government by the people through elected representatives is "atomistic" and superficial. Worse, "[o]ur institutions, democratic in form, tend to favor in substance a privileged plutocracy." Securing the right to private property was central to the Founders' understanding of the purpose of government. For Dewey, private property is the enemy of liberty. Today, "private control of the new forces of production ... would operate in the same way as private unchecked control of political power."[12] (Owners of private property were similarly demonized by President Franklin Roosevelt as "economic royalists."[13]) Instead of protecting the integrity of the private sphere, government must invade and transform it. "There still lingers in the minds of some," Dewey writes, "the notion that there are two different 'spheres' of action and of rightful claims; that of political society and that of the individual, and that in the interest of the latter the former must be as contracted as possible." Democracy is redefined as "that form of social organization, extending to all the areas and ways of living, in which the powers of individuals shall ... be fed, sustained, and directed."[14] Consider that final word: "*directed.*" For Dewey, there is in principle no private action or thought that is not a legitimate object of government control and direction.

Dewey's theory reverses the Founders' view of the relationship between the people and the government. For Dewey, people do not delegate power to the government. Instead, the government empowers the people. Dewey viewed people as essentially needy or disabled, unable to function without the substantial help of government programs. In his view, it is precisely when government leaves people alone that this need or disability is greatest.

Early twentieth century liberalism focused on the needs and disabilities of workers. Starting in the 1960s, government turned to the
needs and disabilities of racial minorities. Women were added to the
growing list of victims in the 1970s, the disabled in the 70s and 80s,
and homosexuals in the 90s. In all of these cases, the role of government is to single out those whom it considers most disabled or victimized to receive special programs and treatment so that they too can
become "free" in this Deweyite sense of freedom.

Dewey's approach to politics was a liberal variation on Hegel's
historicism of progress, with the dogmatic rigor of the Hegelian dialectic abandoned. German political thought swept through American
universities in the late nineteenth century. As men like Wilson and
Dewey openly acknowledged, the universities were deeply affected by
the German attack on the idea of natural right in general, and on the
social compact principles of the founding in particular.[15]

In its American version, this German-inspired denial of human
nature leads away from an understanding of equality in terms of natural
rights. Equality is now understood as something to be produced by
government through *unequal* treatment. President Lyndon Johnson
endorsed this view in a speech at Howard University in 1965: "We
seek ... not just equality as a right and a theory but equality as a fact
and equality as a result."[16] Special programs to take money from haves
and give it to have-nots, especially blacks, were greatly expanded to
meet this demand.

To achieve "equality as a result," rights had to be redefined. For
the Founders, natural rights were rightful claims to one's own talents
and possessions. As James Madison wrote in the tenth *Federalist*, there
is a "diversity in the faculties of men from which the rights of property
originate.... The protection of these faculties is the first object of Government."[17] In the modern liberal view, rights are rightful claims on
the talents and resources of others. The Founders spoke of the natural
rights to life, liberty, and the acquisition of property. To secure these
natural rights, the law must establish civil rights. These included,
among others, the right to free exercise of religion, the right to free
speech, the right to make contracts and start a business, the right to
sue and testify in court, the right to equal protection of the laws, and
the right to trial by jury when one is accused of crime. We today tend
to speak instead of an expanding list of rights that can be obtained

only through government programs that provide citizens with money, goods, and services. These include the right to a decent wage, to housing, to education, to medical care, to food, to day-care, and even, in Franklin Roosevelt's "economic Bill of Rights," a right to recreation.[18] In practice, "rights" have often come to mean that people who are not as hardworking, as talented, as lucky, or as responsible have rightful claims on the work, talent, luck, and responsibility of others.

The principles of modern liberalism are strongly opposed to the principles of the American founding as Dewey and other early liberal theorists knew and sometimes frankly admitted. To see the contrast, consider this typical remark of Jefferson, which could have been authored by almost any member of the founding generation: "To take from one, because it is thought his own industry and that of his fathers has acquired too much, in order to spare to others, who, or whose fathers have not, exercised equal industry and skill, is to violate arbitrarily the first principle of association, the guarantee to everyone the exercise of his industry and the fruits acquired by it."[19] Jefferson's reference to "the first principle of association" is to the basic purpose of government, the protection of one's natural rights to life, liberty, and property. Those rights include the free use and possession of the fruits of one's own talents and industry. The "association" or civil society formed by the social compact is meant to secure those rights against those who would violate them by taking part of one's own income and giving it to someone else. The Founders, of course, were not cruel, and they believed, as Americans still do, that government must provide for extreme cases of destitution. In this minimal "safety net" sense they acknowledged a right to welfare. But they never opposed wealth as such, nor did they promote the redistribution of income to the poor who were able to provide for themselves.[20]

THE INSTITUTIONAL CHARACTER OF MODERN LIBERALISM

The modern denial of human nature and rejection of natural rights undercuts the Founders' idea of constitutionalism. For them, the purpose of constitutionalism is to direct and limit the operations of government in order to protect equal natural rights. Circumstances may call for constitutional amendments; but if the Founders were right, the basic purpose and duties of government will never change. A written constitution that is hard to change becomes an impediment when the government seeks to assert a new vision of social justice, one that requires increased control over what was once regarded as the private sphere.

Early theorists of modern liberalism praised democracy loudly, and they spoke constantly of the supposedly undemocratic features of the Founders' constitutionalism. They promoted direct election of senators instead of election by state legislatures. They advocated party primary elections to replace nominations made by a consensus of locally-based elected politicians. The Progressives urged states to adopt the initiative and referendum to allow direct popular participation in lawmaking.

But other favorite Progressive era reforms were not so "demo-, cratic" in character. The Progressives enacted registration require-ments that cut down on voter participation. Progressives were scath-ingly critical of democratically elected "politicians," a term that came to be equated with "corrupt" and "narrow" and "backward." The overall effect of the Progressive program took power out of the hands of elected officials—the "bad" politicians—and placed it instead into those of "good" administrators, supposedly neutral, "scientifically" educated "experts." The city-manager form of local government, which trans-ferred effectual power over local politics to officials insulated from electoral accountability, was one of the fruits of this movement. In fact, far from believing in democracy in the Founders' sense, Progres-sive intellectuals were deeply suspicious of government by the people, except when the people and their elected representatives were kept far from the actual day-to-day operation of government. Even seem-ingly democratic reforms like the initiative had the effect of removing power from elected officials whose roots were in local communities.

This was a blow to the older American system of local self-gov-ernment as the core of day-to-day democratic politics. In the Consti-tution of 1787, there are no national elections, and elections for the crucial legislative body are local or are conducted by locally elected officials. House elections are by districts, and senators were chosen by states. Since members of state legislatures were even more tied to locali-ties than members of the House of Representatives, the national legisla-ture consisted mostly of members of the middle class who had gained the respect of people in their communities. Progressive intellectuals argued that power should be transferred away from these elected officials, who were often described by Progressive era writers as corrupt and parochial. Instead, power was given to supposedly neutral, scientifically educated "experts." Woodrow Wilson's "The Study of Administration" (1888) argued that America suffers from "the error of trying to do too much by vote." We must learn from the example of Europe, said Wilson, where administrators have far more power than in America. "The cook must be trusted with a large discretion as to the management of the fires and the ovens," and the "cook" is to be a modern university graduate, not a small-town notable or one of his cronies.[21]

James Landis, in agreement with Wilson, attacked the Founders' separation of powers as an obstacle to efficient, scientific government in *The Administrative Process* (1938). This book was a political scientist's defense of the administrative agenda of Roosevelt's New Deal. Landis argued that government expertise will be unable to "control" the "economic forces which affect the life of the community" unless the old separation-of-powers model is discarded. In order for government to direct its powers toward "broad and imaginative ends," the constraints of the rule of law must be overcome. In modern times, Landis writes, government "concerns itself with the regulation of the lives of the people from the cradle—indeed, even ante-natally—to the grave, and being unable itself to deal with all the details, it delegates to the government departments the task of carrying out its policy." Landis explains: "With the rise of regulation, the need for expertness becomes dominant; for the art of regulating an industry requires knowledge of the details of its operation, ability to shift requirements as the condition of the industry may dictate, the pursuit of energetic measures upon the appearance of an emergency."[22]

Landis' overall point is simple: The rule of law was suited to a condition when government was not expected to do much more than protect people from using coercion against each other. But because of a change in historical circumstances (modern industrialization), that is no longer true. The older view was that government should secure the people's natural rights to life, liberty, and property. But in modern times, when private associations like family, church, and business can no longer be trusted to take care of the daily affairs of the nation (as Landis implies), government must involve itself in the details of everyday life that were formerly left to local government and private choice. Landis speaks of the regulation of industry; but his argument, like Dewey's, extends the scope of government in principle well beyond the sphere of business and into every aspect of life. Government cannot deal effectively with this vast mass of concerns through laws passed by a collection of amateur citizen-representatives in Congress. Instead, power must be delegated by Congress to professional experts, presumably educated in advanced institutions such as the Ivy League universities, and they must have a free hand to exercise these vast powers at their discretion. These educational institutions that supply the officials of the liberal state are indeed "neutral" in the perspective of their understanding of science and social science. But they are *not* neutral when it comes to the opposition between liberalism and the older constitutionalism. A major part of the agenda of modern social science is to promote the development and growth of the modern administrative state.[23]

The contrast with the Founders' view is striking. Their theory and practice of government rested on a cautious confidence in human nature, qualified by the sober recognition that through the ages, men in power who operate independently of the people have been all too likely to abuse that power. This applies especially to those who have some credentialed claim to "expertise," such as priestly robes, aristocratic blood, or university degrees. The Founders favored competence in government, of course, but they expected experts to be subordinate to the rule of law. In the case of executive branch administrators, they were to be subordinate to the president's direction. That is, the Founders insisted that all important government policymakers be directly or indirectly responsible to the people through periodic elections.

The confidence of modern liberalism in the authority and power of science leads it into what the Founders would have regarded as a naive forgetfulness about the permanent threat of despotism, a threat that is inherent in human nature itself. As Madison writes in *Federalist* No. 10: "The latent causes of faction"—factions are groups that promote their own selfish interests in opposition to the common good— "are thus sown in the nature of man." Liberals, with their faith in progress, tend to believe, with Francis Fukuyama, that the world is inevitably on the way to democratization everywhere, that there is no going back to the bad old days of tyranny and slavery. Woodrow Wilson frequently affirmed that the question of government had been essentially settled by history. This was on the eve of the century that saw the two most murderous regimes in all human history, Soviet Communism and German Nazism.[24] Had it not been for the United States, one of those two regimes might now be ruling the earth.

The proponents of liberalism did not think of their reforms as undemocratic. Wilson said that it would be a mistake to bring European-style administration to America without keeping it on a democratic leash. But in practice, Landis' proposed transfer of power from private and local control to centralized governmental bodies, substantially insulated from the pressure of elections and responsibility to the people, has proved to be a leading feature of modern government. Indeed, in spite of their democratic rhetoric, the advocates of modern liberalism have often been motivated by their confidence that they alone, free of the supposed bigotry and narrowness of selfish businessmen and fundamentalist Christians, could lead the nation to freedom and justice.

The complete picture of modern government is hard to see, because its scope is so big. But the basic principle is clear. The administrative state is animated by a pervasive distrust of private associations (family, church, business, fraternities, clubs, political parties, and lobbyists) and a corresponding confidence in the capacity of public officials to direct the lives of the people. Government responds to the alleged or real deficiencies of private institutions by setting up agencies, staffed by what it claims to be scientifically trained neutral experts, to oversee the details of one or another of the vast areas of American life that used to be handled by local government or private choice. Since the details of the various activities to be regulated are so extensive, Congress could not pass general laws to deal with them, even if it wanted to. "Once administration was centralized," notes political scientist John Marini, "no legislative body could legislate, in a general manner, all the details of the life of a great nation. Congress had to delegate authority to administrative bodies."[25]

THE ADMINISTRATIVE STATE IN ACTION

Modern liberalism has succeeded in taking over the bulk of the universities, the public schools, the major television networks, the most influential daily newspapers, and the movie and popular music industries. Yet in spite of all that, America today is only partly governed by liberal principles. In fact, the current system is neither the Founders' constitutionalism nor the liberal administrative state. It is an incoherent blend of both. When it comes to theory or science, incoherence is always a vice. But in practical affairs, incoherence has its virtues. In some respects the governments of the United States—of the towns, counties, states, and nation—operate in pretty much the same way now as they were intended to operate from the beginning. In other respects these governments are run today in ways that would have deeply troubled the Founders and presidents like Jackson, Lincoln, Cleveland, Coolidge, and of course Reagan.

To be sure, the Founders' original understanding of constitutional government is not altogether dead. It can be seen every day in the ordinary enforcement of the criminal and civil law in state courts. The legislative branch passes laws defining injuries and setting the penalties—laws against murder, for example. The executive branch, such as the state or local police, investigates crimes and make arrests. Another part of the executive branch, perhaps a county district attorney, indicts the person who is accused of the crime and prosecutes. The judicial branch, the judge and jury, conduct a trial to determine whether the person is guilty or not guilty.

This older way of governing coexists uneasily with the institutional and legal structure advocated by the theorists of modern liberalism. This development is not consistent with the rule of law in the Founders' sense. Political scientists call this new system the *administrative state*. In America today this administrative state exists side-by-side with—and in tension with—the Founders' constitutional order.

Further, much of the power previously held by towns and counties is now exercised by state governments (e.g., public education) and the federal government (e.g., welfare policy). Power previously exercised by states is increasingly federalized (setting of broad educational policies, public health regulations, workplace safety regulations). Activities that were previously thought to be purely private, such as decisions on whether to hire, fire, or promote employees in private businesses, are increasingly controlled by state and federal civil rights law. Power that used to be exercised, at whatever level of government, by officials accountable to the people directly or indirectly through elections, is increasingly held by unelected administrators whose accountability to the public is weakened.

David Schoenbrod is an ex-liberal, a Yale Law School graduate, who was a key player in the environmental movement of the 1970s. Here is his description of his involvement with the National Resources Defense Council (NRDC), a major activist group that was instrumental in developing modern environmental law:

> Congress passed the Clean Air Act in 1970 with hardly a dissenting vote, and President Nixon signed it with great fanfare. But the statute took no concrete action to curb lead as a health hazard. All it did was to erect an abstract ideal—healthy air—and delegate responsibility for realizing that ideal to the newly created Environmental Protection Agency (EPA) ... Should the EPA falter in doing its duty, any citizen could bring suit in federal court. At NRDC, we were set up to do just that.
>
> Here was government the way an elitist like me thought it ought to be. Experts were empowered to achieve an ideal, and I was empowered to make sure they did.[26]

This new understanding of government can also be seen at work in the evolution of civil rights law. In the 1964 Civil Rights Act, preferential treatment by race or sex is banned. But in that act Congress set up an agency, the Equal Employment Opportunity Commission, that it later authorized to write regulations and to handle preliminary adjudication of complaints of discrimination in employment law. This agency's regulations quickly turned the original law on its head, requiring de facto quotas and timetables for hiring by race, and banning many employment tests that were demonstrably useful in predicting job performance (and therefore permitted under the language of the 1964 act) but which had a "disparate impact" on members of certain racial and ethnic groups. What this means is that the actual civil rights "law" that the nation lives by was made not in Congress, but in the EEOC and other federal agencies. Federal courts have largely gone along with this de facto rewrite of the law. Actually, civil rights "law" has been made and remade many times over in several different federal agencies, including the Department of Justice, the Office of Federal Contract Compliance in the Labor Department, and the Office of

Civil Rights in the Department of Education, with plenty of input from the federal judiciary (especially at the District Court level) and from individual members of Congress (but not Congress acting in its constitutional lawmaking role).[27]

Nor is *this* all. Not only are the "laws" of the administrative state often created by agencies rather than by Congress, but enforcement and adjudication are also conducted in part by the agencies. The EEOC investigates businesses that are accused of discrimination, and the EEOC can set what it believes to be an appropriate penalty. The business may only get a jury trial after exhausting the cumbersome and expensive administrative process within the EEOC. Thus all the powers of government—legislative, executive, and judicial—which under the Founders' constitutionalism were to be kept separate, are often united in modern bureaucratic government in a single agency.[28]

But this formula is not quite right. In fact, the agencies, which on paper seem all-powerful, are in practice subject to multiple checks and influences by others. Some political scientists like to say that America has "separated branches sharing powers." In the modern state each of the branches has its say in the administrative process. In this sense, all three branches of government share in all three powers of government: lawmaking, executive prosecution, and adjudication. Responsibility in this system is hard to discern, and the policymaking of the national government is rarely understood. I have hardly ever met an ordinary citizen who understands how federal policies are made today.

We should also note that because the "laws" promulgated by agencies are not "laws" passed by Congress; the agencies easily and often make exceptions to their own rules. "Waivers" have long been a feature of administrative law. Influential groups are in the best position to get them, sometimes with the help of a congressman to whose campaign the group has contributed. What appears to be a general rule often turns out to be negotiable, and those with the best lawyers and the most money are often able to get the best deals.

This, of course, was not the intention of liberal theorists when they recommended the transfer of power to expert agencies. But a form of government originally developed to help the disadvantaged seems often to be more a tool of the Ivy League, the rich, and the well-connected, rather than the government originally set up by the

EEOC has leg. ex. & judicial powers.

Founders, against which the intellectuals of the Progressive era complained so bitterly.

THE TRANSFORMATION OF THE SEPARATION OF POWERS

In the liberal state, each of the three traditional branches of government continues to exist. Each continues to perform its traditional duties some of the time. But each branch has also taken on an altogether new set of duties as a necessary consequence of the new way of making policy in the administrative state.

Congress

The legislative branch was originally intended to devote the bulk of its time to lawmaking. In the administrative state, with its broad delegation of policymaking to executive branch agencies, Congress spends less of its time on policy, and more on administration. That is, congressmen and senators spend growing amounts of time on "pork barreling" and casework, interventions in the bureaucracy for constituents and major donors or simply for their own ideological reasons. Many political scientists now argue that the administrative process, not lawmaking, is "where the action is" in modern government. "Congress and party politics ... matter less and less."[29]

In order to accommodate itself to this new policymaking process, Congress reorganized itself after 1965 by decentralizing power within the institution. This enabled individual congressmen to influence more easily those administrative agencies and policy areas that they specialize in. Congress also expanded its staff dramatically, for two purposes: to expand their oversight of executive branch agencies, and to expand their ability to provide constituent service by intervening in agency decisionmaking.[30]

The Executive

Under the Framers' Constitution, a single person—the president—was in charge of the executive branch. Under today's administrative state, there are multiple executives. Nominally at the center are the heads of the various federal agencies. Realistically, many people other than the official heads of agencies play a large role in the policy process. These include Congress acting through formal votes, especially on the agency budget; individual congressmen acting through committees or on their own; courts of law; and lobbyists, who are given broad authority under modern law to initiate enforcement proceedings. The president himself has considerable say in the administrative process, of course, but he is only one player among many. He is no longer the sole or even the principal boss of the executive branch. In many of these agencies the president is forbidden by law or by court order to direct agency activity. Law also in effect forbids him to fire most federal employees, even if they are working actively against the policies of his administration. Thus the president in these respects is no longer able to fulfill his constitutional duty to "take care that the laws be faithfully executed."

The Judiciary

Under the Framers' Constitution, the job of the courts was to take the laws passed by Congress and the fundamental law of the Constitution, and then to apply them to particular cases in which one party claims that another has committed a legally-defined wrong. Under today's administrative state, the courts have taken on a new role of participating actively in the formation of public policy, in effect giving themselves a legislative and executive role along with the traditional judicial role assigned to them by the Constitution.

The judiciary acquired this legislative-executive role because Congress routinely delegates its lawmaking authority to administrative agencies. Courts become involved in the policy process through lawsuits brought by private groups against the government. Beginning in the 1970s, Congress has encouraged this as a means to get "the public" involved in the administrative process. The result is that the courts have become co-legislators. Jeremy Rabkin shows how the law of school desegregation has been made in effect by the federal judiciary more than by Congress or even the Office of Civil Rights over the past four decades.[31] The original 1964 Civil Rights Act explicitly forbids courts "to issue any order seeking to achieve a racial balance in any school by requiring the transportation of pupils from one school to another." Yet federal courts and agencies have in effect rewritten the Act to mean the exact opposite. One federal court in Missouri has even imposed a tax increase to fund magnet schools in the Kansas City School District. This, as others have noted, violates one of the fundamental principles of the American Revolution, namely, no taxation without representation.[32]

Examples of courts executing the law can also be found in judicial decisions on personnel, equipment, and other details of local school governance (to achieve racial balance) and similar judicial mandates on the details of the design and facilities of state prison systems (to remedy supposed violations of the Eighth Amendment ban on cruel and unusual punishment by improving conditions for prisoners).

In short, the courts not only adjudicate the law, but legislate and execute as well. The president is able to execute some laws, but he finds his powers confined by a bureaucracy partly beyond his control. Congress still makes laws, but it increasingly administers them as well.

THE TRANSFORMATION OF FEDERALISM

Under the Framers' Constitution, the national government was limited to areas of national concern. One could see this in practice by the fact that when bills were introduced in Congress before 1965, there was often a debate about whether they fell within the constitutional powers of Congress. Under today's "living constitution," hardly anything is out of bounds to the national government. Roads, bridges, and schools are paid for in part by federal money and subject to extensive federal regulation. Such traditionally local activities as city dumps, waste treatment, and elementary education are now heavily regulated by the federal government. Running a major business—sometimes even a small one—requires constant attention to what is going on in Washington, D.C. The authority of state and local governments has been much reduced.

It is true that the absolute number of federal employees has not grown much since 1960. That is because the federal government in effect co-opts state and local bureaucracies to run federal programs. For example, the administration of federal welfare programs is conducted largely by local governments operating under federal mandates. As John Marini writes: "The real growth in the power of the national administration ... has occurred through an administrative centralization that mandated an increase of employment at the state and local levels in response to federal directives reinforced by federal grants."[33]

Up to the 1960s, state and local governments tended to resist the expansion of federal authority. Since that time, however, states and localities have become quite friendly to big government. The change is related to bureaucratic patronage. Federal programs to aid local government projects are quite generous. Local governments have become accustomed to their client relationship to the federal patron. The money is often granted directly to state and local administrators, by-passing elected officials and weakening their authority. Administrators tend to find this relationship quite attractive. It frees them in part from the control of elected officials. For this reason there is little resistance in state and local governments against federal intrusion into local affairs. In fact, as political scientist R. Shep Melnick writes: "State administrations often form a powerful alliance with interest groups, federal administrators, and congressional committees to protect and expand federal regulation.[34]

Melnick sums up the overall transformation of federalism in this example:

In 1956, for example, Congress established the interstate highway system in an act only 28 pages long; the federal government placed very few constraints on the use of federal funds. By 1991 the law's 293-page successor, the Intermodal Surface Transportation Efficiency Act, required state and federal administrators not just to finish the remaining highways and improve public transit, but to "relieve congestion, improve air quality, preserve historic sites, encourage the use of auto seat belts and motorcycle helmets, control erosion and storm runoff," reduce drunk driving, promote recycling, hire more women, Native Americans, and members of other disadvantaged groups, and even "control the use of calcium magnesium acetate in performing seismic retrofits on bridges." Prior to the mid-1960s the federal government had used its tax dollars to help states pursue projects they had selected. After the mid-1960s it pursues a wide variety of objectives which often conflict with state and local priorities.[35]

This, then, is the consequence for federal-state relations from the rise of the administrative state. It replaces the limited-government constitutionalism of the Founders with the ever-expanding government of the welfare state. Driven by the ideology of modern liberalism, the administrative state proceeds on the presumption that it must assert control over the ordinary details of daily life because self-governing private associations and local self-government are thought to be incapable of taking care of the ordinary daily needs of the citizens.

CONCLUSION

Before 1965, most Americans were confident that most citizens, acting through self-governing associations such as families, churches, and businesses, could take care of their own daily needs. The job of government was to secure the conditions (peace and order) that would make this possible. In the liberal view that came to predominate after 1965—based on the theories of the Progressive movement—citizens are thought to be unable to manage their own lives without extensive and detailed government regulation of the economy and of social relations. The resulting liberal state has radically altered Americans' way of life. But has it made that way of life better?

It is often said that modern America is too complex to be governed according to an eighteenth century document. As recently as 1965, however, America was already a modern society—wealthy and highly industrialized—and the government was still operating largely under the Founders' Constitution, in accordance with the principles of the Declaration of Independence. It remains a viable choice to return to that way of life today. Whether or not Americans should do so depends on who was right, the Founders of the United States, or the founders of modern liberalism.

Endnotes

1. Christopher Flannery, "Henry Adams and Our Ancient Faith," in *History of American Political Thought*, Bryan-Paul Frost and Jeffrey Sikkenga, eds. (Lanham, Md.: Lexington Books, 2003), 491-503; Charles T. Rubin, "Shoreless Ocean, Sunless Sea: Henry Adams' *Democracy*," in *Challenges to the American Founding: Slavery, Historicism, and Progressivism in the*

Nineteenth Century, Ronald J. Pestritto and Thomas G. West, eds. (Lanham, Md.: Lexington Books, forthcoming).

2. "Mores of the Present and Future," in William Graham Sumner, *Essays*, Albert G. Keller and Maurice R. Davie, eds. (New Haven: Yale University Press, 1934), 1:86. This essay was originally published in 1909.

3. Edward Bellamy, *Looking Backward* (New York: Harper and Brothers, 1959 [originally published in 1888]) (describing a future socialist society and denouncing freedom of contract, private property, etc.); Herbert Croly, *The Promise of American Life* (Boston: Northeastern University Press, 1989 [originally published in 1909]), 180-82 (attacking the Founders' principle of individual rights in the name of "drastic criticism of the existing economic and social order"). For Dewey, see below.

4. Richard Hofstadter, *The American Political Tradition* (New York: Vintage Books, 1948), 16.

5. John Dewey, *Reconstruction in Philosophy* (Boston: Beacon Press, 1957 [originally published in 1948]), 194.

6. John Dewey, *Liberalism and Social Action* (Amherst, N.Y.: Prometheus Books, 2000 [originally published in 1935]), 27.

7. Jefferson, An Act for Establishing Religious Freedom, 1785, in *Writings*, Merrill D. Peterson, ed. (New York: Library of America, 1984), 346.

8. Dewey, *Liberalism and Social Action*, 70.

9. Acts 17:28. Dewey, *Liberalism and Social Action*, 58.

10. Dewey, *Liberalism and Social Action*, 41.

11. Ibid., 34-5.

12. Ibid., 17, 40.

13. Roosevelt, "Acceptance of the Renomination for the Presidency," June 27, 1936, in *Public Papers and Addresses of Franklin D. Roosevelt*, Samuel S. Rosenman, ed. (New York: Random House, 1938), 5:232.

14. Dewey, *Liberalism and Social Action*, 50, 86.

15. Charles Merriam, *A History of American Political Theories* (New York: Macmillan, 1903), 305-316, 321-325, 332-333 (presenting an overview of the American rejection of the founding principles).

16. Lyndon Johnson, "To Fulfill These Rights," June 4, 1965, in *Public Papers of the Presidents: Lyndon B. Johnson* (Washington, D.C.: Government Printing Office, 1966), 2:636.

17. Alexander Hamilton et al., *The Federalist Papers*, introduction and notes by Charles R. Kesler, Clinton Rossiter, ed. (New York: New American Library, Signet Classics, 2003), 73.

18. "Annual Message to Congress," January 11, 1944, in *Nothing to Fear: Selected Addresses of Franklin Delano Roosevelt, 1932-1945*, B. D. Zevin, ed. (New York: Houghton Mifflin, 1946), 397.

19. Letter to Milligan, April 6, 1816, in *Writings of Thomas Jefferson*, Albert E. Bergh, ed. (Washington, D.C.: Thomas Jefferson Memorial Association, 1904), 14:466.

20. See the chapter on poverty and welfare in Thomas G. West, *Vindicating the Founders: Race, Sex, Class, and Justice in the Origins of America* (Lanham, Md.: Rowman and Littlefield, 1997).

21. *The Papers of Woodrow Wilson*, Arthur S. Link, ed. (Princeton: Princeton University Press, 1968), 5:359-380.

22. James M. Landis, *The Administrative Process* (Westport, Conn.: Greenwood Press, 1974 [originally published in 1938]), 8, 13, 18, 23.

23. John Marini, "Theology, Metaphysics, and Positivism: the Origins of the Social Sciences and the Transformation of the American University," in *Challenges to the American Founding*.

24. *The Federalist*, No. 10, 73. Francis Fukuyama, *The End of History and the Last Man* (New York: Free Press, 1992). Wilson, "Study of Administration," 360-2, 367.

25. John Marini, *The Politics of Budget Control: Congress, the Presidency, and the Growth of the Administrative State* (New York: Crane Russak, 1992), 171.

26. David Schoenbrod, "Confessions of an Ex-Elitist," *Commentary* 108 (November 1999): 38.

27. Herman Belz, *Equality Transformed: A Quarter-Century of Affirmative Action* (New Brunswick, N.J.: Transaction Publishers, 1991) tells the story in convincing detail. See also Hugh Davis Graham, *The Civil Rights Era: Origins and Development of National Policy, 1960-1972* (New York: Oxford University Press, 1990).

28. Gary Lawson, "The Rise of the Administrative State," *Harvard Law Review* 107 (1994): 1231-54. Edward J. Erler, *The American Polity: Essays on the Theory and Practice of Constitutional Government* (New York: Crane Russak, 1991), 67, explains why not only Democrats but even Republicans are reluctant to challenge the new method of lawmaking in the administrative state: "No Senator (or House member) wants the Congress to resume its primary role in the formulation of public policy. Congress prefers to defer the difficult and politically risky legislative decisions to the courts and the executive branch."

29. Sidney M. Milkis, "The Presidency, Policy Reform, and the Rise of Administrative Politics," in *Remaking American Politics*, Richard A. Harris and Sidney M. Milkis, eds. (Boulder: Westview Press, 1989), 169. See also Marini, *Politics of Budget Control*, 165-81; Morris P. Fiorina, *Congress: Keystone of the Washington Establishment*, 2nd ed. (New Haven: Yale University Press, 1989).

30. Harold Seidman and Robert Gilmour, *Politics, Position, and Power: From the Positive to the Regulatory State*, 4th ed. (New York: Oxford University Press, 1986), 37-41; R. Shep Melnick, *Between the Lines: Interpreting Welfare Rights* (Washington, D.C.: Brookings, 1994), 23-24, 28-29.

31. *See* Jeremy Rabkin, *Judicial Compulsions: How Public Law Distorts Public Policy* (New York: Basic Books, 1989), 147-181. For an account of the extremes to which judicial policymaking can go, *see* Ross Sandler and David Schoenbrod, *Democracy by Decree: What Happens When Courts Run Government* (New Haven: Yale University Press, 2003), 45-97 (describing how a federal district court took over administration of education for the handicapped in the New York school system from 1979 to at least 2002, when the book was published).

32. Missouri v. Jenkins, 495 U.S. 33 (1990) (describing the facts of the district court takeover of the Kansas City School District, including the order to increase taxes).

33. Marini, *Politics of Budget Control*, 94.

34. R. Shep Melnick, "Federalism and the New Rights," *Yale Law and Policy Review: Yale Journal on Regulation* (Symposium Issue, 1996): 341. See also Seidman and Gilmour, *Politics, Position, and Power*, 199-200: "the governor …[is] undercut by federal regulations, which foster the autonomy of program specialists. It is no coincidence that executive power is likely to be weakest with respect to state agencies that are heavily dependent on federal funds." Also useful is Joseph F. Zimmerman, *Federal Preemption: The Silent Revolution* (Ames: Iowa State University Press, 1991).

35. Melnick, "Federalism and the New Rights," 340-41.

Chapter 2

Theodore Roosevelt on Self-Government and the Administrative State

Will Morrisey

THE AMERICAN UNDERSTANDING OF SELF-GOVERNMENT

In declaring their independence from Great Britain, the greatest imperial state of the day, the American Founders addressed the problem of the modern state in a unique way. They did not oppose Leviathan with Leviathan. Britain intended to subordinate the American colonies firmly within a modern, statist empire; we guess this by seeing what Britain did with the colonies that did not break free at the same time, Ireland and India. The Founders, Tocqueville saw, conceived a new kind of empire, one framed by several institutional innovations. These included popular rather than state sovereignty and the combination of *political* centralization with *administrative* decentralization. Popular sovereignty and administrative decentralization—themselves combined in local self-government of townships and counties—enabled Americans to replace the old intermediate institutions of the titled aristocrats with civil-social structures strong enough to resist encroachments from America's very small and non-sovereign central state. Thus the problem of the relationship of the individual to the state would find its solution in a substantial degree of *self-government*.[1] Self-government in turn would remain true government, and not merely an assertion of the self, because the state would abandon

35

the Machiavellian attempt to convert Christianity into a civil, rather than a prophetic religion; the end of Church establishment would re-animate the personal, Christian spirit in civil society, where Christianity had seen, arguably, its most rapid gains when it had put an end to pagan antiquity.[2] The Declaration's teaching on Creator-endowed unalienable rights, integrated with the laws of Nature and of Nature's God, gave Americans a set of principles that severed national governmental authority from Church membership, thus clearing the way for the exercise of civic duties toward one another that would overcome both religious fanaticism on the one hand and mere "individualism" on the other. American civil society thus preserved some of the ancient and Christian virtues. By adding to these the "bourgeois" virtues of commercial activity, the virtues with which Montesquieu had intended to replace what he deemed the passivity of Christian civil society, this civil society caused Americans to live in an atmosphere of moral tension, but a tension that could be understood by everyone who experienced and lived with it.

America opposed Machiavellian/Hobbesian modernity in civil society, as well. In America there would be no Countess of Forli, and not only because there would be no countesses. American girls, Tocqueville saw, had genuine virtues, not the least of which the ability to know *virtu* when they saw it. They wouldn't play the Machiavellian game, but they did know the score. American women married with their eyes open; feeling the pull of individuality, they knowingly sacrificed it for the sake of families. Their husbands spent their days living tamed-prince lives of acquisition, but at night returned, in exhaustion and relief, to tranquil homes. Together, husbands and wives built the American empire of liberty, opposed to the statist empires of subordination. The glory of that empire would inhere precisely in the equality, the liberty, and the successful pursuit of the happiness of each citizen, not in the exaltation of the prince or the aristocracy.

This is not to suggest that there cannot and should not be a "first among equals." The finest example of this new, American character, the pre-eminent citizen of this new regime, remains for us who it was to his contemporaries: George Washington. Washington's understanding of self-government might be depicted as a set of concentric circles. Everyone's initial sphere of self-government is one's own soul. Each person lives in a family, which also strives to govern itself. Each family lives in a local community—a neighborhood, a village, a town, often characterized by complex economic and other relations among its members. Societies thrive in political communities, countries, with military and civilian dimensions. Countries must govern themselves, assume their equal stations among other countries, the powers of the earth. And the world as a whole exists as part of the natural universe, created by God. In each of these spheres, self-government means the rule of reason.[3]

Thus Washington saw that the human "self" or soul not as some hard-shelled particle, an atom of individualism. The well-ordered human soul radiates its governing energies outward into those other spheres. At the same time, and not only in its childhood and youth, it receives indispensable guidance *from* the wider spheres. The self-governing citizen rules and is ruled, reciprocally. Aristotle teaches that only this relationship deserves the name of *political* rule. All other rule is either parental care or master-slave dominance.

Washingtonian self-government evidently derived from classical models—probably Seneca and other Stoic moralists. But he adapted his maxims to the regime of *commercial* republicanism, telling young correspondents to work for "useful" knowledge, to acquire the "habit of industry," not idleness, to remember that "good company will always be found much less expensive than bad."[4] To his young aristocratic friend Lafayette he offers the most telling advice. Lafayette longed to challenge British officials who spoke disrespectfully of France. Washington praised "the generous Spirit of Chivalry" that remained strong in France, but cautioned, "it is in vain to cherish it." "In our days it is to be feared that your opponent, sheltering himself behind Modern opinion ... would turn a virtue of such ancient date, into ridicule."[5] No less clearly than Tocqueville, decades later, Washington saw that aristocratic souls will need to rethink their condition in the modern world of *embourgeoisement*. There, honor must find a home in principled patriotism, and in the just approbation of one's own people—not in quarreling over a straw.

Whether in the sphere of the government of reason over the passions in the human soul, or in the sphere of the relations of the American states to one another and to the national government in the federal system, or in the sphere of the relations of America with the other powers of the earth, Washington and the other founding presidents sought so to weaken the passions as to enable reason to rule. In exhortation, in action, and in institution building they intended to vindicate rationally perceived natural right by prudentially conceived speech and action, against the liberation of the passions, particularly the passion of *libido dominandi*, effected by Machiavelli and his disciples, partisans of modern statism. The characteristic American passion, the desire for material gain, remains a bourgeois, a "middling," passion, one requiring the government of practical reason (if often of a fairly low, calculating sort) to find its satisfaction.

The political course of events after independence might be described as a series of struggles over the terms and conditions of American self-government, as conceived by the Founders. In the first struggle over the future character of the federal system, the ratification debates of 1787-89, those who asserted the powers and rights of the states over those of the national government did so by appealing to democracy, claiming that the proposed constitution's political centralization would yield eventually a European-like statism. The Confederate project, some seventy years later, asserted states' powers and rights by appealing—at least in the formulations of its principal spokesman, Jefferson Davis—to aristocratic rather than democratic sensibilities, the defense of domestic institutions that included slavery at the service of a new, plantation nobility.[6] But whether democratic, republican, or quasi-aristocratic, Americans from founding to civil war rejected modern statism and opposed it with the regime described in *The Federalist*: an unmixed, commercial, extensive, compound, federal republic, founded upon consent and the rule of law, aimed at securing unalienable rights.[7]

The defeat of the Confederate States of America ended any hope for the constitution of a regime of agrarian "aristocracy" on American soil. But Tocqueville had foreseen another sort of "aristocracy" or oligarchy under conditions of social egalitarianism, namely a commercial-industrial elite, crueler than the old European aristocracy of estate and altar.[8] The triumph of the commercial interests represented in the Republican Party, and the debacle of southern, agrarian Democrats, made this possibility more likely to become real. The industrial elites that formed in the wake of the Civil War also found opportunity in the domination of the national government by Congress, after the murder of Abraham Lincoln. The corrupt "Congressional government" decried in the 1880s by that ambitious young political scientist, Woodrow Wilson, had been criticized as early as 1869 by the young Republican reformer, Henry Adams. But whereas Adams and the other civil service reformers sought to bring the national administrative apparatus back to the principles of the Founders, as the reformers conceived those principles, Wilson famously set out to institute a national bureaucracy founded upon the principle of an impersonal "science of administration"—the indispensable instrument for transforming the American regime into a structure more nearly like the sovereign states of Europe, of which Bismarck's Germany then served as the leading example. Wilson sought to leaven the impersonality of scientific bureaucracy with the personality of the leader, himself led by the personal, loving God of a certain kind of Christianity—a "progressivist" God who works through leaders in what the Founders had called the course of events, and what a series of nineteenth century thinkers had taught Wilson to call "history."[9]

In this conflict between reformist constitutionalism and Wilsonian progressivism, Theodore Roosevelt occupies a central, not to say ambiguous place. Roosevelt had signed on to the reformers' agenda as a young man, an agenda intended to return America to American principles. As an older man, an ex-president, he founded a party *on* "progressivism," in opposition to Wilsonian "progressivism." In contrast to Wilson—who, like his God, revealed his intentions sporadically and worked in mysterious ways, Roosevelt presented himself as triumphantly unguarded, a man of perpetual crescendo. He got the attention of his fellow citizens, all right, but left many of them wondering what the din had been about. Yet Roosevelt's ebullience in the presidential pulpit had a serious political purpose. Roosevelt intended to prepare Americans for the advance of the statist project, here and abroad, by urging them to strengthen their virtues for coming battles against the men of *virtu*. He would strengthen the national state in America, but guard against that strengthening by a concomitant strengthening of individual character and of civil associations.

ROOSEVELT ON SELF-GOVERNMENT IN THE MODERN STATE

In considering self-government as understood by the Founders and the generation of the Civil War, we need to immerse ourselves in controversies somewhat removed from our own: claims of sovereignty by South Carolina, slavery, the concurrent majority, and the like. With Roosevelt we enter a world recognizably our own. Mass communications, urban life, and geopolitics dominate political discourse. Slavery is gone but racial and ethnic tensions persist. To think about the household is to think about the liberation of women from the household and of men who shirk responsibility for their children. Leisure is a problem among members of the middle class; decadence has become democratized.

Roosevelt thought about these matters more acutely than he is credited for having done. Given the scale of contemporary life, he argues, animated as that life is by social forces that overwhelm individuals and small communities, American liberalism, the empire of liberty, must become both more muscular and more intelligent than it had been recently, in the decades following the Civil War. In so doing, Americans must take care not to become illiberal, to mimic the ideologies and movements that threaten them. To govern themselves now, American liberals need to recall the manly, and womanly, thumotic virtues of their forebears, including the great-souled men of the ancient world before liberalism. Like many critics of modern liberalism, Roosevelt harkens to the Greek esteem for balance and magnanimity, and to Biblical sternness and duty. Unlike such critics, Roosevelt refuses simply to abandon liberalism, regarding it as the only decent possibility for modern political life.

For this reason, as a statesman he sought to cultivate not only heroic virtues, but the ordinary, "high average" of virtues that ordinary citizens can attain. He concerned himself with what a later generation would call the problems of political culture, or what Tocqueville before him called "habits of the heart." In so doing, he revived what J. G. A. Pocock and his school call the "republican" tradition of American political thought. Unlike that school, however, he refused to believe this tradition to be fundamentally incompatible with liberalism. He wanted to defend the commercial republicanism of the Founders and of Lincoln, under circumstances much changed.

Perhaps for this reason—the radical changes in modern life since the middle of the nineteenth century—Roosevelt's conception of self-government was more carefully articulated than that of any other major president since Washington. In every "sphere"—the soul, the household, the political economy, the military, the state, the nation, international relations, even man's relationship with nature—Roosevelt explicitly discussed the implications of modern life with respect to self-government. In a sense, defending self-government by declaring our independence from a statist empire had been comparatively easy. Roosevelt operated in a world of much-increased *inter*dependence. Unlike those thinkers who supposed that such interdependence requires compassionate and cosmopolitan humanitarianism, Roosevelt pointed to a robust "Americanism"—to citizen virtues. He sought to show how self-government would survive in conditions of corporatism and geopolitics.

In his words if not in his actions, Roosevelt's insistence on virtue caused him to underplay the importance of institutions, many of which were undergoing profound changes at the time. "I have always been more interested in the men themselves than in the institutions through which they worked."[10] His main "institutional" interest, civil service reform, arose from his moral animus against corruption, not from the "scientific" desire to know, much less to know by means of grasping, creating, or controlling. Although he devoted much of his legendary energy to working at civil service reform "in practice," he did not lay out the theoretical implications of increased bureaucratization on self-government, as did his rival, Woodrow Wilson. In his writings, Roosevelt assured his fellow-citizens that a professional civil service would prove a boon to self-government, without explicitly telling them why or how this would be so. But Roosevelt's understanding of self-government proves less deficient than this one deficiency makes it seem. He concentrated his attention not upon theory, not even on the praxis-science or applied science of "management." He sought to animate administration by practical *morality*. Civil service professionalism looks much less threatening to self-government if viewed from the perspective of Roosevelt's overall project: to destroy the partisan machine politics that interfered with self-government, and to so strengthen citizen virtues as to make the new bureaucrats less numerous and formidable than they would otherwise become.

A comprehensive account of Roosevelt on self-government would exceed the practicable scope of this essay. I shall restrict myself to his account of the relationship of self-government to the modern political economy and the national state.

SELF-GOVERNMENT AND POLITICAL ECONOMY

In Roosevelt's view, political economy rests upon the foundation of household economy. Household economy depends upon "the law of work," "the fundamental law of our being." Unlike the Bible, but like the liberal thinkers following Locke, Roosevelt regarded work "not as a curse but as a blessing," and looked down upon "the idler with scornful pity."[11] The "prime duty" of a man is work outside the house, as that of a woman is work within the house. Children should not work, except at studies, and this prohibition should be enforced by "severe child-labor and factory-inspection laws."[12] The American Revolution itself occurred because the British violated the law of work, "regard[ing] the new lands across the Atlantic as being won and settled, not for the benefit of the men who won and settled them, but for the benefit of the merchants and traders who stayed at home."[13] The law of work entails the right of economic self-government.

The entwining of Americanism with the law of work and the right of property, although just, leaves Americans tending toward a merely commercial mentality. "There is not in the world a more ignoble character than the mere money-getting American, insensible to every duty, regardless of every principle, bent only on amassing a fortune, and putting his fortune only to the basest uses—whether these uses be to speculate in stocks and wreck railroads himself, or to allow his son to lead a life of foolish and expensive idleness and gross debauchery, to purchase some scoundrel of high social position, foreign or native, for his daughter. Such a man is only the more dangerous if he occasionally does some deed like founding a college or endowing a church, which makes those good people who are also foolish forget his real iniquity." To such men, "who measure everything by the shop-till, trade and property are far more sacred than life and honor."[14] Among the many black marks against Woodrow Wilson in Theodore Roosevelt's mind was this sentence, intended to be compassionate: "You cannot worship God on an empty stomach, and you cannot be a patriot when you are starving." "No more sordid untruth was ever uttered," Roosevelt fulminated; "such a sentence as this could be uttered only by a President who cares nothing for the nation's soul, and who believes that the nation puts its belly above its soul." Wilsonian "apostles of the full belly" forget the patriot-soldiers of Valley Forge.

"Is his own soul so small that he cannot see the greatness of soul of Washington and of the Continental soldiers whose feet left bloody tracks upon the snow as they marched toward the enemy?"[15] In fact, Washington himself had voiced similar complaints about the Americans of his own time, including some of his soldiers, and so Roosevelt's rhetoric on the matter has good lineage. More than this, Roosevelt here resists (as Tocqueville would) the nascent materialism of a so-called welfare state, and the passivity, the abandonment of self-government, that such a materialist statism would foster.

To counter the excesses of the commercial ethos, Roosevelt commended those among contemporary workers who continued to exhibit the sterner virtues. "Among the penalties [of "our present advanced civilization"] is the fact that in very many occupations there is so little demand upon nerve, hardihood, and endurance, that there is a tendency to unhealthy softening of fibre and relaxation of fibre." In his time, railroading remained one sector in which "the man has to show the ... qualities of courage, of hardihood, or willingness to face danger, the cultivation of the power of instantaneous decision under difficulties, and the other qualities which go to make up the virile side of a man's character." General William Tecumseh Sherman told him that railroaders would make the best army in the world, given their physical conditioning, courage and "self-reliance."[16] While some technological advances enabled a dangerous ease of living, some of the frontiers of technology still offered physical and moral challenge.

American economic development—a result of self-government—posed still more complex questions for self-government than did the problem of the kind of work now available. "We of this mighty Western Republic have to grapple with the dangers that spring from popular self-government tried on a scale incomparably vaster than ever before in the history of mankind, and from an abounding material prosperity greater also than anything which the world has hitherto seen."[17] This prosperity, occurring at the same time as the closing of the western frontier and the consequent disappearance of free land meant that the problems of industrialization must be faced squarely. The society crystallized by the forces of the modern economy—powered by such technology as steam and electricity, characterized by such phenomena as urban population growth and the general "massification" of life—had replaced yeoman farming and

"self-dependent" small communities[18] with complex, large-scale
networks of "mutualism" or "interdependence"—the last word one
Roosevelt helped to introduce into linguistic circulation.[19] Modern
corporations typify mutualism, bringing "huge wealth" to "a few individuals"; "in no other country in the world had such enormous fortunes been gained."[20] Roosevelt saw what Tocqueville had seen:
although "there have been aristocracies which have played a great
and beneficent part at stages in the growth of mankind," the corporate barons of America were plutocrats; all too often, the laborers they
employ behaved like mobs.[21]

Roosevelt called for moderation, the avoidance of "the Scylla of
mob rule, and the Charybdis of subjection to a plutocracy."[22] "A blind
and ignorant resistance to every effort for the reform of abuses and for
the readjustment of society to modern industrial conditions represents not true conservatism, but an incitement to the wildest radicalism." Indulgence of radicalism, however, will lead to anarchy. "This is
an era of combination alike in the world of capital and in the world of
labor"—seen in the corporations formed by capitalists and the unions
formed by workers. "Each kind of combination can do good, and yet
each, however powerful, must be opposed when it does ill." Neither
could be opposed successfully by mere trust busting.[23] "Corporations
[have] become indispensable in the business world"; it is "folly to try
to prohibit them, but ... also folly to leave them without thoroughgoing control."

The advocates of the Sherman Anti-Trust Act tried "to remedy [the
evil done by big corporations] by destroying them and restoring the
country to the economic conditions of the middle of the nineteenth
century."[24] This "sincere rural toryism," typified by Populists of the
William Jennings Bryan stamp and by some of the later Progressives,[25]
simply did not take account of contemporary economic realities, fail-
ing the test of self-knowledge that members of every self-governing
community must pass. Roosevelt unfailingly required his listeners to
see the realities of modern life, insisting that they think about those
realities and steel themselves for them.

The courts, "for a quarter of a century ... on the whole the agents
of reaction," had "rendered ... decisions sometimes as upholders of
property rights against human rights." In doing so, the courts had
ignored the "corner-stone of the Republic": the determination to "treat

... each man on his worth as a man, paying no heed to his creed, his birthplace, or his occupation, asking not whether he is rich or poor, whether he labors with head or hand," granting "the largest personal liberty consistent with securing the well-being of the whole" by attempting "to secure for each man such equality of opportunity that in the strife of life he may have a fair chance to show the stuff that is in him."[26] Labor precedes capital, and government, including the courts, can only defend capital insofar as government defends labor.

More specifically, the Constitution was framed precisely "to give to some central authority the power to regulate and control interstate commerce," a power overawed after the Civil War by the sheer size of the new corporations.[27] But "the great corporations ... are the creatures of the State and the State not only has the right to control them, but it is duty bound to control them wherever the need of such control is shown."[28] Were the corporations exempt from governmental control, were they ungoverned, they would then become the actual government of every person they affected. That is, America would become an oligarchy. The self-government of the American people would then be at hazard. "Some governmental sovereign"—"which represents the people as a whole"—"must be given power over these artificial, and very powerful, corporate beings."[29] Roosevelt did not mean that government should be made sovereign, in the European sense; to do so would be to explode the corner-stone of the republic. He meant rather that the sovereign people can prevent oligarchy in part by exercising their sovereignty by the means of their government.

Roosevelt therefore advocated cautious regulation of national corporations by a strengthened national government. State governments alone could not govern national corporations, in his opinion. But the threat to self-government posed by corporations must itself be met in the spirit of self-government—"wisdom and self-restraint"—by the regulators. "Our purpose is to build up rather than to tear down. We show ourselves the truest friends of property when we make it evident that we will not tolerate the abuses of property," the tendency of corporations "toward reducing the people to economic servitude."[30] "[I]gnorant meddling" with corporate property—"above all, meddling in a spirit of class legislation or hatred or rancor"—will only injure the prosperity upon which workers depend.[31] To employ Friedrich von Hayek's image, there are actually two "roads to serfdom"—one, as

Hayek sees, paved by statism; the other, as Tocqueville sees, paved by corporate oligarchs.

Where, then, to draw the line? Because he consistently tried to center Americans' thought on morality, not on science, Roosevelt *could* say, "We draw the line at misconduct, not at wealth."[32] Roosevelt had set down the standards for such line-drawing as early as 1900, when still governor of New York. "The true questions to be asked are: Has any given individual been injured by the acquisition of wealth by any man? Were the rights of that individual, if they have been violated, insufficiently protected by law? If so, these rights, and all similar rights, ought to be guaranteed by additional legislation."[33] Typical abuses of individual rights include concealment or misrepresentation of facts connected with the organization of a firm, unscrupulous promotion of a stock offering, "unfair competition," price-fixing, and tyrannical labor practices. Roosevelt styles organizations intent on misconduct "special interests," but "special" interests are not corporate interests as such. "A special interest is one which has been given by law certain improper advantages as compared with the mass of our people, or which enjoys such advantages owing to the absence of needed laws."[34] As president, Roosevelt sought to enact these principles nationally. In so doing he did not, he insisted, extend the authority of the federal government, "for such authority already exists under the Constitution in ample and most far-reaching form": the commerce clause and the popular sovereignty or national self-government implied in the Constitution in which that clause appears.[35] The threat to the nation's self-government by corporations can be met by invoking the nation's supreme act of lawmaking. In any regime, a basic question always is: Who rules? In the United States the people rule under their self-made law, the supreme law of the land; corporations do not rule. If corporations did rule, the regime would change from republic to oligarchy.

Put another way, the administrative decentralization Tocqueville admired—administration lodged in local and county governments—could no longer govern corporate oligarchs. Commerce now appealed not only to modest, bourgeois passions but to *libido dominandi*, to the passion to rule of *individuals* who could now build nationwide industrial empires. Napoleons of industry rather than of arms, the new oligarchs, foreseen by Tocqueville, had escaped local control, and could only be governed with some form of administrative centralization.

Concretely, regulation of corporations should include the require-ment to divulge information about corporate activities, particularly the value of the property in which the public's capital is invested. A Department of Commerce with a cabinet-level secretary should use such data as the basis for regulation (which, Roosevelt told Congress, should include "a law prohibiting all corporations from contributing to the campaign expenses of any party," directly or indirectly).[36] Machiavelli had compared institution building to dams and dikes, and had held out the possibility of mastering Fortuna thereby. Roosevelt was more modest. "You can regulate and control the current [of the Mississippi River]; you can eliminate its destructive features; but you can do it only by studying what a current is and what your own pow-ers are. It is just exactly so in dealing with great tendencies of our great industrial civilization."[37] Regulation must therefore include what later generations would call cost-benefit analysis, as "there can be no equitable division of prosperity until the prosperity is there to divide" and not to destroy.[38]

"I am not advocating anything revolutionary. I am advocating ac-tion to prevent anything revolutionary."[39] The "ignorant or reckless agitator has been the really effective friend of the evils which he has been nominally opposing" by advocating "crude and ill-considered legislation" that would "incur the risk of such far-reaching national disaster that it would be preferable to undertake nothing at all."[40] Such persons are, to borrow a Marxist phrase, objectively pro-busi-ness. "[I]f any seek in their turn to do wrong to the men of means, to do wrong to the men who own those corporations, I will turn around and fight for them in defense of their rights just as hard as I fight against them when I think that they are doing wrong."[41] Just as all corporate conduct is not misconduct, so a man of great wealth is not necessarily a malefactor of great wealth.

This moral—not to say moralizing—quality of Roosevelt's eco-nomic thought, essential to his understanding of self-government, also informed his approach to finance. Finance rests on credit; credit, which means "belief," rests on "confidence," and confidence that is not illu-sory rests on honesty. The self-governing *honnete homme* finds reflec-tion in "an honest business life," of which "an honest currency is the strongest symbol." "Very ignorant and primitive communities"—the United States of the 1780s, under the Articles of Confederation, for example—"are continually obliged to learn the elementary truth that the repudiation of debts is in the end ruinous to the debtors as a class; and when communities have moved somewhat higher in the scale of civilization they also learn that anything in the nature of a debased currency works similar damage." Roosevelt consequently rejected Populist or Bryanist finance; bimetallism, a crude attempt to ease credit by inflating currency in an America without a Federal Reserve Bank or some other reasonable financial system failed not only the "economics" test, but also the moral test of a self-governing people.[42]

Finally, of course, economics and morality cannot be separated, inasmuch as any "demand" for any "supply" remains subject to the scrutiny of "should" and "should not"—the ineluctably moral character of all human action. What distinguished Roosevelt from most capitalists of his time was his insistence that the principle of self-government extends to governmental responsibility for the American financial system. Following the financial panic of 1907, President Roosevelt acknowledged, "[w]hether I am or am not in any degree responsible for the panic, I shall certainly be held responsible." Financial panics are laid at the door of the modern White House, deservedly or not. "At present most of those who thus hold me responsible"—the men of Wall Street—"are bitterly against me anyhow; but of course the feeling will spread to those who have been my friends, because when the average man loses his money he is simply like a wounded snake and strikes right and left at anything, innocent or the reverse, that presents itself as conspicuous in his mind."[43] Nothing if not conspicuous, Roosevelt reasoned that if he were to take the blame he had better have the power to act.

"The big financial men ... seize the occasion [of the panic] to try to escape from all governmental control, and believe they can now thus escape. My judgment is more firmly than ever that they must be brought under control, and that the only way to free them from the undesirable control of the states"—hitherto the primary regulators of corporate activity—"is to secure a more adequate control on the part of the nation."[44] In a special message to Congress in January 1908, Roosevelt advocated measures "to prevent at least the grosser forms of gambling in securities and commodities, such as making large sales of what men do not possess and 'cornering' the market." This sounds rather more like loading the dice than gambling on the roll, but at any rate Roosevelt distinguishes between gambling on the stock market and investing in it. "The great bulk of the business transacted on the exchanges is not only legitimate, but is necessary to the working of our industrial system"; critics of stock trading as such "do not fully realize the modern interdependence in financial and business relations," for example the need to capitalize large corporations for investments to be made on a national scale. Accordingly, in addition to legislation for ensuring honesty in stock transactions, "a central bank would be a very good thing."[45] At the time, Roosevelt judged such a bank politically impossible, as "sooner or later there would be in that bank some insolent man whose head would be turned by his own power and ability ... and would by his actions awaken the slumbering popular distrust and cause a storm in which he would be as helpless as a child, and which would overwhelm not only him but other men and other things of far more importance."[46] Here, characteristically, Roosevelt blended what amounts to a Whiggish discourse against stock-jobbing and of the threat speculation poses to a self-governing people with a hard-headed recognition of the character of modern economies. Again characteristically, he would calculate the distance he could go toward a just and prudent solution, given the political limits imposed by the self-governing American people.

The morality of self-government applies equally to farmers and workers, both needing to form civil associations in order to defend their rights in the new political economy. Victimized by excessive costs imposed by middlemen, farmers needed "the intelligence and energy to work through co-operative societies"; "community self-help is normally preferable to using the machinery of government for tasks to which [government] is unaccustomed." Farm co-ops that own granaries and slaughterhouses can eliminate middlemen and bring farmers a living income. (Middlemen produce nothing, and so failed to engage Roosevelt's sympathies). Insofar as co-ops alone did not suffice, government should use progressive taxation to break-up large landed estates, to make capital available to family farmers, and (rather vaguely) "to care for the woman on the farm as much as for the man, and to eliminate the conditions which now so often tend to make her life one of gray and sterile drudgery."[47] As Tocqueville had seen, by abolishing primogeniture Jefferson and the other Founders had prevented the gentry from forming a titled aristocracy on American soil. Lincoln had ruined the chances of a permanent, slave-based aristocracy. Roosevelt's identical intention addressed the danger of the corporate oligarchy, but in a way he had a harder job. He did not want to destroy it, as it did real good. He wanted to show its potential victims how to stand up to it.

Roosevelt's attention engaged workers' problems far more than those of farmers. As with malefactors of great wealth, so with malefactors of small wealth: "Modern industrial conditions" require "organization of labor in order better to secure the rights of the individual wage-worker," even as such conditions require better organization of capital and of industrial firms. "But when any labor-union seeks improper ends, or seeks to achieve proper ends by improper means, all good citizens and more especially all honorable public servants must oppose the wrong-doing as resolutely as they would oppose the wrong-doing of any great corporation."[48] "The labor problem is a human and a moral as well as an economic problem." Material conditions affect moral conduct, and vice versa. Thus, for example, "the tariff rate must never fall below that which will protect the American workingman by allowing for the difference between the general labor cost here and abroad," so as to foster "the needs of better educated, better paid, better fed, and better clothed workingmen of a higher type"—in intelligence, comfort, "the high standard of civilized living," and "inventive genius"—"than any to be found in a foreign country."[49] Neither the material nor the moral end of the equation should be neglected.

Roosevelt did not posit a moral equivalence with respect to the *situation* of labor and that of business. Again, labor is prior to capital. "The Nation and the Government, within the range of fair play and a just administration of the law, must inevitably sympathize with the men who have nothing but their wages, with the men who are struggling for a decent life, as opposed to men, however honorable, who are merely fighting for larger profits and an autocratic control of big business." The closing of the western frontier with its free land meant that wage earners who want to better their lives are "compelled to progress not by ceasing to be wage-earners, but by improving the conditions under which all the wage-earners in all the industries of the country lived and worked, as well, of course, as improving their own individual efficiency." It was no longer possible to solve economic problems in the cities simply by pulling up stakes and moving toward the horizon. The new frontiers would be those of self-government and productivity within the workplace. Too, the "crass inequality in the bargaining relation between the employer and the individual employee standing alone" threatened not only economic but "simple human rights." A "simple and poor society can exist as a democracy on the basis of sheer individualism," but "a rich and complex industrial society cannot so exist."[50]

Notwithstanding the moral superiority of labor to capital, the moral *character* of workers is "not one whit better" than that of capitalists. "The mass of them on one side is about like the mass on the other; and while the very worst labor people are no worse than the very worst among the capitalists, they so completely outnumber [the capitalists] as to be on the whole as great an element of danger to the community." Socialist newspapers, for example, have even "less regard for truth and for honesty and decency even than the corresponding capitalist papers—if there can be comparatives along the lower levels of baseness."[51] While capitalists, in asserting private property rights, at times refuse to recognize the rights of the public, trade unionists talk of general strikes, which could precipitate "a crisis only less serious than the civil war."[52] Roosevelt's forceful handling of the strike at the anthracite coal mines of Pennsylvania, and of other such disputes in which labor violence occurred, recalled the harsh treatment of rebellion under the administrations of Washington and Lincoln, both of whom brooked no anarchy in the guise of self-government. Roosevelt indignantly rejected the class-war ideology of Marxism, whether expressed in calls for violence, non-violent conflict, or both.

The "Square Deal" meant equal justice for both sides, and that finally meant labor-capital cooperation buttressing a strong nationalism. "There is no reason why any of these economic groups should not consult their group interests by any legitimate means and with due regard to the common, overlying interests of all."[53] State socialism, by contrast, would require "an iron despotism over all workers, compared to which any slave system of the past would seem beneficent, because utterly hopeless"—unless state socialism simply were to cause mass starvation, the destruction of the society it proposed to transform. "The worst wrongs that capitalism can commit upon labor would sink into insignificance when compared with the hideous wrongs done by those who would degrade labor by sapping the foundations of self-respect and self-reliance." The very materialism of Marxism and of other forms of modern socialism makes them "not only indifferent, but at bottom hostile, to the intellectual, the religious, the domestic and moral life; it is a form of communism with no moral foundation, but essentially based on the immediate annihilation of personal ownership of capital, and, in the near future, the annihilation of the family, and ultimately the annihilation of civilization." The socialist mixture of materialism and quasi-religious spiritedness yields an odd dogmatism that compromises the life of the mind, resulting in a disconnection between the mind and actual experience in the world: "Too many thoroughly well-meaning men and women in the America of today glibly repeat and accept—much as medieval schoolmen repeated and accepted authorized dogma in their day—various assumptions and speculations by Marx and others which by the lapse of time and by actual experiment have been shown to possess not one shred of value."[54] Such socialist reforms as child labor laws, better working hours, sanitation, worker safety, and employers' liability are entirely just. But they can be had without statism, and with self-government.

Class consciousness, so called, "is merely another name for the odious vice of class selfishness"—"equally noxious whether in an employer's association or in a working man's association."[55] A people "genuinely skilled in and fitted for self-government ... therefore will spurn the leadership of those who seek to excite this ferocious and foolish class antagonism," animated by "envy and arrogance," which are "but different developments of the same spirit."[56] Given that "the foundation of our whole social structure rests upon the material and moral well-being, the intelligence, the foresight, the sanity, the sense of duty, and the wholesome patriotism of the wage-worker," such "mutual misunderstanding," such "failure to appreciate one another's point of view," must be remedied by the "fellow feeling, sympathy, brotherhood" that "comes by association." "Our prime need as a nation is that every American should understand and work with his fellow citizens, getting into touch with them, so that by actual contact he may learn that fundamentally he and they have the same interests, needs, and aspirations."[57] In this advocacy of labor-capital association, Roosevelt departs from the familiar Madisonian argument concerning faction, set down in *Federalist* 10; Madison would not unite the extended republic but rule it by letting it divide, and letting its divisions compete with, and so regulate, one another. Madison would have regarded Roosevelt's project as overly ambitious, likely to be dangerous in failure or success alike. Roosevelt never explicitly replied to Madison. Had he done so, he might have argued that national corporations and the technologies they themselves controlled had in one sense united the republic in a way the Founders could not foresee. Larger civil-associational units, working in cooperation with corporations when possible, against them when necessary, alone could defend individuals on the level of the social sphere.

Although corporations may unite Americans on terms amenable to oligarchs, Roosevelt sees that in another sense modern life is even more specialized and compartmentalized than in Madison's time; not only new trades, but also new workers consisting of new (to America) ethnic identities have proliferated. In addition to stronger civil-associational ties, correspondingly stronger state and national governments are also needed to hold vast and ever-more diverse populations together: "a governmental control that will check the corporation when it is doing wrong and check the labor-union when it is doing wrong." "[D]isregard[ing] equally the apostles of ultracollectivism and the doctrinaires of ultra-individualism," acknowledging that "the extreme capitalistic tyranny which once treated trades-unions as illegal and sought to make of the laborer a serf was largely responsible for the subsequent outbreaks of labor-union tyranny which in certain places and at certain times have taken the form of criminal conspiracies against society,"[58] Americans should consider the German example. In Germany the state has regulated the corporations, "securing justice and reasonably fair treatment among capitalists, managers, salaried experts, and wage-workers—*all of whom had some voice in, some control of, at least certain parts of their common business.*" Large-scale corporations with some degree of worker self-government—"a shift in control which will mean that the competent workers become partners in the enterprise," sharing not only profits but "the guidance and management" of the firm—and large-scale cooperatives among small-scale merchants, farmers, and workers will dominate "small individualistic business[es]" in many sectors. Government can "make the people a partner of both" the corporations and the labor unions, "supervis[ing] the relations of each to the other and of both to the general public." "When the tool-user has some ownership in and some control over the tool, the matter of opposition to labor-saving machinery," and to "scientific management" generally, "will largely solve itself"; "for then a substantial part of the benefit will come to the working man, instead of having it all come as profit to the capitalist, while the working man may see his job vanish." Such "industrial democracy" will not entail "handing over the control of matters requiring expert knowledge to masses of men who lack that knowledge," but rather will depend upon "the men in the ranks hav[ing] sufficient self-knowledge and self-control to accept and demand expert leadership as part of the necessary division of labor." Otherwise, democracy, "whether in industry or politics," will "simply show that it is unfit to survive." Thus "though the conditions of life have grown so puzzling in their complexity ... yet we may remain absolutely sure of one thing, that now, as ever in the past, and as it ever will be in the future, there can be no substitute for the elemental virtues, for the elemental qualities to which we allude when we speak of a man as not only a good man but as emphatically a man." Manliness or *andreia* would enable Roosevelt's contemporaries to have the courage to see unflinchingly the *necessity* of acting in accordance to the new conditions of economic life.[59]

Roosevelt recalled the legacy of Abraham Lincoln to garner support for his policies. In Roosevelt's estimation, in recognizing the priority of labor to capital, Lincoln was right. In recognizing the need for the recognition of individual or natural rights of men as such, Lincoln again was right. But under modern conditions so different than those that prevailed in the mid-nineteenth century, Lincoln's principles need a new application. "Lincoln's teachings, applied to the facts of today, mean that if alive now he would lead toward a working combination of collective control and liberty, just as he once led toward a working combination of individual control and liberty."[60]

SELF-GOVERNMENT AND THE NATIONAL STATE

Roosevelt endorsed popular sovereignty limited by civil rights, and natural rights. He distinguished between civil and natural rights, saying that "it is simple idle folly to talk of suffrage [for example] as being an 'inborn' or 'natural' right." At a minimum, he continued, even the most civilized society will impose age limits on suffrage.[61] Although "I would not be willing to die for what I regard as the untrue abstract statement that all men are in all respects equal, and are all alike entitled to the same power ... I would be quite willing to die—or better still, to fight so effectively that I should live—for the proposition that each man has certain rights which no other man should be allowed to take away from him, and that in certain great and vital matters all men should be treated as equal before the law and before the bar of public opinion."[62] To this qualified natural and civil equality, consistent with the principles of the Founders, Roosevelt added liberty. "The distinguishing feature of our American governmental system is the freedom of the individual" from the oppression of the one or the many. Finally, government must provide a framework conducive to the pursuit of happiness ("government agencies must find their justification largely in the way in which they are used for the practical betterment of living and working conditions among the mass of the people").[63]

Unlike the Founders, for whom property rights clearly number among the human rights, Roosevelt distinguishes between property rights and human rights. The need for such a distinction probably stems from the increased importance of large corporations, and their treatment as legal "persons" entitled to property rights. The "rights of man"—worship, to engage in politics, and to work—trump the rights of property, when they conflict with it.[64]

Human or natural rights are secured by the Constitution, or, as Roosevelt put it: "The Declaration of Independence has to be supplemented in the first place by that great instrument of constructive and administrative statesmanship—the constitution under which we now live."[65] Constitution making is "the fundamental work of self-government."[66] The Declaration of Independence also introduces institution building as a means of securing unalienable rights, so Roosevelt's argument here generally tracks the reasoning of the second paragraph of the Declaration, although he is ambiguous on natural right. "All constitutions ... are designed, and must be interpreted and administered so as to fit human rights, as Lincoln had done and as Buchanan had not.[67]

But there is an ambiguity here. For the Founders, natural rights provided the stable foundation for civil rights because human nature, and thus the rights inherent in it, does not change. In Roosevelt's more "progressivist" moods, human rights inhere in a humanity characterized by "the eternal forces of human growth."[68] If pressed, this could end in John Dewey's historicized natural right, finally identical to historicism. Roosevelt, however, does not develop this thought. His progressivism or historicism thus seems quite limited in comparison to more ambitious notions of so many twentieth century political "leaders" and ideologues. It may be that Roosevelt, a lifelong student of nature—moreover a student who studied nature directly, out "in nature," not only in books—had a more sober sense of how much effort survival and growth require than did so many of his contemporaries.

With regard to the strengths of the American regime, Roosevelt acknowledged the significance of the Founders' understanding of the extended republic—of both its extensiveness and its republicanism taken together. "The nations of antiquity, the nations of the middle ages, that tried the experiment of self-government ... rarely lasted long, never rose to a pitch of greatness, such as ours, without having suffered some radical and, as it proved ultimately, fatal change of structure. Until our Republic was founded it had proved impossible in the long run to combine freedom for the individual and greatness for the nation."[69] Monarchy is not necessarily evil; the last Dutch colonial governor of New York, Peter Stuyvesant, was a "brave and gallant old fellow," a "kindly tyrant"; the crowned heads of Europe Roosevelt met during his 1911 tour were polite and responsible folk. But Stuyvesant lacked the popular support to defend his outpost against British ships, and the European monarchs "were like other human beings in that the average among them was not very high as regards intellect and force."[70] Indeed, "I have not much sympathy with Hamilton's distrust of the democracy," despite democracy's weakness for demagoguery. "[T]he highly cultivated classes, who tend to become either cynically worldly-wise or to develop along the lines of the Eighteenth Century philosophers, and the moneyed classes, especially those of large fortune, whose ideal tends to be mere money, are not fitted for any predominant guidance in a really great nation."[71] Only the people themselves provide the material foundation for greatness, but their rule "is good only if the majority has the will and the morality and the intelligence to do right"—which condition has not occurred in most countries at most times.[72] Roosevelt's often-remarked moralism addresses this danger. He deliberately made his moralism impossible to miss, and I have found no reader who has. He links national greatness firmly to republicanism and to citizen virtue in a decidedly un-Machiavellian manner. Politically and individually, self-government "is in its essence the substitution of self-restraint for external restraint." As Lincoln saw, "in a self-governing democracy those who desire to be considered fit to enjoy liberty must show that they know how to use it with moderation and justice in peace"—of "self-control and of learning by their mistakes"—"and how to fight for it when it is jeoparded by malice domestic or foreign levy."[73] Mutuality of service and of respect for service rendered,[74] both founded upon "equality of opportunity as far as it is humanly possible to secure it," is not only a right but a duty, representing "the triumph of orderly liberty."[75]

As noted, Roosevelt sought to extend the power of the American national government. He did not want to be understood as a statist, again separating himself from the Machiavellian line. Not only are "vigorous forms of self-government in state and city" desirable, but the national government itself must be democratized. "What is meant by the nationalization of the democratic method is the giving to the whole people themselves the power to do those things that are essential in the interest of the whole people."[76] "[A] strong central government [is] perfectly compatible with absolute democracy."[77] Three years before Herbert Croly published *The Promise of American Life*, with its famous formula, "Hamiltonian means, Jeffersonian ends," Roosevelt said, "while I am a Jeffersonian in my genuine faith in democracy and popular government, I am a Hamiltonian in my governmental views, especially with reference to the need of the exercise of broad powers by the National Government."[78]

Contemporary social conditions require a more prince-like American president, with respect to the exercise of executive power. This requires the unMachiavellian Roosevelt to find some means other than institutions to control the president. Separation of powers, between states and the national government and even among the branches of the national government itself, now matters less than *responsibility* of government officers to the people. "What is normally needed is the concentration in the hands of one man, or of a very small body of men, of ample power to enable him or them to do the work that is necessary; and then the devising of means to hold these men fully responsible for the exercise of that power by the people." That is true "self-government" and "good government."[79] "The danger to American democracy lies not in the least in the concentration of administrative power in responsible and accountable hands. It lies in having the power insufficiently concentrated, so that no one can be held responsible to the people for its use." Concentrated power that is "palpable, visible, responsible, easily reached, quickly held to account" will not compromise democracy but save it from secrecy-loving oligarchs.[80] What scholars now call "the modern presidency"—the opinionated, publicized, personalized presidency—arose from this need for a real national government in which the apparatus of the bureaucratic state serves responsible self-government by means of elected representatives who are sufficiently conspicuous to be both heard and watched.

The empowered and responsible executive officer of the national government should be "the steward of the public welfare" and, in "great national crises," "the steward of the people." Roosevelt borrows stewardship from the Bible, particularly from the Book of Luke, chapters 12 and 16—the parables of the faithful steward and the shrewd steward, respectively (the latter concluding in a sharp contrast between stewards faithful to God and stewards faithful to Mammon). A steward rules the household by serving his lord. He has latitude for "executive action," but also full responsibility to the lord. In his executive latitude, the steward-president "is bound to assume that he has the legal right to do whatever the needs of the people demand, unless the Constitution or the laws explicitly forbid him to do it." This, Roosevelt claims, is the model of the presidency followed by Andrew Jackson and Abraham Lincoln, and it contrasts with the example of James Buchanan, who claimed that he could perform no actions except those explicitly permitted him under the Constitution.[81] He had in mind the Christian distinction between fidelity to the spirit of the Law and fidelity to the letter of the Law.

The duties of the steward-executive spill into the legislative sphere. Because the president "is or ought to be peculiarly representative of the people as a whole," he should "take a very active interest in getting the right kind of legislation" in addition to his strictly executive work. He can do this "only by arousing the people, and riveting their attention" on what must be done—the use of the executive office as the celebrated "bully pulpit."[82] This conception of the executive lends itself to a routinization of emergency or, to put it differently, the fomenting and/or proclaiming of crises that cry out for—or, more precisely, that the executive cries out in behalf of—bold management.

Given Roosevelt's own forcefully stated reservations about popular sovereignty—particularly, the danger of majority tyranny resulting from demagoguery—and given also his impatience with the doctrine of separation of powers—the stewardship theory gave some observers pause. The most prominent of these, sometime friend and ally William Howard Taft, wrote: "The wide field of action that this would give to the Executive one can hardly limit." Lincoln, by contrast, acting under "the stress of the greatest civil war in modern times," "always pointed out the source of the authority which in his opinion justified his acts"— for example, the constitutional warrant for suspending the writ of habeas corpus, which was in the event confirmed by Congress, albeit after the fact. Although "there is little danger to the public weal from the tyranny or reckless character of a President who is not sustained by the people," Taft continued, there is some danger from one who is. Fortunately, "this condition cannot probably be long continued," as the people themselves will desert the would-be tyrant or overreaching democrat.[83] In Roosevelt's defense one might reply that his conception of the executive cannot be separated from his conception of the right kind of political man who will be the executive, nor from the right kind of private men and women whom the executive will serve. A self-governing president in alliance with a self-governing people—in the full, Rooseveltian sense of the term—will scarcely present a danger to minorities. But this drifts far from the Madisonian sense of the frailties of even the best public men, and the best peoples.[84] Both those men and those peoples might go to the spirited wells of thumotic passion too habitually, losing the inclination of prudence that the Founders, and Washington above all, required in themselves. Human nature must indeed "grow" or progress in order to make progressivism feasible. This, again, is what Roosevelt's rhetoric from the bully pulpit was for.

With respect to the other branches of government, Roosevelt had little of interest to say about the legislative branch, confining himself to accounts of how it can act corruptly and to recommendations that honest legislators always hit their enemies hard.[85] In this, Roosevelt seems to have shared the estimate of many Progressives and of reformers generally: that Congress, having gained dominance after the assassination of Lincoln, tended to corruption, and other opaque dealings out of the public view. The judiciary branch, however, came under more serious scrutiny. Roosevelt frankly and publicly said that judges should be selected not only for their character—"such elementary virtues as honesty, courage, and fair-mindedness"—but for their "economic and social philosophy." Every interpretation reflects such "philosophy"; "judges, like executives and legislators, should hold sound views on the questions of public policy which are of vital interest to the people."[86] A judge should be "a party man, a constructive statesman, constantly keeping in mind his adherence to the principles and policies under which this nation has been built up and in accordance with which it must go on; and keeping in mind also his relations with his fellow statesmen who in other branches of the government are striving in cooperation with him to advance the ends of government."[87] Roosevelt did, at times, commend the restriction of judicial activity to interpretation of the law. "A law may be unwise and improper, but it should not for these reasons be declared unconstitutional by a strained interpretation, for the result of such action is to take away from the people at large their sense of responsibility and ultimately to destroy their capacity for orderly self-restraint and self-government";[88] indeed, the decisions of state supreme courts should be subject to popular revision by means of initiative and referendum.[89] But at other times he conceded that judges make law. "In judging Marshall and Taney, for instance, I think the difference between them was not the technical propriety of their interpretation of law, but in their wisdom in what was really creating law."[90] The discrepancy may be explained by noticing the public character of Roosevelt's "judicial restraint" expression, and the private character of his "judicial legislation" expressions.

Of such "party men" as Roosevelt mentions, there are essentially two categories in American history since the founding. The Democrats have stood for the people, but not often for the people as a whole. They have been mired in localism. Localism yields not the pure, citizen virtue the gentlemanly Jefferson envisioned but the corrupt bossism and spoilsmanship instituted by Jackson and perfected by the Little Magician, Martin Van Buren. The paradox of the Democratic conception of democracy may be seen in the election of Van Buren himself; the party machine of "the democracy" produced a president no one would otherwise have voted for.[91] In his own day, Roosevelt wrote, the Democratic Party still bore the scars of antebellum corruption: "In no long time I believe that the division between the forces of wise progress and of reaction in the Democratic Party will become so marked as to render it evident to the people of this country that that party is powerless to work effectively for the common welfare of all the citizens of this nation."[92] Of course, much the same could be said—and Roosevelt eventually did say it—about the Republican Party, "which in the days of Abraham Lincoln was founded as the radical progressive party of the Nation," which rightly resisted the "foolish and ill-judged mock radicalism" of the Populists in the last decade of the nineteenth century, and remained strongly nationalist.[93] When Roosevelt left the Republican Party in 1912, he may have intended to rally all "progressives" from both parties, an event that would have led to a straightforward ideological party system consisting of a "progressive" and a conservative or "reactionary" party. Alternatively, the Republican Party might have been purged of its "reactionary" elements, which would have gone over to the Democrats and driven the "progressives" out of that party. As happens so often in politics, the dialectic never played out so neatly.

Indeed, for Roosevelt there seems to have been no *historical* dialectic that could "play out." "Progress" for Roosevelt requires a real fight for principles grounded in morality, but one can lose that fight. Roosevelt does take political life to be a form of the struggle for survival by "the fittest," as so many of his generation in America did. But unlike Wilson, Roosevelt holds out no assurance, guaranteed either by Providence or by History, that "the fittest" will be morally right, that human nature really will grow in the right direction, that some inevitable triumph of the *good* awaits us at the "end of history." "Progress" to him meant movement toward what he called "realizable ideals," but such ideals will not *necessarily* be realized. Roosevelt heeds Tocqueville's warning against the democratic tendency toward "necessitarian" doctrines, and remains within the American theme of self-government.

Roosevelt's understanding of civil service reform becomes clearer if seen in the light of this moral and partisan struggle. Civil service reform was Roosevelt's remedy for Democratic machine politics. Historian William Henry Harbaugh sees that "civil service reform was at once the most confirmed and most sustained cause of Roosevelt's career." "The bulk of government is not legislative but administrative," Roosevelt said. The attempt to set part of government beyond the reach of partisanship was, then, itself a partisan move—a move that would end the old partisanship of spoils and force political struggle to a higher moral plane.[94] Roosevelt acknowledged the appeal, and even the merit, of machine politics. "There is often much good in the type of boss, especially common in the big cities, who fulfills towards the people of his district in rough and ready fashion the position of friend and protector." For immigrants in particular, city life has something in common with the frontier West: these are "men and women who struggle hard against poverty and with whom the problem of living is very real and very close." They understandably prefer the man who gets them jobs, loans them money, and organizes clambakes to the reformer who talks about "good government." "They would prefer clean and honest government, if this clean and honest government is accompanied by human sympathy, human understanding. But an appeal made to them for virtue in the abstract, an appeal made by good men who do not really understand their needs, will often pass quite unheeded, if on the other side stands the boss, the friend and benefactor, who may have been guilty of much wrong-doing in things that they are hardly aware concern them, but who appeals to them, not only for the sake of favors to come, but in the name of gratitude and loyalty, and above all understanding and fellow-feeling."[95] Human life is neither a matter simply of "idealism" nor of "utility"; the Democratic Party had understood this for a long time, and had deployed such sentiments not only among the would-be aristocrats of the south but with more justice among the cities of the north.

What Paul Eidelberg has called "the politics of compassion"[96] among the Progressives begins with the attempt to reconfigure government so as to combine the honesty and efficiency esteemed by the civil service reformers with the sympathetic sentiments displayed by the bosses. The desire for governmental honesty and efficiency, the consequent desire to replace the spoils system with a professional civil service, and the desire "to break up the alliance between crooked business and crooked politics,"[97] the Wall Street-Tammany Hall nexus of "mutual payment and repayment," will never be satisfied if the concrete "human sympathy" and "human understanding" that animates bossism cannot be replicated by the reformers.[98] Toward this end, the civil service merit system of hiring and advancement will democratize government. More specifically, it will make government more truly a means of self-government by "filling these offices by an open and manly rivalry, into which every American citizen has the right to enter, without any more regard being paid to his political than to his religious creed, and without being required to render degrading service to any party boss."[99] "The boss does not develop in a community thoroughly fit for self-government," a population prepared for such open and manly rivalries.[100] Such communities may be brought to such fitness by a combination of reform politics with the reform economics of the Square Deal.

To democratize the civil service by opening civil service jobs to competitive examinations will not alone ensure that the resulting professional civil service will govern democratically, however. Reform politics will yield reformed government, but that reformed government must then yield a reformed politics. With civil service in place, "we can make political contests be fought and decided on public questions purely, and not be mixed up with undignified scrambles for patronage."[101] Then, Roosevelt predicts with pardonable partisan exaggeration, "the Republican party can and shall be made now what it was made under Lincoln—a great instrument for the achievement of righteousness through the rule of the plain people."[102] Such "progressive" measures as initiative, referendum, and recall would further ensure this "purified" popular control over government, even as—because—government officers themselves became professionals and experts.[103] "There never was a straighter fight waged for the principle of popular rule than that which we are now waging."[104] Why would money not then flow to the parties for the sake not of jobs but for the purpose of influencing the new, issues-oriented politics? Given the much higher stakes of a far-reaching "politics of compassion," given the enhanced power of the executive and of administration to enact policies consistent with that politics, why would corporations and labor unions not have all the more incentive to bankroll partisan campaigns? As noted above, Roosevelt supported a ban on corporate contributions to political campaigns. As for individual contributions, he judged them acceptable so long as there were "no strings attached"—a criterion that one might be excused for regarding as theoretically sound but practically flimsy. As a matter of fact the Republican Party accepted large sums of money from corporations in Roosevelt's 1904 campaign for the presidency, although at the time Roosevelt sharply denied any such goings on.[105] The point is not to convict Roosevelt of hypocrisy, which is rather too easy to do with anyone, but to note any reform at best does what the Founders expected: re-channel but not remove selfish and material incentives from public life. If self-government can rise only to the moral level of the "selves" doing the governing, then the use of the presidency as a pulpit makes sense. In his pulpit Roosevelt preached not religion but "the New Nationalism." The novelty of the new nationalism consisted in its rejection of racial and ethnic distinctions as morally and politically relevant categories, a rejection implicit in but not fulfilled by the founding. Thus in the end Roosevelt's "progressivism" points back to the principles of the founding in a way that Wilson's did not.

CONCLUSION

Against Machiavellian statism, the American Founders combined the "tamed-prince" strategy, encouraging a commercial civil society (a strategy laid out most elaborately by Montesquieu) with the civil associational strategy, including the proliferation of Christian churches, a strategy whose effects Tocqueville best describes. To this they added still another element, the "ancient" or "classical" virtues praised by Aristotle and the Stoics, and embodied by the greatest statesman among them, George Washington. Roosevelt to a considerable extent wanted to preserve the spirit of the founding—the combination of these three "spirits," in a world in which Machiavellianism had advanced impressively, a world of large industrial corporations and of formidable, centralized nation-states, both empowered by technology of global reach and by bureaucratic efficiency unknown as late as a half-century before. Rightly or wrongly, he judged that America would need increased administrative centralization to go with its existing political centralization, in order to continue to stand up to the Machiavellian challenge. The hazards of his project, of an empowered if not sovereign national state and, particularly, of an empowered national executive, struck thoughtful friends such as Taft, and continue to worry observers of the American presidency today.

Roosevelt's impatience with his critics most likely issued from his sense of the urgency of this project. His over-boiling indignation of Wilson—no friendly critic—probably issued from Roosevelt's driving conviction that the instruments of intentions of contemporary and future Machiavellians would require a considerable toughening of the American spirit, a muscular Christianity and a muscular liberalism that would stand at Armageddon to do *battle* for the Lord—that Americans could not allow themselves the luxury of supposing that Europeans had fought the battle already with the Great War, and that Americans need now only lead the chastened and war-weary in the spirit of the lamb. In this estimation of his own and of future times he turned out to have been right.

To understand Roosevelt as he understood himself, then, one must concentrate on his work as a political moralist. As a theorist, he left behind a farrago of liberalism, utilitarianism, Lamarckian progressivism; if one turns to him to resolve the theoretical questions his moralism raised, one turns in vain.[106] Because the shortcomings of Roosevelt's hardheaded progressivism have been noticed adequately by others, and remarked in passing here, I prefer to end by pointing to its one greatest merit. Roosevelt unfailingly pointed Americans toward real things—real nature, real battle, the realities of modern economics and nation-states and geopolitics. He always refused to let Americans hide behind comforting ideologies. Libertarianism, socialism, providentialisms sacred and profane—none of these could stand, and he scorned them all. Neither inevitable progress nor nostalgic return would do. He said this to Americans repeatedly, in a thousand ways. To the extent that he succeeded, won his hearing, he avoided the fate of Cassandra by leavening his realism with a spirit of generosity, even of magnanimity, that could serve as a charming, but not merely charming, countercharm to the ideological seductions he fought.

Endnotes

1. Alexis de Tocqueville, *Democracy in America*, trans. Harvey C. Mansfield Jr. and Delba Winthrop (Chicago: University of Chicago Press, 2000), I.i.5.82-93.

2. Ibid., II.ii.9.278-288.

3. See Will Morrisey, *Self-Government, The American Theme: Presidents of the Founding and the Civil War* (Lanham, Md.: Lexington Books, forthcoming), chapter 1.

4. George Washington, Letter to George Steptoe Washington, March 23, 1789, in *The Collected Writings of George Washington*, John Kirkpatrick, ed. (Washington, D. C.: United States Government Printing Office, 1931), 30.246-247.

5. Ibid., Letter to the Marquis de Lafayette, October 4, 1778. See also Richard Brookhiser, *Founding Father: Rediscovering George Washington* (New York: The Free Press, 1995), 116-119.

6. See Will Morrisey, *Self-Government, The American Theme*, chapter 5.

7. See Will Morrisey, *A Political Approach to Pacifism* (Lewiston, N.Y.: Edwin Mellen Press), 1996, 30-44.

8. Tocqueville, *Democracy in America*, II.ii.20.530-532.

9. See Henry Adams, "Civil Service Reform," *North American Review* 109 (October 1869): 443-475, and Brooks Adams, "The Platform of the New Party," *North American Review* 119 (July 1874): 33-60. I am indebted to my colleague Robert Eden for bringing these, and other writings of the civil service reformers, to my attention. Dr. Eden will be publishing the results of his study of the reformers in due course, in conjunction with his ongoing work on Woodrow Wilson.

10. Theodore Roosevelt quoted in William Henry Harbaugh, *Power and Responsibility: The Life and Times of Theodore Roosevelt* (New York: Farrar, Straus and Cudahy, 1961), 57.

11. Theodore Roosevelt, "The Strenuous Life," in *The Works of Theodore Roosevelt*, Herman Hagedorn, ed. (New York: Charles Scribner's Sons, 1923-26), 15.325, 330.

12. Ibid., "Fourth Annual Message to Congress," December 6, 1904, 17.265.

13. Ibid., *The Winning of the West*, 10.33-34.

14. Ibid., "Realizable Ideals," 15.10-12.

15. Ibid., "Fear God and Take Your Own Part," 20.521-523.

16. Roosevelt, Speech at Topeka, Kansas, May 1, 1903, in *A Compilation of the Messages and Speeches of Theodore Roosevelt*, Henry Alfred Lewis, ed. (Washington: Bureau of National Art and Literature, 1906), 318. See also Roosevelt, "Speech to the Brotherhood of Locomotive Firemen," Chattanooga, Tennessee, September 8, 1902, in *Works*, 18.204-206.

17. Roosevelt, "The Settlement at Jamestown," Address at the Jamestown Exhibition, Jamestown, Virginia, April 26, 1907, in *Works*, 12.593.

18. Roosevelt, Speech at Providence, Rhode Island, August 23, 1902, *A Compilation*, 74-75.

19. Roosevelt, "Eighth Annual Message to Congress," December 8, 1908, in *Works*, 17.604.

20. Ibid., "Eighth Annual Message to Congress," December 8, 1908, 17.604; *Autobiography*, 22.481.

21. Ibid., *Autobiography*, 22.483-484.

22. Roosevelt, Letter to Arthur Hamilton Lee, December 26, 1907, in *The Letters of Theodore Roosevelt*, Elting E. Morison, ed. (Cambridge: Harvard University Press, 1951-54), 6.874.

23. Roosevelt, "Eighth Annual Message to Congress," December 8, 1908, in *Works*, 17.587.

24. Ibid., *Autobiography*, 22.483.

25. Ibid.; see also Letter to Alfred W. Cooley, August 29, 1911, quoted in George E. Mowry, *The Era of Theodore Roosevelt: 1900-1912* (New York: Harper and Row, 1958), 55.

26. Roosevelt, *Autobiography*, in *Works*, 22.481-482.

27. Ibid., *Autobiography*, 484.

28. Roosevelt, Speech at Providence, Rhode Island, August 23, 1902, *A Compilation*, 79.

29. Roosevelt, "Fifth Annual Message to Congress, December 5, 1905, in *Works*, 17.317.

30. Ibid., "The Settlement at Jamestown," 12.595.

31. Roosevelt, Speech at Providence, Rhode Island, August 23, 1902, *A Compilation*, 79.

32. Roosevelt, "Second Annual Message to Congress," December 2, 1902, in *Works*, 17.164.

33. Ibid., "Annual Message to the New York State Legislature," Albany, New York, January 3, 1900, 17.46-47, 52-53.

34. Ibid., *Nationalism and Progress*, 19.142.

35. Ibid., "Seventh Annual Message to Congress," December 3, 1907, 17.487.

36. Ibid., "Sixth Annual Message to Congress," December 3, 1906, 17.401. See also "First Message to Congress," December 3, 1901, 17.1-3,105, 107.

37. Roosevelt, Speech at Banquet given by Attorney-General Knox, Pittsburgh, Pennsylvania, July 4, 1902, *A Compilation*, 50.

38. Roosevelt, "Progressive Democracy," essay, November 11, 1904, in *Works*, 14.222.

39. Roosevelt, Speech at Symphony Hall, Boston, Massachusetts, August 25, 1902, *A Compilation*, 69.

40. Roosevelt, "Progressive Democracy," essay, November 11, 1904, in *Works*, 14.222.

41. Ibid., "With Malice Toward None," Speech at Oyster Bay, New York, July 4, 1906, 18.9.

42. Roosevelt, Speech at Logansport, Indiana, September 23, 1902, *A Compilation*, 165.

43. Roosevelt, Letter to Alexander Lambert, November 1, 1907, *Letters*, 5.826.

44. Ibid.

45. Ibid., "Special Message of the President of the United States," January 31, 1908, 6.1578.

46. Ibid., Letter to Henry White, November 27, 1907, 5.858-859. In the event, without a government-controlled financial system to work with, Roosevelt dispatched Treasury Secretary George B. Cortelyou to the New York bankers headed by J. P. Morgan and made a deal: to save a key New York brokerage house whose ruin would have threatened the ruin of the New York Stock Exchange (an event that would have converted the financial panic into an economic depression), Morgan's United States Steel Corporation would be allowed to purchase the brokerage house's imperiled investment, the Tennessee Coal and Iron Company. No anti-trust action would be taken. In addition, Treasury issued $150 million in bonds and Treasury certificates for sale to banks on credit. The panic subsided, and there was no depression. See George E. Mowry, *The Era of Theodore Roosevelt*, 219.

47. Roosevelt, *The Foes of Our Own Household*, in *Works*, 21.114-115, 118.

48. Ibid., "Fourth Annual Message to Congress," December 6, 1904, 17.252-253.

49. Roosevelt, Speech at Logansport, Indiana, September 23, 1902, *A Compilation*, 168.

50. Roosevelt, *Autobiography*, in *Works*, 22.537-540, 547-548.

51. Roosevelt, Letter to Winston Churchill, August 4, 1915, *Letters*, 8.958-959.

52. Ibid., Letter to Winthrop Murray Crane, October 22, 1902, 3.362.

53. Roosevelt, *Autobiography*, in *Works*, 22.552-553.

54. Ibid., "Socialism," essay, March 20 and 27, 1909, 18.556-563.

55. Ibid., "Eighth Annual Message to Congress," December 8, 1908, 17.595.

56. Ibid., Speech at the State Fair, Syracuse, New York, September 7, 1903, 18.61-63.

57. Ibid., "The Labor Question," Speech at the Labor Day Picnic, September 3, 1900, 16.509-519.

58. Ibid., *The Foes of Our Own Household*, 21.69-70, 84-94.

59. Ibid., *The Foes of Our Own Household*, 21.70.

60. Ibid., *Gouverneur Morris*, 8.386-387.

61. Roosevelt, Letter to Lyman Abbot, July 26, 1904, *Letters*, 4.866.

62. Roosevelt, *Autobiography*, in *Works*, 22.526.

63. Ibid., Speech at Lincoln Day Banquet, New York, February 12, 1913, 19.485.

64. Roosevelt, Speech at a Banquet Given by Attorney-General Knox, Pittsburgh, Pennsylvania, July 4, 1902, *A Compilation*, 46.

65. Roosevelt, Address before the Ohio Constitutional Convention, Columbus, Ohio, February 2, 1912, *Works*, 19.163.

66. Ibid., 165.

67. Ibid., Speech at Lincoln Day Banquet, New York, February 12, 1913, 19.485.

68. Roosevelt, Speech before the Minnesota Legislature, St. Paul, Minnesota, April 4, 1903, *A Compilation*, 249.

69. Roosevelt, *New York*, in *Works*, 9.246, 256. See also Roosevelt, "Speech at the Dedication of the State Arsenal of Springfield, Illinois," June 4, 1903, *A Compilation*, 478-479.

70. Roosevelt, *New York*, in *Works*, 9.246.

71. Roosevelt, Letter to Frederick Scott Oliver, August 9, 1906, *Letters*, 5.352.

72. Ibid., Letter to Charles Dwight Willard, April 28, 1911, 7.256.

73. Roosevelt, "The Men of Gettysburg," Address at Gettysburg, Pennsylvania, May 30, 1904, in *Works*, 12.609-610. See also Address at Carnegie Hall, New York, March 20, 1912, 19.200.

74. Ibid., *The Great Adventure*, 21.372.

75. Ibid., "The Wisdom of Hope in National Affairs," Speech at Cairo, Illinois, September 3, 1907, 18.17.

76. Ibid., "Progressive Democracy," essay, November 18, 1914, 14.218.

77. Ibid., *Gouverneur Morris*, 8.383.

78. Roosevelt, Letter to William Plumer Potter, April 23, 1906, *Letters*, 5.216-217.

79. Roosevelt, *Autobiography*, in *Works*, 22.204-205.

80. Ibid., "Eighth Annual Message to Congress," December 8, 1908, 17.586.

81. Ibid., *Autobiography*, 22.411, 481, 530.

82. Ibid., 22.322-323.

83. William Howard Taft, *Our Chief Magistrate and His Powers* (New York: Columbia University Press, 1925), 142-155. See also John Morton Blum, *The Republican Roosevelt* (New York: Atheneum, 1968), 123; Lewis

L. Gould, *The Presidency of Theodore Roosevelt* (Lawrence: University of Kansas Press, 1991), 198. For a recent, brief restatement of the Taft criticism, see Charles Kesler, "Bearish on Teddy," review of H. W. Brands, *T.R.: The Last Romantic*, in *The National Interest* 51(1999): 105-109.

84. On this point see Harbaugh, *Power and Responsibility*, 262 and Howard K. Beale, *Theodore Roosevelt and the Rise of America to World Power* (Baltimore: Johns Hopkins University Press, 1956), 453.

85. Roosevelt, *Autobiography*, in *Works*, 22.84-85, 103.

86. Ibid., "Eighth Annual Message to Congress," December 8, 1908, 17.601-602.

87. Roosevelt, Letter to Henry Cabot Lodge, July 10, 1902, *Letters*, 3.289.

88. Roosevelt, "Eighth Annual Message to Congress," December 8, 1908, in *Works*, 17.603.

89. Ibid., Address before the Ohio Constitutional Convention, Columbus, Ohio, 19.188.

90. Roosevelt, Letter to Frederick Getman Fincke, June 7, 1901, *Letters*, 3.89.

91. Roosevelt, *Thomas Hart Benton*, in *Works*, 8.53-55, 138-139.

92. Roosevelt, Letter to Robert Scadden Vessey et al., January 22, 1913, *Letters*, 7.692.

93. Roosevelt, *Autobiography*, in *Works*, 22.397-398.

94. Harbaugh, *Power and Responsibility*, 75; Roosevelt quoted in Blum, *The Republican Roosevelt*, 17.

95. Roosevelt, *Autobiography*, in *Works*, 22.180-181.

96. Paul Eidelberg, *A Discourse on Statesmanship: The Design and Transformation of the American Founding* (Urbana: University of Illinois Press, 1974), 342-346. Roosevelt attempted to combine what for Eidelberg are polar opposites, the politics of compassion and the politics of magnanimity.

97. Roosevelt, Speech at Elmira, New York, October 14, 1910, in *Works*, 19.43, 59.

98. Ibid., *Autobiography*, 22.155-156, 176-177.

99. Ibid., "The Merit System versus the Patronage System," essay, February 1890, 16.158-159.

100. Roosevelt, Letter to Francis Cabot Lodge, March 16, 1900, *Letters*, 2.1228-1229. On the extent of Roosevelt's efforts to expand the classified civil service during his presidential administration, see Gould, *The Presidency of Theodore Roosevelt*, 199.

101. Roosevelt, Letter to Rufus R. Dawes, October 24, 1890, *Letters*, 1.236.

102. Ibid., Letter to Joseph Moore Dixon, March 8, 1912, 7.522.

103. Roosevelt, Speech to the Progressive Party Convention, Chicago, Illinois, August 6, 1912, in *Works*, 19.364-365.

104. Roosevelt, Letter to Joseph Moore Dixon, March 8, 1912, *Letters*, 7.523.

105. Ibid., Letter to Moses Edwin Clapp, August 28, 1912, 7.623. See also Mowry, *The Era of Theodore Roosevelt*, 178-179.

106. A good example of the potential theoretical confusion Roosevelt spreads may be seen in his letter to the German-born Harvard Professor Hugo Munsterberg, written during the First World War, before America's entry. "I do not believe that the Americanism of today should be a mere submission to the American ideals of the period of the Declaration of Independence. Such action would be not only to stand still, but to go back....I have actively fought in favor of grafting onto our social life, no less than on our industrial life, many of the German ideals" (Letter to Hugo Munsterberg, February 2, 1916, *Letters*, 8.1018). That looks like a smoking gun held over the corpses of Washington and Jefferson, but it turns out that the one example Roosevelt offers of an "ideal" he wanted to graft onto American social life was "the German type of club," which had admitted women as well as men, before American clubs did. He assured Munsterberg that there were many more such "German ideals" that he advocated, without specifying any. He sharply criticized German militarism, and of course called insistently for American entry into the war.

·⌣Chapter 3⌣·

Frederick Douglass' Natural Rights Constitutionalism: The Postwar, Pre-Progressive Period

Peter C. Myers

INTRODUCTION

To reflect on the career of Frederick Douglass is to be reminded of a famous self-description attributed to one of his great contemporaries. "I am not *an* American," Mark Twain wrote in his journal, "I am *the* American." In his most popular speech, "Self-Made Men," Douglass ranks Americans among the world's exemplary self-made peoples, having risen by their own virtues to freedom and greatness, from low beginnings and against great odds. In other words, Americans stand out as perhaps humankind's exemplary *revolutionary* people. Properly understood, the American people's revolution follows a broad Lockean course. It consists, first, in their assertion of natural liberty against subjection to arbitrary, hereditary power, and second, in their renunciation of natural liberty in favor of civil, constitutional liberty. Likewise, Douglass presents his personal revolution as the primary theme of his autobiographies. "You have seen how a man was made a slave," he says, preparing the unforgettable story of his morally self-liberating battle with the slavebreaker Covey; "you shall see how a slave was made a man" (N 75; cf. BF 138, 151-52; LT 124, 126, 143).[1] And just as his countrymen's first revolution required a second—his recovery of natural liberty also required completion by a further revolution. As readers of Douglass' first autobiography witness the revolutionary self-transformation of a slave into a man, so his second autobiography shows us, in the story of his renunciation of Garrisonian disunion, the beginning of a more important revolution: the transformation of a man into a citizen. The bearer of natural liberty becomes an apostle of constitutional liberty.

The essential question for America's revolutionary founding, however, or for any attempt to establish constitutional liberty on the basis of a claim to natural liberty, concerns its stability. As Lincoln framed it at Gettysburg, the essential question is whether any nation conceived in liberty and dedicated to the proposition that all men are created equal can long endure. Must the modern American revolution, commenced in the name of natural human rights, beget further revolutions antagonistic to those rights and purporting to supersede them? This question, central to the present volume, is also a prominent question for Douglass.

It is a prominent question for Douglass not mainly in the more thoroughly studied, antebellum period of his constitutional thought, but rather in his postwar arguments. After 1865 as before, Douglass defended the Constitution and urged the broad reading and full application of national powers to vanquish slavery altogether, in spirit as well as in form. Yet, also during the postwar years, he occasionally ventured more general reflections on the nature of republican government and, in this context, advanced a serious critique of the Founders' Constitution as insufficiently democratic. In several important respects, Douglass' critique resembles the deeply damaging critique advanced shortly thereafter by leaders of the Progressive movement. Hence the question arises whether the evolution of Douglass' personal career epitomizes that of his nation—or at least of its ruling elites—in this respect, too, in affirming initially the principles of natural equality and liberty and the constitutional order constructed upon them, only subsequently to be lured astray by the god of historical Progress.

In the discussion that follows, I consider two main elements of Douglass' constitutional thought in the postwar period. Each embodies a challenging argument, and each, as we will see, is in important respects problematic. Yet, whatever its difficulties and despite some appearances to the contrary, I conclude that Douglass' postwar constitutionalism remains grounded in his continuing agreement with, not any rejection of, the Founders' fundamental principles. However "progressive" he may have found his critique of the Founders' Constitution, Douglass was never a forerunner of Progressivism in his fundamental principles. From the 1850s until his death in 1895, Douglass insisted on reading the Constitution in the light of the first principles of moral and political philosophy, and he never wavered from the conviction that those first principles could be no other than those the Founders originally declared, the laws of nature and of nature's God or the principles of natural human rights. In ordering my discussion of Douglass' postwar constitutionalism, it is convenient to begin with his interpretations of constitutional powers and rights after 1865 and thereafter to consider his ideas for constitutional reform.

Interpreting the Postwar Constitution

The Civil War and its immediate aftermath seemed to herald the grand, comprehensive triumph of Douglass' antebellum, antislavery constitutional arguments. Mindful of the Emancipation Proclamation's limitations, he was yet convinced that its deep, ultimate meaning "was the entire abolition of slavery" (*LT* 354). Beginning with the Proclamation and extending through the Fifteenth Amendment, the abolition of slavery and the securing of equal civil rights, grounded in natural rights and guaranteed by national citizenship, gained explicit constitutional status. More broadly, the outcome of the Civil War signified to Douglass the triumph of the principle of national Union, especially over the disintegrative alternatives proposed by the likes of John Calhoun and Stephen Douglas. The War rendered Calhounian, Confederate notions of government "anachronisms and superstitions." At a stroke, it swept away the notion of state sovereignty along with the larger allegiance to sectionalism (*LT* 434, *FDP* 5.400). At a still deeper level, the Union victory effectively discredited (at least until the late twentieth century) Stephen Douglas' paradoxical but seductive appeals to "diversity" as the Union's unifying principle. It heralded the end of all hitherto deep, pernicious divisions in American political life—divisions by race and, ultimately, gender as well as by state and section—and the emergence, for the first time, of a truly unified American nation. The War would "make us a homogenous [*sic*] people" (*FDP* 4.280; also 4.524; *LW* 3.274, 4.306).

Especially in its immediate aftermath, Douglass interpreted the promise of the Civil War in grandly enthusiastic terms. Its greatest, deepest object was to effectuate the vision of human unity common to the Constitution, the Declaration of Independence, and the Bible itself. At its origin and now fortified by the postwar amendments, the Constitution contains "nothing of a narrow description." It stands "free from bigotry, free from superstition, free from sectarian prejudices, caste or political distinction. In the eye of that great instrument we are neither Jews, Greeks, Barbarians or Cythians, but fellow-citizens of a common country, embracing all men of all colors" (*FDP* 4.153). The Fourteenth Amendment reaffirms the Declaration's principle of the equality of human persons; Douglass reassured his "Democratic friends" in 1870 that Thomas Jefferson was its true author (*FDP* 4.272). While it justly claimed roots in the Declaration, however, Douglass' understanding of the American nation's universalist meaning and mission clearly expanded upon that of (the colonizationist, anti-integrationist) Jefferson himself. The "plain and unmistakable" American mission, Douglass declared in an 1869 speech, is to provide the most "perfect national illustration of the unity and dignity of the human family that the world has ever seen." Our national "greatness and grandeur will be found in the faithful application of the principle of perfect civil equality to the people of all races and of all creeds" (*FDP* 4.253).

As he reflected, at the close of the War, on the momentous accomplishment of abolition and all that it promised, Douglass even experienced along with his great joy a moment of wistful sadness. With "the deepest desire and the great labor of my life" thus fulfilled and completed, he confessed, "I felt that I had reached the end of the noblest and best part of my life; my school was broken up, my church disbanded, and the beloved congregation dispersed, never to come together again" (*LT* 373). But his feeling of sadness could be only momentary, as Douglass would soon realize again what he had anticipated before the War's end (e.g. *LW* 3.290-91, 421). In very important respects, formal abolition marked not the end but only the end of the beginning. Much work remained for him to do.

It would soon become all too clear that the legal victory of Douglass' position remained incomplete. In keeping with his antebellum constitutionalism, Douglass regarded the legal changes effected by the Civil

War as a clarification or authoritative restoration, not a revolution of constitutional meaning. "We have had justice enough in our Constitution from the beginning to have made slavery impossible," he reminded his audience at an 1872 Republican rally. "The trouble never was in the Constitution, but in the administration of the Constitution. All experience shows that laws are of little value in the hands of those unfriendly to their objects" (*FDP* 4.341; also 83, 299). If the problem had always been the enforcement, not the meaning, of the Constitution's provisions, then why place antislavery hopes in constitutional amendments? To say the least, it was surely prudent to doubt that their subjection to military conquest had made the former slaveholding class and its supporters any friendlier to the Constitution's true objects than they had been before the War. "We may conquer Southern armies by the sword; but it is another thing to conquer Southern hate" (*LW* 3.421). While Lincoln's Proclamation and the Thirteenth Amendment, backed by superior military force, could bring an end to the formal institution of chattel slavery, they clearly could not dispel the spirit of slavery or of racial supremacy, which would continue to obstruct the nation's pursuance of equal justice for all.

Warning against an excessive faith in parchment guarantees, Douglass insisted that "the very essence of the Thirteenth, Fourteenth, and Fifteenth Amendments is in the grant of power to Congress to enforce them by 'appropriate legislation.' Without legislation these provisions may be evaded and practically rendered null and void" (*FDP* 4.341; also 328-29). Accordingly, he devoted most of his political energies during the postwar period to campaigning for the election of Republican majorities and to persuading congressional majorities and presidents to secure the full freedoms guaranteed by those amendments. Excepting only relatively brief commentaries on Supreme Court rulings, Douglass' constitutional reasoning during this period appears, for the most part, inferentially in his statements supporting various proposed exertions of national power.

"What the negro wants," Douglass declared in an April 14, 1875 address, "is, first, protection to the rights already conceded by law, and, secondly, education" (*FDP* 4.413). The proper objects of national power correspond to the two general objects of political life: protection against oppression and moral elevation. Given his emphasis on congressional enforcement of the recent Amendments, foremost among the rights to be protected, for Douglass, was the right of suffrage. In January, 1865, with the War's formal end in view, he urged the "'immediate, unconditional, and universal' enfranchisement of the black man, in every State of the Union." As we will see further below, it is significant that Douglass placed greater, more urgent emphasis on the right to vote than on any of the other rights attendant upon citizenship. Although the Thirteenth and Fourteenth Amendments held vast potential importance, the latter in particular guaranteeing an extraordinarily broad array of basic rights, the Fifteenth Amendment— properly enforced— represented the *sine qua non* of black liberation. Vividly envisioning likely legislative evasions of the Thirteenth Amendment, Douglass insisted simply: "Slavery is not abolished until the black man has the ballot." The right to vote meant, literally as well as metaphorically, the right to life. Douglass greeted the news of the Fifteenth's ratification with great (and premature) exuberance: "Henceforth we live in a new world.... We have ourselves, we have a country, and we have a future in common with other men.... Never was revolution more complete." Congress' enactment also in 1870 of the Enforcement Act, protecting the vote against both states' and private individuals' attempts to deny it, appeared to solidify this vital constitutional protection. Douglass' grateful delight permitted only a single, muted note of caution: it "seems almost too good to be true" (*FDP* 4.62, 82-83, 175, 266-67).

Beyond the voting right, the protection of rights that Douglass demanded included protection of the various civil rights associated with security of person and property, along with equal access, without racial discrimination, to public accommodations—the rights guaranteed by the Fourteenth Amendment and the Civil Rights Acts of 1866 and 1875. Douglass exulted over the passage of the 1875 Act in particular, which, despite Congress' weakening of it,[2] marked "an era in the history of American justice, liberty, and civilization" (*LW* 4.305). He also urged the exercise of expansive federal powers to remedy hardships produced by specific or general acts or systems of injustice. He called for federal reimbursement of depositors to the failed Freedmen's Bank, for instance, along with national assistance for the resettlement of black laborers migrating from the South; he decried discrimination against blacks by labor unions and demanded equitable compensation for black laborers (*LW* 4.387-88, 438, 282-85, 381-86; *FDP* 4.231-

37). Still further, Douglass called for federal measures to assist blacks in achieving a degree of self-sufficiency at least equal to that of whites. He proposed the establishment of a federally chartered company for the purchase of tracts of land to be resold or leased to freedmen, and, most importantly, he declared it imperative that Congress establish a system of universal education (*LW* 4.31-32, 386-87).

Douglass conceived of public education and other forms of federal assistance primarily in terms of rights, or as imperatives of compensatory justice, and secondarily as expressions of public charity or of national interest. In support of a pending education bill,[3] for instance, he wrote in 1890 that the measure's enactment would represent "at least a recognition of a great national duty towards a people to whom an immeasurable debt is due. It will tell that people and all others that the nation has the disposition if not entire ability to do the Negro right and justice" (*LW* 4.459; cf. 225, also 438; *FDP* 5.543, 557, 624). Although he objected strongly to the idea that the nation should try to do *everything* for the freedmen, it is clear that Douglass did not intend literally his repeated postwar demands that the nation "do nothing with the Negro" and simply "let him alone" (e.g. *LW* 4.272, *FDP* 4.68, 202-03). For a nation historically accustomed to federalism, tending to regard the nationalizing implications of the recent War with diffidence if not outright hostility, his proposals reflected an extraordinarily expansive conception of federal power.[4]

The question naturally arises concerning the constitutional bases of Douglass' proposed assertions of national powers. In an 1888 speech, Douglass expressed a measure of frustration with such questions, or with the overly fastidious construction of national power that sometimes inspired them: "whenever an administration has had the will to do anything, it has generally found constitutional power to do it" (*FDP* 5.369). His frustration reflected not a cynical or exploitive attitude toward constitutional interpretation but rather an enduring, though often-disappointed, faith that the Constitution supplies powers sufficient for the national government to enact such measures as justice and the nation's well-being may require. But out of the materials that he supplied in various occasional arguments, it is possible to construct his more specific answer. First, with respect to education in particular, Douglass appeared to find in the General Welfare Clause of Article I, section 1, a broad authority to commit national resources to the achievement of the general objects of the Constitution's Preamble. In his 1890 letter endorsing the Blair Educational Bill then pending in the House of Representatives, he referred to two of those objects: the bill would do justice to black Americans, as noted above, and it would "promote the general welfare of diffusing knowledge and enlightenment, in the darkest corners of the Republic where it is most needed."[5] He added a broader suggestion that the power to enact such measures may be inferred from the general presumption in favor of liberty that had become still more explicit in the postwar Constitution. "If the national Government had the power ... to protect slavery in the states while Slavery existed, it has the right to assist in the education and improvement of the newly emancipated and enfranchised citizens, now that Liberty had become the base line of the Republic and the fundamental law of the land" (LW 4.458-59). These arguments would serve as well to justify the further national powers that Douglass advocated.

Douglass appears also, like other radical Republicans, to have found a broad grant of national protective and remedial powers in the Thirteenth Amendment. The basis for this reading was a broad conception of the slavery that the Amendment prohibits. Already in 1874, he complained to Gerrit Smith of the "murderous warfare going on against the newly emancipated citizens and their friends at the South," thus suggesting an effective continuation of slavery, itself a profound state of war (LW 4.308).[6] To the delegates to the 1876 Republican National Convention, he declared that the freedmen's case "is the most extraordinary case of any people ever emancipated on the globe.... you turned us loose to the wrath of our infuriated masters" (FDP 4.442; also 413; LT 503). In the 1880s, he complained repeatedly that the freedmen so-called were in fact half-free at best (FDP 5.225, 419; LW 4.430). The southern practice of compensation by "store orders" gave the old master class "complete mastery" over its nominally emancipated laborers (FDP 5.419). A kind of slavery persists, Douglass maintained, wherever blacks are deprived of the right to vote and wherever the word "white" appears in legislation (FDP 4.62, 81-82). By conceiving of various postbellum southern laws, policies, and practices as effective forms of slavery, Douglass implicitly invoked the Thirteenth Amendment. By providing Congress the power to enforce its prohibition of slavery or involuntary servitude, that Amendment provides power sufficient for Congress to prevent slavery's reappearance in any of its various disguises.

Douglass addressed somewhat more directly the meaning of the Fourteenth Amendment, once again finding therein a broad grant of national powers to protect a broad array of rights. With respect to this most complex postwar Amendment, his claims came mainly in reaction to two major rulings from the U.S. Supreme Court. Commenting briefly on *The Slaughterhouse Cases* (1873), he objected to the Court's severe diminution of the concept of national citizenship and the rights pertaining thereto.[7] To Gerrit Smith in 1874, he complained of the ruling's endorsement of an "impractical doctrine of two citizenships," which effectively means "no citizenship. The one destroys the other.... The nation affirms, the state denies, and there is no progress. The true doctrine is one nation, one country, one citizenship and one law for all the people" (*LW* 4.306).

In a well-known 1883 speech, Douglass commented more extensively on the *Civil Rights Cases*, in which the Court invalidated the 1875 Civil Rights Act and thus left southern blacks especially exposed to racial discrimination in public accommodations. Taking care to urge cautious and prudently reserved speech in response, Douglass yet lamented: "We have been, as a class, grievously wounded ... in the house of our friends." The ruling advanced the causes of "slavery, caste, and oppression," striking a blow at human progress. It diminished the American nation as it allowed for the humiliation of American blacks: "It presents the United States before the world as a Nation utterly destitute of power to protect the rights of its own citizens upon its own soil."

Even as he vigorously denounced the injustice the ruling protects, Douglass claimed to reserve judgment on its basis in law. "I am not here to discuss the constitutionality or unconstitutionality of this decision.... The decision may or may not be constitutional." He proceeded immediately, however, to challenge the ruling's legal soundness on various grounds. The ruling disregarded the intentions of the framers, who had meant the Fourteenth Amendment "to protect the newly enfranchised citizen from injustice and wrong, not merely from a State, but from the individual members of a State." It was also inconsistent with the Court's own precedents, so far as the latter, in the antebellum period, assigned the greatest interpretive weight to the framers' (supposedly proslavery) intention. Most fundamentally, it violated the rules of legal interpretation, which require judicial deference toward any law favoring liberty and justice: "the reasons for declaring such a law unconstitutional and void, should be strong, irresistible and absolutely conclusive." Finally, it reinstated a disintegrative logic discredited by the larger meaning of the War, so that the parts or individual constituents of a state regained a license to commit injustices forbidden to the whole (*FDP* 5.111-121). In a later speech, Douglass concluded that the Supreme Court in this case had "essentially modified" the Fourteenth Amendment (*FDP* 5.244-45; also *LW* 4.423-24, *LT* 539-40).

Republican Government and Constitutional Reform

In this way, in a series of somewhat scattered, fragmentary, and summative suggestions, Douglass made tolerably clear his understanding of the general meaning of the Civil War Amendments. Yet the relative paucity of his constitutional commentary in the postwar years is notable, especially in contrast to the more focused and elaborate argumentation that he presented in the prewar period. On the whole, Douglass' constitutional arguments during the postwar period are significantly less sustained, thematic, and energetic, less attentive to powerful objections, and more fragmentary and summative, than were his arguments during the decade preceding the War. It seems particularly surprising that in a speech specifically devoted to the ruling in the *Civil Rights Cases* that Douglass declined to develop a more thorough legal argument. He described the latter ruling as a "moral cyclone," comparable in importance to *Dred Scott v. Sandford*, in response to which in 1857 he had developed an elaborate argument of protest covering constitutional as well as moral and political grounds (*FDP* 5.112; *LW* 2.407-24). He seems likewise to have offered only the cursory denunciation of *The Slaughterhouse Cases* cited above and to have made no significant public comment on *U.S. v. Reese* and *U.S. v. Cruikshank*, a pair of 1876 cases in which the Court severely limited the national government's powers to enforce the Fourteenth and Fifteenth Amendments, as specified in the Enforcement Act of 1870.[8] Given his opinion that the essence of these Amendments lay in the enforcement powers that they provided to Congress, Douglass could hardly have failed to see the momentous importance of these rulings too. In his last great speech, "Lessons of the Hour" in 1894, he declared that the Civil War had been effectively lost in the postbellum years; among the indications and causes of this loss was the fact that "the Supreme Court has, in a measure, surrendered" (*LW* 4.511).

Seemingly puzzling in view of these developments, Douglass' failure to present more developed arguments with respect to postwar constitutional interpretation is in fact revealing. This neglect in the postwar years proceeds partly from considerations of practical, political interest. But it also reflects more fundamental, principled considerations concerning the meaning of republican constitutionalism and republican citizenship. These latter considerations, again less developed than one might wish, moved Douglass beyond the sphere of constitutional interpretation into that of suggested constitutional reform. An exploration of his arguments for reform leads us shortly to consider the resemblance of Douglass' postwar constitutionalism to the program of the purported constitutional reformers who would shortly assume control of American political life under the banner of Progressivism. But it ultimately reveals that, for Douglass, the principle of republican government properly—more radically—understood represents the true center of the Constitution's design to protect individual natural rights.

In the postwar years, as in the antebellum years after 1851, Douglass mainly devoted his argumentative powers to the cause of building, strengthening, and energizing voting majorities opposed to slavery in all its forms and vestiges. In the postwar years, that meant endeavoring to promote and to educate the Republican Party. Fully aware of and increasingly troubled by their shortcomings, Douglass nonetheless unwaveringly supported the Republicans, to whom alone could be entrusted any realistic hopes for the cause of racial justice. "For colored men the Republican Party is the deck, all outside is the sea" (*FDP* 4.298).[9] With respect to constitutional argument, however, there is a significant difference between the two periods. During the prewar years, Douglass needed to persuade various elements of antislavery opinion that a legislative majority representing them would *possess* the constitutional power to end slavery. In the postwar years, by contrast, Douglass needed mainly to persuade Republican majorities to *use* the constitutional powers that they knew they possessed to complete and preserve the victory over slavery. In the earlier period, marshaling effective arguments concerning constitutional interpretation had been an urgent antislavery imperative, whereas in the later period arguments concerning moral and civic duty and political interest acquired more immediate practical importance.

This prudential, pragmatic explanation of Douglass' later de-emphasis of constitutional interpretation may appear exposed to an obvious objection. As we have observed, for most of the 1860s through the early 1870s, a legislative majority approximating the one Douglass desired did control the Congress. A brief period of presidential obstruction notwithstanding, it did enact significant portions (though by no means all) of the antislavery, pro-civil rights legislative program that Douglass urgently advocated. It did so, moreover, in confidence that a Supreme Court consisting of Republican appointees—the "house of our friends" to which Douglass refers glumly in 1883—would sustain its reforms against constitutional challenges. And within a short few years, nonetheless, it saw those reforms nullified or seriously diminished by that same Supreme Court. Thence arises the objection: in view of such assertions of judicial supremacy, would not prudence dictate a renewed, even intensified preoccupation in the postwar years with influencing (directly or indirectly) the federal judiciary, and therewith a redoubled interest in constitutional interpretation?

To this objection, one might respond that the relevant history did not confirm the notion of judicial supremacy. Although the 1870s and 1880s demonstrated the power of the Supreme Court temporarily to overturn legislative attempts at reform, the 1860s and early 1870s, in particular the fate of the *Dred Scott* ruling, demonstrated the power of determined legislative and constitutional majorities to overturn the actions even of a hostile Supreme Court. Douglass himself sometimes seemed to endorse such a response. Reflecting in 1869 on the crisis through which the Republic had lately passed, for instance, he observed that the "real trouble with us was never our system or form of government, or the principles underlying it, but the peculiar composition of our people" (*FDP* 4.244). As in the 1850s, so in the postwar years, the urgent task for Douglass was to reform the public opinion that permitted governmental deviations from the true principles. With that fundamental task accomplished, the proper realignment of the Congress, then of the courts, would follow each in its turn.

At least in the postwar years, however, Douglass was not wholly satisfied to view errors by the judiciary, or by any other branch of government, as mere, particular anomalies in a generally sound constitutional order. In response to adverse particular rulings, he did, as always, attempt to persuade the Justices and whoever else might listen to adopt sounder, more just and humanitarian readings of the Constitution. So he longed in 1883 "for a Supreme Court which shall be as true, as vigilant, as active, and exacting in maintaining laws enacted for the protection of human rights, as in other days was that Court for the destruction of human rights" (*FDP* 5.121). But even as he argued for more favorable rulings from the high court, he also argued at a deeper level in support of diminishing the courts' powers, for good or ill, to override the will of legislative majorities. Whereas the sovereignty of the American people may become active, at extraordinary moments, in overturning Supreme Court rulings that it believes contrary to its principles, the fact remains that in ordinary circumstances, for practical purposes the Supreme Court *is* "the Supreme Power of the Nation" (*FDP* 5.115). Notwithstanding his reaffirmations of constitutional faith, Douglass contended that at a deeper level, the problem really *was* with the form of government that the framers designed, in its imperfect embodiment of the genuine republican principle. Douglass' diminished interest in constitutional interpretation, in the postwar years, reflects an expanded interest in substantial constitutional reform.

In an extraordinary speech delivered to numerous audiences in the winter of 1866-67, Douglass considered the "Sources of Danger to the Republic"—to the American Republic and to republics in general. A great advantage of the republican form in America, he observed, is that the Constitution makes no "divine pretension" and claims no "superstitious reverence." It is instead "a purely human contrivance, designed with more or less wisdom, for human purposes," and as such invites critical examination (*FDP* 4.152). This Jeffersonian reflection introduced a discussion of important lingering defects in the Constitution, which became a recurrent theme in Douglass' postbellum thought. For the first time since 1851, Douglass spoke disapprovingly of some aspect of the Founders' Constitution. Douglass' public critique of the Constitution emerged in response to the Reconstruction conflict between Congress and President Andrew Johnson. While substantially a partisan matter between a Republican legislature and a Democratic executive, the problem lay deeper than the substantive positions taken by President Johnson. Its root lay in the constitutional grant of broad, independent powers to the president. Douglass responded by calling not simply for the election of a Republican president in 1868 but also for fundamental, structural constitutional reform. With Johnson endeavoring to thwart the progressive aims of congressional Republicans and to enhance his own political fortunes by the use of various presidential powers, Douglass called, in sum, for the abolition of the independent chief executive, and with it, of major elements of the constitutional system of checks and balances as designed by the framers. In particular, he proposed the elimination of the presidential veto as "alien to every idea of republican government." Likewise, he proposed the abolition of the president's power to pardon and eligibility for re-election, along with the office's immense patronage powers. He proposed even to abolish the office of vice-president, viewing it as supplying an institutionalized incentive to conspire against the president. Disclaiming any personal charge against Johnson in this respect, Douglass yet claimed that "the men" who assassinated President Lincoln "knew Andrew Johnson as we know him now" (FDP 4.162-170).

There is an obvious danger of making too much of these proposals. Douglass issued them in a state of intense anger and alarm at Johnson's effort, as he saw it, to undo in peacetime the War's great and costly gains. He made no sustained campaign to secure their enactment. In most particulars, he did not repeat them beyond this brief season. To this extent, one may agree with Douglass' biographer, Benjamin Quarles, in viewing them as uncharacteristic, a momentary loss of balance on Douglass' part.[10]

Yet, although Douglass' specific assault on the independent executive did not extend beyond the Johnson presidency, one cannot explain it away as simply the unfortunate expression of a momentary passion. The basic principle beneath that momentary assault informed Douglass' thinking well beyond the Johnson years. It reappeared in the 1880s in a different application as Douglass responded to the Supreme Court's disappointing ruling in the Civil Rights Cases.[11] Douglass showed notably greater caution in this later context, disclaiming any denunciation of the Court itself and insisting on patient reform and fidelity to the rule of law. Nonetheless, while he specifically advocated no constitutional reform of the Court's structure or powers, he laid the principled groundwork for it in objecting not only to the Court's specific reading of the Constitution and to this particular instance of judicial review but also, implicitly, to its very possession of that power. As the president was in the late 1860s, so the Supreme Court in the early 1880s (and other times) is "the autocratic point in our National Government. No monarch in Europe has a power more absolute" than has the Court. What "His Holiness, the Pope, is to the Roman Catholic Church, the Supreme Court is to the American State" (*FDP* 5.122, 113, 115). Such a characterization is not consistent with an acceptance of the legitimacy of the power of judicial review in any truly republican constitutional order.[12] But the principle from which it was based entails, as Douglass well understood, a critique of the Founders' Constitution extending well beyond the practice of judicial review.

In this more radical dimension of Douglass' postwar argument, the judiciary's assertions of constitutional supremacy, like the fully independent executive, proceed from a serious defect in constitutional design. In his 1867 "Sources of Danger" speech, he explained the defect in the Constitution as itself symptomatic of a still deeper defect in our natural constitution. "Such is the constitution of the human mind, that there can be no such thing as immediate emancipation, either from slavery or from monarchy." As Douglass and fellow abolitionists had argued all along, the issue in the war against slavery was at bottom the same as the issue in the (first) American Revolution. Slavery, like absolute monarchy, signified an assertion of irresponsible power (*FDP* 1.311, 4.519; *LW* 4.505), a claim to rule others without their consent. Just as the current antislavery generation is finding it difficult to eradicate slavery in its entirety, Douglass argued, so the revolutionary fathers were born under monarchy and remained in some measure under its influence even as they waged war against it. "They gave us a Constitution made in the shadow of slavery and of monarchy, and in its character it partakes in some of its features of both those unfavorable influences." Against the argument of *The Federalist*,[13] then, Douglass held that the American Republic was in fact not a pure republic but instead a mixed constitutional form, and its main weaknesses were traceable to its admixture of nonrepublican elements. Its "first source of weakness" was its incorporation of "the one-man power"—not simply the literal rule of one but more generally the spirit of "Monarchical man-worship" and the various forms of irresponsible power in which it issued (*FDP* 4.157-58, 472). Whether explicitly, as in 1866-67, or only implicitly, as in 1883, Douglass' argument necessarily entailed a call for dramatic changes in the American government's constitutional structure. The American Revolution could not be complete until all of the Constitution's lingering autocratic, monarchic, or aristocratic—all of its nondemocratic or countermajoritarian—features were expunged.

The only truly legitimate form of government, Douglass came to believe, the form that the Constitution imperfectly embodies and points toward, is not a constitutionally mixed or balanced system but rather a purely popular government. He introduced himself in the "Sources of Danger" speech in an amusing but revealing way: "I am here tonight as a democrat, a genuine democrat dyed in the wool." A genuine republic, for Douglass, was "a genuine *democratic* republic" (*FDP* 4.158; emphasis supplied). With respect to institutional design, Douglass' conception of democratic-republican government entailed, first, the primacy of the legislative power relative to the other powers of government. Congress stands for the soul of the American Republic; it is "the true index to the character and mental resources of the nation" (*FDP* 4.470). So far Douglass remained in agreement with most of the original framers; and he further agreed with Publius that Congress' dependence on the people provides the primary check against abusive legislation. He rejected Publius' further insistence, however, on the need for "auxiliary precautions" in the form of checks wielded by the other branches. Legislative primacy meant, for Douglass, that the other subordinate branches need not and should not function as checks upon congressional power. "We are great on checks," he observed sarcastically in the 1867 speech. In his 1883 speech on the *Civil Rights Cases*, he made, to similar effect, a most surprising and historically puzzling claim: "All men who have given any thought to the machinery, the structure, and practical operation of our Government, must have recognized the importance of absolute harmony between its various departments of powers and duties. They must have seen clearly the mischievous tendency and danger to the body politic of any antagonisms between its various branches" (*FDP* 5.114). In striking contrast to the famous argument in *Federalist* No. 51, Douglass holds that harmony, not competitive ambition or defensiveness, should characterize the three branches' interrelations. He warmly approved of an energetic executive and an activist judiciary, so long as that energy and activism operate to enforce national statutory and constitutional laws against disobedient private parties and state governments, not to overrule the will of the national legislature.

Douglass rejected the framers' design of balanced government, in these postwar arguments, because he rejected, at a more basic level, their general design of removing government from direct control by popular majorities. In response to the concern, rooted in traditional liberal constitutionalism and shared by Publius, that the electoral majority to which a representative legislature is responsible may be itself tyrannical, Douglass issued a qualified but emphatic denial. "[We] have recently been told that majorities can be as destructive and more arbitrary than individual despots....If this be so ... I think that we ought to part with Republican government at once." Acknowledging the obvious truth that "majorities can be despotic and have been arbitrary," he yet asked: "arbitrary to whom?" He answered that whenever majorities are arbitrary, it is "always to unrepresented classes." The remedy for governmental arbitrariness is simply a "consistent republic in which there shall be no unrepresented classes" (*FDP* 4.164-65). The essential, defining, necessary-and-sufficient characteristic of a genuine republic is universal representation, so that "every man subject to it is represented in it." Absent such representation, the constitutional system of checks and balances had not sufficed to secure equal rights for all; with it, no additional checks would be needed (*FDP* 4.154-56).

DOUGLASS AND PROGRESSIVISM

Reflecting on the evolution of Douglass' constitutional commentary, one may be tempted to infer that in this further respect, too, Douglass' own career epitomizes his country's—or at least that of his country's egalitarian or progressive elements. In the postwar era, his antebellum dedication to the Founders' antislavery Constitution evolved into a purified, simplified democratic partisanship. In particular, Douglass' postwar constitutionalism appears similar in important respects to the radical democratic nationalism whereby leaders of the Progressive movement a few decades later sought to supersede the work of the Founders.

Perhaps the most obvious point of resemblance concerns the antagonism to constitutional checks and balances. Leading Progressive political scientist and politician Woodrow Wilson commented, for instance, that the Founders "constructed the federal government upon a theory of checks and balances which was meant to limit the operation of each part and allow to no single part or organ of it a dominating force; but no government can be successfully conducted upon so mechanical a theory." Like Douglass, Wilson held that harmonious cooperation rather than competitive ambition and mutual wariness must characterize the interrelations of governmental departments. "Their cooperation is indispensable, their warfare fatal."[14] In Wilson's reading, the original scheme of checks reflects the Founders' preoccupation with constitutionally limited government, itself a legacy of English Whigs' insistence upon constitutionally limited monarchy. "The revolution which separated America from England was part of a great Whig contest with the Crown for constitutional liberties."[15] Deriding the notion of effective constitutional restraints upon government action as a mere "literary theory," Wilson echoed and indeed went well beyond Douglass in his expansive conception of national powers. "Government does not stop with the protection of life, liberty, and property," Wilson observed approvingly; "it goes on to serve every convenience of society. Its sphere is limited only by its own wisdom, alike where republican and where absolutist principles prevail."[16] Campaigning for the Republican presidential nomination in 1912, Theodore Roosevelt proclaimed, in a similar spirit, that the device of constitutional checks and balances does not signify any delegation of power to officials in any department of government to frustrate the popular will. To the contrary, "the people in their legislative capacity have the power to enact into law any measure they deem necessary for the betterment of social or industrial conditions."[17]

In Wilson's perspective, the Founders' Whig constitutionalism was less erroneous or ill-conceived than it was outdated. In its deeper underpinnings, it represented an application to political law—"a sort of unconscious copy"—of the then-current Newtonian view of the natural universe. But the true conception of government had become visible only after the passing of the Founders' Newtonian world, with the emergence of Darwinian evolutionary science. "In our own day, whenever we discuss the structure or development of anything, whether in nature or in society, we consciously or unconsciously follow Mr. Darwin." The crucial insight that Darwinian natural science lent to political science was the conception of government as a living, evolving being. "Governments are living things and operate as organic wholes," such that their naturally, historically evolving powers and purposes cannot be assigned any fixed, unchanging definition or limits by a written constitution. Hence "the Constitution of the United States ... is a vehicle of life, and its spirit is always the spirit of the age."[18]

The direction in which the constitutional order was evolving, as Progressives saw it, marks a further apparent convergence between Douglass' postwar constitutionalism and their own principles. We have noticed Douglass' affirmation of unchecked democracy, along with his career-long constitutional nationalism. In his hopeful expectation, the Civil War heralded the end of sectional and racial divisions, the achievement of fundamental national homogeneity, and the vigorous exercise of expansive national powers for truly national purposes. Representing again the Progressive view, Wilson argued that constitutional government presupposes the existence of a national community, conscious of common interests and able to form common purposes. Such a community was only partially in existence in founding era America; but in the relatively brief course of national evolution, "our life has undergone radical changes ... and almost every change has operated to draw the nation together." The great effect of the Civil War, above all other causes, was that "the nation was made, in social institutions, at last homogeneous." By the turn of the twentieth century, Wilson wrote in *The State*, Americans had become "in the fullest organic sense a nation." This acceptance of national unity as an accomplished fact is the underlying premise for the Progressives' affirmation of unchecked democracy. "Self-government"—truly democratic government—"is the last, the consummate stage of constitutional development."[19] Conceiving of the United States as, in the decisive respects, a unified, homogeneous nation, the Progressives conceived of democracy in post-Civil War America not as the rule of majorities over minorities but rather as the rule of the whole.[20] Hence they understood their primary constitutional imperatives to include not the securing of minority rights against abusive majorities but, to the contrary, purging all lingering, regressive special interests, removing constitutional limits on the powers of the nation's elected representatives, and promoting the efficient governmental administration of the popular will.[21]

Such resemblances between Douglass' postwar constitutionalism and that of major representatives of the Progressive movement are impressive and significant in their way, but in the final analysis, the differences are deeper and more important than the similarities. Their sharp divergence in understanding the significance of the Civil War and its aftermath can serve as a signpost to the deeper differences. Although Wilson did allow that slavery is incompatible with modern democracy, he yet maintained that the achievement of national homogeneity was *the* great effect of the War, thereby implying that mere dividedness had been the great deficiency in national life to that point.[22] By contrast, although Douglass warmly approved the prospect of true national unity, he insistently opposed elevating the cause of Union or unity over the antislavery cause. The great, singular evil had always been slavery itself, and Emancipation was the War's transcendent achievement. Moreover, from Douglass' perspective, the Progressives' sanguine pronouncements concerning the postwar achievement of national unity could only have signified a striking, if depressingly familiar, blindness to the persisting reality of racial division and injustice. At roughly the same time that Wilson was celebrating the purported fact of national homogeneity in *The State*, Douglass was declaiming angrily against a spreading reign of mob violence, predominantly but not exclusively in the South, against black citizens. In his last great speech, "The Lesson of the Hour," Douglass revived in 1894 the spirited indignation of his prewar antislavery agitation.

> The presence of eight millions of people in any section of this country, constituting an aggrieved class, smarting under terrible wrongs, denied the exercise of the commonest rights of humanity, and regarded by the ruling class of that section as outside of the government, outside of the law, outside of society, having nothing in common with the people with whom they live, the sport of mob violence and murder, is not only a disgrace and a scandal to that particular section, but a menace to the peace and security of the whole country. (*LW* 4.491-92; also *FDP* 5.358ff., 403-26)

For Douglass, the post-Reconstruction "harmony" between North and South—the harmony that Progressives like Wilson celebrated—was made possible only by the nullification of the postwar Amendments and the willful disregard of blacks' rights (*FDP* 5.443; also *LT* 536).[23]

The Progressives' blithe presumption of postwar American unity reflects in part their Darwinian tendency to conceive of nations as racial units.[24] Their general failure to recognize blacks as true, full American citizens reflects not only their Darwinian racialism, however, but also their Darwinian or historicist skepticism of any notion of natural, universal, permanent principles of justice. For Wilson above all, the notion of a moral natural law or of unalienable natural rights was little more than a superstition lingering from a prescientific era. The term "natural law," in his view, properly refers only to "generalized statements of physical fact"—to the purely immanent, necessary, invariant relations of material and efficient causation among physical bodies. Political laws therefore could only be customary or cultural, not natural, in their foundations, representing expressions of communal will rather than rules discovered by reason. "Law is the will of the State," mirroring or reflecting the will of the "organic community" that the State represents.[25]

In keeping with his high regard for discovery as the pre-eminent human virtue (*LW* 4.487; *FDP* 3.472, 4.572, 5.355-56), Douglass took considerable interest in emergent trends in science and philosophy, including Darwinian science and (at least indirectly) Hegelian philosophy. Yet, whatever the fascination such innovations may have held for him, none could ever disturb his bedrock conviction of the permanent, universal truth of the principles of natural human rights. From the beginning to the end of his long career, Douglass affirmed consistently and incessantly the unchanging truth of those principles. The true principles of right and wrong, virtue and vice, he observed as a young man, do not depend on time and place. Likewise, he reiterated as a much older man, conditions may vary, but human nature is permanent.

The "sublime and glorious truths" affirmed in the Declaration of Independence represent, in summary, "the eternal principles of truth, justice, and humanity." Recognize and protect the natural rights of all, Douglass urged his countrymen one last time in 1894, and "your Republic will stand and flourish forever" (*LW* 5.110; *FDP* 5.338; *LW* 4.523).

Douglass' abiding affirmation of the permanent truth of the classical natural rights doctrine sets him apart, too, from important particular elements of the Progressive program. As he could never have approved Wilson's skepticism concerning natural inalienable rights, so it is unlikely that he would have endorsed Herbert Croly's and Theodore Roosevelt's broad attacks on property rights as antagonistic to human rights or to the general welfare.[26] He would likely have regarded as grossly misbegotten the latter's analogy between plutocrats and slaveholders, just as he had earlier rejected socialists' attempts to subsume the abolitionist cause into a generalized assault on private property (LT 228; LW 1.110-12, 5.105; FDP 3.376). Like the Progressives, Douglass clearly favored the nationalization and centralization of political power. Nationalized, centralized government answered an urgent imperative to meet the needs of the day, in his view, and represented a natural outgrowth of the nation's commitment to universal, humanitarian principles of justice. So long as the American people possessed the ballot, national power posed far smaller dangers to the republic than did the persisting spirit of sectionalism (FDP 4.405, 452-53). But Douglass' general support for an energetic, reformist national government signified neither a hostility toward property rights nor an endorsement of constitutionally unlimited governmental power. In 1871, advocating vigorous federal action to ensure "fair play," he could yet "accept that political faith universally believed in, but nowhere practiced, that that government is best which governs least—and altogether regret that other theory which assumes that, because governments are good for something, they are, therefore, good for everything." Douglass, who had read and admired Tocqueville's *Democracy in America*, did not allow his experience under the hard despotism of slavery to blind him to the danger of despotism in a softer form. His postwar programmatic proposals reflect a wary optimism concerning the national government's powers to secure rights, remedy injustice, and promote moral elevation. They are significantly tempered, above all, by his wariness of fostering dependency, the great bane of personal virtue, individual rights, and self-government, among the purported beneficiaries (LW 4.272; FDP 4.202-03, 419-22, 5.406).

Moreover, as Douglass was resolute in defense of natural rights, so he insisted on the formality of direct, universal popular consent as the indispensable protection for those rights. This marks a further point of significant contrast with Progressives, whose commitment to democratic consent is ambiguous. Wilson and Roosevelt alike endorse a conception of government as ministerial in nature, deploying constitutionally unlimited powers as efficient executor of the popular will.[27] But they also seem to affirm a Rousseauan distinction between the true, progressive popular will and the consciously held, directly expressed judgments of actual voters, so that government becomes the leader or shaper, not mere executor, of the popular will.[28] This latter conception of rule by presidential stewardship, deriving its ends from a free divination of the popular will or the spirit of the age, and given its concrete substance by a body of unelected administrative experts, is plainly incompatible with Douglass' understanding of democratic governance. Douglass would surely have regarded it as essentially a refurbished, more sophisticated incarnation of "the one-man power" that he denounced in 1867 in his "Sources of Danger" speech.

With this consideration of the concept of consent, we come to the fundamental significance of Douglass' critique of the Founders' Constitution. As noted, Douglass offered particular, institutional suggestions only occasionally, making virtually no effort to campaign for dramatic structural changes in the Constitution as a near-term goal.[29] His serious practical purpose was less to abolish the system of governmental checks and balances than to provoke a renewed, enlivened public consideration of the first principles of republican citizenship— above all, of the relation of rights and popular consent. Contrary to the leading Progressives, Douglass argued for constitutional reform not to remove all fetters on governmental power but rather to emphasize and to strengthen what he understood to be the only effective mode of protection against arbitrary government. Viewed from this perspective, the significant effect of his assault on the system of checks and balances was to assimilate, at a very basic level, the condition of the American voting majority with that of their black minority. His critique implied that the Founders' Constitution, with its autocratic Supreme Court and perhaps, too, with a quasi-monarchic presidency, erodes the American people's power of self-government in a manner closely related in principle (although incomparably milder in practice) to the outright disfranchisement to which the black minority had always been subjected. From the reformist point of view, congressional representatives were obstructed by presidential vetoes and adverse

Supreme Court rulings, making the American people subjects rather than real citizens; they were politically dependent on a few individuals who represented them at best very imperfectly and indirectly (*FDP* 4.165). In this they had some kinship with—and, Douglass hoped, some sympathy for—their black fellow countrymen, who had long endured such dependence in its extremity, benefiting from American governments only very unevenly and often only as the "step-children" (see *FDP* 4.432), not the voting constituents, of public officials who bore no effective responsibility to them.

Douglass' attack on checks and balances served thus to illustrate and to universalize the importance of effective voting rights. The core of unfreedom, for whites and blacks alike, is a condition of dependence, or subjection to an irresponsible power. "No man can be truly free whose liberty is dependent upon the thought, feeling, and action of others....I know of no class of my fellow men, however just, enlightened, and humane, which can be wisely and safely trusted absolutely with the liberties of any other class" (*LT* 377). The only effective remedy, Douglass maintained, is the fully representative, democratic republic. The only truly effective, dependable freedom is the freedom of self-government, at the center of which is the guarantee of universal suffrage. For these reasons, the Fifteenth Amendment represents for Douglass the keystone to the arch of liberty (*LT* 379, *FDP* 4.201), and virtually all the bitter disappointments of the postbellum years resulted from its nonenforcement and effective nullification in the South. The voting right is *the* fundamental right of citizens, the conjunction of natural and civil rights, indispensable to human liberty and human dignity. It is a vital instrument of self-protection (*LW* 2.520, 3.420, 4.298; *LT* 379-80), and more fundamentally, it is a property of all self-owning beings. "I want to vote," Douglass declared finally, "because I am a rational being" (*FDP* 4.119, 183; also *FDP* 5.255).

CONCLUSION

The foregoing arguments suffice to show that, in his vision of constitutional reform as well as his arguments of constitutional interpretation, Douglass viewed his nationalist, democratic republicanism as perfecting, not transcending a constitutionalism grounded in the Declaration of Independence. While he stands apart, in his vision of republicanism, from both his predecessors the Founders and his successors the Progressives, his differences with the former are in the nature of a family dispute, proceeding from principles internal and fundamental, not alien, to the Founders' political thought. Yet, although Douglass' new republicanism does not suffer from the fundamental infirmities of that of the Progressives, it does appear exposed to a familiar and powerful objection from the Founders' perspective. But it is useful in closing to reflect just a bit further on the objection and Douglass' responses, as one finds thereby that a significant weakness in Douglass' republicanism is closely related to an important strength.

In fairness to Douglass, let us recall that his majoritarian faith is significantly qualified. He placed his trust not in any majority but only in those that affirm equal rights of representation to all adult members of society. Nonetheless, one might object that Douglass treated dismissively the argument, from such weighty authorities as Madison and Tocqueville, that unchecked democratic majorities are prone to act tyrannically to enfranchised as well as to disfranchised minorities. Out of Douglass' various arguments, one can reconstruct various possible responses to this objection. As we have seen, one of those responses reflects Douglass' realist doubt of the ultimate efficacy of constitutional restraints: as the *Dred Scott* ruling could not survive the attack of a determined majority opposed to it, so the *Civil Rights Cases* and other damaging postwar rulings would not survive, if a determined majority could be aroused against them. In the American democratic republic, "all power … is in the hands of the people. Public opinion, is in this sense omnipotent" (*LW* 5.229).[30] At a deeper level, Douglass' critique of constitutional restraints on majorities rests on the contention that even supposing their efficacy, the most well-intentioned restraints may be at best accidentally related to the achievement of justice. They may serve the cause of justice in protecting Madison's minorities of innocent property-holders in the eighteenth century or in vindicating the claims of black citizens in the 1950s and 1960s; but they may be equally useful to the minority of slaveholders in the 1850s or the unreconstructed white supremacists of the 1870s and beyond.

The foregoing responses to the Madisonians' objection may not suffice entirely to overcome it. But while Madisonian fears of unchecked majorities may be very well founded, Douglass' faith in majorities yet reflects a fundamental strength of his own argument, so far as his objection to constitutional checks on the elective branches derives from his spirited, healthy disdain for the *minoritarian* politics that such checks make possible. At the deepest level, Douglass disdains appeals to constitutional protections of minorities, at least where avoidable, as not only futile, in the long term, but also dispiriting. To depend, in one's hopes for justice, upon favorable rulings from the Supreme Court is little different from depending on the interests or judgments of legislators and executives whom one holds no power to elect. The practitioners of nonelectoral, minoritarian politics remain in a condition of demeaning, dispiriting dependency that is not fundamentally different from the condition of those excluded altogether from political society.[31] Douglass' entire history of constitutional, political advocacy suggests that the only truly reliable and dignifying security of individual rights is found in active republican citizenship—in regular participation in partisan, electoral contests, endeavoring to form a majority coalition capable of governing on its own initiative and responsibility. Douglass' urgent insistence on the active self—on self-liberation, self-elevation, and self-government—represents the constant, unifying theme of his constitutionalism in the prewar and postwar periods. For the citizen no less than the slave: "He who would be free, must himself strike the blow" (*FDP* 2.86, *LW* 4.381).

Endnotes

1. Citations of Douglass' works appear in the text, abbreviated as follows, with text and page references:

BF — *My Bondage and My Freedom*, William L. Andrews, ed. (Urbana: University of Illinois Press, 1987).

FDP — *The Frederick Douglass Papers*, John Blassingame and John McKivigan, eds., Series 1 (New Haven: Yale University Press, 1979-1992).

LT — *The Life and Times of Frederick Douglass*, Rayford Logan, ed. (New

York: MacMillan Publishing Company, 1962)
LW — *The Life and Writings of Frederick Douglass*, Phillip Foner, ed. (New York: International Publishers, 1950-1975).
N — *Narrative of the Life of Frederick Douglass: An American Slave*, David W. Blight, ed. (Boston: Bedford Books, 1993).

2. Often derided as an attempt to mandate "social equality" or integration, the bill was regarded by many Republicans as a political liability, who removed from its original proposal provisions prohibiting racial discrimination in public schools and churches. A lame-duck Republican majority enacted it into law largely as a final tribute to its recently deceased author, Senator Charles Sumner. See James MacPherson, "Abolitionists and the Civil Rights Act of 1875," *The Journal of American History* 52.3 (December, 1965): 493-510.

3. The Blair Bill, Foner notes, "provided for federal aid and supervision of education to do away with illiteracy in the South. It was shelved by the Republicans" (*LW* 4.555n48).

4. Cf. David Blight, *Frederick Douglass' Civil War* (Baton Rouge, La.: Louisiana State University Press, 1989), 179.

5. Earlier he implicitly suggested that public education promotes a third object of the Preamble, the formation of a more perfect Union, as he referred to public schools as "a common platform of nationality" (*FDP* 4.302).

6. On slavery as a state of war, see *FDP* 2.267; 3.127, 317; 2.327.

7. The Slaughterhouse Cases (83 US 36).

8. U.S. v. Reese, 92 US 214 (1875). U.S. v. Cruikshank, 92 US 542 (1875).

9. This support for the Republicans derives in no small part from Douglass' loathing of their major partisan adversaries, the Democrats, for whom he finds "no place for soft speech." A memorable example of how harsh his anti-Democrat speech could be appears in an 1880 address commemorating emancipation: "Had the doors of all the prisons in the land been opened, and all the thieves, thugs and murderers turned loose to prey upon the country, the evil would have been far less than that inflicted by the Democratic party" (*FDP* 4.575, 579; see also *FDP* 5.225).

10. Benjamin Quarles, *Frederick Douglass* (New York: Atheneum, 1969 [originally published in 1948]), 235.

11. Civil Rights Cases, 109 U.S. 3 (1883).

12. As Leslie Friedman Goldstein observes, Douglass' 1857 attack on the *Dred Scott* decision carefully targeted the Supreme Court's "slaveholding wing" and Chief Justice Taney in particular—not the Court as an institu-

tion (See Leslie Friedman Goldstein, "The Political Thought of Frederick Douglass" [Ph.D. Dissertation, Cornell University, 1975], 123ff.). In this respect, his call for restraint notwithstanding, his response to the *Civil Rights Cases* carries far more radical implications.

13. See especially *Federalist* No. 39, "we may define a republic to be, or at least may bestow that name on, a government which derives all its powers directly or indirectly from the great body of the people, and is administered by persons holding their offices during pleasure for a limited period, or during good behavior." Alexander Hamilton, James Madison, and John Jay, *The Federalist Papers*, introduction and notes by Charles R. Kesler, Clinton Rossiter, ed. (New York: New American Library, 1999), 209.

14. Woodrow Wilson, *Constitutional Government in the United States* (New York: Columbia University Press, 1908), 54, 57; also 199-200.

15. Ibid., 198.

16. Ibid., 70; Wilson, *The State: Elements of Historical and Practical Politics* (Boston: D. C. Heath, 1904), 621.

17. Theodore Roosevelt, *Social Justice and Popular Rule* (New York: Arno Press, 1974 [originally published in 1925]), 166, 168. See also Herbert Croly's statement in *The Promise of American Life* (New York: The MacMillan Company, 1909), a work Roosevelt much admired: "every popular government should in the end ... possess the power of taking any action, which, in the opinion of a decisive majority of the people, is demanded by the public welfare. Such is not the case with the government organized under the Federal Constitution." *The Promise of American Life*, 35-36.

18. Wilson, *Constitutional Government*, 54-55, 69. Cf. *The State*, 555, 575-76, 603.

19. Wilson, *Constitutional Government*, 25, 46, 51-52; *The State*, 467. Wilson's affirmation of national homogeneity is more qualified in his later *Constitutional Government* than in *The State*. In the later work, to the question "Are [sic] the United States a community?" he answered, "In some things, yes; in most things, no." He proceeded immediately to add, however, that only "highly developed, self-conscious communities" can be self-governing, and he affirmed that the United States is already self-governing. *Constitutional Government*, 51-52.

20. Cf. R. J. Pestritto, "Woodrow Wilson, the Organic State, and American Republicanism," in *History of American Political Thought*, Bryan-Paul Frost and Jeffrey Sikkenga, eds. (Lanham, Md.: Lexington Books, 2003), 556.

21. On the theme of purging special interests, see especially Theodore Roosevelt, *The New Nationalism*, William E. Leuchtenberg, ed. (Englewood Cliffs, N.J.: Prentice-Hall, 1961), 25-27, 32-35. On the advocacy of un-

checked democracy, see also Roosevelt's speech "A Charter of Democracy," in *Social Justice and Popular Rule*, 163-97. On the need for efficient government, see Croly, *The Promise of American Life*, 33-35.

22. Wilson, *The State*, 582, 467.

23. For Wilson's utter lack of interest in the nonenforcement of the Fourteenth and Fifteenth Amendments, see *The State*, 485, 490-91, 532.

24. For Wilson's racialism, see *The State*, 1-2, 18-24, and Pestritto, "Woodrow Wilson," 552, 557. On Roosevelt's, see Jean Yarbrough, "Theodore Roosevelt and the Stewardship of the American Presidency," in *History of American Political Thought*, Frost and Sikkenga, eds., 538-40.

25. Wilson, *The State*, 606, 587, 603.

26. See Croly, *The Promise of American Life*, 38, 148-54; Roosevelt, *The New Nationalism*, 32-34, 37. Roosevelt did profess a belief in the ultimate coincidence of property rights and human rights (171), but the significance of such professions appears dubious in view of his endorsement of an effectively unlimited governmental regulatory power. See also *Social Justice and Popular Rule*, 168-77.

27. Wilson, *The State*, 576: "Government is merely the executive organ of society." See also *Constitutional Government*, 23-24; Roosevelt, *Social Justice and Popular Rule*, 163, 190-91.

28. Wilson, *Constitutional Government*, 68-69; also Pestritto, "Woodrow Wilson," 557; Roosevelt, *The New Nationalism*, 36.

29. Cf. Leslie Friedman Goldstein's observation, "Morality & Prudence in the Statesmanship of Frederick Douglass: Radical as Reformer," *Polity* 16.4 (Summer 1984): 610: "Douglass's overall strategy can be simply stated: Do not burden yourself with more than is necessary and use all the legitimate weapons available."

30. Compare Lincoln's statement at Ottawa, in the first of his 1858 debates with Stephen Douglas: "In this and like communities, public sentiment is everything. With public sentiment, nothing can fail; without it nothing can succeed." In *Abraham Lincoln: Speeches and Writings 1832-1858* (New York: The Library of America, 1989), 524-25.

31. Explaining the superiority of his "direct-action" strategy to the NAACP's more elitist, implicitly minoritarian strategy of litigation, Martin Luther King makes an argument similar to Douglass'. See *Why We Can't Wait* (New York: New American Library, 1964), 33-34, 42.

·⁓Chapter 4⁓·

Regimes and Revolutions: Madison and Wilson on Parties in America

Scot J. Zentner

> I am persuaded that the good sense of the people will always be found to be the best army. They may be led astray for a moment, but will soon correct themselves. The people are the only censors of their governors: and even their errors will tend to keep these to the true principles of the institution. To punish these errors too severely would be to suppress the only safeguard of the public liberty.—Thomas Jefferson[1]

James Madison famously argued against parties in *The Federalist*, but only a few years later just as eloquently defended the formation of the first national party movement. He nicely embodies the ambivalence, but also the coherence, of the view of parties during the American founding. Woodrow Wilson, on the other hand, is perhaps the best representative of the Progressive view of parties, even though most Progressives were opposed to organized political parties. Given the inevitability of parties in democracies, his defense of a "responsible" party system was more realistic than the attack on parties by his fellow Progressives. He represents as well as any other figure the Progressive refounding of America in the early twentieth century. Both Madison and Wilson were especially influential with respect to the development of political parties in their respective eras. Examining the differences between these two prominent politicians and thinkers regarding parties is instructive for understanding the origin and transformation of American politics.

Madison's approach is largely a continuation of traditional political science.[2] In this view, politics is understood to be mainly a competition between different classes or parties (e.g., democrats versus oligarchs) representing distinct types of regimes. These parties present claims to rule on the basis of opposed conceptions of the good or the just. Madison similarly argues that there is a "natural" division of society into these parties of principle. In particular, he argues that there are those who are more dedicated to republicanism and those who are less dedicated. When the party conflict becomes "most interesting," i.e., most intense, the political community returns to a debate over first principles, to the question of the regime itself.[3] When the differences between the parties are fundamental and one party defeats the other in a major election or series of elections, a regime change of sorts occurs. This phenomenon has come to be called a party "realignment," often thought of as a peaceful revolution by electoral means.[4] In this sense, Madison's Republican Party of the 1790s was a revolutionary institution. He likely agreed with Jefferson's well-known characterization of the party's great victory over the Federalists: "The Revolution of 1800 was as real a revolution in the principles of our government as that of 1776 was in its form."[5] The Republican Party was more than just one part of a larger system of parties; it was an agent for a kind of regime change.[6]

Wilson's view, on the other hand, is quite the opposite. His idea of partisanship is predicated on the eclipse of regime politics altogether. He believed that fundamental disputes were finally settled in favor of the modern idea of democracy and the modern institution of the democratic state. All that is left, according to Wilson, are questions of detail, i.e., questions of administration. Administration, he says, was formerly "put aside as 'practical detail' which clerks could arrange after doctors had agreed upon principles." The larger and more pressing issue had been about the regime. "The question," Wilson notes, "was always: Who shall make law, and what shall that law be?" But in his rather Hegelian view, he suggests that such fundamental questions no longer play or should play the central role in politics. He thinks that America no longer lives in an age of "dogmatized" politics.[7] That is, politics need no longer be viewed as a harsh or dramatic conflict over fundamentally opposed principles. We had passed into the final stage of history, in which "the leaders of the people themselves became the government, and the development was complete."[8] Government could now concentrate on the increasingly complicated business of administrative adjustment.[9] Instead of contending over regime principles, political parties would now offer different policies regarding mainly technical and bureaucratic matters. Party and policy positions would lie along an ideological continuum from liberal to conservative. Even though the two major parties would compete with one another, the differences between them would be in degree, not in kind.

Today's party system in many ways reflects Wilson's ideas. Like other Progressives, he objected to certain aspects of the mass party system that had developed in the nineteenth century and which tended to discourage the emergence of ideological parties. As a result of Progressive reforms in the twentieth century, there is now a more issue-oriented party system. But Madison, too, objected to elements of the party machines that he saw emerge in the Jacksonian era.[10] He might even have agreed with some of the modern reforms. In fact, as some scholars have noted,[11] today's party system is—at least in terms of its institutional arrangements—closer in form to the first party system than is often recognized. Today's system is more open to principled appeals than perhaps was the case several generations ago. Yet, in spite of this, Madison would favor a partisanship of republicanism over Wilson's partisanship of progress.

MADISON

In *Federalist* 10, Madison uses the terms *faction* and *party* interchangeably. He argues that factions are inevitable because they are natural. A faction or party exists where a group of individuals with a shared passion or interest acts collectively against the public good or the private rights of others. In a republic, Madison argues, a faction is especially dangerous if it becomes a majority of the society. His well-known solution to the problem is to allow a proliferation of such groups so as to render the emergence of a majority faction unlikely.[12] For this reason, Madison is sometimes thought to advocate a kind of pluralism which rests upon the idea that the public good is nothing more than the result of the interplay of competing private interests. In this view, the advocacy of a true common interest or single authoritative opinion is considered either dangerous or futile.

Yet, Madison's argument in *Federalist* 10 is actually compatible with a principled form of partisanship; he implicitly distinguishes between parties as mere factions and parties of principle. It is important to note that he limits the causes of faction to passion and interest, but not opinion. Passion-based factions, in particular, result from the coincidence of both passion and false opinion. The consequence is a "zeal for different opinions concerning religion, concerning government, and many other points, as well of speculation as of practice."[13] Such zeal can be destructive. However, if a party's opinion were true and just, then the passionate zeal of that party would be in the service of truth and justice: such passion would be the basis of public spiritedness, not of factionalism. People form different wrong opinions because of their fallible reason, not necessarily because of the mingling of passion and reason. As Charles Kesler has noted, Madison "emphasizes that fallible men typically make mistakes in their reasoning ... not that they are biased or unjust."[14] Even though reason is fallible, it should not always be distrusted. This implies the possibility of some right opinion upon which there may be general agreement.

On Madison's terms, one can conceive of a majority party based upon right opinion. *Federalist* 10 subtly suggests what would become more explicit in his defense of the Jeffersonian-Republican Party: because opinion formation itself is not necessarily corrupted by the passions, public opinion is educable. Kesler argues that the "refusal to reduce opinions or reason to the effect of prerational or subrational causes is characteristic of *Federalist* 10's argument, and lays the groundwork for the politics of public opinion—of republicanism—that *The Federalist* is constructing."[15] From the beginning Madison was not opposed to the cultivation of, or even a passion for, right opinion. The fight for ratification, to say nothing of the Revolution, exhibited such passion.[16] He concludes *Federalist* 10 with a certain invocation to a principled partisanship: "In the extent and proper structure of the Union, therefore, we behold a republican remedy for the diseases most incident to republican government. And according to the degree of *pleasure and pride we feel* in being republicans ought to be our *zeal* in cherishing the spirit and supporting the character of federalists."[17] Such "pleasure and pride" are part of a robust republicanism. Madison's words suggest the consistency of his thought: his pleasure and pride in the partisan cause of the original Federalists anticipate his zeal in defense of the Republican Party just a few years later. As Edward Erler concludes: "It may be only a short step from the partisan zeal that Madison invokes in support of the Constitution to a political party devoted to the partisanship of republican principles."[18]

It was, indeed, a short step from a partisanship in support of the Constitution to a partisanship in defense of republicanism. In his essays for the *National Gazette* in the early 1790s, Madison explicitly associates the Republican Party with the Founding Fathers. Indeed, he notes the correspondence between exceptional partisan moments in American history up to that time:

> The most interesting state of parties in the United States may be referred to three periods: Those who espoused the cause of independence and those who adhered to the British claims, formed the parties of the first period.... The Federal Constitution ... gave birth to a second and most interesting division of the people.... This state of parties was terminated by the regular and effectual establishment of the federal government in 1788; out of the administration of which, however, has arisen a third division, which being natural to most political societies, is likely to be of some duration in ours.[19]

These exceptional periods are distinct from the normal politics described in *Federalist* 10, with its extended republic of multiple interests. From "1783 to 1787," Madison observes, "there were parties in abundance, but being rather local than general, they are not within the present review."[20] He almost certainly had such local parties in mind when he wrote *Federalist* 10. The Federalist and Republican parties of the 1790s, on the other hand, are different in kind from these mere factions.[21]

Parties during exceptional periods are "general" in more than a geographic sense because the issues dividing them concern the form of the regime itself. Indeed, it is the agitation of the regime question that makes the party conflict at such times "most interesting." As Madison notes, the "antirepublican" Federalists are

> those, whom from particular interest, from natural temper, or from the habits of life, are more partial to the opulent than to the other classes of society; and having debauched themselves into a

persuasion that mankind are incapable of governing themselves, it follows with them of course, that government can be carried on only by the pageantry of rank, the influence of money and emoluments, and the terror of military force.[22]

The Republican Party, on the other hand, believes in the "doctrine that mankind are capable of governing themselves," hates "hereditary power," and is offended at policies that do not appeal "to the understanding and to the general interest of the community." Such measures should be "conformable to the principles, and conducive to the preservation of republican government."[23] In this sense, the struggle between Federalists and Republicans reflects in form the contest between monarchy and republicanism present at the Revolution.

Party conflict is always present to some degree and therefore is "natural," only growing more pronounced during the "most interesting" periods. We are reminded of Aristotle's explanation of parties and regimes.[24] He suggests that political communities naturally are made up of competing elements, with one usually ruling and the others ruled. These elements roughly correspond to classes (democrats, oligarchs, etc.), but they form themselves into distinct voices in the community. Usually the offices of government and the very way of life in the city as a whole are guided or determined by a particular party or class. However, because they are concerned with the general question of the regime itself, such parties are unlike the localistic or particularistic factions of *Federalist* 10.

Madison's regime politics is similar to that of Aristotle, albeit with certain important differences. In *Federalist* 43, the central number of *The Federalist*, Madison asks: "On what principle the Confederation, which stands in the solemn form of a compact among the States, can be superseded without the unanimous consent of the parties to it?" That is, why or in what sense were the framers of the Constitution justified in discarding the Articles of Confederation? Madison answers by turning to the revolutionary origins of the regime, "by recurring to the absolute necessity of the case; to the great principle of self-preservation; to the transcendent law of nature and of nature's God, which declares that the safety and happiness of society are the objects at which all political institutions aim and to which all such institutions must be sacrificed."[25] He cites the Declaration of Independence because he understands the regime question specifically in terms of the social contract, a concept for the most part rejected by Aristotle. But Madison agrees with Aristotle insofar as the sacrifice of existing institutions is a kind of regime politics, which serves to affirm or reject some ultimate claim to justice.[26] This did, indeed, occur as a result of the revolutionary leadership of the framers. And this is all to the good, according to Madison, as an expression of regime, as opposed to factional, partisanship.

But the social contract basis of the American republic adds an element to party politics missing from the classical understanding. For Aristotle, there is some measure of justice in the claims of the different parties, such as the claim of freedom by democrats or of wealth by oligarchs. The best practical regime, therefore, admits of some mixture of the parties so as to combine, however imperfectly, the elements of justice out of the various incomplete claims. Madison, like most of the other Founders, rejects this idea. Unlike Aristotle's mixed regime, American republicanism is legitimated by more than merely *political* justice. It is legitimated by its adherence to *natural* justice, the Declaration's "transcendent law of nature and of nature's God," according to which the social contract is created. As a practical matter, this requires fidelity to written constitutions as expressions of that contract. Madison remarked that the constitutions of the United States are the "political scriptures" of the people and are "the most sacred part of their property."[27] In this very important respect, constitutions are more than just formative influences on the society (although they are that too, as Madison makes clear in *Federalist* 49); they are also the principal possessions of the people, objects which express their fully formed opinions about the ends of government and society.[28]

One is reminded of John Locke's teaching on revolution: "Men can never be secure from Tyranny if there be no means to escape it, till they are perfectly under it: And therefore it is, that they have not only a Right to get out of it, but to prevent it."[29] The people need not remain idle in the face of emerging tyranny. The Virginia Resolutions and the Virginia Report were the climax of Madison's defense of this role for the people. There he makes clear the radical implications for partisanship contained within the social contract. The Resolutions declare that "*the powers granted under the constitution, being derived from the people of the United States, may be resumed by them, whensoever the same shall be perverted to their injury or oppression; and that every power not granted thereby, remains with them and at their will.*"[30] Of course, in this defense of "interposition," Madison famously and controversially argues that the states are "parties to the compact from which the powers of the Federal Government result." But the controversy is resolved in principle with his insistence that "states" here "means the people composing those political societies, in their highest sovereign capacity."[31] This is the majority of the entire nation that establishes the formal social contract, but is itself the necessarily informal or "ultraconstitutional"[32] expression of the primordial and natural right of the people to govern themselves. However complicated the arrangement of "the people" may be through the respective states, according to Madison, the underlying premise is the same: the people are the sovereign authority and, therefore, "can explain, amend, or remake"[33] the constitutional compact. Madison here follows the logic of social contract theory. Locke, for example, notes that, "*[W]hen the government is dissolved*, the People are at liberty to provide for themselves, by erecting a new Legislative, differing from the other, by the change of Persons, or Form, or both as they shall find it most for their safety and good."[34] One might say that Locke's change of "Persons" foreshadows Jefferson's revolution in "principles."

It is important to note that the Republican revolution of 1800 was more than a matter of electoral politics. The Republican movement was closely tied to the Virginia Resolutions, and the doctrine of interposition contained therein.[35] Thus, it did more than attempt to "arrest the progress of the evil [of the Alien and Sedition Acts] thro' the elective process according to the forms of the Constitution." Madison distinguishes between turning to the "influence of the Ballot-boxes & Hustings," on the one hand, and resorting to the greater "power that made the Constitution," on the other.[36] Insofar as it was an instrument of interposition, the Republican Party clearly was a vehicle for representing the latter. Until the 1790s, Americans had used conventions for this constitutional purpose. As Gordon Wood has noted, the conception of the "constituent convention" was formed through a sense of "civil disobedience" and during a period of "pervasive mistrust of the representational process."[37] In *Federalist* 40, Madison exhibited something of this spirit, arguing in defense of the Constitutional Convention that "in all great changes of established governments forms ought to give way to substance; that a rigid adherence in such cases to the former would render nominal and nugatory the transcendent and precious right of the people to 'abolish or alter their governments as to them shall seem most likely to effect their safety and happiness'..."[38] The state conventions followed upon this principle as completion of the fundamental legislative power embodied in the Philadelphia Convention.

However, in the 1790s, the national institution used to fulfill this role was not the Congress, nor even the state legislatures in their conventional and collective capacity, even though they provided to some extent the medium for expression of the popular will through documents like the Virginia Resolutions. Instead, the Republican Party became that institution. Indeed, Madison likely thought of his role in the party much as he conceived of his role in the Convention: as one of those "patriotic and respectable ... number of citizens" that occasionally must propose to the people "plans for their safety and happiness."[39] The difference between electioneering and interposition is important. In the latter case, which is rarer and clearly more extreme, the existing government may come to stand against the society as if in a state of nature. The government in such circumstances comes precariously close to being "dissolved," to use Locke's term. It may, therefore, legitimately be resisted by the people. Madison suggests this argument in the "Report" when, in defense of interposition, he remarks that "the resolution of the General Assembly relates to those *great and extraordinary* cases, in which *all the forms of the constitution may prove ineffectual* against infractions dangerous to the essential rights of the parties to it."[40] The threat is not so much from the Constitution as from the faction or cabal in control of the actual institutions of the prevailing government.

It is noteworthy that Madison uses similar language in *Federalist* 49, arguing that "a constitutional road to the decision of the people ought to be marked out and kept open, for certain *great and extraordinary* occasions."[41] He refers there to the formal amendment procedures in Article V of the Constitution. But in the midst of the war crisis of the late 1790s, Madison casts doubt upon the relevance of the Constitution itself. The situation is, in a sense, a greater and more extraordinary moment than what he anticipated in *The Federalist*. The precise problem in the crisis, at least as Madison perceives it, is that the constitutional forms themselves may have proven too weak to secure the ends of society. The action called for in the "Resolutions" and the "Report" is defined less by the form it takes, such as through constitutionally sanctioned conventions or amendment procedures, and more by the extraordinary events themselves, by the necessity of the case. Indeed, it remains unclear at what point the party, as the embodiment of the people in their "highest sovereign capacity," moves from being an agent of electoral politics to an instrument of interposition, and from there to a revolutionary body in the most extreme sense.

Scholars understandably question the coherence and clarity of Madison's doctrine of interposition. Neal Riemer, for example, suggests that the "exact nature of this ultraconstitutional remedy—this extreme remedy to be employed only in rare cases—remains somewhat mysterious. Madison never spelled out its exact nature."[42] If interposition does not amount to the natural right of revolution by any segment of the society, is it merely a call for electoral victory, much like the organized mass partisanship that would emerge in the 1830s? Madison does argue that the Virginia Resolutions serve as "expressions of opinion, unaccompanied with any other effect, than what they may produce on opinion, by exciting reflection."[43] The "interposition of the parties, in their sovereign capacity," he maintains, "can be called for by occasions only, deeply and essentially affecting the vital principles of their political system." It should not come about "in a hasty manner, or on doubtful and inferior occasions," but only when there is a *"deliberate, palpable* and *dangerous* breach of the Constitution."[44] Nevertheless, Madison's assertion that the people in their constituent capacity may *resume* the powers that they have granted to the government is quite radical. The only clear limit that he suggests, the only thing that seems to distinguish it from nullification or revolution outright, is the requirement that it be carried out by the majority of the people, not merely a minority.[45] It remains otherwise unclear just what the limits of the power of resumption are or what such a power might look like when fully exercised. The "object of the interposition," Madison argues, is "solely that of arresting the progress of the *evil* of usurpation, and of maintaining the authorities, rights and liberties appertaining to the states, as parties to the constitution."[46] But how exactly can the people, even a majority of the people throughout the nation, "arrest" the progress of the evil?[47] Madison ostensibly argues that the goal is preservation of the Constitution, not its destruction. But that point may be moot, for he has suggested that the Constitution itself may be irrelevant because it has become ineffective, that there is, as a practical matter, little left of the Constitution to preserve. This at least seems to be the logic of his argument. Such is the potentially radical nature of regime politics.

Madison's radicalism is evident throughout the 1790s, not just in the crisis over the Alien and Sedition Acts. In the *National Gazette* essays, for example, he prefigured his more controversial discussion in the "Resolutions" and the "Report." In these essays, he recognized that the extended sphere of *Federalist* 10, which does so much to thwart majority faction, may also prevent the creation of majorities that actually can "watch over" the government. Since in the large republic it is "less easy" for the country's "real opinion to be ascertained,"[48] the government may be left free to acquire undue power. This may especially be the case under the able leadership of someone like Alexander Hamilton.[49] To counter the Federalists' attempted "consolidation of the states into one government," Madison calls for a "consolidation" of the "interests and affections" of the people:

> [The] less the supposed difference of interests, and the greater the concord and confidence throughout the great body of the people, the more readily must they sympathize with each other, the more seasonably can they interpose a common manifestation of their sentiments, the more certainly will they take the alarm at usurpation or oppression, and the more effectually will they *consolidate* their defence of the public liberty.[50]

This interposition by the "great body of the people" does not reflect the normal politics described in *Federalist* 10, with its emphasis upon shifting coalitions and more narrow, primarily local and economic, interests. The conflict now is analogous to the great struggle of the Revolution. Much as the Declaration referred to "abuses and usurpations;" Madison here refers to "usurpation or oppression." As the Declaration affirmed the existence of "one people" against the British, so Madison now asks the people to "interpose a common manifestation of their sentiments" against the Federalists. The division between state and society in his partisanship is clear. If necessary, the people may act *against* their government, rather than merely *through* it.

But normally this radical role for parties is not necessary. The more moderate politics of *Federalist* 10 usually prevails. Because the "most interesting" state of parties is exceptional in nature, the regime parties themselves need not (and perhaps should not) exist in perpetuity. When Jefferson said in his First Inaugural Address that "we are all Federalists, we are all Republicans," he really meant that his party's victory signaled the end of the other party. He was correct. By 1820, the Federalist Party had all but disappeared. This made sense to Jefferson and Madison, for they did not conceive of the Federalists as either a legitimate majority or, after 1800, even a loyal opposition.

The notion of a party *system* as it would later be understood did not really exist for the early partisans. Federalists were forced to adopt Republican rhetoric and policies after 1800. The end of party competition meant, in turn, the end of parties altogether.

An actual system of political parties did not emerge in America until the 1830s. In response to the electoral "chaos"[51] that resulted from the demise of two-party competition in the 1820s, Martin Van Buren and others consciously set about to create what came to be the modern mass party system. This system lasted in more or less the same form until the 1960s. Its chief characteristic was the party machine, led by unelected party bosses and sustained by the spoils system. Van Buren intended this "party-in-control"[52] to cure the problem of "personal factions"[53] that had erupted so controversially in the 1824 presidential election. His goal was to channel the ambitions and careers of individual politicians through the disciplined parties. Yet, "occasionally" such parties are able to "respond to a powerful issue outside the current party mainstream, and pursue policies that require radical changes, extending possibly to the constitutional fabric itself." That is, the mass party system was open to the kind of "convulsive regime politics"[54] that marked the initial party conflict between Federalists and Republicans. This openness to radical change was most evident in the party realignments associated with the critical elections of 1860 and 1932, and to a lesser extent those of 1828 and 1896. This occasional emergence of regime politics is consistent with Madison's suggestion that the fundamental division in society is natural and, therefore, destined to return in "most interesting" ways.

WILSON

Woodrow Wilson's goal of party reform has been seen by some as an attempt to bring about significant political and governmental change much more frequently than under the Van Burenite party system. This is seen most clearly in his repeated calls for visionary and centralized political leadership.[55] Political scientists Dean McSweeney and John Zvesper summarize this interpretation of Wilson's view:

> The mature party system provided opportunity for major policy change and party realignment, but the assumption was that such opportunities would not be used very often; in the reformed system the assumption is that major policy change will frequently

be needed. Therefore party power, especially at the state and local levels, must be made to yield to candidate and leader power.[56]

Wilson's view can be understood, in this sense, as a more open and extreme version of the implicit and periodic radicalism of Madison's interposition doctrine. Some of Wilson's latter-day critics concentrate upon his turn to a plebiscitary leadership style for the president, one which opens the door to democratic excesses dangerous to the republican and constitutional order. Indeed, it has been suggested that the modern "rhetorical presidency" has perhaps displaced that order, with unfortunate results.[57]

Yet, while there is truth in this interpretation, Wilson's emphasis upon change must be distinguished very clearly from the regime politics of Madison, or even that of Van Buren. While Madison likened the "natural" division between Federalists and Republicans to the Revolution, Wilson argues that revolutions as such are now improbable. In fact, the American Revolution itself was really only one moment—if a rather dramatic one—in a long transitional period within what Wilson calls "constitutional development." Relying upon a kind of "Darwinian" determinism, he suggests that we must "understand our own institutions as they cannot be understood in any other way," as a result of the "whole process" of history.[58] This history, he believes, is made up of four "stages." In the first stage, absolute rule predominated. In the second stage, such "mastery" still prevailed, but largely with the voluntary submission of the people (he has in mind the benevolent rule of monarchs like Queen Elizabeth I). But in the third stage, "both sorts of mastery failed" and the government "found itself face to face with leaders of the people who were bent upon controlling it, a period of deep agitation and full of the signs of change."[59] Eighteenth century America was one such period. In this tumultuous stage, Wilson argues: "Governments find themselves ... in the presence of *Agitation*, of systematic movements of opinion which do not merely flare up in spasmodic flame and then die down again, but burn with an accumulating ardor which can be checked and extinguished only by removing the grievances and abolishing the unacceptable institutions which are its fuel."[60] With those institutional changes, "the leaders of the people themselves became the government, and the development was complete."[61] Wilson's conception of history, then, necessarily precludes regime parties, for the regime question itself has been decided with the transition to the final stage of constitutional development. Indeed, for Wilson, this is really *regime* development, which ends in the modern democratic state.

Wilson may be considered a "conservative" insofar as he is rather closed to the possibility or desirability of regime politics; he does not foresee future change of such magnitude. Indeed, as he describes it, even the regime politics of the third stage of agitation seems more evolutionary than revolutionary. Similarly, however contentious modern politics in the final stage might appear, Wilson is confident that it will not boil over into regime politics:

> We are so accustomed to agitation, to absolutely free, outspoken argument for change, to an unrestrained criticism of men and measures carried almost to the point of license, that to us it seems a normal, harmless part of the familiar processes of government. We have learned that it is pent-up feelings that are dangerous, whispered purposes that are revolutionary, covert follies that warp and poison the mind; that the wisest thing to do with a fool is to encourage him to hire a hall and discourse to his fellow citizens.[62]

The final stage apparently can risk such unrestraint because the "long discipline" and "habit" of orderly government is so engrained in the people; they have come to their "political maturity."[63] Wilson's preference for vigorous leadership and frequent policy change should be understood in this light. Such volatility, he suggests, is to remain within the confines of the social and political order, or at least that order as it is found at the end of history. In fact, because of his reverence for this order, many historians view Wilson as anything but a radical. Some argue that, given his apparent contentment, he should not even be considered a Progressive.[64]

But political scientists and theorists are right to point out that Wilson's Darwinian views necessarily entail the central historicist and evolutionary elements of Progressive thought, elements clearly at odds with the natural law principles of Madison and the Founders.[65] On the other hand, we know that Wilson disagreed with many Progressives on several points, especially regarding the value of political parties. So we might conclude that Wilson is somewhere between the Founders and the Progressives. Yet, this is also inadequate and inaccurate, for he certainly is a Progressive, if only of a certain kind. I suggest that an appeal to philosophical categories is helpful here.[66] As Madison echoes Locke and Aristotle, the Progressives may reasonably be associated with Rousseau and Marx, figures known for their radicalism. Wilson, however, may be likened to Hegel, who shares some of the same historicist premises of Rousseau and Marx, but who also can appear rather moderate by comparison. That is, Wilson identifies a kind of Hegelian evolution of republican institutions in American politics and government. The party system, as he sees it, is an integral element of this evolving order. This should be kept in mind when examining both Wilson's evaluation of the mass party system and his specific prescriptions for its reform.

Wilson's view of American parties is informed, as is just about every aspect of his political thought, by his negative appraisal of government diversity in America, including the separation of powers and, what is "vastly more important,"[67] the multiplication of elective offices in the federal system. Such diversity, he believes, thwarts the national will. Yet, he praises the Van Buren system of machine politics for its ability to overcome much of this problem.[68] It brought, in his view, a much needed discipline and national scope to the political system. Wilson describes how the political parties had done so much to unify the vast country, to bring together in some working order the disparate parts of the federal and constitutional system. "There is," he suggests, "a sense in which our parties may be said to have been our real body politic."[69] The parties organized caucuses and conventions, chose the nation's policy and personnel, integrated its decentralized institutions, and brought together the separate government branches.[70]

The main purpose of Wilson's party reform, then, is not simply to overcome government diversity, for the mass party system largely accomplished that goal. He was more concerned with the "irresponsibility" of the party bosses. Only in the United States, he wrote, did the party, as then constituted, amount to a "distinct authority outside the formal government, expressing its purposes through its own separate and peculiar organs and permitted to dictate what Congress shall undertake and the national administration shall address itself to."[71] The parties, thus, did not represent the will of the people. Wilson actually was not concerned so much with the nationalizing force of the party system, for that was its strength: "Party organization is no longer needed for the mere rudimentary task of holding the machinery together or giving it the sustenance of some common object, some single cooperative motive." Instead, he emphasized the need to "examine the network of party in detail and change its structure without imperiling its strength." Such an examination would provide clues as to the means to make the parties responsible to the people.[72] The goal was to join the responsibility of holding public office with the organizational structure of the political parties.

From the beginning of his career, Wilson held to this opinion, although his practical prescriptions changed over time. He originally thought that the best form of government to ensure responsibility was the parliamentary system based on the British model. He conceived of a government in which members of Congress would serve in the cabinet, executive branch officials would serve leadership roles in both houses of the legislature, and the houses would function and deliberate on the British model. He aimed to make the officers of government hold real political power, which until then, he thought, had largely been held by the party bosses.[73] Responsibility to public opinion would be found through the test of parliamentary debate.

Some observers conclude that this desire for responsibility indicates Wilson's hope for a more plebiscitary political system. But his goal of responsible parties was not simply a matter of democratic accountability. For example, his early preference for cabinet government was largely motivated by his belief, not entirely unlike that of Madison and the Founders, that debate and deliberation ought to characterize lawmaking. Such a system, he argued, would encourage competition and deliberation among the governmental elite, leading to principled leadership and statesmanship.[74] This would result in the formation of a quasi-aristocratic leadership class. Similarly, for years he objected to the adoption of direct primaries because he thought they might undermine the coherence and stability of the parties; he really only changed his view after entering politics.[75] More generally, Wilson lamented the emergence of universal suffrage.[76] Indeed, he thought that the people were "selfish, ignorant, timid, stubborn, or foolish."[77] He objected to the idea that government ought simply to mirror the passions of the people, as would be the case in a plebiscitary system. Responsibility, at least as he explained it, meant more than immediate responsiveness to the changing whims of the majority. He hoped, however unrealistically, that Progressive leadership would be deliberate and moderate.

Wilson explained his conception of leadership in his well-known essay, "Leaders of Men." He stressed the conservatism of his approach, arguing that "the instructed few may not be safe leaders, except in so far as they have communicated their instruction to the many, except in so far as they have transmuted their thought into a common, a popular thought."[78] The political leader must actively work to educate public opinion. But Wilson also argues that "leadership, for the statesman, is interpretation. He must read the common thought: he must test and calculate very circumspectly the preparation of the nation for the next move in the progress of politics."[79] Even though the leader must instruct the many, this notion of "interpretation" suggests that the leader is bound by the current state of public opinion, that he should guard against pressing for too much change. Leadership should be evolutionary, not revolutionary.

Wilson's conception of leadership is closely related to his theory of historical development. It centers upon the emergence of the modern state, which has progressed beyond the more raw regime politics of Madison, the Founders, and the age of "agitation." Unlike the Constitution that can be changed, Wilson argues, "there is a law greater than it that cannot be changed." This law is embedded in the forces of historical development, a "law written on our hearts which makes us conscious of our oneness as a single personality in the great company of nations."[80] Human consciousness itself has been so transformed that the citizen's relationship to the state takes on a character wholly different than that conceived of by Madison. Wilson believes that the people should not so much "watch over" the state as they should actualize themselves through it. It goes without saying that he rejects the possibility of a fundamental antagonism between government and society. Instead, he maintains that the modern state is the "first among the few polities which are for the future." That is, the modern state has achieved an "ideality" of "political salvation." Such salvation is found in the recognition of the freedom and dignity of all the people, in a kind of secular analogue to Christian salvation. This recognition occurs through the state, but by means of "self-expression through personality" in "the persons of trusted leaders."[81] For Wilson, each person in the modern democratic state is to enjoy recognition through the leaders of the state. Statism, and not democracy, is the real heart of his political theory.

There is a striking similarity here between Wilson's terms and Hegel's. He seems to echo Hegel's emphasis upon the "personality" of the state, and the relationship of the people to it:

> [Personality], like subjectivity in general, as infinitely self-related, has its truth (to be precise, its most elementary, immediate, truth)

only in a person, in a subject existing "for" himself, and that exists "for" itself is just simply a unit. It is only as a person, the monarch, that the personality of the state is actual. Personality expresses the concept as such; but the person enshrines the actuality of the concept, and only when the concept is determined as person is it the Idea or truth.[82]

In the "artificial person" that is any political community or association, personality, as Hegel seems to define it, has "not achieved its true mode of existence." This leads him to conclude that, "taken without its monarch and the articulation of the whole which is the indispensable and direct concomitant of monarchy, the people is a formless mass and no longer a state."[83] Similarly, Wilson thinks that his proposed reforms will facilitate the reconciliation of the universal interests of the state and the particular interests of individuals within the state.[84] Unlike Hegel's monarchy, however, Wilson thought that this reconciliation could be achieved through a republican form of government.

Wilson's reform proposals naturally centered upon the president, who, somewhat like Hegel's monarch, is the official best situated to embody the "personality" of the American people. Not surprisingly, in his early scheme for cabinet government, Wilson thought that the president's tenure of office should be made "permanent." "Otherwise," he argued, "we would be exposed to all the perils of instability. There would be no permanent centre to our system, no central pillar of support."[85] In *Constitutional Government*, the last major work of his academic career, Wilson sharpens this view, suggesting that the president is "a man who will be and who will seem to the country in some sort an embodiment of the character and purposes it wishes its government to have." The presidential leader is one "who understands his own day and the needs of the country, and who has the personality and the initiative to enforce his views both upon the people and the Congress." "The nation as a whole has chosen him," Wilson adds, "and is conscious that it has no other spokesman. His is the only national voice in affairs." The president's "position takes the imagination of the country. He is the representative of no constituency, but of the whole people.... If he rightly interpret the national thought and boldly insist upon it, he is irresistible." The "clear logic of our constitutional practice," Wilson argues, tends toward this central role for the president.[86]

It is worth noting that in Wilson's early scheme for cabinet government, the president "would be lifted above the passing caprice of party spirit."[87] He would represent the whole nation, not just a partisan majority. By the time of *Constitutional Government*, Wilson had refined his thoughts on party government even further. The president, not the unified party government of the parliamentary model, was to be the chief source of governmental unity. Wilson came to believe that the party system as a whole existed to provide the basis from which leaders, especially the president, could guide the public will, but that the party would be less of a constraint on the president than perhaps it had been in the past. Yet, Wilson does not advocate rule by plebiscite as that is normally understood. Instead, he conceives of a broader system of public opinion formation in which presidents and presidential candidates would participate. He never dispenses with the idea of a stabilizing party system. Instead, each major party should come to fulfill a new and important role: the representation of distinct ideological views. This, however, would require a substantive transformation of the parties. "The chief obstacle to their reform," Wilson maintains, "the chief thing that has stood in the way of making them amenable to public opinion, controllable by independent opposition, is the reverence with which we have come to regard them."[88] It is much more important, he believes, to see that the parties have a new, more ideological role; they are no longer to have sectional or sentimental ties:

> [With] changing generations feelings change. We are coming now to look upon our parties once more as instruments for progressive action, as means for handling the affairs of a new age. Sentimental reminiscence is less dominant over us. We are ready to study new uses for our parties and to adapt them to new standards and principles.[89]

Wilson's party system is to be drawn on explicitly "progressive," i.e., ideological, lines. The "independent opposition" presumably refers to a division between liberal and conservative parties, the goal being a simplification of the framework within which public opinion will be shaped and formed. He argues that we must, among other things, "decrease the number and complexity of the things the voter is called upon to do; concentrate his attention upon a few men he can make responsible, a few objects upon which he can easily centre his purpose; make parties his instruments and not his masters by an utter simplification of the things he is expected to do."[90]

But this means in practice that the party system as a whole, and not just Wilson's own Democratic Party, is to act in the service of the State. The parties do this by clarifying and supporting the general will and opinion of the people. Through the test of party competition, leaders, primarily presidents and presidential candidates, would emerge who could then prepare the "nation for the next move in the progress of politics." In this sense, Wilson's parties act together as a certain adjunct to the Hegelian president, cultivating and clarifying the popular will. Both parties are legitimate representatives of the people, and together serve as democratic and competitive means for achieving unanimity of opinion.[91] One might say that the difference between the early and late Wilson is that in the former case the competition for leadership occurs within the government, while in the latter case the competition occurs much more publicly, in election campaigns and in the media. His purposes, however, remain the same.

Central to Wilson's view is his rejection of Madison's idea that conflict between majority and minority, between the major parties, can erupt into regime politics, not to mention revolution. The parties compete, but they do not divide on questions of fundamental importance. A ruling opinion need not be fought for, but only identified, or "interpreted." Indeed, the problem of majority faction is overcome in the final, democratic stage of constitutional development. The key, Wilson argues, is that "this democracy—this modern democracy—is not the rule of the many, but the rule of the whole.... Democracy is truly government by the whole—for the rule of the majority implies and is dependent upon the cooperation, be it active or passive, of the minority."[92] But he speaks of "modern democracy" only, which, he says, "is the nation come to its majority, conscious of its authority, and in clear sight of its aims."[93] In effect, the majority party no longer really rules the minority party. One might say that the parties have more in common—especially a belief in the nation's progress—than not. Indeed, Wilson says, "the Whole, too, has become self-conscious, and by becoming self-directive has set out upon a new course of development."[94] Regime politics, according to Wilson, is replaced by the acceptance of the progressive idea of the democratic state, the belief that the modern state is the final stage of political development. Indeed, the whole has direction precisely because, as in Hegel's view, it is a "self." Wilson, then, accepts what is impractical for Madison: that faction may be overcome, in effect, by giving everyone the same opinions, passions, or interests.[95]

Much like Hegel, Wilson conceives of history as a rational process, i.e., there is a rationality embedded in the customs and traditions of peoples that becomes more evident through time and emerges fully in modern democratic states.[96] Regime politics, therefore, eventually comes to an end. In a very instructive passage he notes that "through democracy thus genuinely grown, the cycle of Aristotle is impossible."[97] Aristotle held that a regime's defects would likely result in its decline and, eventually, change to another regime. In other words, he thought that permanent defects attend the human condition, that human nature is limited. Wilson, on the other hand, holds that modern democracy will avoid decline into an inferior regime because it is now understood as rule by the whole of the nation, not rule simply by the majority. It "is thus no accident," he asserts, "but the outcome of great and permanent causes, that there is no more to be found among the civilized races of Europe any satisfactory example of Aristotle's Monarchies and Aristocracies."[98] Wilson overcomes the limitations of human nature implied in regime politics by assuming the end of history.

The conflict between Wilson's thought and Madison's is clear. Wilson believes that the modern state is the embodiment of rationality and justice and, therefore, rejects the abstractions of the social contract theory. In a particularly striking passage, he notes that we think of the Declaration as a "highly theoretical document, but except for its assertion that all men are equal it is not." Instead, he says that it is "intensely practical," essentially the same as Magna Carta, which secures only "such freedom and privilege as Englishmen already of right enjoy." Not unlike Hegel (and the great conservative Burke), Wilson laments the appeal to abstract notions of rights, such as is reflected in the "revolutionary ardor of French leaders."[99] According to Wilson, the Declaration's social contract principles provide no justification or excuse for revolution. Instead, the state embodies and enforces rationality; only through it do men find their freedom and happiness; and this is so precisely because it is a "practical" manifestation of the wisdom embedded in the historical "process." Nature as such, but especially human nature, provides no real standard for politics or morality.

Madison, on the other hand, argues that just and free government relies upon an adequate understanding of human nature, its pitfalls as well as its potential. As he suggests in *Federalist* 10, men have varying natures, which at times allow their opinions to be erroneously derived and passionately held. The differing views of individuals ought to be secured in a system of representative institutions and thereby moderated, but never actually overcome or subsumed into some greater whole. Public spiritedness and a consensus in favor of republican government are necessarily precarious things. As Madison notes in the *National Gazette* essays, there remains the primary "natural" distinction between those more and those less confident about republican government. There is no one "personality" shared by the people, though the people individually participate in a public or common good. The separation between state and society remains clear in Madison's mind. The people, he says, must "watch over" their government not only to protect their freedom, but to maintain the integrity of their regime.

Conclusion

Today's party system, while not exactly identical to what Wilson envisioned, largely follows the spirit of his work. Consistent with his view, contemporary American politics usually centers upon administrative questions rather than regime questions. In particular, the central government tends to focus on the often utilitarian and mundane tasks of business regulation and maintenance of the economy. The role of the parties mirrors that of the government itself, with Republicans and Democrats often quarrelling over narrow issues of policy that have little, if any, connection to what one might properly call a regime question. While the party system today is competitive and popular debate can sometimes be rancorous, the public tends to look upon the principles of both parties as essentially legitimate.[100] Voters rarely are called upon to choose in a decisive way between fundamentally opposed principles. Indeed, the current era represents the longest period without a major party realignment in America. The New Deal realignment, which largely brought into being the administrative state desired by Wilson and other Progressives, would appear to have ushered in the end of regime politics, and the end of parties of principle.[101]

Consider, for example, the typical debate over taxes. Very often the argument concerns what the macroeconomic impact of tax cuts or increases might be, which is reasonable in itself, but which also is divorced from any distinct regime question. Republicans, who ostensibly are opposed to the progressivism of the modern administrative state, often defend tax cuts for their stimulative effect on the economy, rather than for their intrinsic justice as a matter of natural right. Compare this, for example, to Madison's argument against government manipulation of the economy, which he dislikes not simply because it may retard economic growth, but because it encourages "fashion" and disrupts the "order of society" essential for a free people to govern itself.[102] Both parties today, on the other hand, seem to accept the essential legitimacy of the modern state, the inherent paternalism of which Madison likely would condemn as contrary to republicanism.

This is not to say, of course, that there are no moral arguments in political and partisan debates today, for surely there are. Despite what Wilson thought, history has not ended. Yet, these debates tend to be framed in Progressive terms. For example, "culture" often replaces "morality" in discussions of morality proper. Moreover, "moral" issues are often mistakenly distinguished from "economic" issues, where the latter are thought of as matters of necessity and the former matters of idiosyncratic choice. The idea of ordered liberty, so central to republicanism, is lost in this language. Republican Party leaders, in particular, are often perplexed and ineffective in a rhetorical framework that naturally works against them, both as to public policy and to public relations. This is the inevitable problem for the "conservative" party in a progressive political order as it necessarily always stands just behind the curve of history, conceding in some essential respect the moral high ground, such as it is, to the liberal party.

Wilson himself, as I have suggested, can be interpreted as a conservative, if we assume a thoroughly progressive view. Not surprisingly, he is, as already mentioned, sometimes considered to be an unfaithful Progressive. But this only highlights the problem from the point of view of Madison's regime partisanship. One can reasonably argue that the Democratic and Republican parties are more liberal and conservative, respectively, than they are democratic and republican, i.e., they are not essentially animated by the regime question. In this way, the Republicans, the party that might be expected to challenge progressivism itself, is locked into a largely self-defeating role in the party system.

The answer to this problem would seem to require a return to Madison's republicanism and a rejection of Wilson's progressivism. But such a return, oddly enough, would be ineffective if understood to be a merely conservative enterprise. In order to have a chance to succeed, the return likely would have to follow the example of the Founders themselves and appeal not to tradition or law, but to the "transcendent" principles of the Declaration. It remains to be seen whether the "necessity of the case" today would render such an appeal successful.

Endnotes

1. *Thomas Jefferson: Writings*, Merrill D. Peterson, ed. (New York: Library of America, 1984), 880. On the relationship between partisanship and the right of revolution, from which much of the argument of this paper derives, see Harry V. Jaffa, *A New Birth of Freedom* (Lanham, Md: Rowman and Littlefield, 2000), especially chapter one.

2. For a helpful discussion of the traditional political science of regimes and American politics, see James Ceaser, *Liberal Democracy And Political Science* (Baltimore: Johns Hopkins University Press, 1990).

3. Madison, "A Candid State of Parties," in *The Papers of James Madison*, William T. Hutchinson, et al., eds. (Chicago: University of Chicago Press, 1962), 14:370-71.

4. See Walter Dean Burnham, *Critical Elections and the Mainsprings of American Politics* (New York: Norton, 1970); V.O. Key, Jr., "A Theory of Critical Elections," *Journal of Politics* 17 (February 1955): 3-18; David R. Mayhew, *Electoral Realignments: A Critique of an American Genre* (New Haven: Yale University Press, 2003); and, especially, Harry V. Jaffa, *Equality and Liberty: Theory and Practice in American Politics* (Claremont, Ca.: The Claremont Institute, 1999), 32-41.

5. Letter to Spencer Roane, Sept. 6, 1819, in *The Writings of Thomas Jefferson*, Andrew Lipscomb and Albert Bergh, eds. (Washington, D.C.: Jefferson Memorial Association of the United States, 1903-1905), 15:212.

6. For a related discussion, see Jaffa, *Equality and Liberty*, 3-32.

7. Woodrow Wilson, "The Study of Administration," in *The Public Papers of Woodrow Wilson: College and State*, R. S. Baker and W. E. Dodd, eds. (New York: Harper and Brothers, 1925), 1:131-32.

8. Woodrow Wilson, *Constitutional Government in the United States* (New York: Columbia University Press, 1908), 28.

9. Wilson, "The Study of Administration," *College and State*, 133.

10. Madison, Letter to Edward Coles, Aug. 29, 1834, in *The Writings of James Madison*, Gaillard Hunt, ed. (New York: G. P. Putnam's Sons, 1904), 9: 539.

11. See, for example, John Aldrich, *Why Parties? The Origins and Transformations of Party Politics in America* (Chicago: University of Chicago Press, 1995).

12. *Federalist* 10, in Alexander Hamilton, James Madison, and John Jay, *The Federalist Papers*, introduction and notes by Charles R. Kesler, Clinton Rossiter, ed. (New York: New American Library, 1999), 45-52.

13. Ibid., 47.

14. Charles R. Kesler, "*Federalist* 10 and American Republicanism," in

Saving the Revolution, Charles R. Kesler, ed. (New York: The Free Press, 1987), 26.

15. Ibid., 27, 38. Kesler notes that: "When it is seen that [Madison] is contending not for a multiplicity of factions but of interests, and these informed by a common opinion, the way from *Federalist* 10 to republican politics ... opens up."

16. See also, for example, the peroration to *Federalist* No. 14.

17. *Federalist* No. 10, 52 (emphasis added).

18. Edward J. Erler, *The American Polity* (New York: Crane Russak, 1991), 35.

19. "A Candid State of Parties," *Papers of James Madison*, 14:370-71.

20. Ibid., 14:370.

21. Madison's leadership of the Republican Party, then, no more contradicted *The Federalist* than *The Federalist* contradicted the Revolution. Some scholars do say that the Constitution and *The Federalist* represent a movement away from the principles of the Revolution, although Madison appears not to have thought so. See the "classical republican" school in American historiography, especially J. G. A. Pocock, *The Machiavellian Moment: Florentine Political Thought and the Atlantic Republican Tradition* (Princeton: Princeton University Press, 1975), and Gordon Wood, *The Creation of the American Republic, 1776-1787* (Chapel Hill: University of North Carolina Press, 1969).

22. "A Candid State of Parties," *Papers of James Madison*, 14:371.

23. Ibid.

24. Aristotle, *Politics*, trans. Carnes Lord (Chicago: University of Chicago Press, 1984), Books 3 and 4.

25. *Federalist* No. 43, 247.

26. Harry Jaffa notes that the "safety and happiness of society" referred to in the Declaration are the "alpha and omega of political life in Aristotle's *Politics*." Jaffa, "Aristotle and Locke in the American Founding," *Claremont Review of Books* (Winter 2001), 10.

27. *Papers of James Madison*, 14:192, 218. On these passages, see Colleen Sheehan, "Madison's Party Press Essays," *Interpretation: A Journal of Political Philosophy* 17 (Spring 1990): 355-377.

28. Madison remarks that after establishing a government, the people "should watch over it, as well as obey it." *Papers of James Madison*, 14: 426. See John Zvesper, *Political Philosophy and Rhetoric: A Study of the Origins of American Party Politics* (Cambridge: Cambridge University Press, 1977).

29. John Locke, *Two Treatises of Government*, intro. Peter Laslett (New York: New American Library, 1965), 460 (*Second Treatise*, sec. 220).

30. *Papers of James Madison*, 17:345 (italics original).

31. Ibid., 17:309.

32. Neal Riemer, *James Madison: Creating the American Constitution* (Washington, D.C.: Congressional Quarterly, 1986), 148.

33. "Notes on Nullification," in *Writing of James Madison*, 9:597.

34. Locke, *Two Treatises*, 459 (*Second Treatise*, sec. 220).

35. Madison suggested that the "Resolutions" and the "Report" were instruments of the organized Republican Party, not simply of the Virginia legislature. Late in his life, for example, he noted "the reception given to the proceedings [i.e., the Resolutions and the Report] by the Republican party every where, and the pains taken by it, in multiplying republications of them in newspapers and other forms." "Notes on Nullification," in *Writings of James Madison*, 9:595.

36. "Notes on Nullification," *Writings of James Madison*, 9:59.

37. Wood, *The Creation of the American Republic, 1776-1787*, 328.

38. *Federalist* No. 40, 220-21.

39. Ibid., 221.

40. *Papers of James Madison*, 17:311 (emphasis added).

41. *Federalist* No. 49, 282 (emphasis added).

42. Riemer, *James Madison*, 148.

43. "Virginia Report of 1800," *Papers of James Madison*, 17:348.

44. "Ibid., 17:310.

45. For Madison's most thorough account of this point, see his extensive "Notes on Nullification," *Writings of James Madison*, 9:573-607, which he wrote to explain the difference between his interposition doctrine and John Calhoun's nullification doctrine. There he argues forcefully that interposition can only exist in order to affirm and defend the existing Constitution. And in accordance with social contract principles, it does so only by marshalling the opinion of the majority of the whole people of the states, not just one state or a minority of the people.

46. "Virginia Report of 1800," *Papers of James Madison*, 17:310.

47. Jaffa intimates the delicacy of this question:

[E]lections are not, in and of themselves, an alternative to "blood and revolution." The threat or menace of revolution remains an integral element of the pressure brought to bear in and through the electoral process. That threat or menace, however, consists less in the fear of the force that might be brought to bear than in the reminder of the role of the right of revolution in the theory on which the American Revolution was grounded.... [*Federalist* 43's] appeal to the right of revolution is purely peaceful and rational. Madison in the *Federalist* legitimates subsequent appeals, such as those in the Kentucky and Virginia Resolutions, against the very government whose adoption he is recommending. These appeals are at once revolutionary, threatening, peaceful, and rational. The natural right of revolution, we may say, is the right whose recognition and understanding are supremely necessary if "reflection and choice" are to replace "accident and force" in the government of mankind.

A New Birth of Freedom, 59-60. The aim is a "peaceful and rational" society, but the achievement of this aim requires, in some way, the "threat or menace of revolution." One might say that this threat or menace indicates the seriousness of the question facing the society, of what I have called the regime question. Madison's doctrine of interposition was, I suggest, perhaps the most extreme instance of this appeal. On the other hand, Jefferson's initial Kentucky Resolutions, with their sanction of single-state nullification, seem to be more akin to an outright revolutionary appeal.

48. "Public Opinion," *Papers of James Madison*, 14:170.

49. "In such a state of things, the impossibility of acting together, might be succeeded by the inefficacy of partial expressions of the public mind, and this at length, by a universal silence and insensibility, leaving the whole government to that *self directed course*, which, it must be owned, is the natural propensity of every government." Madison, "Consolidation," in *Papers of James Madison*, 14:138.

50. Ibid., 14:138-39. "Let the latter [those who may be more inclined to contemplate the people of America in the light of one nation] employ their utmost zeal, eradicating local prejudices and mistaken rivalships, to consolidate the affairs of the states into one harmonious interest; and let it be the patriotic study of all, to maintain the various authorities established by our complicated system, each in its respective constitutional sphere; and to erect over the whole, one paramount Empire of reason, benevolence and brotherly affection."

51. Roy F. Nichols, *The Invention of the American Political Parties* (New York: MacMillan, 1967), 262-78.

52. Aldrich, *Why Parties?*, 97-125.

53. Martin Van Buren, *Inquiry into the Origin and Course of Political Parties in the United States* (New York: Augustus M. Kelley, 1967 [originally published 1867]), 4.

54. Dean McSweeney and John Zvesper, *American Political Parties: The Formation, Decline and Reform of the American Party System* (London: Routledge, 1991), 51. See also James Ceaser, "Political Change and Party

Reform," in *Political Parties in the Eighties*, Robert A. Goldwin, ed. (Washington, D.C.: American Enterprise Institute, 1980).

55. The most important early statement is Wilson's 1890 essay, *Leaders of Men* (Princeton: Princeton University Press, 1952 [from the 1890 manuscript]). With its emphasis on a central role for the presidency, *Constitutional Government* is the culmination of his academic study and advocacy of vigorous leadership.

56. McSweeney and Zvesper, *American Political Parties*, 54.

57. Jeffrey K. Tulis, *The Rhetorical Presidency* (Princeton: Princeton University Press, 1987), 173-204.

58. Wilson, *Constitutional Government*, 57, 12.

59. Ibid., 28.

60. Ibid., 37.

61. Ibid., 28.

62. Ibid., 38.

63. Ibid., 52.

64. See, for example, Eldon Eisenach, *The Lost Promise of Progressivism* (Lawrence, Kan.: University Press of Kansas, 1994).

65. See Ronald J. Pestritto, "A New Look at the New Freedom," paper prepared for the Annual Meeting of the American Political Science Association, Boston, 2002.

66. I am less interested in Wilson's philosophical pedigree than with simply understanding his thought. He had many influences, Hegel among them.

67. Wilson, *Constitutional Government*, 41.

68. On how the Founders intended to forestall the creation of a mass democracy, see Colleen Sheehan, "Madison's Party Press Essays," 355-77.

69. Wilson, *Constitutional Government*, 218.

70. Ibid., 211.

71. Ibid.

72. Ibid., 220.

73. Wilson, "Cabinet Government in the United States," *College and State*, 1:19-42; "Committee or Cabinet Government?" ibid., 1:95-129.

74. Wilson, "Cabinet Government in the United States," *College and State*, 1:28-29, 34-37.

75. See the discussion in Henry Bragdon, *Woodrow Wilson: The Academic Years* (Cambridge: Harvard University Press, 1967), 400.

76. Wilson, *The Papers of Woodrow Wilson*, Arthur S. Link. ed. (Princeton: Princeton University Press, 1966), 1:352-53, 493-94.

77. Wilson, "The Study of Administration," in *College and State*, 1: 142.

78. Wilson, *Leaders of Men*, 41-2.

79. Ibid., 42.
80. *Papers of Woodrow Wilson*, 5:61-2.
81. Ibid., 5:69.
82. G. W. F. Hegel, *Philosophy of Right*, trans. T. M. Knox (London: Oxford University Press, 1952), 181-2.
83. Ibid., 182-83.
84. In this connection, consider Wilson's language describing Daniel Webster's reply to Robert Hayne on the question of union:

There is a sense in which it may almost be said that Mr. Webster that day called a nation into being. What he said has the immortal quality of words which almost create the thoughts they speak. The nation lay as it were unconscious of its unity and purpose, and he called it into full consciousness. It could never again be anything less than what he had said that it was. (*Constitutional Government*, 49.)

For a discussion of the relationship between the individual and the state in Wilson's thought, see Zentner, "Liberalism & Executive Power: Woodrow Wilson & the American Founders," *Polity* (Summer 1994): 579-99.
85. *Papers of Woodrow Wilson*, 1:571.
86. Wilson, *Constitutional Government*, 65, 68, 72.
87. *Papers of Woodrow Wilson*, 1:571.
88. Wilson, *Constitutional Government*, 220.
89. Ibid., 221.
90. Ibid., 221-22.
91. This point is explained at greater length in Scot J. Zentner, "Progressivism and the Party System," paper delivered at the Annual Meeting of the American Political Science Association, Boston, 2002.
92. *Papers of Woodrow Wilson*, 5:76.
93. Ibid.
94. Wilson, *The State: Elements of Practical and Historical Politics* (Boston: D. C. Heath and Co., 1889), 609.
95. *Federalist* 10, 78.
96. Wilson's history text, *The State*, in many parts reads like a simplified account of Hegel's philosophy of history.
97. *Papers of Woodrow Wilson*, 5:76.
98. Wilson, *The State*, 608-09.
99. Wilson, *Constitutional Government*, 4, 8, 16.
100. Byron E. Shafer and William J. M. Claggett, *The Two Majorities: The Issue Context of Modern American Politics* (Baltimore: Johns Hopkins

University Press, 1995).

101. See Sidney Milkis, *The President and the Parties: The Transformation of the American Party System Since the New Deal* (New York: Oxford University Press, 1993).

102. "Fashion" and "Republican Distribution of Citizens," in *Papers of James Madison*, 14:257, 245.

Chapter 5

Montesquieu, the Founders, and Woodrow Wilson:
The Evolution of Rights and the Eclipse of Constitutionalism

Paul Carrese

RIGHTS, THE JUDICIALIZING OF POLITICS, AND CONSTITUTIONALISM

Is Woodrow Wilson, architect of the liberal-democratic administrative state, at all responsible for the intellectual and political troubles besetting judicial power in America and beyond—and thus for larger problems in liberal constitutionalism? Wilson's "constitutional government" eschews the constitutionalism of Montesquieu and the American Founders by treating rights and courts as mere means to a progressive state. How could this doctrine be responsible for the extraordinary prominence in America of rights claims and of the political and social battles waged through courts?

In its third century, and at the height of its power, modern liberal democracy faces this paradox about its claim to champion the rule of law: independent judiciaries have risen to extraordinary political power even while modern liberal jurisprudence has descended into a coliseum of competing theories, on and off the bench.[1] Indeed, the advocates of judicial power appear to think there can never be too much of a good thing, even as the dominant varieties of legal realism in modern liberal jurisprudence argue that juridical law has no stable, uncontested meanings. When jurists and political scientists look only at a particular Supreme Court case or line of cases, or we enter the fray about liberal or conservative judicial activism, we can lose sight of the larger sweep of jurisprudence and judicial power in the liberal democracies in the past half-century. These narrower professional perspectives also can obscure the signs that a century of revolutionary jurisprudence is having unintended, but not entirely unpredictable, consequences for judicial power and constitutional governance.

For America, the war on terrorism largely pushed aside the political and legal controversy over the Florida and the United States Supreme Court rulings in the 2000 presidential election, in which one court or the other was determined to decide a presidential election no matter how much each court fractured over a legal rationale. Still, rulings during the most recent term of the U.S. high court remind us that the Court and the legal community have grown accustomed to the Court setting public policy on many issues about which the Constitution provides little juridical guidance. Lacking this authoritative anchor such rulings often turn on subtle interpretations or elaborations of recent precedents; the Constitution fades into the background while a Court which is not working off the same page, in any sense, splinters into competing opinions—a small majority or plurality, then multiple concurrences and dissents. To be fair, the jurists and scholars who dissent from the most progressive rulings often have adopted a polemical tone and narrowly originalist lines of argument, which have not always aided a broader fidelity to constitutionalism and the Constitution. Decades of aggressive progressivism and an aggressive rearguard reaction thus have made the Supreme Court a complex bureaucracy, comprised of the justices and clerks, the bar, the professors, the press—a policymaking arena and process not unlike that centered around the E.P.A., or I.N.S., or F.C.C. Practitioners of the burgeoning field of judicial process, and advocates of various theories of judicial policymaking, openly admit this phenomenon.

This judicialized mode of politics and bureaucratized mode of judging are most evident in Court rulings on claimed rights to privacy, autonomy, and dignity. These new rights are not easily discovered in the Constitution, as all admit. The Court and its bar nonetheless have set national policy in recent decades on issues ranging from abortion to equality for homosexual and heterosexual acts; from what kinds of religious presence are permissible in public education to whether race is a permissible factor for admissions in public higher education; from admission of women in military academies to the broad rights of expression afforded for indecent or violent "speech." This tendency to find that the Constitution commands protection for individual privacy, autonomy, or dignity has fostered a larger constitutional and legal spirit, in which the Court tends to take the law out of judging and the politics out of politics.[2] The sophisticated quasi-lawlessness of modern courts is theoretically described as realist or sociological judging (Oliver Wendell Holmes, Jr., Benjamin Cardozo), or judging with moral integrity (Ronald Dworkin), or a high politics of judging (Bruce Ackerman, Sanford Levinson); other scholars defend this development through more openly post-modernist theories of legal power (Randall Kennedy, Lief Carter). Whatever the name or theory, the pattern remains: a quasi-lawlessness in which courts decide controversial social issues by narrow majorities, with a multitude of competing rationales and opinions in a case or a line of cases, through ever-evolving conceptions of newly minted rights. There is no anchor in natural law, tradition, text, or consent of the governed; the new breed of court implicitly claims that such characteristic sources and qualities of law can be replaced by itself and its recent precedents. A second tendency arises from this new spirit of law, the urge to save political life from the dangers and irrationalities of politics. The Supreme Court now tends to find—apart from its narrowly achieved federalism rulings of the past decade—that the Constitution deeply distrusts self-governing citizens, ruling and being ruled in turn through debate, elections, and complex institutions. Policies about sexuality, public morals, religion, and race, among other categories of rights, must be decided by courts alone.[3] By deciding to decide such cases the Court decrees an elastic conception of individual rights that trumps the complex modes of governance once characteristic of American constitutionalism. This doctrine has grown ever more dominant, from Holmes' rulings on free speech to the mystical dimensions of the right of privacy.

The new jurisprudence has brought controversy, legal and political. Whatever the latest opinion polls tracking confidence in the Supreme Court over time, much evidence suggests that in recent decades America's appellate judiciary and her realist or post-modern legal theorists have spent the coin of legitimacy more quickly than they have replenished it. The stridency and jurisprudential narrowness of some prominent rearguard voices may have hindered the search for

a pathway out of this dilemma, but the boldness of progressive jurisprudence has provoked such spirited responses. The final 2000 election
rulings, *Gore v. Harris* (Florida 2000) and *Bush v. Gore* (U.S. Supreme
Court), extended this judicialized politics and jurisprudence of individualism even further into election and equal protection issues,
beyond the bold rulings in state and federal courts of recent decades
on the right to vote and racial redistricting policies. Both supreme
courts held that each individual's right to vote, and equal protection
for that right, must trump all other constitutional considerations about
election to the most powerful office in the land, indeed, the world.
Judicialism doesn't get much bolder: judges of all stripes, from separate courts, took the bait served up by the bar and the scholars—that
one or the other court *must* decide the contest, one way or the other.
During the current presidential campaign the losing party in 2000
increasingly will make a campaign issue of the judicial resolution of
the last election, thus reminding Americans of these contentious issues about judicial power.

Compounding this are three additional phenomena. We can expect, as usual, one or more striking rulings from the Court in its coming
term about some deeply controversial issue of national politics; a bruis-
ing political fight is expected come the next Supreme Court vacancy;
and, a fight already is simmering in the Senate and editorial pages
over several nominees for the court of appeals. The steady diet of
confirmation fights that began with Judge Robert Bork in 1987 thus
has grown only steadier, and spread to the appellate level. During the
past decade nearly all senators of both parties on the Judiciary Committee, and many more senators besides, have opposed the judicial
activism they find in the other party's nominees. A bipartisan plurality
of the Senate, and perhaps a majority, clearly has lost confidence that
the legal profession and judiciary can conduct the courts according to
law. These confirmation fights, coupled with the congressional distrust evident in successive rounds of judicial sentencing guidelines,
indicate that the judiciary and courts are paying a significant price for
the legal realism and post-modernism of twentieth century American
law. Indeed, the open squabbling this year on the Sixth Circuit Court
of Appeals confirms the worst fears of critics of legal realism or positivism and of legal post-modernism. The twin phenomena of growing
judicialism and growing controversy prevails abroad as well, from the

European Court of Human Rights to the several United Nations war crimes tribunals, and from the new International Criminal Court to particular judges wielding new notions of international human rights law against officials from other sovereign states. This past year it was clear that Liberia's civil war had festered, at the cost of many lives, because the tyrant Charles Taylor had been indicted by a U.N. war crimes tribunal—an indictment announced at a peace conference arranged by diplomats to secure Taylor's voluntary exile to a neighboring state. His eventual exile was secured only through the quiet promise of his host country, Nigeria, to effectively ignore the court's indictment. Never have courts been so powerful in political affairs, domestically and internationally, yet never have the legal principles upon which they exercise their power been more novel, controversial, and unsettled, on and off the bench.

What's Wilson got to do with it? The main moral and intellectual impetus for this judicializing of politics and bureaucratizing of judging is the new conception of rights that grew out of, or alongside, two further developments in nineteenth century law and constitutionalism. These are legal realism, legal positivism and pragmatism embodied by Oliver Wendell Holmes, Jr., and a democratic political science of constitutional development, embodied by Woodrow Wilson. Both of these novel theories, along with the new concept of rights, are related to Progressivism, although neither Holmes nor Wilson are pure Progressives akin to Louis Brandeis or Herbert Croly. Still, even a whirlwind tour through traditional principles of constitutionalism and judicial power confirms just how revolutionary were these new conceptions of law, rights, and courts. A century hence it may be easier to see that the principles of Montesquieu and of the American Founders, particularly Hamilton, ultimately are more theoretically and practically sound, not least because they were designed to avoid the constitutional instability and fusion of law and politics which the Progressive reformers have brought to our courts and our polity.

MONTESQUIEU'S COMPLEX RIGHTS AND MODERATE CONSTITUTIONALISM

Montesquieu's *The Spirit of the Laws* (1748) was the foremost philosophic influence upon the framers of the 1787 Constitution, and his tempering of Lockean liberalism also shaped the statement of American principle in the Declaration of Independence.[4] The spirit of Montesquieu's philosophy, its guiding principle, is moderation, understood as the achievement of balance and appropriate complexity in both thought and action: "I say it, and it seems to me I have brought forth this work only to prove it: the spirit of moderation ought to be that of the legislator; the political good, like the moral good, is always found between two limits."[5] The fact that Montesquieu reserves remarks on moderation until Book 29, near the end of the reader's long, complicated journey through *The Spirit of the Laws*, suggests not confusion but respect for the world's complexity, and signals his effort to moderate the more doctrinaire moments of earlier liberal philosophy.[6] Similarly, the American framers found in Montesquieu not the single source of their political principles but a persuasive rationale for blending diverse authorities and principles to justify revolution and then to form a constitutional republic. The framers blended liberalism and modern republicanism, as well as classical philosophy, Christianity, and classic common law, to form a distinctly American amalgam of principles. Schools of theory or practice tend to emphasize one element of America's character at the expense of others, but such moderation or balance in fact pervades American constitutionalism, informing not just separation of powers, federalism, and bicameralism but also the complexity of American life and thought, as is evident in our blending of pluralism and principle, rights and public purposes.[7]

Montesquieu's principle of moderation directs the complex character of his liberalism, and of his view of natural rights. He is a modern liberal philosopher, but he incorporates some ancient and medieval principles. Some scholars suggest that Montesquieu is an historicist or communitarian who eschews rights, while others effectively reduce his view of natural right to Hobbes, Spinoza, Locke, or some other modern philosophy.[8] Montesquieu does indeed endorse natural rights, and largely through the lens of modern liberalism, but he considered aspects of contractarian philosophy immoderate in both theory and practice. His complicated remarks on natural rights, and the complex constitutionalism he devised for best protecting these, together emphasize that fundamentalism about individual rights can be as dangerous to a tranquil, decent political order as can the explicit rejection of rights by political or theological despotism.

Montesquieu's approach to natural right or natural law in Book 1 of *The Spirit of the Laws* thus resembles as much Montaigne's complex humanism as Cartesian, deductive rationalism. The Preface and Book 1 together introduce the blend of ancient and modern ideas he discerns in politics and which inform its spirit. The aim is to moderate early modern efforts to establish new foundations for political philosophy upon abstract analyses of man and right in a state of nature. Like Plato, Aristotle, and Cicero, and Tocqueville after him, Montesquieu grasps natural right through the complexity of human experience, found both in our probable primitive condition and in large, complicated societies. Contrary to those who would reduce his philosophy to Hobbes or Locke, Montesquieu opens *The Spirit of the Laws* by insisting upon his philosophic originality; likewise, those who find only sociology or historicism overlook his early pronouncement that philosophy can help man to discover "his own nature" despite erroneous philosophies that obscure it (Preface, 230; cf. 29.19). Montesquieu elaborates his conception of natural right not only in the early, quasi-contractarian analysis in Book 1 but throughout *Spirit*, a method that itself links natural right with complexity. His view of natural right unfolds throughout his grand text, a work that begins and ends with quotations from Virgil's *Aeneid* and grasps human affairs in a manner almost as indebted to the epic tradition as to Hobbes. The hero of this investigation of nature and politics is the philosopher-legislator who watches over mankind by inculcating prudence about how to moderate politics and make it more humane (Preface; 1.1; 24.10).

Although the final aim of Montesquieu's new science of politics is liberty and the protection of natural rights, a distinctively modern concept of moderation is the crucial condition for securing these. His negative idea of liberty, as tranquility or freedom from fear (11.6), follows Hobbes in defining human nature more by aversion to insecurity than by orientation to a higher end. However, against Hobbes he argues that liberty requires political moderation, and that our nature is open to higher aims, even to the divine (1.1-2; see also 4.2, 5.12, 24.1). Proper liberty entails moderation, the avoidance of any structural imbalance of forces or any stagnation of motion—avoidance, that is, of both despotism and instability. Here Montesquieu's different conception of rights propels his departure from both the proto-constitutionalist sovereignty of Hobbes and the streamlined constitutionalism of Locke, which lacks federalism, bicameralism, and a separate judiciary, but is fond of revolution. To protect mankind's complex rights and our natural law Montesquieu formulates his most noted political doctrine, a constitutional politics of separated powers in a dynamic equilibrium, one that serves both tranquility and moderate satisfaction of the passions. In this complicated, factional politics the checking of each force by another "strains" all the springs of the governmental order, producing actions and reactions that keep the system moving and avoids the inertness of despotism or the chaos of civil war (5.1, 11.13, 19.27). Montesquieu's account of rights and constitutionalism thus tempers the abstract and more extreme tendencies of earlier modern liberalism with some elements of classical and medieval philosophy. Whatever the allure of Machiavellian efficacy or of the certainty in sovereignty and contractarian rights, all rulers and citizens ultimately are governed by a higher law. On the other hand, observation of nature and human nature cannot support the moralism of classical and medieval natural law. In this way Montesquieu provides the lineaments of a modern "common sense" philosophy, neither teleological nor reductive, of the sort evident in the Declaration of Independence. The American Founders balanced its Enlightenment doctrines with appeals to Providence, legal tradition, duty, and honor throughout, echoing a philosophical moderation that assimilates moderns and ancients, liberalism and classic common law.

A sketch of Montesquieu's specific remarks on rights confirms these larger brush strokes about his constitutionalism and complex liberal philosophy. The complicated argument of Book 1 of *The Spirit of the Laws* begins a redefinition of natural right in the non-Hobbesian terms of man's most basic feelings, including sentiments toward family and friends, a modification confirmed by the very next usage of *droit naturel* in the work (3.10, 260).[9] In his chapter on the laws of nature, which discusses the natural law for humans, Montesquieu examines "the constitution of our being" by initially referring to the "law that impresses on us the idea of a creator and thereby leads us toward him." This is the first natural law "in importance" but not "in the order of these laws," and he drops any treatment of divinity (1.2, 235). He then sketches four laws of "our being" which define humans as passionate animals with some potential for rational, higher aims. Peace is "the first natural law"—first in historical appearance—since by nature each man "feels himself inferior" and would hardly attack his fellows. He explicitly criticizes Hobbes for projecting such a "complex" idea as desire for power and domination upon natural, pre-political man (1.2, 235). The second law of nature is "nourishment," since "man would add the feeling of his needs to the feeling of his weakness" (236). The "natural entreaty" that men "always make to another," or man's natural sociability, is the third law, although this has a complex root in fear, pleasure, and sexual charm. Man's natural timidity and fear prompts recognition of "mutual fear," which would "soon persuade them to approach one another." Alternately, "the pleasure one animal feels at the approach" of "its own kind" would foster sociability. This third drive for community thus is the increase in such pleasure brought about by "the charm that the two sexes inspire in each other by their difference" (236). Montesquieu closes the account by noting that beyond "sentiment" or feeling, "which belongs to men from the outset," men eventually gain "knowledge." This is no end in itself, but another "bond" that other animals lack, "another motive for uniting," and thus "the desire to live in society" is the fourth natural law (236). Man is naturally rational in that he develops this capacity through historical experience. While a modern view, this is not the Rousseauan historicism of a malleable humanity, nor is it the anti-foundationalist or sociological view Hannah Arendt and others find. Montesquieu's view lies between a Thomistic view of rational and political man, a Hobbesian view of rational but apolitical man, and a Rousseauan view of irrational and apolitical man developing toward reason and society.

This conception of natural rights informs Montesquieu's argument that the genius of politics—the spirit of laws—is to constitute laws that will best preserve our nature in all its complexity. The first recourse to "natural right" after Book 1 confirms this humane revision of earlier liberalism. Natural right primarily involves neither self-preservation nor self-defense, nor even individual liberty. Rather, it concerns "natural feelings," such as "respect for a father, tenderness for one's children and women, laws of honor, or the state of one's health;" such standards of "natural right" are just what a despot eschews, even if he might be checked by religious doctrines (3.10, 260).[10] By thus avoiding extremes of rationalism and skepticism, Montesquieu's political science grasps the multiplicity, complexity, and diversity of phenomena affecting politics while insisting that natural right is a crucial standard for them. He deems a complex, moderate constitution the best government, both for peoples disposed toward it by nature and history and for those who could gain it through gradual reforms (Book 11, chs. 8, 11). He broadens liberalism by insisting that its aims are achieved by "Gothic" constitutions that are "well tempered" through their "true distribution" of legislative, executive, and judicial powers among a "free people" (11.8, 409; 11.11, 411). Nature indicates that politics must be structured in terms of multiple powers and perspectives that at once check and facilitate the free movement of political passions and energies. This humane tale of moderation and balance, recommending devices that range from independent judges and commerce to toleration and the complexities of the medieval French constitution, is the great theme of the work. The philosophy of moderation informing Montesquieu's view of natural right and politics directly shaped such statements of American pluralism and political balancing as *Federalist* No. 10 and No. 51; it is no accident that he is extensively discussed in the less famous essays informing these, Nos. 9 and 47. A related innovation is his insistence that one of the independent powers be a judiciary that secures the tranquility of each individual's feelings about security for their rights, especially for liberty. This is the complex version of liberal constitutionalism that he bequeathed to American constitutionalism, politics, and political theory, both directly and through his disciple Blackstone.

HAMILTON ON RIGHTS AND CONSTITUTIONALISM: BEYOND LOCKE TO MODERATION

Montesquieu's conceptions of moderation and natural rights directly shaped America's quasi-legal revolution of 1776, defending traditional rights as a duty of "sacred honor," in contrast to the more rationalist line of Locke and Rousseau, and of France after 1789. That complex spirit led America's Founders to further transcend Locke through a complex constitutionalism of federalism, tripartite powers, and bicameralism. As both the Declaration and the Preamble to the Constitution attest, and the Bill of Rights later affirmed, the framers saw constitutionalism as a means to the protection of natural rights, although in another sense they affirmed both as ends. Inherent in their

Montesquieuan conception of constitutionalism was the lively inter-action of various powers and citizens, such that the right to liberty was not just served by the rule of law but was identical with it—a more constitutionalist and less volatile conception of rights and how to secure them than Locke had propounded.

Locke's constitutionalism also lacked an independent judiciary, and one might say that the Herculean judiciary of twentieth century jurisprudence and the Lockean, judicial restraint school that opposes it are precisely the extremes that the framers, following Montesquieu and Blackstone, sought to avoid. The original American understand-ing defined judges neither as legislators nor mere clerks, but as pow-erful officers in a constitutionalism of separated and limited powers. It was this conception which granted life tenure and a power of con-stitutional review to judges, and only this understanding would justify perpetuating such position and power. Study of Washington, Jefferson, Madison, and other framers, and of the Constitutional Convention and ratification debates, obviously are important for fully understanding the framers' ideas about rights and constitutionalism, but Alexander Hamilton's arguments on these matters are as crucial as they are now overlooked. Hamilton makes the most thematic case for Article III power during the debates over the Constitution, and lays the ground for a constitutional review power intimated by earlier American courts and later secured by Chief Justice John Marshall. Hamilton did so in the context of expounding a tripartite separation of powers and federal-ism as providing the complex constitutionalism most conducive to securing the life, liberty, and pursuit of happiness for which he had fought during the Revolution. This leading statesman-jurist of the American founding owes a significant debt to Montesquieu, albeit one tempered by other influences. The deeper complexity to American conceptions of rights, constitutionalism, and judicial power is most evident in the writings of Hamilton and Tocqueville, and while Tocqueville liberally drew upon the former, they both had recourse to a blend of Montesquieuan liberalism and traditional common law ju-risprudence.[11]

General Hamilton was not known for his personal moderation, but the constitutionalism embodied in his writings as a lawyer and leading citizen, and especially in *The Federalist*, is deeply imbued with Montesquieu's principle of seeking a sound philosophical and political balance. Even the briefest sketch reveals his adoption of a blend of liberal and common law principles drawn from Blackstone, Montesquieu, and even Coke, especially regarding the role of independent courts in securing rights. Both Federalists and Anti-Federalists marshaled Montesquieu's support for their views of the Constitution, but Hamilton demonstrates the greater affinity with Federalist principles in his debate with the Anti-Federalist reading of *The Spirit of the Laws* in *Federalist* No. 9. Indeed, Montesquieu's distinctive political philosophy pervades *The Federalist*, often in explicit citations on federalism (Nos. 9, 43), separation of powers (No. 47), and an independent judiciary (No. 78). This extends to the blending of a realist political psychology with a factional political dynamic in Nos. 10 and 51. *The Federalist* cites Blackstone, Montesquieu's most famous disciple, almost as much as Montesquieu, but not Hobbes, Locke, Sidney, or Harrington even once.

Hamilton's defense of a "next to nothing" federal judiciary in *Federalist* No. 78 and the quiet but steady endorsement of judicial power throughout the essays epitomize the American adaptation of Montesquieu's cloaking of power—the project to secure rights and political moderation by elevating a non-partisan judiciary to separate and equal status with the executive and legislative powers. Hamilton's profession as a lawyer and advocate in court was not merely preliminary to his executive ambitions, nor only a consolation after his political career ended; it is rightly said that he "deserves a statue in front of the Supreme Court almost as much as his statue at the Treasury Department."[12] He worked to establish judicial power not only in *The Federalist* (1787-88) but in making the first widely noted argument for judicial review to protect rights, citing Coke, in *Rutgers v. Waddington* (New York, 1784), and still later in criticizing Jefferson's plan to repeal the 1801 Judiciary Act. Before his death he defended both newspapers and courts as forums for discerning truth, and for protecting rights against majority tyranny, in *The People v. Croswell* (New York, 1804). There, in the spirit of Coke, Hamilton defined common law as: "Natural law and natural reason applied to the purposes of society," and urged an appellate court to view Blackstone's speech-restrictive doctrine of libel as "being against reason and natural justice, and contrary to the original principles of the common law." Many great dramas of Hamilton's life did concern war, commerce, and executive statesmanship, and he did decline Washington's entreaty to become Chief Justice in 1795. Still, the extraordinary claims made for judicial power in *The Federalist* are consistent with important thoughts and deeds throughout his life.[13] Before serving in Washington's army, his "Farmer Refuted" (1775) defended America's cause as grounded in "natural rights" and "the law of nature," as expounded by "Grotius, Puffendorf, Locke, Montesquieu, and Burlemaqui." At age eighteen he repudiates the legal positivism of "Mr. Hobbs" for denying "a supreme intelligence, who rules the world, and has established law to regulate the actions of his creatures." Such phrases, and references to the "despotic kingdoms" of Turkey, Russia, France, and Spain, confirm his early study of Montesquieu at King's College (later Columbia), and the essay quotes Blackstone twice at length, on natural law and the rights of individuals.[14]

After the Constitutional Convention Hamilton conceived the idea for a series of essays in the New York papers to defend the proposed Constitution, and upon securing the collaboration of John Jay and James Madison, he wrote two-thirds of the 85 essays that became *The Federalist*. Hamilton, Madison, and Jay all were black-letter common law lawyers, trained in both Coke and Blackstone, and Jay would become the first Chief Justice of the United States. It is not surprising, then, that the importance of an independent, federal judicial power arises early in the essays and percolates throughout, culminating in Hamilton's exposition in Nos. 78 to 83.[15] After Jay emphasizes the need for a stable rule of law across all thirteen states for both internal and external affairs of the Union (No. 3), Hamilton underscores the point in No. 9 while arguing that the Constitution's superiority to ancient republics lies in the "great improvement" achieved in the "science of politics" in modern times. The central principle of the five essays that define the new American constitutionalism is "the institution of courts composed of judges holding their offices during good behavior."[16] Hamilton further emphasizes independent judging when arguing that the Constitution at last establishes the proper rule of law in America's federal republic (No. 15), when declaring the administration of justice the "great cement of society" (No. 17), and by proclaiming that "[a] circumstance which crowns the defects of the Confederation" is "the want of a judiciary power" (No. 22). After recourse to "the celebrated Montesquieu" in No. 47 on separation of powers, Publius examines in No. 49 how to enforce a constitutional distribution of powers against attempted encroachments by one branch or another. In 47 and 48 Madison argues, citing Jefferson's *Notes on Virginia* (1784), that because the legislature is closest to the people it represents the greater danger to any constitutional limits. In No. 49 Publius—probably Madison, perhaps Hamilton—criticizes Jefferson's proposal in the *Notes* for ensuring separation through recourse to popular conventions, which could alter a constitution or correct breaches of it (No. 49, 321-22). The first objection echoes Aristotle and the common law doctrine of precedent, that frequent changes in the laws, especially the fundamental law, will undermine that reverence for laws so crucial for developing the political habit of being ruled by law. If a later reader could not already detect how great a departure Holmes or Woodrow Wilson made from the constitutionalism of the Founders then the sequel may help, for Publius criticizes plebiscitary government more bluntly: the passions of the people might overwhelm their more considered judgment now that the dangers of revolution are gone and more self-interested, partisan interests have arisen. The crucial objection, however, is that popular appeals will not restore the constitutional "equilibrium" endangered by any encroachments. The legislature is most likely to breach such limits and the people likely will concur with any legislative majority; we might say now that Publius is no friend of "the living constitution." His constitutionalism thus associates the executive and judiciary with the *"reason"* of the people and the legislature with the *"passions"* that can overwhelm both reason and those branches (No. 49, 322-25).

The groundwork for Hamilton's famous exposition of judicial power as a bulwark of rights against majoritarianism or republican passions is laid, then, throughout *The Federalist*. A crucial argument is added in No. 51 when Publius announces the not very Jeffersonian (or Wilsonian) principle that a sound constitutional order "must first enable the government to control the governed; and in the next place oblige it to control itself." Dependence on the people is the root of republican government, but the constitutional framework needs "auxiliary precautions" and "inventions of prudence" to ensure that both citizens and officials are governed by law (331-32). Publius thus defines the three least obviously republican branches, the unelected Judiciary and the indirectly elected Senate and Executive, as keeping the House—

and, one infers, the more populist governments of the states—within the bounds of the constitutional order, and safe for rights (332-33). A simply negative view of power checking power does not adequately answer the question raised by No. 49, regarding how to ultimately ensure legal protections for rights or the rule of law more generally. The answer given by No. 51 in itself, without the constitutional argument developed in the subsequent essays on Senate, Executive, and Judiciary, would tend toward gridlock or crisis, thus increasing the likelihood of either recourse to powers outside the community or government, or a collapse into populism. The analysis of separation of powers in Nos. 47 to 51 thus quietly prepares for the more positive conception of the principle developed in the essays on the Senate, Executive, and Judiciary, largely written by Hamilton. The positive conception uses the principle of a division of labor to argue that distinct powers will perform each function better, while also maintaining within a complex constitutionalism the negative conception of separation usually termed checks and balances. While remaining republican *The Federalist* increasingly emphasizes the positive view, ultimately rooted in Aristotle's conception of separate functions in a polity, after initially stressing the negative conception drawn more from Locke and Montesquieu.[17]

This background allows the widely studied exposition of judicial power in No. 78 to be seen anew, and, to quickly summarize, to appreciate its three distinct strands of argument that interweave throughout. First, Hamilton defends an independent judiciary with a negative conception of separation of powers, on the Montesquieuan premise that professional judges must be bulwarks for rights and for a stable constitutionalism—indeed, for the Constitution itself—against the populist abuses likely to come from the legislative power in a republic. The second strand draws upon Coke as much as Montesquieu, arguing that the Constitution implies a distinctly common law character for the federal judiciary, a body of lawyers elevated to the bench and serving as a depository not of force or will but legal judgment— thus further affirming its role as protector of the Constitution against the mutability of popular government. The first strand proposes the novel power of judicial review, but it is the second that explains why common law judges in a republic could have such a power and be entrusted with it, a shift from negative to positive conceptions of the separation of powers. The third strand, often overlooked, amplifies both of these elements through a more fully positive conception of separation of powers. Hamilton ultimately blends Montesquieu's juridical liberalism with an Aristotelian appreciation for practical legal wisdom, defining the judiciary as not only the guardian of the Constitution but as schoolmasters of moderation and constitutionalism. One particular argument should be noted, however, to highlight the contrast with later doctrines of a living Constitution. Hamilton's brief for judicial review begins precisely by arguing that independent courts are "peculiarly essential in a limited Constitution," defined as "one which contains certain specified exceptions to the legislative authority" (No. 78, 497). While it seems Lockean to emphasize a written constitution, only the likes of Coke, Montesquieu, or Blackstone would suggest that the very integrity of constitutionalism and the rule of law in a republic hinges upon the right kind of judicial power. Indeed, for Hamilton, constitutional limits on the legislature "can be preserved in practice no other way than through the medium of the courts of justice, whose duty it must be to declare all acts contrary to the manifest tenor of the Constitution void."

Before turning to Woodrow Wilson's deconstruction of these concepts of rights and constitutionalism, a word might be said about how Hamilton's jurisprudence inoculates Montesquieuan constitutionalism against a weakness that later Darwinian thought would exploit, or aggravate. Montesquieu may be partly responsible for the subsequent decline of his constitutionalism in liberal thought, since his humane conception of natural right to some degree dilutes our conceptions of human nature and natural law. Holmes, the main architect of the pragmatism or positivism now predominant in American law—repudiating both natural right and a fixed constitutionalism—found in Montesquieu only doctrines of historical change and that dominant communal forces should prevail over time in the factional contests of a free society.[18] This suggests that the redefinition of natural right in *Spirit of the Laws* in terms of affections and familial attachments lends itself to reductionist, skeptical consequences not originally intended. As Tocqueville expounded, an emphasis on individual tranquility and security permits the rival extremes of individualism and majority tyranny, which undermine the very constitutionalism and concern for mores characteristic of Montesquieu's political science.

Since it is clear that Tocqueville drew many of his insights about judicial power from Hamilton, it is fair to note that the American jurist had quietly sought to modify Montesquieuan jurisprudence to temper these tendencies of the modern liberal republic.

WILSON'S "CONSTITUTION," EVOLVING RIGHT, AND POLITICAL IMMODERATION

In American law and constitutionalism Oliver Wendell Holmes, Jr., exemplifies the revolutionary advocacy of a positivistic, evolutionary conception of law and judicial power. Woodrow Wilson, his contemporary, embodies a revolutionary political science that harnessed popular democracy with administrative science to achieve a progressive societal development beyond the confines of an eighteenth century Constitution. Much legal and constitutional writing has diagnosed the consequences for law and judging of Holmesean legal realism and the new conception of the politicized judge.[19] Wilson's parallel advocacy of new conceptions of the presidency and administration are also well known, as components of his organic, progressive conception of constitutional government.[20] Less noted is Wilson's indirect and perhaps direct role in fostering a new conception of judicial power which buttressed, consciously or not, the rise of Holmesean legal realism and judicial policymaking.[21] One paradox shared by Holmes and Wilson is that their aim to liberate the spirit of democracy from the confines of an outdated, Montesquieuan constitution nonetheless required prodding, or command, by legal-bureaucratic experts. In Rousseau's spirit, that of the French Revolution, the evolving spirit of democracy must be forced to be free. After a century of the growing dominance of their views of law, constitutionalism, and political science another paradox is apparent, that the scientific, value-free analyses of the dominant judicial process school have permitted or aided a moralistic fervor for individual privacy, autonomy, and dignity achieved by judicial policymaking. Holmes instructs judges to anticipate and foster an enlightened society purging itself of backward notions and backward strains, while Wilson emphasizes presidents, parties as their instruments, and administrators as means to his own ideas of progress. Still, the fervor of Wilson's project to rejuvenate constitutional government spilled over from executive politics to the judiciary, for even such venerable concepts as rights and law could not escape this transformation.

Anti-Federalists and Jefferson had criticized Montesquieu's separation of powers constitutionalism for fostering the aristocratic, inegalitarian tendencies in the Federalists. A century later Wilson radicalized these views, taking aim not only at Montesquieu but at the very Constitution informed by this anachronistic philosophy. The chapter on the presidency in his *Constitutional Government in the United States* (1908) opens by repudiating the Newtonian, mechanistic paradigm behind Montesquieu's separation of powers and the 1787 Constitution. Such a political science is outdated in the wake of Darwinian evolution, Hegelian liberal progress, and Rousseau's more democratic vision for constitutional government. Wilson's new political science thus defined the presidency in the non-constitutional terms of popular leadership and scientific administration, making it the key to moving the Constitution beyond its framers' obsolete doctrines to a higher plane of democratic politics. This would liberate the organic, living Constitution from its bondage to the "Whig" or "literary" theory of the text embodied by *The Spirit of the Laws*, and this call for emancipation later informed Wilson's conduct as president.[22]

Wilson's theory of constitutionalism propounded a new doctrine to replace the fundamental idea of securing rights through stable principles of law: "Living political constitutions must be Darwinian in structure and practice." He had saved this radical formulation for the third chapter, on the presidency, but the seeds of a turn away from fixed principles of fundamental law, and from natural rights, were evident in the work's opening: "A constitutional government is one whose powers have been adapted to the interests of its people and to the maintenance of individual liberty."[23] Wilson's earlier work, *Congressional Government* (1885), did not address courts or rights in analyzing the failure of separation of powers constitutionalism to provide America strong executive leadership. *Constitutional Government* begins instead by emphasizing liberty and the protection of individual rights as the aim, Magna Charta as its historical root, and independent courts as the indispensable institution of such governments: "Indeed there is a sense in which it may be said that the whole efficacy and reality of constitutional government resides in its courts" (*PWW*, 18:80, ch. I; see 69-80). This sounds like Montesquieu or Hamilton, not Rousseau or Darwin, although even the traditional advocates of courts did not so openly speak of placing this one power above the others. However, Wilson lays the groundwork for his formulation of the presidency as the most dynamic agent of the living Constitution with this emphasis upon process and organicism, thereby quietly redefining traditional constitutionalist concepts. Liberty is not a natural right, one self-evident to politically decent men in all times and places; rather, "[o]ur definition of liberty is that it is the best practicable adjustment between the powers of the government and the privileges of the individual; and liberty is the object of constitutional government" (*PWW*, 18: 80, ch. I). Coke, Locke, and Montesquieu are superseded by Bagehot's Darwinian, loosely Hegelian definition of the unwritten English constitution as a more efficient, enlightened instrument of popular agency and administrative skill than is the cumbersome American Constitution.[24] Indeed, Wilson cites Bagehot three times in *Constitutional Government*, once each in its first three chapters; in the opening one he nearly recasts the American Constitution as, in effect, the unwritten and ever-evolving British one:

> The underlying understandings of a constitutional system are modified from age to age by changes of life and circumstance and corresponding alterations of opinion. It does not remain fixed in any unchanging form, but grows with the growth and is altered with the change of the nation's needs and purposes. The Constitution of England, the original and typical constitutional government of the world, is unwritten except for its statement of individual right and privilege in Magna Carta, in the Bill of Rights, and in the Petition of Right; is, in other words, only a body of very definite opinion, except for occasional definitions of statute here and there.... and even around a written constitution there grow up a body of practices which have no formal recognition or sanction in the written law, which even modify the written stipulations of the system in many subtle ways and become the instrument of opinion in effecting a slow transformation. If it were not so, the written document would become too stiff a garment for the living thing (*PWW*, 18: 83, ch. I).

This doctrine transforms the essence of constitutionalism propounded by traditional sources ranging from Coke and Locke to Montesquieu and Blackstone, who emphasized binding and stable law to protect immutable natural law and natural rights. Coke, Montesquieu, and Blackstone incorporated the notion of reform and refinement into their views of constitutionalism, partly but not wholly through the agency of courts, but understood such change in the spirit not of Rousseau or Hegel but of Aristotle and the classic common law. Practical wisdom and professional legal understanding, in executives and legislatures as well as in courts, could adjust fixed principles of law to meet the requirements of natural rights in particular circumstances, and such legal wisdom could become more refined over time. The Aristotelian, common law, and Montesquieuan strains of constitutionalism did not imply, however, that the very aims of constitutionalism were fundamentally mutable, or that rights were the evolving epiphenomena of a constitutional order rather than its anchor, or that a constitution was meant to facilitate, not govern or check, the opinions and passions of ever-changing moments. Wilson reduces a constitution to the processes of parliamentary agency and the development of public opinion, since even the basic rules of these activities are not confined or guided by any fundamental law, natural or positive.

Wilson continues to take the law out of law, and the Constitution out of constitutionalism, in his chapter on the courts. The second chapter elevates the historical development of constitutionalism to a separate and grand theme, and his re-founding of executive power drives home this point, defining the president as the prime agent of transformation in American constitutional government. The increasing boldness of his constitutionalism peaks after his analyses of the American presidency, House, and Senate when he finds in the courts the same spirit of Darwin and of process that defines, or ought to define, executive and legislative agency. His earlier oscillation between traditional and novel characterizations of judicial power continues here, with the courts deemed at once the bulwark of individual rights and liberty through their "non-political" discipline of law and a crucial "balance-wheel" in the process of transformation that is constitutionalism. Courts of law "maintain that nice wheel of adjustment between individual rights and governmental powers which constitutes political liberty" (*PWW*, 18: 162, 167, ch. VI).

It becomes clear that the moving wheel or central gear of judicial power continually transforms the meaning of rights themselves. What made rights a central concept in the history of jurisprudence, their fixed quality and their anchor in human nature, now is deemed to unreasonably impede political growth and progress. Courts must be liberated from these confining notions, and understood instead as "a means of energy for the individual citizen" to take the initiative against the government or a fellow citizen. Courts "keep our singularly complex system at its right poise and adjustment" by providing individuals "a complete administration of its safeguards." He mentions Tocqueville's observation about the legal character permeating American politics, the expectation that every citizen know something about protecting oneself through the law and courts, but Wilson's larger aim is to cast courts in terms of energy and motion: courts are "the people's forum" where each individual tugs the government in his preferred direction (*PWW*, 18: 166-69, ch. VI). This is not exactly Tocqueville's praise of a professional judiciary as the bulwark for rights and the rule of law against democratic commotion, majoritarianism, and passion.[25]

Whereas Tocqueville, in the spirit of Coke, Montesquieu, and Blackstone, celebrates the complexity and the enduring principles of law, Wilson celebrates the ability of courts to keep up with the changing needs of society and government. This analysis of courts as a policymaking arena thus recommends reforms of courts toward greater accessibility, and toward simplification in the law. "[O]ur immediate duty is to amend and simplify our processes of justice," so that the poor can better withstand the cost, length, and complexity of trials and thus be included in this great process of policymaking (*PWW*, 18: 169-70, ch. VI). This note of reform leads to the chapter's boldest theme, the recasting of American constitutional law and of its embodiment, John Marshall, as agents of the same transformative spirit Wilson finds in the executive. The power to pronounce on the constitutionality of statutes makes the courts the repository of "the statesmanship of control," but this traditional judicial function must now be understood to carry with it a more dynamic power, "the statesmanship of adaptation" (*PWW*, 18: 172-79, ch. VI). Here an implicit contrast to Holmes, and to other Progressives, is telling. Holmes famously dismissed John Marshall in a 1901 speech as a jurist stuck firmly in his time, without vision, dutifully carrying out the legal orders issued by Washington and Hamilton.[26] Herbert Croly, in *The Promise of American Life* (1909), railed against the legal establishment and courts—"the monarchy of the Constitution" and individual rights—as obstacles to democratic participation, to economic fairness, and to societal progress. Eldon Eisenach notes that Wilson thus was oddly conservative, even reactionary, for arguing in *Constitutional Government* that traditional ideas of constitutional law, individual liberty, and rights were the best basis for American progress, and that federal commerce power should not be extended at the expense of local police power.[27]

Wilson, however, follows the spirit of Holmes more than was perceived by Croly or other Progressives. His reformulation of judicial review and courts in *Constitutional Government* paved the way for the Constitutional Revolution of 1937 and full-blown Holmesean realism in American law, with the Supreme Court baptizing New Deal nationalism and federal economic regulation, and the Court becoming the agent of a living Constitution.[28] Wilson buttressed this Holmesean revolution by countering Holmes on a crucial point: that progressive jurisprudence need not see Marshall as embodying the backward, mechanical constitutionalism of Montesquieu and *The Federalist*. Wilson depicts Marshall as agreeing that "[t]he Constitution is not a mere lawyers' document: it is, as I have more than once said, the vehicle of a nation's life."

> We can say without the least disparagement or even criticism of the Supreme Court of the United States that at its hands the Constitution has received an adaptation and an elaboration which would fill its framers of the simple days of 1787 with nothing less than amazement.... each generation of statesmen looks to the Supreme Court to supply the interpretation which will serve the needs of the day (*PWW*, 18: 172-73, ch. VI).

Marshall, then, was not a mere lawyer. As the great Chief Justice he exercised "the statesmanship of control" by holding government and citizenry to the blueprint of the Constitution, but he also exercised, more importantly, "the statesmanship of adaptation" by transforming the blueprint itself. Marshall understood that the Court's role, and the agency of constitutional law, concerned not static rights but issues of policy, particularly how to adapt governmental powers to achieve changing societal needs and aims. It was Marshall who "gave to our federal government its scope and power," who combined "imagination" and "a large vision of things to come" with "the conscience of a lawyer." It is on Marshall's model that American constitutionalism has "married legislation with adjudication," and this is why we "look for statesmanship in our courts" (PWW, 18: 172, 179-80, ch. VI).

Throughout the twentieth century this became the standard reading of Marshall in constitutional law scholarship, that he was the first great judicial activist and judicial legislator.[29] Beyond revisionist readings about Marshall's cunning in establishing judicial review by fiat in *Marbury*, scholars cited dicta in *McCulloch v. Maryland* (1819) about the Constitution and broad national aims to prove his activism—that "we must never forget that it is a constitution we are expounding," one "intended to endure for ages to come, and, consequently, to be adapted to the various crises of human affairs." Less frequently cited from *McCulloch* was Marshall's warning to those who think the Constitution utterly elastic, one of several affirmations of federalism and the substantial sovereign powers reserved to the states: "Should congress, in the execution of its powers, adopt measures which are prohibited by the constitution; or should congress, under the pretext of executing its powers, pass laws for the accomplishment of objects not entrusted to the government; it would become the painful duty of this tribunal, should a case requiring such a decision come before it, to say, that such an act was not the law of the land."[30] Wilson's aggressive misreading, or creative adaptation, of Marshall's jurisprudence suggests that, although initially trained in the law, he does not genuinely have the lawyer's spirit as Tocqueville defined it. While the latter does describe American judicial statesmanship, he does so by means of an accurate conception of Marshall as a jurist serving and bound by the Constitution, not sitting above it as one who adapts it—that is, who discards it and invents a new one deemed useful for the given moment. Of course, on these terms, Holmes did not have the lawyer's spirit, nor do a good many leading professors of law, courts, and jurisprudence today.

Wilson's misunderstanding or transformation of the traditional notions of rights and judicial power inherited by the founders of the American bar and bench brings us full circle. Just after this sweeping revision of Marshall's judicial legacy in *Constitutional Government* he advocates a more narrowly legal view of federalism and of the police power of the states, specifically defending the limited view of the federal commerce power that the Supreme Court grudgingly abandoned only by 1937. One wonders how Wilson thought he could endorse constitutional legislating from the bench and then advise the courts to resist the calls to allow the federal commerce power to adapt to new national necessities (*PWW*, 18: 181, ch. VI). Similarly, one wonders how proponents of legal realism and judicial legislating from Justice Holmes to Justice Brennan could think that the other powers of federal and state governments would passively allow jurists to adapt the Constitution as the jurists see fit, without legislatures or executives playing hardball in response—either to capture the judiciary for their own explicit political aims, or, to make sure that the other party does not capture it through their appointments to the bench, no matter the damage done to the judiciary. The scorched-earth option only begs the question, however, of whether the real damage done to the judiciary is self-inflicted, by having effectively invited such political brawls. After aggressively cloaking political power by judicializing politics, it is odd to take cover behind the cloak of legal dignity and apolitical judicial integrity. The intellectual justifications for legal positivism and for judicial legislating became increasingly sophisticated throughout the twentieth century and into the twenty-first, perhaps because prior efforts could not adequately explain how law and courts can enjoin obligations upon the political branches and citizenry if the law is radically unstable and contested, and the courts have effectively become policy bureaucracies. Not only is it theoretically unconvincing to try to take the qualities of law out of law, but a century of replacing constitutionalism with adaptability is reaping clear consequences for the courts and constitutional law.

Ours is a paradoxical moment in which, just when liberal democracy is at the peak of its global power and influence, we see the new forms taken by old maladies that first were diagnosed by Thucydides, Plato, and Aristotle millennia ago, diagnoses recently reaffirmed by Tocqueville. Democracies ever are bosoms of paradox: the people claim to rule, but are led by the few who persuade them through claimed expertise and clever rhetoric to sacrifice self-government for efficient attainment of desired ends; moreover, the rule of law seeks to perpetuate democracy and prevent the restoration of ruling families or aristocracies, but the characteristic freedom or commotion of democratic opinions erodes the very stability of law. Further paradoxes are more specific to American jurisprudence a century after the positivist and realist revolution: now that historicism and judicial policymaking have brought many new rights and rulings, their advocates want to reinstate stability to preserve such gains. In this view wholesale legal instability is fine, but particular instances of retail stability somehow can be preferred to prevent a subsequent revolution from canceling an earlier one. In the plurality opinion in *Planned Parenthood v. Casey* (1992) which both defended substantial revision of *Roe v. Wade* (1973) and rejected arguments to overturn it, several justices came close to saying that *Roe* must be preserved, *ipse dixit*, for otherwise the Court would lose its capacity to pronounce new rights or make other rulings *ipse dixit*. Time will tell if the Court extends its latest ruling of that ilk, *Lawrence v. Texas* (2003), which comes close to saying that the Court, upon the authority of its own recent precedents, must have the final say on all matters of sexual morality and distinctions between persons.

As a matter of political theory it is highly debatable whether this right of privacy jurisprudence is good for liberal democracy, or any human society, in the long term.[31] As to judicial power itself, the new jurisprudence of privacy is a main cause of the now endemic, and occasionally furious, political battles about courts. If the Supreme Court draws back from extending this jurisprudential revolution to marriage it will not be for any discernible legal principle of restraint included in its earlier policy rulings on privacy, but probably in response to political and majoritarian pressures. If this can be called judicial statesmanship it certainly is not the kind that Hamilton, Marshall, and Tocqueville praise, and it is hard to see how it is good for the law or for courts in the long term. We put at risk this great achievement of Western civilization, the rule of law and protection of rights enforced by independent courts drawn from and working with a professional bar, as one pillar of a free but stable constitutional order.

Endnotes

1. This article draws upon several lines of argument about Montesquieu and the American founding, and about more recent views

of judicial power, from my book *The Cloaking of Power: Montesquieu, Blackstone, and the Rise of Judicial Activism* (Chicago: University of Chicago Press, 2003).

2. A recent argument for fusing political and juridical activity, as a mode of democratic political development, is Christopher Eisgruber, *Constitutional Self-Government* (Cambridge: Harvard University Press, 2001). Keith Whittington distinguishes judicial interpretation from the representative activity of construction, and diagnoses problems when the two are confused, in *Constitutional Interpretation: Textual Meaning, Original Intent, and Judicial Review* (Lawrence, Ka: University Press of Kansas, 1999); and *Constitutional Construction: Divided Powers and Constitutional Meaning* (Cambridge: Harvard University Press, 1999).

3. The leading lines of debate include Ronald Dworkin, *Taking Rights Seriously* (Cambridge: Harvard University Press, 1977) and *Freedom's Law: The Moral Reading of the American Constitution* (Cambridge: Harvard University Press, 1996), versus Mary Ann Glendon, *Rights Talk: The Impoverishment of Political Discourse* (New York: Free Press, 1991) and Michael Sandel, *Democracy's Discontent: America in Search of a Public Philosophy* (Cambridge: Harvard University Press, 1996).

4. See Donald Lutz, "The Relative Influence of European Writers on Late Eighteenth-Century American Political Thought," *American Political Science Review* 78 (1984):189-97; James W. Muller, "The American Framers' Debt to Montesquieu," in *The Revival of Constitutionalism*, James W. Muller, ed. (Lincoln, Ne.: University of Nebraska Press, 1988), 87-102; and Judith Shklar, "A New Constitution for a New Nation," in *Redeeming American Political Thought*, Stanley Hoffman and Dennis F. Thompson, eds. (Chicago: University of Chicago Press, 1998), 158-69.

5. *De l'Esprit des Lois*, Book 29, ch. 1, in *Œuvres complètes*, Pléiade edition, ed. Caillois, 2 vols. (Paris: Gallimard, 1949-51), 2: 865. Subsequent references are parenthetical, citing part of the work and page in the Pléiade edition. I have checked my translations against *The Spirit of the Laws*, Cohler et al. eds. (Cambridge: Cambridge University Press, 1989) and the translation of Thomas Nugent (New York: Hafner, 1949 [1750]), often using a more literal, precise rendering.

6. This section of my essay is adapted from my article "Montesquieu's Complex Natural Right and Moderate Liberalism: The Roots of American Moderation," *Polity* 36 (January 2004). I have omitted most of the notes and extensive citations.

7. For the American founding as an incoherent "plethora of views," see Isaac Kramnick, "The Great National Discussion," *William and Mary Quarterly*, 3d series 45, no. 1 (January 1988): 3-32. Arguments that the

American amalgam is principled include James Stoner, *Common Law and Liberal Theory: Coke, Hobbes, and the Origins of American Constitutionalism* (Lawrence, Kan.: University Press of Kansas, 1992), especially at 176-96, and Hans Eicholz, *Harmonizing Sentiments: The Declaration of Independence and the Jeffersonian Idea of Self-Government* (New York: Peter Lang, 2001).

8. In "Montesquieu's Complex Natural Right" I argue that Arendt, Hulliung, Manent, and Kingston find sociology, or communitarianism, or anti-foundationalism at the core of his philosophy; Lowenthal, Pangle, and Zuckert find Hobbes and Locke; Waddicor, Tuck, and Courtney find Grotius and modern natural law. See also Mark Waddicor, *Montesquieu and the Philosophy of Natural Law* (The Hague: Martinus Nijhoff, 1970), 16-17 for another typology of scholarly views.

9. Thomas Pangle overlooks this passage in *Montesquieu's Philosophy of Liberalism* (Chicago: University of Chicago Press, 1973), 309-10, and in "The Philosophic Understandings of Human Nature Informing the Constitution," in *Confronting the Constitution*, Allan Bloom, ed. (Washington, D.C.: AEI Press, 1990), 15-18, 24-37.

10. See also the emphasis upon honor in 4.2 and 5.12, and the analyses by Sharon Krause in "The Politics of Distinction and Disobedience: Honor and the Defense of Liberty in Montesquieu," *Polity* 31 (1999): 469-99, and *Liberalism With Honor* (Cambridge: Harvard University Press, 2002).

11. This section draws upon my chapter "Hamilton's Common Law Constitutionalism and Judicial Prudence," in *The Cloaking of Power*, 185-210. I have omitted most notes and citations.

12. Richard Brookhiser, *Alexander Hamilton: American* (New York: Free Press, 1999), 9-10; see also 55-60, 169-74, 204-06 on Hamilton's legal career and debt to the common law tradition of Coke.

13. See Charles Warren, *The Supreme Court in United States History* (Boston: Little, Brown, 1924), 1:125.

14. "The Farmer Refuted," February 23, 1775, in *Selected Writings and Speeches of Alexander Hamilton*, Morton Frisch, ed. (Washington, D.C.: AEI Press, 1985), 19-22.

15. Analyses of Publius on judicial power include Stoner, "Constitutionalism and Judging in *The Federalist*," in *Common Law and Liberal Theory*, 197-211, and Sotirios Barber, *The Constitution of Judicial Power* (Baltimore: Johns Hopkins University Press, 1993), 26-65.

16. Alexander Hamilton, John Jay, and James Madison, *The Federalist*, Robert Scigliano, ed. (New York: Modern Library, 2000), No. 9, 48. Scigliano incorporates the McLean (1788) and Gideon (1818) revisions to the newspaper essays, and most of the Hopkins (1802) revisions; he also notes Hamilton's possible authorship or joint authorship of some disputed

essays, upon reviewing the evidence and twentieth century scholarship; see Editor's Introduction, vii-xlviii, Note on the Text, xlix-lii. See also the helpful Introduction, Bibliography, and notes in Charles R. Kesler's revision of the Rossiter edition, *The Federalist Papers*, Clinton Rossiter, ed. (New York: Mentor, 1999 [1961]), and in *The Federalist: The Gideon Edition*, George Carey and James McClellan, eds. (Indianapolis: Liberty Fund, 2001 [originally published in 1818]).

17. See Harvey C. Mansfield, *America's Constitutional Soul* (Baltimore: Johns Hopkins University Press, 1991), 122, and Paul Rahe on Hamilton's defense of the executive and judicial powers as mixing classical and modern political science, in *Republics Ancient & Modern*, vol. 3, *Inventions of Prudence: Constituting the American Regime* (Chapel Hill: University of North Carolina Press, 1994), 3:67-72.

18. Oliver Wendell Holmes, "Montesquieu," in *Collected Legal Papers*, Harold Laski, ed. (New York: Harcourt Brace, 1920), 250-65.

19. Recent works include Albert Alschuler, *Law Without Values: The Life, Work, and Legacy of Justice Holmes* (Chicago: University of Chicago Press, 2000); David F. Forte, "The Making of the Modern Supreme Court: Oliver Wendell Holmes, Jr., and Louis D. Brandeis," in *History of American Political Thought*, Bryan-Paul Frost and Jeffrey Sikkenga, eds. (Lanham, Md.: Lexington Books, 2003), 569-584; James Stoner, "Common Law and Constitution: Original Understanding, Republican Synthesis, and Modern Transformation," in *Common Law Liberty: Rethinking American Constitutionalism*, James Stoner, ed. (Lawrence, Ka: University Press of Kansas, 2003), 9-29; and Carrese, "Holmes and Judicialized Liberalism," in *The Cloaking of Power*, 231-56. Two classic expositions are Robert Faulkner, "Justice Holmes and Chief Justice Marshall," in *The Jurisprudence of John Marshall* (Princeton University Press, 1968), 227-268, and Walter Berns, "Oliver Wendell Holmes, Jr.," in *American Political Thought: The Philosophic Dimension of American Statesmanship*, Morton Frisch and Richard Stevens, eds., (New York: Charles Scribner's Sons, 1971), 167-90. A recent defense of Holmes is Richard Posner, "Introduction," in *The Essential Holmes: Selections from the Letters, Speeches, Judicial Opinions, and Other Writings of Oliver Wendell Holmes, Jr.*, Richard Posner, ed. (Chicago: University of Chicago Press, 1992).

20. See Herbert Storing, "Political Parties and the Bureaucracy" and "American Statesmanship: Old and New," in *Toward a More Perfect Union: Writings of Herbert J. Storing*, Joseph Bessette, ed. (Washington D.C.: AEI Press, 1995), 307-26, 403-28; Niels Aage Thorsen, *The Political Thought of Woodrow Wilson, 1875-1910* (Princeton: Princeton University Press, 1988); and Ronald J. Pestritto, "Woodrow Wilson, the Organic State,

and American Republicanism," in *History of American Political Thought*, Frost and Sikkenga, eds., 549-68.

21. A helpful exception is Christopher Wolfe, *The Rise of Modern Judicial Review: From Constitutional Interpretation to Judge-Made Law*, rev. ed. (Totowa, N.J.: Littlefield Adams, 1994 [originally published in 1986]), 205-16. See also David K. Nichols, "'Merely Judgment': The Supreme Court and the Administrative State," in *The Supreme Court and American Constitutionalism*, Bradford Wilson and Ken Masugi, eds. (Lanham, Md.: Rowman and Littlefield, 1998), 211-31, and more generally, Morton Horwitz, *The Transformation of American Law, 1870-1960: The Crisis of Legal Orthodoxy* (New York: Oxford University Press, 1992).

22. Woodrow Wilson, "The President of the United States," chapter III in *Constitutional Government in the United States* (New York: Columbia University Press, 1908), reprinted in *The Papers of Woodrow Wilson*, Arthur S. Link, ed. (Princeton: Princeton University Press, 1974) 18:104-23, especially 104-109. Further studies of Wilson's idea of "the living Constitution" include James Ceaser, Glen Thurow, Jeffrey Tulis, and Joseph Bessette, "The Rise of the Rhetorical Presidency," *Presidential Studies Quarterly* 11 (1981): 158-71, and Jeffrey Tulis, *The Rhetorical Presidency* (Princeton: Princeton University Press, 1987).

23. *Papers*, 18: 106 (ch. 3), 69-70 (ch. 1). Hereafter, references to *Congressional Government* will be made parenthetically in the text as (*PWW*, 18:106, ch. 3). See Niels Aage Thorsen, *Political Thought of Woodrow Wilson: 1875-1910* (Princeton: Princeton University Press, 1988), 201-03 on Wilson's legal realism and distinction between Constitution and constitutionalism.

24. See Thorsen, *Political Thought of Wilson*, 31, on Bagehot's influence upon Wilson's political science.

25. See Harold Levy, "Lawyers' Spirit and Democratic Liberty: Tocqueville on Lawyers, Jurors, and the Whole People," in *Tocqueville's Defense of Human Liberty: Current Essays*, Peter Lawler and Joseph Alulis, eds. (New York: Garland Publishing, 1993), 243-63; Bruce Frohnen, "Tocqueville's Law: Integrative Jurisprudence in the American Context," *American Journal of Jurisprudence* 39 (1994): 241-72; and my chapter, "Tocqueville Judicial Statesmanship and Common Law Spirit," in *The Cloaking of Power*, 211-30.

26. "John Marshall," in *The Mind and Faith of Justice Holmes*, Max Lerner, ed. (Boston: Little, Brown and Company, 1943), 382-85.

27. Eldon J. Eisenach, *The Lost Promise of Progressivism* (Lawrence, Kan.: University Press of Kansas, 1994), 122-29; see also 107, 216. Two helpful studies of politics and judicial power in the era are William G. Ross, *A Muted Fury: Populists, Progressives, and Labor Unions Confront the*

Courts, 1890-1937 (Princeton: Princeton University Press, 1994), and the study of Brandeis by Edward A. Purcell, *Erie, The Judicial Power, and the Politics of the Federal Courts in Twentieth-Century America* (New Haven: Yale University Press, 2000).

28. See Wolfe, "Origins: The Felt Need for Adaptation," in Rise of Modern Judicial Review, and Eisenach, *Lost Promise of Progressivism,* 262-66.

29. See Robert L. Clinton, *Marbury v. Madison and Judicial Review* (Lawence, Ka.: University Press of Kansas, 1989), 188-99, citing among others Vernon Parrington (*Main Currents in American Thought,* 1927), Dean Alfange (*The Supreme Court and the National Will,* 1937), and Robert H. Jackson (*The Struggle for Judicial Supremacy,* 1941).

30. McCulloch v. Maryland, 4 U.S. 316 (1819), 407, 415, 423. Also little noted is Marshall's ruling in Willson v. Black Bird Creek Marsh Co., 27 U.S. 245 (1829), that federal commerce power does not trump state authority to control predominantly intra-state affairs. For traditional interpretations of Marshall after the Progressives see, in addition to the works by Faulkner, Wolfe, and Clinton cited above, Matthew Franck, "Union, Constitutionalism, and the Judicial Defense of Rights: John Marshall," in *History of American Political Thought,* Frost and Sikkenga, eds., 248-68.

31. John Rawls provides a broad theoretical defense in *Political Liberalism* (New York: Columbia University Press, 1993), especially in Lecture VI, 231-40, 212-13; Sandel sharply criticizes judicially-enforced individualism in *Democracy's Discontent* at 28, 39-47, 92-101, 279-80, 286-88. Policy studies critical of judicial legislating include Donald L. Horowitz, *The Courts and Social Policy* (Washington, D.C.: Brookings, 1977), Jeremy Rabkin, *Judicial Compulsions: How Public Law Distorts Public Policy* (New York: Basic Books, 1989), and R. Shep Melnick, *Between the Lines: Interpreting Welfare Rights* (Washington, D.C.: Brookings, 1994).

Chapter 6

Marbury v. Madison and the Progressive Transformation of Judicial Power

Edward J. Erler

"there would always have to be present in the city something possessing the same understanding of the regime as you, the lawgiver, had when you were setting down the laws."—Plato, *Republic* 497c-d

"those who are to be really guardians of the laws must really know the truth pertaining to them and capable of sufficiently interpreting it in argument and following it in deed, judging the things that come into being nobly and those that do not, according to the standard of nature."—Plato, *Laws* 966b

Chief Justice William Rehnquist recently remarked that "[t]he opinion in *Marbury v. Madison* is a remarkable example of judicial statesmanship.... The doctrine of judicial review—the authority of federal courts to declare legislative acts unconstitutional—is established, but in such a self-denying way that it is the Court's authority which is cut back."[1] There can be little doubt that Marshall's decision in *Marbury* was a consummate act of "judicial statesmanship," but there is considerable uncertainty as to whether its ... statesmanship resides in the establishment of "judicial review." So far from establishing "judicial review," Marshall argued in *Marbury* that the judicial power of the courts to declare laws in conflict with the Constitution void was a power that was intrinsic to the very idea of a written constitution and thus a part of the "judicial power of the United States." "Judicial review" was therefore recognized but not "established" by the *Marbury* decision.

Whether the *Marbury* decision was "self-denying" is open to dispute. But what is not disputable is the fact that since the Warren Court era, judicial review has been transmogrified from an element of judicial statesmanship into a vehicle of judicial aggrandizement. For Marshall, the judicial power was always in the service of constitutional principles; in the contemporary universe of liberal jurisprudence judicial review has almost replaced the Constitution—to say nothing of constitutional principles. The Constitution, we are assured, is constantly evolving, and the Supreme Court is the engine of that evolution. Its role, in short, is to serve as a "continuing constitutional convention," revising and updating the Constitution to meet evolutionary demands. The Constitution, Justice William Brennan argued, must be kept abreast of the "evolution of our concepts of human dignity." The "evolutionary process," Justice Brennan assures us, "is inevitable and, indeed, it is the true interpretive genius of the text" since "the demands of human dignity will never cease to evolve." Given the inevitability of progress, it is impossible to rely on the original intent of the framers. "The genius of the Constitution," Brennan asserts, "rests not in any static meaning it might have had in a world that is dead and gone, but in the adaptability of its great principles to cope with current problems and current needs. What the constitutional fundamentals meant to the wisdom of other times cannot be their measure to the vision of our time."[2] Thus, a constitutional jurisprudence that "is rooted in the text of the Constitution as illuminated by those who drafted, proposed and ratified it" is wholly inadequate for a world that is constantly evolving toward more refined conceptions of human dignity.[3]

Many commentators agree that the high point of judicial supremacy was the Supreme Court's use of *Marbury* in *Cooper v. Aaron* (1958). "It is necessary," the Court announced in an opinion signed by nine justices, "only to recall some basic constitutional propositions which are settled doctrine."

> Article VI of the Constitution makes the Constitution the "supreme Law of the Land." In 1803, Chief Justice Marshall, speaking

for a unanimous Court, referring to the Constitution as "the fundamental and paramount law of the nation," declared in the notable case of *Marbury v. Madison* ... that "it is emphatically the province and duty of the judicial department to say what the law is." This decision declared the basic principle that the federal judiciary is supreme in the exposition of the law of the Constitution, and that principle has ever since been respected by this Court and the Country as a permanent and indispensable feature of our constitutional system. It follows that the interpretation of the Fourteenth Amendment enunciated by this Court in the *Brown* [*v. Board of Education*] case is the supreme law of the land.[4]

Thus the Constitution was transmogrified by the Court's irrefragable logic into constitutional law. But as a matter of logic, the Court's "syllogism" is rendered defective when it is recalled that Marshall concluded his opinion in *Marbury* that "it is apparent that the framers of the constitution contemplated that instrument as a rule for the government of courts, as well as of the legislature."[5] If, however, constitutional law rather than the Constitution becomes "the supreme law of the land," the Constitution would cease to be "a rule for the government of courts." It is significant to note that the Court in *Cooper* said that judicial supremacy had become an "indispensable feature of our constitutional *system*." In this calculus of judicial supremacy, the Constitution has been converted into mere process without purpose, a process that is wholly indifferent to ends.

An enthusiastic supporter of judicial activism, Kenneth Karst, was forced to admit that the logic of *Cooper* "was not self-evident." Indeed, Karst notes, the conclusion that "*Brown* was the supreme law of the land ... carried the assertion of judicial power further than *Marbury* had taken it." And while the reasoning was not sound as a "doctrinal" matter, it did serve, according to Karst, a crucial "political" role: it "galvanized northern opinion" against racial segregation on the eve of the 1960 presidential election which "brought to office a president committed to a strong civil rights program."[6] This open defense of a politicized and activist Supreme Court seemed shocking when it was published nearly twenty years ago, but such arguments have become legion among the proponents of judicial activism. It seems almost quaint at this late date to recall Marshall's argument that since the Constitution resulted from the "original and supreme will" of the people, its principles must be "deemed fundamental [and] permanent."[7] Under the tutelage of liberal jurisprudes, however, constitutional law has replaced the authority of the Constitution. The idea that the Constitution contains permanent principles derived from natural law or natural right is regarded as the merest delusion of an earlier age that also believed in ghosts.[8] This transmogrification was not, however, the work of *Cooper v. Aaron*, but stems directly from *Brown v. Board of Education*, the first case to declare in explicit terms the irrelevance of the Constitution.[9]

Karst notes that

> *Brown* was ... the beginning of a new ordering of our institutions of government, one in which the judiciary—and the Supreme Court in particular—would play a more active role in articulating the nation's fundamental values and defending those values in the name of the Constitution....
>
> The authoritative status of the Supreme Court's articulation of our national values is an undeniable fact in the American political order. In the nation's early days, the Supreme Court spoke with authority largely because it spoke in the name of the Constitution. Today, in contrast, our constitutional rights take at least some of their authority from the Court that declares them.[10]

The language here is almost breathtaking; *Brown* is a new constitutional order that takes the name, but not the substance, of the Constitution. *Brown* was a judicial revolution establishing new "fundamental values" that are legitimately defended only "in the name of the Constitution." Marshall's fundamental and permanent principles have been replaced by mere "values." The advantage of substituting values for principles, from the point of view of the judicial activists, is that "values" don't have to be defended by reason—indeed, they cannot be defended by reason because they are merely idiosyncratic preferences or choices. The idea that reason can decide between competing values is a mere chimera that seemed to have an unbreakable grip on the consciousness of the founding era. As we will see later, however extreme Karst's analysis of *Brown* might seem, his assessment is far too restrained.

STATE CONSTITUTIONS AND LEGISLATIVE SUPREMACY

Many observers have noted that Marshall's assertion of the power to declare acts of Congress void was not novel. The way had been prepared, it is claimed, by previous federal cases and was accepted as an ordinary function of the judiciary by several states.[11] Marshall, of course, cites neither federal nor state precedents in support of his conclusion in *Marbury* that "an act of the legislature, repugnant to the constitution, is void."[12] Rather, the idea that legislative acts in conflict with the Constitution are void seems to Marshall to be an irrefragable conclusion from "the principles and theory of our government."[13] Marshall does obliquely refer to *Hayburn's Case* (1792), but that case, producing a variety of opinions among the justices on circuit, had no value as precedent and Marshall used it only on the issue of the appropriateness of mandamus as a remedy.[14]

Much energy, ingenuity and effort has been expended in canvassing the various state precedents that Marshall might have used to buttress his argument. It is sometimes argued that an understanding of the state precedents is essential to understanding Marshall's opinion. The assumption here is that Marshall would certainly have known about the state precedents and would have accepted them at face value. After an exhaustive review of the historical record, William Crosskey concluded that the precedents are "[i]n large part imaginary." Many of the cases relied upon are unreported and attempts to reconstruct the opinions suffer from various defects. Even in those cases where records survive, Crosskey alleges that they

> actually established no more, at most, than a right in the courts, in two or, possibly, three of the thirteen states, to carry on their own constitutional functions, in what seemed to them the way their state's constitution required; and, hence their right to disregard any act of their legislature, which in their judgment, sought to compel them to proceed differently.... And so far as is known, there was not a single instance when the Convention met, or even when it adjourned, in which any American court openly—or successfully, even in a covert way—had reversed a legislature's determination as to the nature of its powers, where no infraction of the reviewing court's own powers, or of the constitutionally required mode of its exercise of its own powers, had not been concerned.[15]

Robert Clinton, although disagreeing about the reliability of the state precedents, nevertheless agrees with Crosskey that judicial review, to the extent it existed in the states, was used by the courts only as a defensive mechanism in defense of judicial independence. This involved nothing more than "the idea of limiting legislative power by judicial nonapplication of statutes in certain cases."[16] The "certain cases" were only those of a "judiciary nature," involving questions of the independence of the judiciary. Leonard Levy's review of the state cases also led him to the conclusion that "[j]udicial review emerged ... mainly in cases relating to the province of the judicial department or trial by jury. The precedents tend not to show that the courts could pass on the constitutionality of the general powers of the legislatures."[17] But even this limited notion of judicial review, Levy argued, "seemed novel, controversial, and an encroachment on legislative authority. Its exercise, even when imagined, was disputed and liable to provoke the legislature to retaliation."[18] As Marshall surely must have realized, there were no state precedents where judicial review had been exercised by a truly independent judiciary. And, there is no doubt that Marshall shared the view of both Madison and Hamilton that an independent judiciary was an essential ingredient of the separation of powers. Marshall's opinion in *Marbury* was principally an attempt to establish judicial independence in the Constitution's scheme of separated powers. It is doubtful that Marshall saw any of the state cases as providing any precedent.

A serious question thus arises about the relevance of the authority of pre-Convention precedents. In the "early State constitutions," Edward Corwin argued, the "legislature ... *was practically omnipotent.*"[19] As Madison argued pointedly in *The Federalist*, none of the states had provided for an effective separation of powers, relying in almost every instance on mere "parchment barriers." "[I]n no instance," Madison alleged, "has a competent provision been made for maintaining in practice the separation delineated on paper." But as Madison forcefully argued, "experience assures us" that such reliance "has been greatly overrated." Some mechanisms are necessary for fortifying "the more feeble against the more powerful members of the government. The legislative department is everywhere extending the sphere of its activity and drawing all power into its impetuous vortex."[20] Thus, legislative supremacy will result unless the executive and judicial branches can be sufficiently "fortified." "Energy in the executive" and an "independent" judiciary are the indispensable fortifications against legislative encroachments. Legislative supremacy is an inherent problem of republican government, whether at the state or federal level, because of its "supposed influence over the people" (No. 48 at 309) who are the "only legitimate fountain of power" (No. 49 at 313). "[I]t is against the enterprising ambition of [the legislative] department," Madison warns, "that the people ought to indulge all their jealousy and exhaust all their precautions" (No. 48 at 309).

At the Constitutional Convention, Madison had argued that one of the objects of "a National Government" was to provide "more effectually for the security of private rights, and the steady dispensation of Justice. Interferences with these were evils which had more perhaps than any thing else, produced this convention. Was it to be supposed," Madison queried, "that republican liberty could long exist under the abuses of it practiced in some of the States?"[21] Madison, of course, reiterated this argument and brought it to perfection in the tenth *Federalist*. At the Convention, Madison proposed a national negative on state legislation as a remedy for state abuses. The proposal would have given the national congress the power "to negative all laws passed by the several States contravening ... the articles of Union."[22] By this proposal, Congress would have become the final arbiters of the federal relationship. Madison

> considered the negative ... as essential to the efficacy & security of the Genl. Govt. The necessity of a general Govt. proceeds from the propensity of the States to pursue their particular interests in opposition to the general interest. Nothing short of a negative on their laws will controul it ... Confidence can not be put in the State Tribunals as guardians of the National authority and interests. In all the states these are more or less depend[en]t on the Legislatures ... In R. Island the Judges who refused to execute an unconstitutional law were displaced, and others substituted, by the Legislature who would be willing instruments of the wicked & arbitrary plans of their masters.[23]

Madison was emphatic in his insistence that no reliance could be placed in state judiciaries because none were sufficiently independent from legislative control. He alludes to the Rhode Island case of

Trevett v. Weeden which had been decided in 1786 (reports of the decision were being widely circulated in pamphlet-form during the Philadelphia Convention). In *Trevett*, the Rhode Island court had asserted the power to declare laws in violation of the constitution to be void, although in the actual decision the justices resorted to a technicality to avoid making a decision. This mild assertion of judicial power enraged the legislature and the judges were summoned to give an account of their pretended power. Finding that the judges were unable to acquit their pretensions, a motion was made to dismiss the judges from office. The motion failed because a persuasive argument was mounted that, under the Rhode Island Constitution, judges could be dismissed only on criminal charges. At the next annual election of the legislature, however, four of the offending justices were removed from the bench and four others more compliant to the wishes of the legislature were selected to replace them.[24] In Madison's view, an independent judiciary was a necessary ingredient in providing a robust separation of power and he did everything in his power at the Constitutional Convention to devise constitutional checks on both state and federal legislative power.

Gouverneur Morris, however, argued against the provision, noting that " the proposal ... would disgust all the States. A law that ought to be negatived will be set aside in the Judiciary department and if that security should fail; may be repealed by a National law."[25] Morris' argument eventually carried the vote and the proposal was rejected. On July 17, 1787 the first version of the Supremacy Clause was introduced as a substitute for the congressional negative. As it eventually emerged from the Convention, Article VI reads, in pertinent part, that:

> This Constitution, and the Laws of the United States which shall be made in Pursuance thereof; and all Treaties made, or which shall be made, under the Authority of the United States, shall be the supreme Law of the Land; and the Judges in every State shall be bound thereby, any Thing in the Constitution or Laws of any State to the Contrary notwithstanding.

Madison was bitterly disappointed by the Convention's failure to pass the national negative, and his concerns were only partially assuaged by the addition of the Supremacy Clause.

Writing to Jefferson shortly before the Convention adjourned, Madison was pessimistic about the prospects of the new Constitution: "I hazard an opinion ... that the plan should it be adopted will neither effectually answer its national object nor prevent the local mischiefs which every where excite disgusts ag[ain]st the state governments."[26] Madison's next letter to Jefferson, written a little over a month after the end of the Convention, explained in greater detail the effects he anticipated from the failure of the federal negative. "Without such a check in the whole over the parts," Madison argued, "our system involves the evil of imperia in imperio." "It may be said," Madison speculated,

> that the Judicial authority under our new system will keep the States within their proper limits, and supply the place of a negative on their laws. The answer is, that it is more convenient to prevent the passage of a law, than to declare it void after it is passed; that this will be particularly the case, where the law aggrieves individuals, who may be unable to support an appeal ag[ain]st a State to the Supreme Judiciary; that a State which would violate the Legislative rights of the Union, would not be very ready to obey a Judicial decree in support of them, and that a recurrence to force, which in the event of disobedience would be necessary, is an evil which the new Constitution meant to exclude as far as possible.[27]

Madison always maintained the necessity of a final arbiter to determine the boundaries of the federal system in cases of conflict, and in *The Federalist* he argued that the judiciary would indeed supply the national negative. In controversies relating to the boundaries between state and federal power, Madison conceded, "the tribunal which is ultimately to decide is to be established under the general government ... The decision is to be impartially made, according to the rules of the Constitution, and all the usual and most effectual precautions are taken to secure this impartiality. Some such tribunal is clearly essential to prevent an appeal to the sword and a dissolution of the compact; and that it ought to be established under the general rather than under the local governments, or, to speak more properly, that it could be safely established under the first alone, is a position not likely to be combated" (No. 39 at 245-246). Many years later, reflecting on the work of the Convention, Madison wrote that "the General Convention" vested authority "in the Judicial Department as a final resort in relation to the States, for cases resulting to it in the exercise of its functions." This intention, Madison continued, is "expressed by the articles declaring that the federal Constitution & laws shall be the supreme law of the land." This, Madison contended "was the prevailing view of the subject when the Constitution was adopted and put into execution." Madison punctuated his recollection with the statement that "I have never yielded my original opinion in the 'Federalist' No. 39 ... [to] this construction of the Constitution."[28]

Marshall took a similar view in the Virginia Ratifying Convention when he asked a series of rhetorical questions in responding to critics of the proposed jurisdiction of the federal courts. "Is it not necessary," Marshall queried, "that the federal courts should have cognizance of cases arising under the Constitution, and the laws, of the United States? What is the service or purpose of a judiciary, but to execute the laws in a peaceable, orderly manner, without shedding blood, or creating a contest, or availing yourselves of force? If this be the case, where can its jurisdiction be more necessary than here?"[29] Many years later in *Cohens v. Virginia* (1821)[30] Marshall answered these rhetorical questions and brought to perfection the argument derived from the Supremacy Clause that the Supreme Court was to play the dominant role in policing the federal relationship.[31]

Marshall, however, used an argument derived from the Supremacy Clause to justify judicial review that is not found anywhere in the writings of Madison. In the peroration to *Marbury* Marshall recognized "the principle, supposed to be essential to all written constitutions, that a law repugnant to the constitution is void; and that courts, as well as other departments, are bound by that instrument."[32] Marshall's previous paragraph had noted that "in declaring what shall be the supreme law of the land, the constitution itself is first mentioned; and not the laws of the United States generally, but those only which shall be made in pursuance of the constitution have that rank." Marshall thus understood the word "pursuance" as "in accordance with" or "in conformity with" the Constitution. Thus inferior laws not in "pursuance" of the Constitution were not the "supreme law of the land" and were thus null and void. Any other interpretation would merely render the Constitution form without substance and would ultimately dissolve the distinction between the Constitution as fundamental law and those ordinary acts of legislation authorized by the Constitution. It would convert the Constitution into mere process devoid of any purpose; in a word, it would utterly confuse means and ends. Throughout his career, Marshall's judicial statesmanship focused on securing the position of the Constitution as "fundamental" and "superior" law. As Charles Hobson has rightly noted, "[t]he formation of a supreme law as the original and deliberate act of the people was the indispensable basis for a theory of judicial review that was compatible with the principles of popular government."[33]

The proposal for a Council of Revision was another attempt on Madison's part to prevent the development of legislative supremacy in the proposed constitution. The Council would have been composed of "the executive" and "a convenient number" of the national judiciary.[34] Since the phrase "a convenient number" implied at least two members of the Supreme Court would be included on the Council, the Judiciary, as Nathaniel Gorham pointed out, would have predominance.[35] The Council's principal function would be to provide a "revisionary check on the Legislature" through the prior review of legislative proposals. It would, Madison argued, provide a defensive mechanism against "Legislative encroachments" for both the executive and judicial branches.[36] "Experience in all the States," Madison insisted, "had evinced a powerful tendency in the Legislature to absorb all power into its vortex. This was the real source of danger to the American Constitutions."[37] James Wilson, a future Supreme Court justice, and George Mason wished to extend the revisionary power beyond a mere checking function. "Laws may be unjust, may be unwise, may be dangerous, may be destructive," Wilson argued, "and yet not be so unconstitutional as to justify the Judges in refusing to give them effect." A share in the revisionary power, however, will give judges "an opportunity of taking notice of these characters of a law, and of counteracting, by the weight of their opinions the improper views of the Legislature."[38] Madison agreed: the Council of Revision "would ... be useful to the Community at large as an additional check against a pursuit of those unwise & unjust measures which constituted so great a portion of our calamities."[39]

A majority of the Convention, however, reasoned that such a mixture of executive and judicial power would make "statesmen of the

Judges."[40] Elbridge Gerry alleged that it was "foreign" to the "nature" of the judiciary to involve judges in "the policy of public measures."[41] In any case, Gerry argued, the revisionary council was superfluous because "the Judiciary ... will have a sufficient check against encroachments on their own department by their exposition of the laws, which involved a power of deciding on their Constitutionality."[42] Gerry distinctly anticipated judicial review as a defensive measure against "encroachments" on the judiciary. Clearly, however, the Council of Revision was intended to be something far more extensive. Luther Martin described the mixing of powers as "a dangerous innovation." "As to the constitutionality of laws," he averred, "that point will come before the Judges in their proper official character. In this character they have a negative on the laws. Join them with the Executive in the Revision and they will have a double negative."[43] The proposal was thus defeated primarily because of the delegates' reservations about the integrity of the principle of separated powers.

Madison considered the failure to secure the revisionary council to be a major defeat. Madison seemed almost desperate in his attempts to provide adequate checks on legislative power. The legislature, Madison knew, was all too prone to overstep its constitutional limits in its attempt to aggrandize power. A fortified judiciary, and to a lesser extent, a fortified executive was needed to police the boundaries of the Constitution's separated powers. The Council of Revision was to provide a kind of pre-screening of legislation that amounted to judicial review before the fact. With the defeat of the council proposal did Madison also see this power devolving upon the Supreme Court in a similar way he saw the national negative resulting by default to the judiciary?

In *The Federalist*, Madison criticized Jefferson's plan, included in his draft constitution for Virginia and published in the *Notes on the State of Virginia*, to call constitutional conventions "for altering the Constitution, or *correcting breaches of it*" (No. 49, at 313). In one sense, Madison argued, the plan is "strictly consonant to the republican theory" since it recurs "to the same original authority, not only whenever it may be necessary to enlarge, diminish, or new-model the powers of government, but also whenever any one of the departments may commit encroachments on the chartered authorities of the others" (No. 49, at 314). Madison's principal criticism was that a frequent appeal to the people would, by implying "some defect in the government," "deprive the government of that veneration which time bestows on everything, and without which perhaps the wisest and freest government would not possess the requisite stability." Recurrences to the people are thus "experiments ... of too ticklish a nature to be unnecessarily multiplied" (No. 49, at 315). Frequent appeals would not only undermine reverence for the Constitution, but "would inevitably be connected with the spirit of pre-existing parties" so that "passions ... not the reason of the public would sit in judgment." But constitutional government is designed to elevate reason over passion: "it is the reason alone, of the public, that ought to control and regulate the government. The passions ought to be controlled and regulated by the government" (No. 49, at 317). Madison concluded that the separation of powers must be maintained only "by so contriving the interior structure of the government as that its several constituent parts may, by their mutual relations, be the means of keeping each other in their proper places" (No. 51, at 320). The institutional structure of the judiciary would render it least likely to be "connected with the spirit of pre-existing parties" and better placed to exercise reason in the control and regulation of the government.

Madison does not detail here the particular role of the judiciary, but there is little reason to doubt that he agreed with the principal points of Hamilton's analysis of the judiciary in the *Federalist* No. 78. Hamilton argued that an important function of the judiciary was "to guard the Constitution" by serving as the bulwark "of a limited Constitution against legislative encroachments" (No. 78, at 469). This was the precise role that Madison had envisioned for the revisionary council rejected by the Convention. Since guardianship of the Constitution cannot be entrusted to the people directly, there must be some agency within the separated powers that would serve as an institutional substitute for a frequent "recurrence to the people." This was the role that Hamilton envisioned for the Supreme Court when he thrust it in the role as the "bulwark" and "guard" of a limited Constitution. The principal function of the Supreme Court, therefore, is to serve as a sentinel over the "original" will of the people, thus making frequent "recurrence" to the people—with its attendant dangers—unnecessary. Any recurrence to the people—the ultimate sovereign—will be reserved for the most extraordinary occasions.

There was no indication in Hamilton's exegesis that the guardianship of the Constitution was necessarily limited merely to defenses of judicial power, although at the Convention, Madison on one occasion had intimated that the judicial power "ought to be limited to cases of a Judiciary Nature," and that the "right of expounding the Constitution in cases not of this nature ought not to be given to that Department."[44] This would seem to limit Hamilton's more sweeping charge that the Supreme Court be the guardian not only of individual rights but the rights of the Constitution as well. But there can be no doubt that Hamilton's detailed explication of judicial power in the *Federalist* No. 78—however much it may have expanded Madison's analysis—had a profound influence on Marshall's opinion in *Marbury v. Madison*.

Oliver Ellsworth, a future Chief Justice of the Supreme Court, had "approved heartily" of the motion to create a Council of Revision at the Convention.[45] The extent to which he believed that the Supreme Court might still fill something of the role contemplated in the defeated revisionary council was indicated in his comments before the Connecticut ratifying convention. "The Constitution defines the extent of the powers of the general government," Ellsworth argued.

> If the general legislature should at any time overleap their limits, the judicial department is a constitutional check. If the United States go beyond their powers, if they make a law which the Constitution does not authorize, it is void; and the judicial power, the national judges, who, to secure their impartiality, are to be made independent, will declare it to be void. On the other hand, if the states go beyond their limits, if they make a law which is a usurpation upon the general government, the law is void; and upright, independent judges will declare it to be so.[46]

Several months later, speaking before the Virginia ratifying convention, John Marshall, who would succeed Ellsworth as Chief Justice, was somewhat more circumspect when he contended that if the federal government "were to make a law not warranted by any of the powers enumerated, it would be considered by the judges as an infringement of the Constitution which they are to guard. They would not consider such a law as coming under their jurisdiction. They would declare it void."[47] Marshall's statement is noteworthy because it identifies the principal role of the Court as a guardian of the Constitution—not just the judiciary—against legislative usurpations. This was to become the primary theme of Marshall's opinion in *Marbury*.

It is important to note that there was no independent judiciary in the theories of Locke or Montesquieu, the two political philosophers who most influenced the framers. The creation of an independent judiciary was the exclusive work of the framers. Montesquieu's jury system was converted into a permanent and independent judiciary, and the judiciary was to serve a crucial role in the scheme of separated powers by providing a check on legislative power. The framers drew little from the experience of the states where separation of powers, while honored in theory by all state constitutions, was rarely honored in practice. Legislative supremacy in state governments, as Madison warned, was the principal cause of the "prevailing and increasing distrust of public engagements and alarm for private rights which are echoed from one end of the continent to the other" (No. 10 at 77-78). It was this legislative tyranny, abetted by majority faction, that the framers were determined to avoid in the new constitution, and an independent judiciary was crucial in preventing legislative usurpations.

Principles Long and Well Established

The concluding section of Marshall's *Marbury* opinion can only be described as a resort to first principles. "The question," Marshall wrote,

> whether an act, repugnant to the constitution, can become the law of the land, is a question deeply interesting to the United States; but, happily, not of an intricacy proportioned to its interest. It seems only necessary to recognize certain principles, supposed to have been long and well established, to decide it.[48]

It almost goes without saying that Marshall does not rely on state or federal precedent for the explication of the "certain principles, supposed to have been long and well established." Rather, he immediately moves to the explication of these first principles in terms of the social compact theory of the origins of civil society. One of the staple precepts of social compact theory is the distinction between fundamental law and ordinary law. Marshall, of course, doesn't explicitly refer to social compact, but his analysis, asserting the "original right" of the people to establish "their future government" on "such principles, as, in their opinion, shall most conduce to their own happiness" is the unmistakable language of social compact. This "original right," Marshall continues, is the basis upon "which the whole American fabric has been erected." William Nelson notes that Marshall "at no point in the opinion" invoked "the language of natural rights."[49] While it is true that the phrase "natural rights" is never used in the opinion, the "language of natural rights" is evident in the use of the term "original right" as well as reference to the "fundamental" principles of the Constitution which do not derive from the Constitution itself.

According to the Declaration of Independence "Governments are instituted among Men, deriving their just powers from the consent of the governed." This is the familiar language of social compact, as is the invocation of the "Right of the People to alter or to abolish" government when it becomes "destructive" of the "ends" for which it was established—the "Safety and Happiness" of the people. Madison frequently expressed the opinion that "the idea of compact ... is a fundamental principle of free Government." "The original compact," Madison explained,

> is the one implied or presumed, but nowhere reduced to writing, by which a people agree to form one society. The next is a compact, by which the people in their social state agree to a Government over them. These two compacts may be considered as blended in the Constitution of the U.S.[50]

Thus, Madison pointedly noted in *The Federalist* that the principal features of the Constitution were rooted in "the first principles of the social compact" (No. 44, at 282). Professor Harry Jaffa has rightly noted that "[t]he idea of compact is at the heart of American constitutionalism. It is at the heart of the philosophical statesmanship that made the Revolution, of which the Constitution is the fruit. In the most fundamental respect, compact is an inference from the proposition 'that all men are created equal.'"[51] The number of public documents and public statements by eminent statesmen of the founding period make it impossible to gainsay the importance attached to social compact, "whether expressed or presumed." But it is also important to understand that the framers understood social compact as an expression of natural right—the theory of social compact is derived from the principles of human nature. Marshall's reliance on the social compact is, I believe, essential to understanding the deepest level of his analysis in *Marbury*.

Marshall writes that the "original right" of the people to form civil society "is a very great exertion; nor can it, nor ought it, to be frequently repeated."[52] This is clearly an echo of the Declaration's doctrine that "prudence" should govern the exercise of "original right": "Prudence, indeed, will dictate that Governments long established should not be changed for light and transient causes; and accordingly all experience hath shown, that mankind are more disposed to suffer, while evils are sufferable, than to right themselves by abolishing the forms to which they are accustomed." Marshall's eminently reasonable conclusion is that "[t]he principles" established by this "great exertion" must be "deemed fundamental. And as the authority from which they proceed is supreme, and can seldom act, they are designed to be permanent."[53] Thus the principles of the Constitution, consistent with the requirements of prudence, must be "deemed" permanent. This does not, of course, foreclose any future resort to "original right," but because these principles emanate from the supreme authority of the people they are "designed to be permanent" and in fact are a permanent expression of the superior will of the people acting in their original capacity. This superior will can only be displaced when the people resume their original capacity and "alter or abolish government." It is the object of statesmanship, rightly understood, to supply the prudence that the people can exercise only on extraordinary occasions. Prudence, or practical wisdom, would calculate the application of permanent principles to changing circumstances and is an essential part of all three branches of government, but most particularly of the legislative and judicial branches.[54] From this point of view, guardianship of first principles—"the original will" of the people expressed in the Constitution—would seem to be the primary role of courts.

Marshall seemed to have understood the guardianship of first principles as the principal object of original intent jurisprudence. Corwin was only slightly exaggerating when he wrote that Marshall "was thoroughly persuaded that he knew the intentions of the framers of the Constitution—the intentions which had been wrought into the in-strument itself—and he was equally determined that these intentions should prevail. For this reason he refused to regard his office merely as a judicial tribunal; it was a platform from which to promulgate sound constitutional principles, the very cathedra indeed of constitu-tional orthodoxy."[55] With his penchant for understated hyperbole, Corwin might as well have argued that Marshall's conception of the Supreme Court's role was not unlike that envisioned for the Nocturnal Council in Plato's *Laws*.[56] In *Cohens v. Virginia* (1821) Marshall argued that the "American people, in the conventions of their respective states, adopted the present constitution." The Constitution thus is expressed in "the authoritative language of the American People."[57] The "mainte-nance" of the "principles established in the constitution ... in their purity, is certainly among the great duties of the government. One of the instruments by which this duty may be peaceably performed, is the judicial department. It is authorized to decide all cases of every description, arising under the constitution or laws of the United States."[58] Significantly, Marshall does not qualify the judicial department's role in maintaining the principles of the Constitution by limiting jurisdiction to cases of a "judiciary nature."

Marshall was not hesitant to draw arguments "from the nature of government, and from the general spirit of the Constitution,"[59] al-though he insisted that the spirit of the Constitution must be drawn from the words of the Constitution itself. "[A]lthough the spirit of an instrument, especially of a constitution, is to be respected not less than its letter," Marshall contended, "yet the spirit is to be collected chiefly from its words. It would be dangerous in the extreme to infer from extrinsic circumstances, that a case for which the words of an instrument expressly provide, shall be exempted from its operation."[60] The spirit of the Constitution as Marshall knew—and as Abraham Lincoln was later to argue—was derived from the "original will" of the people expressed in the social compact principles of the Declaration of Independence and embodied in the language of the Constitution. The words of the Constitution can only be understood and construed as expressions of those principles. Lincoln spoke of the "philosophi-cal cause" of the founding, and in a much cited passage Lincoln said the principles of the Declaration were words *"fitly spoken"* which have "proved an 'apple of gold' to us. The *Union* and the *Constitution*, are the *picture* of *silver,* subsequently framed around it. The picture was made, not to *conceal,* or *destroy* the apple; but to *adorn,* and *preserve* it. The *picture* was made *for* the apple—*not* the apple for the picture."[61] Thus, in Lincoln's view—and I say Marshall's as well—the Constitution was meant to preserve the principles of the Declaration; those principles are thus the authoritative guide to the construction of the language of the Constitution.

"This original and supreme will," Marshall cogently argued in *Marbury,* "organizes the government, and assigns to different departments their respective powers. It may either stop here, or establish certain limits not to be transcended by those departments."[62] What seems therefore to be intrinsic to government derived from the exercise of "original will" is the separation of powers. As Madison had famously remarked in *Federalist* No. 47, "[t]he accumulation of all powers, legislative, executive, and judiciary, in the same hands, whether of one, a few, or many, and whether hereditary, self-appointed, or elective, may justly be pronounced the very definition of tyranny" (No. 47 at 301). For all of his vaunted argument about representative government in *Federalist* No. 10, Madison knew that the principle of representation was not enough to secure constitutional government. "[W]hile a dependence on the people is, no doubt, the primary control on government," Madison cautioned, "experience has taught mankind the necessity of auxiliary precautions" (No. 51, at 322).

But the separation of powers was not just an "essential precaution" against tyrannical government; it was also the key to "good government." The functional specialization of the branches would situate each branch so that each part would do its work well. The multi-membered legislature, representing diverse interests, would be suitable for deliberation; the single executive for execution; and the independent supreme court for judgment. The key, according to Madison, was the independence of the branches. In remarks at the Constitutional Convention, Madison argued that "if it be a fundamental principle of free Govt. that the Legislative, Executive & Judiciary powers should be *separately* exercised; it is equally so that they be *independently* exercised."[63] Indeed, the Declaration lists as one of its grievances against the King that "he has made Judges dependent on his Will alone, for the tenure of their offices, and the amount and payment of their salaries." This grievance is offered as one of the elements of the accumulated evidence that "evinces a design to reduce [the people] under absolute Despotism."

For Madison, the key to maintaining a separation of powers in practice was checks and balances—giving each department a mechanism of self-defense against the encroachments of coordinate branches. A complete separation of powers would be effective only in a mixed regime where the different powers of government could be distributed to the different classes in society. There the different branches of government would serve as a check on one another because they would reflect on the level of government the natural class antagonisms that existed in society. But in a regime where all power is derived either directly or indirectly from the people, some substitute for the mixed regime principle had to be found. That substitute was checks and balances, the principal means devised to republicanize the separation of powers.[64] But in this scheme, the Supreme Court appears not to have been apportioned any defensive weapons beyond "permanency in office." Judicial review, however, seems to have been widely regarded as an intrinsic part of constitutional government understood as limited government. Hamilton argued that "this doctrine is not deducible from any circumstance peculiar to the plan of convention, but from the general theory of a limited Constitution" (No. 81, at 482). There can be little doubt that this was also a part of Marshall's understanding when he referred to "principles long and well established."

THE DEFENSE OF JUDICIAL POWER: FEDERALIST NO. 78

Hamilton argued in *Federalist* No. 78 that "the judiciary from the nature of its functions, will always be the least dangerous to the political rights of the Constitution" because it has "neither FORCE nor WILL but merely judgment; and must ultimately depend upon the aid of the executive arm even for the efficacy of its judgments" (No. 78, at 465). Indeed, "the natural feebleness of the judiciary" places it "in continual jeopardy of being overpowered, awed, or influenced by its coordinate branches" (No. 78, at 466). Some method of fortifying the judiciary must therefore be devised because "[t]he complete independence of the courts of justice is peculiarly essential in a limited Constitution" (No. 78, at 466). The "courts of justice are to be considered as the bulwarks of a limited Constitution against legislative encroachments" and "the permanent tenure of judicial offices" will "contribute ... to that independent spirit in the judges which must be essential to the faithful performance of so arduous a duty" (No. 78, 469). In short, a "permanency in office" will be "an indispensable ingredient" to the "firmness and independence" of the judiciary (No. 78, at 466).

But while permanent tenure is a necessary condition of independence, it doesn't appear to be a sufficient condition. A "limited Constitution" Hamilton remarks, is "one which contains certain specified exceptions to the legislative authority" (No. 78, at 466). He mentions only two examples, bills of attainder and ex post facto laws, remarking that "[l]imitations of this kind can be preserved in practice no other way than through the medium of courts of justice, whose duty it must be to declare all acts contrary to the manifest tenor of the Constitution void. Without this, all the reservations of particular rights or privileges would amount to nothing" (No. 78, at 466). If it might be argued that "the legislative body are themselves the constitutional judges of their own powers and that the construction they put upon them is conclusive upon the other departments it may be answered that this cannot be the natural presumption where it is not to be collected from any particular provisions in the Constitution" (No. 78, at 467). Such a presumption would allow the legislature to judge in its own cause, enabling "the representatives of the people to substitute their will to that of their constituents." Rather, "[i]t is far more rational to suppose that the courts were designed to be an intermediate body between the people and the legislature in order, among other things, to keep the latter within the limits assigned to their authority" (No. 78, at 467).

In the separation of powers, "the interpretation of the laws is the proper and peculiar province of the courts." The Constitution is "fundamental law" and must be so "regarded by the judges" (No. 78, at 467). It belongs to the judiciary, therefore, to ascertain the meaning of the fundamental law as well as those legislative acts authorized by the fundamental law, and "[i]f there should be an irreconcilable variance between the two, that which has the superior obligation and validity ought, of course, to be preferred; or, in other words, the Constitution ought to be preferred to the statute, the intention of the people to the intention of their agents" (No. 78, at 467).

Hamilton was quick to add that the duty to interpret the law did not imply a superiority of the judiciary over the legislative branch, but rather "only supposes that the power of the people is superior to both, and that where the will of the legislature, declared in its statutes, stands in opposition to that of the people, declared in the Constitution, the judges ought to be governed by the latter rather than the former. They ought to regulate their decisions by the fundamental laws rather than by those which are not fundamental" (No. 78, at 468). Thus, the distinction between "fundamental laws," the product of what Marshall described as the "original and supreme will," and ordinary acts of legislation, the product of an inferior and subordinate will, is fundamental to any notion of limited government. If the "courts of justice are to be considered as the bulwarks of a limited Constitution against legislative encroachments," the distinction between fundamental law and non-fundamental law must serve as the first principle of all its activities.

The possibility of a judicial encroachment upon legislative power, Hamilton says, is "in reality a phantom" (No. 81, at 484). This conclusion is supported by reflections on the "general nature of the judicial power," "the objects to which it relates," "the manner in which it is exercised," a proper understanding of the "comparative weakness" of the judicial branch and the recognition of "its total incapacity to support its usurpations by force" (No. 81, at 485). Besides, Hamilton avers, the "important constitutional check" of impeachment is "alone a complete security" against judicial usurpations (No. 81, at 485).

The judiciary's role in serving as a check on the legislative branch was described by Hamilton as defending the "political rights of the Constitution" (No. 78, at 465, 470-1; No. 73, at 443, 445). Hamilton seems to have distinguished the "political rights of the Constitution" from "the rights of individuals." As he pointedly remarked, the "independence of the judges is *equally requisite* to guard the Constitution and the rights of individuals ... " (No. 78, at 469 [emphasis added]). And here Hamilton makes a curious allusion to the Declaration of Independence, remarking that "I trust the friends of the proposed Constitution will never concur with its enemies in questioning that fundamental principle of republican government which admits the right of the people to alter or abolish the established Constitution whenever they find it inconsistent with their happiness" (No. 78, at 469). This is a reminder that the most fundamental right of the people is the right of revolution and that the right of revolution is ultimately the right which guarantees all other rights. The judiciary should always be animated by the idea that its role in the vindication of "the rights of individuals" is to stand as "an intermediate body between the people and the legislature." The judiciary is to protect the "original will" of the people against any subsequent and subordinate will.

The greatest problem, as Hamilton gravely notes, is majority faction. Here the courts are to play a crucial role in preventing majority factions from denying rights of individuals and minorities. Madison had argued in *Federalist* No. 10 that the prospects of republican government depended on finding a cure for the disease of majority faction. Republican governments, of course, have a natural and general tendency to faction, but while minority factions are compatible with republican government, majority faction is utterly incompatible with the existence of the "public good and private rights" (No. 10 at 80). Madison argued that the primary cure for the disease of majority faction was a governmental structure that would produce constitutional majorities as opposed to mere numerical majorities. In short, the problem was to find some method of insuring that the majority ruled in the interest of the whole of society rather than merely in the interest of a part. A diverse regime inculcating a multiplicity of interests would be the primary solution. Majorities would rule, but no majority would be animated by a single interest or passion. The competition between the various and interfering interests in society would insure that no majority would develop a sense of its own self interest *as a majority*. Such majorities—coalitions of various minority interests— would have little interest in invading the rights of minorities or of individuals. But as we have already seen, Madison believed that some "auxiliary precautions" were also necessary. It was left to Hamilton to argue that the courts would play a crucial role in minimizing the effects of majority faction not only on the "rights of the Constitution" but on the "rights of individuals" as well. The only alternative to judicial statesmanship, Hamilton seems to suggest, is resort to the right of revolution where the people resume, to use Marshall's phrase, their "original and supreme will."

Marshall was clear that in cases properly before it, the Court had a constitutional duty to decide. The Constitution, Marshall notes, "does not extend the judicial power to every violation of the constitution which may possibly take place, but to 'a case in law or equity', in which a right, under such law, is asserted in a court of justice. If the question cannot be brought into a court, then there is no case in law or equity, and no jurisdiction is given by the words" of Article III. But where jurisdiction does exist, the Court is obligated to render a decision. "It is most true," Marshall concedes,

> that this court will not take jurisdiction if it should not; but it is equally true, that it must take jurisdiction if it should. The judiciary cannot, as the legislature may, avoid a measure because it approaches the confines of the constitution. We cannot pass it by because it is doubtful. With whatever doubts, with whatever difficulties, a case may be attended, we must decide it if it be brought before us. We have no more right to decline the exercise of jurisdiction which is given, than to usurp that which is not given. The one or the other would be treason to the constitution.[65]

Here it is clear that the court's guardianship of the Constitution is limited to justiciable cases—this is a separation of powers requirement. But as the holding and the argument of *Cohens* indicates, the Court will approach the issue of justiciability with great latitude.

We should remind ourselves here of the dual function that Hamilton assigned to the judiciary—to protect the "rights of the Constitution" as well as "the rights of individuals." It is not clear from Hamilton's analysis whether these two different functions give rise to two different conceptions of judicial power or whether the vindication of the "rights of individuals" is at one and the same time the vindication of the "rights of the constitution." The charge that courts are "to be considered as the bulwarks of a limited Constitution against legislative encroachments" is, however, an extensive one and seems to extend beyond the "rights of individuals."

THE SOLE PROVINCE OF THE JUDICIARY

Marshall seems to have believed—at least as a preliminary matter—that "[t]he province of the court is, solely, to decide on the rights of individuals."[66] Madison expressed the same view when he introduced legislation to create a bill of rights in the first Congress on June 8,

1789. Madison distinguished "positive rights"—"those that result from the nature of the compact"—from natural rights which he described as "any one of the pre-existent rights of nature."[67] Positive rights in the Constitution are derived from natural rights, but they are positive rights to the extent that they depend on the social compact—the Constitution—for their existence. Trial by jury, Madison notes, is a positive right rather than a natural right. Yet it is "as essential to secure the liberty of the people as any one of the rights of nature." Rights, both natural and positive, when they are "incorporated in the Constitution" will be the special province, Madison argues, of the courts. "Independent tribunals of justice," he explained, "will consider themselves in a peculiar manner the guardians of those rights; they will be an impenetrable bulwark against every assumption of power in the legislative or executive. They will be naturally led to resist every encroachment upon the rights expressly stipulated for in the constitution by the declaration of rights."[68] Madison's position here seems to comport fully with both Hamilton's and Marshall's understanding of the role of the judiciary in the protection of individual rights.

As opposed to questions of individual rights, Marshall argued, "[q]uestions in their nature political, or which are, by the constitution and laws, submitted to the executive, can never be made in this court."[69] Thus the Court seemingly eschews jurisdiction wherever discretion is a proper part of the exercise of constitutional power. Many constitutional duties require the exercise of political discretion and the Court will only review the exercise of constitutional duties, not the discretion attached to it, as long as the exercise of discretion itself doesn't violate the rights of individuals. William Nelson argues that Marshall's "creative act" in the *Marbury* decision was "the distinction between law and politics" and that this distinction became "the foundation of Marshall's constitutional jurisprudence."[70] But it is clear from Marshall's careful language that the determination of which questions are "in their nature political" and those "which are, by the constitution and laws" is to be made by the judiciary. As one perceptive commentator notes: "While the courts might not meddle in the political sphere, they alone determine how far the forbidden sphere extends. By their authority to interpret the Constitution and laws they can limit law-maker and law-executor alike. The national courts thus not only judge under the laws but magisterially preside over them."[71]

What appears at first glance, then, to be a statement disclaiming "all pretensions" to "jurisdiction" where political questions are involved, actually extends the jurisdiction of the courts by asserting the pretension of authority to define what is merely political and discretionary and what is required by the Constitution and law. Besides other considerations, Marshall must surely have regarded the Constitution itself as "political" in the most decisive respect as the product of "reflection and choice" (No. 1, at 33). In short, Marshall certainly knew that the debate over ratification involved regime questions. There can be little doubt that Marshall believed that the defense of the Constitution demanded the partisanship of republican principles. Marshall wrote with similar studied ambiguity some sixteen years later in *McCulloch v. Maryland*: "Should Congress," he speculated, "in the execution of its powers, adopt measures which are prohibited by the constitution; or should Congress, under the pretext of executing its powers, pass laws for the accomplishment of objects not entrusted to the government, it would become the painful duty of this tribunal, should a case requiring such a decision come before it, to say that such an act was not the law of the land."[72] Marshall here doesn't limit the "painful duty" to cases of a "judiciary nature." This statement reads as a comprehensive duty on the part of the courts to exercise general supervision over matters involving the constitutional separation of powers.

It is not reasonable from a constitutional perspective to allow the means to defeat the end, so even though Marshall seems to insulate political discretion from review, the exercise of discretion cannot be considered an end in itself. It must pursue constitutional purposes and be free from any implication that individual rights are being violated. Since executive discretion was properly and completely exercised, Marbury had acquired a vested right to his commission. And the very notion of the rule of law—indeed the core of constitutional government itself—demands that whenever government or the law has created an injury it must also afford a remedy. As Marshall noted,

[t]he very essence of civil liberty certainly consists in the right of every individual to claim the protection of the laws, whenever he receives an injury. One of the first duties of government is to afford that protection ...

The government of the United States has been emphatically termed a government of laws, and not of men. It will certainly cease to deserve this high appellation, if the laws furnish no remedy for the violation of a vested legal right.[73]

The proper remedy by legal usage and law was clearly a writ of mandamus ordering the Secretary of State to perform his non-discretionary duty to deliver the commission to Marbury.

THE CONSTRUCTION OF ARTICLE III

Marshall, of course, held that Section 13 of the Judiciary Act of 1789 which purported to authorize the Court to issue such a mandamus was unconstitutional and therefore void. It was unconstitutional because it attempted to add to the Court's original jurisdiction by an ordinary act of legislation. The list of original powers in the Constitution, Marshall reasoned, must be read as an exclusive list. Congress' power to make "exceptions" applied only to appellate and not to original jurisdiction. Confronted with such a conflict between fundamental law and ordinary law, the Court was obliged to adhere to the Constitution and ignore the law. As Marshall noted, in one of the most cited passages of the opinion, "[i]t is emphatically the province and duty of the judicial department to say what the law is. Those who apply the rule to particular cases, must of necessity expound and interpret that rule."[74] In the event of a conflict between the fundamental law of the Constitution and an act of legislation, the Court must, of course, choose the fundamental law. "Between these alternatives," Marshall argued, "there is no middle ground. The constitution is either a superior paramount law, unchangeable by ordinary means, or it is on a level with ordinary legislative acts, and, like other acts, is alterable when the legislature shall please to alter it."[75] If the Constitution is "superior paramount law," then "a legislative act contrary to the constitution is not law; if the latter ... be true, then written constitutions are absurd attempts, on the part of the people, to limit a power in its own nature illimitable." The "theory" of limited government presupposes as a fundamental principle of a written constitution that "an act of the legislature, repugnant to the constitution, is void." And in determining whether an ordinary act of legislation is "repugnant," judges "in some cases" must look into and interpret the Constitution, but presumably only to the extent necessary to decide the particular "case or controversy" before the Court. Thus, the duty of the judiciary to "say what the law is" also includes the duty to say what the Constitution as "fundamental law" is. No doubt the same principles of interpretation apply even though the superiority of the Constitution as "fundamental law" makes it a different kind of law. The principles of interpretation are the principles of reason—whether derived from common law principles or principles of natural right—and those principles must take into account the fundamental distinction between superior and inferior law.

Several commentators maintain that Marshall deliberately misconstrued the Constitution in order to enhance judicial power. The distinction between original and appellate jurisdiction, it is argued, is merely preliminary and "Congress may except certain cases otherwise subject only to the Court's appellate jurisdiction by *adding them to the Court's original jurisdiction*, which, it might be added, is precisely what Congress did in Section 13 of the Judiciary Act."[76] But if the "exceptions clause" authorizes Congress to make original what was in the Constitution merely appellate, then it would, in Marshall's terms, also authorize the Congress, by a parity of reasoning, to make what was original to the Court only appellate.

Evidence of the fact that the "distribution of jurisdiction" is merely provisional is said to be provided by the language of the Constitution itself—it is general and "it contains no negative or restrictive words." Thus counsel for Madison argued that there is no logical necessity to read the positive words assigning original jurisdiction as having a restrictive or exclusive force. The principle of interpretation that the inclusion of one thing is necessarily the exclusion of the other has no application here. The absence of any particular exclusion, it is purported, will support the interpretation that the list is provisional and can be expanded under the aegis of the exceptions clause.

But, as Marshall countered, "[a]ffirmative words are often, in their operation, negative of other objects than those affirmed; and in this case, a negative or exclusive sense must be given to them, or they have no operation at all."[77] Marshall's conclusion seems to be irresistible: "If congress remains at liberty to give this court appellate jurisdiction, where the constitution has declared their jurisdiction shall be original; and original jurisdiction where the constitution has declared it shall be appellate; the distribution of jurisdiction, made in the constitution, is form without substance."[78] "Form without substance," of course, is incompatible with the idea of a written constitution, because "[i]t cannot be presumed that any clause in the constitution is intended to be without effect."[79] Rendering some provision "without effect" is tantamount to an amendment of the Constitution by interpretation alone.

Thus, while Marbury has a vested right to his commission, the Supreme Court cannot afford him a remedy because Section 13 of the Judiciary Act authorizing the Court to issue writs of mandamus is unconstitutional. Since in its nature the power of mandamus is an original, not an appellate power, Section 13 is unconstitutional as an attempt to amend the Constitution by an ordinary act of legislation. The Supreme Court need only refuse to act in order to enforce its opinion here. Section 13 applied only to the judiciary and the Court's refusal to exercise power under that section is sufficient to enforce its decision. And, although the case arose in the context of individual rights, it was not resolved on that basis since the Court ruled it had no means under the Constitution to compel the vindication of Marbury's legal right. The legislative attempt to add writs of mandamus to the arsenal of the Court's original powers was, in some sense, an attempt at aggrandizement—the increase of legislative power at the expense of the Constitution's express command to the contrary. Thus, one could argue that the Court did serve as a "bulwark" against legislative encroachment but it failed in its attempt to secure the rights of Marbury, because it was necessary to purchase the first achievement at the expense of the second.

JUDICIAL STATESMANSHIP

Many commentators have noted that Marshall could have avoided ruling on the constitutional issue by declaring that the Supreme Court had no jurisdiction to decide the case. But I think it is too obvious for argument that Marshall went out of his way, not so much to assert the power of judicial review, but to give the nation an authoritative discourse on the fundamental principles of the Constitution. In the wake of the election of 1800 and the attacks on the judiciary that followed in its train, this was a necessary act of judicial statesmanship. Indeed, Marshall's conception of judicial statesmanship was to provide, on appropriate and propitious occasions, a powerful and authoritative explication or exegesis of fundamental constitutional principles. Marshall at least on one occasion referred to the Constitution as a "sacred instrument,"[80] and he seemed to have conceived of judicial statesmanship as providing authoritative commentary on the funda- mental—and even sacred—law of the nation.[81] Creating reverence for the fundamental law was Marshall's most powerful contribution to making the Constitution an instrument "framed for ages to come, and ... designed to approach immortality as nearly as human institutions can approach it."[82] The "framers must be unwise statesmen indeed," Marshall continues, "if they have not provided [the Constitution], as far as its nature will permit, with the means of self-preservation from the perils it may be destined to encounter."[83] It is in the explication and defense of the fundamental law that Marshall lodged the "mea- sure of self-preservation" in the Supreme Court.

Any attempt, of course, to issue a mandamus in the vindication of Marbury's claim would have ended in failure, since as we have seen the judiciary "must ultimately depend upon the aid of the executive arm even for the efficacy of its judgments" (No. 78, at 465). *Marbury* is an example of the Court's power to make a final determination about the meaning of the Constitution because the statute in question was addressed to the Court. The Court merely had to refrain from acting to make its decision—and its interpretation of the Constitution—final. In other cases, where the cooperation of the legislative and executive branch is required, the Court's construction of the Constitution would not have the same air of finality.

The executive and legislative branches equally have the power and responsibility of constitutional construction. Congress, presum- ably, would not pass a law that it believed was unconstitutional, nor would the president sign a bill that he deemed unconstitutional. Courts also make judgments about the constitutionality of laws that come before them in the context of particular cases or controversies. Judges, of course, are bound by their constitutional oaths no less than presi- dents and members of Congress and are duty-bound not to apply laws they deem to be unconstitutional. But are the decisions of judges final? Does the judiciary because of its "peculiar province" to say what the law is occupy a superior position with respect to the determination of constitutionality?

Whenever the Court declares a law unconstitutional it does so in the context of the vindication of particular constitutional rights. If, as Marshall noted, "[t]he province of the court is, solely, to decide on the rights of individuals" and the Constitution imposes a case-or-controversy rule on the Court's jurisdiction, then power to "open the Constitution" is limited to the resolution of particular cases. And, as Marshall argued, the Court can open the Constitution only as far as necessary to vindicate individual rights. The vindication of individual rights will usually mean that any legislation which is void because it is judged to be unconstitutional will bring dismissal of the case against the individual. It is a necessary inference, however, that all those similarly situated will receive the same judgments. But the Court's decision in the context of a particular case will be binding only on the parties. Does the Court's decision in a particular case control the legislative and executive branches as well? *Marbury's* emphasis on the rights of individuals seems to indicate that the decision would be binding on the other branches to the extent that the Court has the last decision, if not the final decision. In a case of dispute between the branches, each acting on its own interpretation of the Constitution, the only possible resolution would be a political one—unless the dispute was severe enough to warrant impeachment of the judges. If the executive continued to enforce the law, and even if Congress cooperated in the enforcement of the law in contravention of the Supreme Court's ruling, the issue would ultimately be decided in elections as the issue would be appealed to the people for ultimate resolution.

ABRAHAM LINCOLN AND JUDICIAL POWER

This appears to be what Abraham Lincoln had in mind when he remarked in his First Inaugural, March 4, 1861 that

> I do not forget the position assumed by some, that constitutional questions are to be decided by the Supreme Court; nor do I deny that such decisions must be binding in any case, upon the parties to a suit, as to the object of that suit, while they are also entitled to very high respect and consideration, in all parallel

cases, by all other departments of the government. And while it is obviously possible that such decision may be erroneous in any given case, still the evil effect following it, being limited to that particular case, with the chance that it may be over-ruled, and never become a precedent for other cases, can better be borne than could the evils of a different practice. At the same time the candid citizen must confess that if the policy of the government, upon vital questions, affecting the whole people, is to be irrevocably fixed by decisions of the Supreme Court, the instant they are made, in ordinary litigation between parties, in personal actions, the people will have ceased, to be their own rulers, having, to that extent, practically resigned their government, into the hands of that eminent tribunal.[84]

Four years earlier Lincoln had said, in explicit reference to the *Dred Scott* decision, that the Supreme Court's

decisions on Constitutional questions, when fully settled, should control, not only the particular cases decided, but the general policy of the country, subject to be disturbed only by amendments of the Constitution…. More than this would be revolution. But we think the Dred Scott decision is erroneous. We know the court that made it, has often over-ruled its own decisions, and we shall do what we can to have it to over-rule this….

If this important decision had been made by the unanimous concurrence of the judges, and without any apparent partisan bias and in accordance with legal public expectation, and with the steady practice of the departments throughout our history, and had been in no part, based on assumed historical facts which are not really true; or, if wanting in some of these, it had been before the court more than once, and had there been affirmed and reaffirmed through a course of years, it then might be, perhaps would be, factious, nay, even revolutionary, to not acquiesce in it as a precedent.

But when we … find it wanting in all these claims to the public confidence, it is not resistance, it is not factious, it is not even disrespectful, to treat it as not having yet quite established a settled doctrine for the country.[85]

Lincoln's view of the judicial power here is fully consistent with *Marbury's* insistence that the province of the Court is solely to decide individual rights. Lincoln, however, seems never to have questioned the fact that the *Dred Scott* case was properly before the Court.

Unlike the *Marbury* decision, however, the *Dred Scott* ruling sparked a political firestorm. *Marbury*, although couched in general terms, was a narrow decision invalidating an attempt on the part of Congress to increase the judicial power of the Supreme Court. *Dred Scott*, on the other hand, was nothing less than "a summons to the Republicans to disband."[86] The Republican Party was organized almost exclusively around opposition to the extension of slavery to the territories and the restoration of the Missouri Compromise slavery restrictions. As Harry Jaffa points out:

> The election of 1856 had revealed that the Democratic party was now a minority party in the nation as far as the presidential vote was concerned. The Whig and Know-Nothing parties were break-ing up rapidly, and it was highly probable that the Republican party would become the majority party in the not very distant future.... The elections of 1856 carried the clear portent of an impending realignment of political strength in the nation, such as had not happened since 1800.[87]

The equivalent analogy for *Marbury v. Madison*, Jaffa argues, would be the declaration by the Marshall Court that "the repeal of the Judiciary Act of 1801 by Jefferson's party had been unconstitutional."[88] The *Dred Scott* decision branded the Republicans as the party of revolution against the Constitution. In many respects, Chief Justice Roger Taney's opin-ion in *Dred Scott* reads as an extended criticism of the Republican Party platform of 1856, and it was the Court's foray into politics that was the focus of Lincoln's opposition.[89]

Lincoln, of course, opposed the *Dred Scott* decision from the mo-ment it was announced. In the first of many such accusations, Stephen A. Douglas, Lincoln's arch-nemesis, accused him of waging a "cru-sade against the Supreme court of the United States on account of the Dred Scott decision."[90] In the third Lincoln-Douglas debate, Douglas argued, in language suggestive of the decision in *Cooper v. Aaron*, that "[i]t is the fundamental principle of the judiciary that its decisions are final. It is created for that purpose, so that when you cannot agree

among yourselves on a disputed point you appeal to the judicial tribunal which steps in and decides for you, and that decision is then
binding on every good citizen. It is the law of the land just as much
with Mr. Lincoln against it as for it."[91] Lincoln gave an extended reply
in the sixth debate: "We oppose the Dred Scott decision in a certain
way," Lincoln stated. "We do not propose that when Dred Scott has
been decided to be a slave by the court, we, as a mob, will decide him
to be free. We do not propose that, when any other one, or one thousand, shall be decided by that court to be slaves, we will in any violent
way disturb the rights of property thus settled, but we nevertheless do
oppose that decision as a political rule, which shall be binding on the
voter, to vote for nobody who thinks it wrong, which shall be binding
on the members of Congress or the President to favor no measure that
does not actually concur with the principles of that decision ... We
propose so resisting it as to have it reversed if we can, and a new
judicial rule established upon this subject."[92] Lincoln was thus mindful of the fact that "[j]udicial opinions are merely explanations of the
judge's reasons, and are no more 'the law' than the statement a president may issue when he signs a bill. Only the judgment is the legally
operative act. The opinion is not itself a legally operative act, though
it is significant because it helps predict how the court will rule in later
cases. Consequently, though the court's *judgment* may bind other
branches, its *opinion* is no more binding than a press release."[93]

Thus Lincoln's opposition was to the decision "as a political rule,"
to be overturned, if possible, by political means. In Lincoln's view, the
decision was factually wrong, the product of a split court and derived
from no precedent. It was thus politically vulnerable and Lincoln made
a political issue of *Dred Scott*, eventually skewering Douglas on the
contradiction between his advocacy of popular sovereignty—the right
of local majorities to vote slavery "up or down"—and the Court's prohibition against voting slavery down because it deprived a slaveowner's
right to property.

Lincoln was convinced that approval of the decision in the election of 1860 would lead to a "second Dred Scott decision" which would
legalize slavery in every state as well.[94] Lincoln's logic was uncontest-
able: *Dred Scott* held that "the right of property in a slave is distinctly
and expressly affirmed in the Constitution." Under Article VI of the
Constitution, "the Judges of every State shall be bound by it, any law

or Constitution of any State to the contrary notwithstanding." "There-fore," Lincoln concluded, "nothing in the Constitution or laws of any State can destroy the right of property in a slave."[95] Lincoln may or may not have known of the California Supreme Court case decided in January 1858 that made precisely this argument in upholding a slaveowner's right to take his slave to a free state.[96] In *Ex Parte Archy*, Justice Peter H. Burnett, citing *Dred Scott*, noted that "[I]t must be con-cluded that where slavery exists, the right of property of the master in the slave must follow as a necessary incident. The right of property is recognized by the Constitution of the United States. The right of prop-erty, having been recognized by the supreme law of the law, certain logical results must follow this recognition." Those "logical results" dictated that slave property must be protected as much as any other form of property and that "[n]o distinction can be made ... between the different descriptions of private property." Thus, despite the fact that the California Constitution prohibited slavery, "in virtue of the paramount sovereignty of the United States, the citizens of each State have the right to pass through the other States, with any property whatever."[97]

Lincoln certainly knew, however, of a case, making its way to the Supreme Court from New York that presented the same issue.[98] Refer-ence to *Lemmon v. The People*, decided by the New York Court of Ap-peals in March 1860, was made in the printed version of the "Cooper Union Speech." Although the speech was delivered before the deci-sion was handed down, a note in the pamphlet reproducing the speech—a publication that Lincoln supervised—referred to the case. The New York Court of Appeals had held that a slave brought from Virginia, even merely as a sojourner, was freed by a New York law and that the privileges and immunities clause of the Federal Constitu-tion could not be construed to give a citizen of another state "rights superior to those of any citizen of New York."[99] Lincoln's annotation to the "Cooper Union Speech" accurately stated that "the State of Virginia is now engaged in carrying this, the Lemmon case, to the Supreme Court of the United States, hoping by a decision there, in accordance with the intimations in the Dred Scott case, to overthrow the Constitution of New York."[100]

The logical necessity of a "second Dred Scott decision" was a constant theme of Lincoln's beginning with the "House Divided Speech" in June of 1858.[101] His fears were not merely fanciful nor the product of an over-active conspiratorial imagination. The nationalization of slavery, of course, would have meant that the framers' intentions with regard to slavery—that freedom is the rule and slavery the exception in the Constitution—would have been overthrown. Lincoln fought mightily to return the issue of slavery to the position that the framers had left it—toleration by necessity until it was politically possible to exclude it entirely. The Constitution, Lincoln insisted, when understood in the light of the principles of the Declaration, had put slavery on the road to ultimate extinction.[102]

Lincoln's principal quarrel with the *Dred Scott* decision was Taney's egregiously mistaken view of the framers' intent on the issue of slavery in the territories. Lincoln's proof that the framers contemplated congressional regulation of slavery in the territories was derived from "contemporaneous construction" by the framers themselves. In his "Cooper Union Speech" Lincoln noted that sixteen of the thirty-nine members of the Constitutional Convention served in the first Congress of the United States and all supported the passage of the Ordinance which "forever prohibited" slavery in the Northwest Territory. Since, as Lincoln noted, the bill "went through all its stages without a word of opposition, and finally passed both branches without yeas and nays," this was "the equivalent to an unanimous passage."[103] These sixteen framers were also present when the Fifth Amendment was passed. The *Dred Scott* decision, of course, had held that the Missouri Compromise law—which used the same "forever prohibited" language of the Northwest Ordinance—was unconstitutional because it deprived a slaveowner of his property without due process of law in violation of the Fifth Amendment. Thus, Taney concluded, "[t]he only power conferred" on Congress by the Constitution "is the power coupled with the duty of guarding and protecting the owner in his rights."[104] But if the same Congress that passed the Northwest Ordinance also passed the Fifth Amendment it is impossible, Lincoln argued, to conclude that the two legislative acts contradict one another. Obviously the Congress—including sixteen framers—believed that the two acts were compatible and that regulation of slavery in the Northwest Territory was not a violation of due process. Lincoln's argument, it seems, is a complete refutation of Taney's decision in *Dred Scott* on the basis of a superior understanding of original intent.[105]

For Lincoln, the Court's decision in a particular case is not conclusive in all other cases, especially when the ruling of the Court is disputed and where there have been no authoritative precedents. Political opposition—to be decided ultimately in elections—is the proper remedy, Lincoln suggests, in those cases where the Court has overreached or has plainly made mistakes. Lincoln makes no reference to the constitutional remedy that Hamilton thought conclusive, the power of impeachment. Lincoln does, however, mention revolution and thus reminds us that the ultimate political authority rests in the "original and supreme" right of the people "to alter or abolish" government. Jaffa has noted that for Jefferson—whom Lincoln said was "the most distinguished politician of our history"[106]—"the right of revolution would forever underlie the right of free elections and would supply a compelling reason why governments ought to have such elections as authentic expressions, not only of the people's will, but also of those rights that are the authority of the people's will. That is to say, the wholesome fear of the people by governments would also be a wholesome fear informing the majority in its dealings with minorities."[107] This was Lincoln's view as he expressed it in the First Inaugural. "A majority, held in restraint by constitutional checks, and limitations, and always changing easily, with deliberate changes of popular opinions and sentiments, is the only true sovereign of a free people. Whoever rejects it, does, of necessity, fly to anarchy or to despotism."[108] "This country with its institutions," Lincoln continued, "belongs to the people who inhabit it. Whenever they shall grow weary of the existing government, they can exercise their *constitutional* right of amending it, or their *revolutionary* right to dismember, or overthrow it."[109]

Thus consent of the governed is not only the basis for the establishment of government, but is required for its operation as well. Elections provide the mechanism for periodic renewal of consent and the opinion that informs that consent is the "real sovereign" in every constitutional regime. Lincoln, as Jefferson before him, was always mindful that constitutional rights ultimately depend upon the right of revolution, a right which, as Marshall noted in *Marbury*, "seldom acts" but is always reserved by the people. It is a right which must be exercised with prudence, but it must never recede too far from the public consciousness.

Some have maintained that the Civil War itself was the second battle in the Revolutionary War, a completion of the principles announced in 1776.[110] Lincoln's whole political career was an effort to perpetuate the principles of the Declaration—the principles of social compact—as the foundation of the Constitution. The Constitution was fundamental law—"organic law" as Lincoln occasionally termed it—because it was an expression of natural right principles embodied in the Declaration, those principles that provided the implicit and explicit referent points for Marshall in *Marbury*. Lincoln's restoration of those principles during the succession crisis, however, was only momentary. Almost immediately after the Union forces proclaimed victory, the forces of Continental thought—principally Hegel and Darwin—overwhelmed the constitutional jurisprudence inspired by Lincoln and the principles of the Declaration. The forces of Continental thought were eventually concentrated in the Progressive movement, a movement that aspired, more than anything else, to read the natural right and natural law principles out of the founding and out of America's constitutional life.[111]

PROGRESSIVISM AND THE CONSTITUTION: FUNDAMENTAL LAW AND ORGANIC WILL

In the universe of the Progressives, history—or progressive history—had supplanted nature or natural right as the standard for morality and politics. Carl Becker, along with Charles Beard the most talented of the progressive historians, wrote in his seminal work *The Declaration of Independence*, first published in 1922, that the naive faith of the framers in universal principles derived from natural right or natural law "could not survive the harsh realities of the modern world,"[112] particularly after the "great discover[ies] of Darwin."[113] The unquestioned premise of Becker's thesis is that all thought is historically conditioned and limited to the historical circumstances that produced it. All thought is merely the epiphenomena of historical forces. Therefore "[t]o ask whether the natural rights philosophy of the Declaration is true or false is essentially a meaningless question."[114] It is "meaningless" because it ignores the historical insight that no thought can be said to "transcend" its own historical epoch. Becker himself never seems to have considered the possibility that this insight was itself the product of his own historical epoch. Rather, he asserted the truth of the insights of the historical school as true for all thought. If all thought is "historical," why not his own? Becker and the historical school seemed either unaware of this question or utterly untroubled by it.

The Progressives took up the theme that the Constitution is process without purpose—whatever purpose there is in the world is assigned by evolutionary or progressive history, not framers of constitutions. The explicit goal of Progressivism was to free the Constitution from its moorings in the founding, most particularly from what were termed the "static" doctrines of the Declaration and its reliance on natural right.

In Madison's constitutional vision, the "reason ... of the public" was the foundation for the moral and political order; it was particularly the foundation for limited government and the rule of law. For it is "reason alone," Madison argued, "that ought to control and regulate the government. The passions ought to be controlled and regulated by the government" (No. 49, at 317). The Progressives sought to elevate administration over government and thus replace limited government with the administrative state. The administrative state grounded itself, not in the "reason of the public," but in the "organic will" of the community. Organic law—the Constitution—is thus transformed into organic will. And, as everyone seems to realize, government derived from "organic will" requires unlimited government since there are no reasoned limits to what can be willed.

Woodrow Wilson, a leader of the Progressive movement, argued that the views of the framers had been exposed by Darwinian thought to be hopelessly outmoded—and dangerously naive. Darwin had made it possible to replace the "static" universe that informed the politics of the framers with one that viewed politics as a "living organism." "Liberty fixed in an unalterable law," Wilson said, "would be no liberty at all."[115] Wilson reserved particular animus for the constitutional separation of powers because it divided the "organic will" of the nation.

> [G]overnment is not a machine, but a living thing. It falls, not under the theory of the universe, but under the theory of organic life. It is accountable to Darwin.... No living thing can have its organs offset against each other as checks, and live. On the

contrary, its life is dependent upon their quick cooperation, their ready response to the commands of instinct or intelligence, their amicable community of purpose. Living political constitutions must be Darwinian in structure and in practice.[116]

This Progressive critique of the founding finds its most powerful expression today in the rhetoric of the "living constitution," which must evolve and adapt to changing circumstances and especially to changing (and progressive) notions of morality.

The only principle of liberty that can be recognized within the Darwinian universe is the freedom to change or progress; but it is a change or progress that has no particular end or purpose. The Darwinian view makes it impossible to distinguish between liberty and necessity. And it is the conflation of liberty and necessity that forms the basis of the administrative state. It is necessity, not liberty and the consequent centrality of moral choice, that is the motive force at the core of the administrative state. Rights are no longer understood as the irrefragable dictate of human nature—that "all men are created equal"—but as simply "needs" or "values" competing for recognition in the political marketplace.

In the arena of constitutional law, nothing epitomizes the Progressive world-view more than Justice Oliver Wendell Holmes' dissenting opinion in *Gitlow v. New York* (1925). "If, in the long run," Holmes argued, "the beliefs expressed in proletarian dictatorship are destined to be accepted by the dominant forces of the community, the only meaning of free speech is that they should be given their chance and have their way."[117] An eminent scholar has recently declared that this statement, so often celebrated in the circles of ideological liberalism, "may be the single most disgraceful sentence in our jurisprudence."[118] The reason this commentator regards the statement as "disgraceful" is because its author (and Justice Louis Brandeis who joined the dissent) "seem to have forgotten that our system of government is based on an original agreement (implemented by popular ratification) to unite in accepting only a form of government specifically designed to protect the inalienable rights of every citizen. Every system of government opposed to such an end is considered fundamentally illegitimate and inherently antagonistic to our own."[119] Thus Holmes would subordinate the "original and supreme will" of the people to a subsequent and inferior will, thereby undermining the very foundation of the Constitution.[120]

Holmes seemed to argue that the people were free to use freedom of speech and free elections to destroy freedom. Freedom of speech was regarded by the framers, not as an end in itself, but as a means to secure free government. Free government was the end for which freedom of speech existed. In Holmes' analysis the means can be a mechanism for destroying the ends. The Holmesean position that free speech has no particular ends or purposes would be eminently sensible if the Constitution had no ends or purposes. The framers certainly believed that the Constitution was designed to protect liberty, not destroy it. And they were not disillusioned about the difference between freedom and slavery—freedom was not just another "fighting faith." It would be foolish to allow the indispensable means of preserving free government, freedom of speech, to destroy the ends of free government. But if ends disappear from the universe of constitutional discourse, it is difficult—indeed impossible—to discriminate among the means. Holmes, of course, did not believe that reason could determine moral principles nor in any way settle the question between competing moral claims. Moral principles were in Holmes' language merely "fighting faiths" competing for recognition in the public arena. The principles of the American Constitution as understood by its framers are no less a "fighting faith" than communism, fascism or wahhabism. "Fighting faiths" merely depend upon acceptance or commitment. And it is the strength of the commitment, not its intrinsic reasonableness, that determines whether it is accepted by the "dominant forces" of the community. Thus, in Holmes' view—the view that prevails in today's constitutional jurisprudence—all "fighting faiths" must be tolerated because reason cannot decide between them. Toleration seems therefore to be a value that transcends "fighting faiths." But how, in a universe where there are only "fighting faiths," does "toleration" find any ground of exemption? Surely Holmes must have realized that the dictatorship of the proletariat would have been the end of toleration. But he seems not to have thought the issue through adequately—he merely accepted the historicist premises of the movement of which he was, wittingly or unwittingly, a part. Today, Holmes' view is reflected in the Supreme Court's doctrine that "[u]nder the First Amendment there is no such thing as a false idea."[121]

BROWN V. BOARD OF EDUCATION AND THE CONSTITUTION

If Holmes understood the Constitution as merely instituting a process for decisionmaking that was indifferent to the decisions that were produced by the process, it was only a short step to reading the Constitution out of constitutional law entirely. That, I believe, was the work of *Brown v. Board of Education* (1954). The holding in *Brown* was eminently correct; any reasonable interpretation of the equal protection clause would have concluded that racial classifications can play no role in constitutional government simply because race is an accidental rather than an essential feature of human nature and the principles that flow from human nature—those principles adumbrated in the Declaration. There is abundant evidence that the framers of the Fourteenth Amendment believed it to be a completion of the founding in the sense that it finally brought the Constitution into formal harmony with the principles of the Declaration.[122]

William Nelson writes that "[i]n *Brown*, the Supreme Court rejected the narrow version of judicial review focusing on adherence to precedent, framers' intentions, and the Constitution's text." Nelson also rightly notes that *Brown* was a pivotal case in the Court's doctrinal move away from its main focus on the protection of individual rights to the protection of the group rights of "discrete and insular minorities."[123] The Supreme Court thus abandoned one of the primary injunctions of *Marbury* that "[t]he province of the court is, solely, to decide on the rights of individuals ..." The Court's new role as "virtual representative" of "discrete and insular minorities" made forays into the area of politics and policy far easier for the Court.[124]

Chief Justice Earl Warren's opinion in *Brown* is utterly indefensible. In one of the most curious arguments ever mounted in a Supreme Court opinion, Warren asserted that "we cannot turn the clock back to 1868 when the [Fourteenth] Amendment was adopted."[125] The reason is that the intentions of the framers of the Fourteenth Amendment are "[a]t best ... inconclusive."[126] "The most avid proponents of the post-War Amendments," Warren noted, "undoubtedly intended them to remove all legal distinctions ... Their opponents, just as certainly, were antagonistic to both the letter and the spirit of the Amendments and wished them to have the most limited effect. What others in Congress and the state legislatures had in mind cannot be determined with any degree of certainty."[127] Why the opponents of the Fourteenth Amendment are included in the argument is something of a mystery—after all, they lost! To aver that there was opposition to the amendment and that this opposition renders the discovery of intent doubtful defies logic. What is even more puzzling is the fact that the Chief Justice admitted that the "most avid proponents"—presumably including those who drafted the amendment—"*undoubtedly* intended" to remove all legal distinctions among American citizens. Yet in the light of the undoubted intentions of the framers, Warren casually rejects the reliability of such intentions and turns to the more reliable evidence of modern psychology.[128]

Once it is assumed that the intentions of the framers can play no role in the decision of the case, it becomes necessary to find some other authoritative source as ground for the opinion. Warren found this in the authority of modern social science, specifically modern psychology. Modern psychology buttresses the idea that "separate is inherently unequal" because the mere fact of separation "generates" among school children "a feeling of inferiority as to their status in the community that may affect their hearts and minds in a way unlikely ever to be undone."[129] Thus, "[w]hatever may have been the extent of psychological knowledge at the time of Plessy v. Ferguson, this finding is amply supported by modern authority."[130] *Plessy* had held that any "assumption that the enforced separation of the two races stamps the colored race with a badge of inferiority is not by reason of anything found in the act, but solely because the colored race chooses to put that construction upon it."[131] The difference between the *Brown* decision and *Plessy* was in the interpretation of the facts, not in the principle of constitutional construction. *Plessy* had held that a "feeling of inferiority" was not a fact of inferiority from the point of view of the equal protection clause. *Brown*, on the basis of the findings of modern psychology, held that a feeling of inferiority must now be regarded as a "fact" of inferiority. But modern psychology can hardly provide the stable ground for constitutionalism that is available in the Constitution itself. The tenets of modern psychology change—or "progress"—frequently; the principles of the Constitution were designed, in Marshall's memorable phrase to be "permanent."

In his dissenting opinion in *Grutter v. Bollinger*, Justice Clarence Thomas complained about the fact that the majority opinion "relies heavily on social science evidence to justify" its decision on diversity. Thomas cited credible studies that "heterogeneity actually impairs learning among black students ... and that black students experience superior cognitive development at Historically Black Colleges."[132] Does this new evidence require a new Supreme Court ruling resurrecting the "separate but equal doctrine?"

The reliance on social science evidence makes it easy—indeed necessary—to ignore the Constitution. Once the Constitution can be safely ignored, then there is no reason not to adopt other constitutions that might seem to be more attractive at the moment. References to international law and international conventions—as well as international public opinion—are becoming more frequent in Supreme Court decisions. In a recent speech to the American Constitution Society, Justice Ruth Bader Ginsburg stated that "[o]ur island or lone ranger mentality is beginning to change." Justices, she said, "are becoming more open to comparative and international law perspectives."[133] Indeed, in her concurring opinion in *Grutter v. Bollinger* (2003), Ginsburg cited the International Convention on the Elimination of All Forms of Racial Discrimination in support of the decision to uphold an affirmative action program at the University of Michigan law school.[134] The Court cited the opinion of "the world community" in *Atkins v. Virginia*, holding that the execution of the mentally retarded violates the Eighth Amendment's restrictions against "cruel and unusual punishment,"[135] and Justice David Souter—in a most incredible display of myopia— even relied upon the Zimbabwe Supreme Court to buttress his opinion that excessive delays in executing the death penalty amount to "cruel and unusual punishment."[136] More importantly, Justice Anthony Kennedy cited cases from the European Court of Human Rights as evidence that homosexual sodomy "has been accepted as an integral part of human freedom in many other countries." Kennedy used this evidence to conclude that "[t]here has been no showing that in this country the governmental interest in circumscribing personal choice is somehow more legitimate or urgent."[137] Justice Antonin Scalia in an acerb dissent warned that "[t]he Court's discussion of these foreign views (ignoring, of course, the many countries that have retained criminal prohibitions on sodomy) is therefore meaningless dicta. Dangerous dicta, however, since 'this Court ... should not impose foreign moods, fads, or fashions on Americans.'"[138]

Scalia's point about the danger of using foreign—even European—precedents is well taken. It suffices only to recall Justice Taney's opinion in *Dred Scott*. Taney relied on the "public opinion … which prevailed in the civilized and enlightened portions of the world at the time the Declaration of Independence and … the Constitution of the United States was framed and adopted" to buttress his argument that no black of African descent could ever become a citizen of the United States. "[T]he public history of every European nation," Taney reports, "displays … in a manner too plain to be mistaken" that blacks had "been regarded as beings of an inferior order; and altogether unfit to associate with the white race, either in social or political relations; and so far inferior that they had no rights which the white man was bound to respect; and that the Negro might justly and lawfully be reduced to slavery for his benefit." The "fixed and universal" opinion "in the civilized portion of the white race" regarded blacks of African descent as mere articles of "merchandise and traffic" to be "bought and sold … whenever a profit could be made by it."[139] Reliance on European opinion, rather than the language of the Declaration and the Constitution interpreted according to the true intentions of the framers, led Taney to the wholly erroneous conclusion that blacks of African descent were not included in the Declaration's injunction that "all men are created equal" and therefore could never be citizens of the United States. Lincoln's refutation of Taney's reasoning in the "Standard Maxim Speech" and the "Cooper Union Speech" is unassailable. But Lincoln's unassailable logic did not prevent civil war—and may have precipitated it.

It would be bold (and perhaps hyperbolic) to argue that the increased reliance on European opinion that seems to be making headway in the Supreme Court is the *terminus ad quem* of the *Brown* decision and the Progressive revolution it culminated. But the evidence ineluctably points in that direction.

Endnotes

1. William H. Rehnquist, "Remarks of the Chief Justice: My Life in the Law Series," *Duke Law Journal* 52 (2003): 789-90.

2. William Brennan, "The Constitution of the United States: Contemporary Ratification," Text and Teaching Symposium, Georgetown University, October 12, 1985, reprinted in *The Great Debate: Interpreting Our Written Constitution* (Washington, D.C.: The Federalist Society, 1986), 19, 25, 23.

3. Ibid., 35. Curiously enough, Brennan asserts that there is one constitutional principle that is "fixed and immutable"—that capital punishment "is under all circumstances cruel and unusual punishment prohibited by the Eighth and Fourteenth Amendments." This "fixed and immutable" view, however, is at odds with the literal language of the Constitution which lists "capital" crimes in the Fifth Amendment along with a due process requirement for depriving a person of life, liberty or property. It almost goes without saying that the Fifth Amendment was passed contemporaneously with the Eight Amendment's ban on "cruel and unusual punishment." This seems to be proof that the framers did not regard capital punishment as cruel and unusual. Brennan wisely does not attempt to explain the unexplainable: how it is possible for one "fixed and immutable" point to exist in a constitutional universe that is constantly evolving.

4. Cooper v. Aaron, 358 U.S. 1, 17 (1958).

5. Marbury v. Madison, 5 U.S. (1 Cranch.) 137, 179-80 (1803).

6. Kenneth Karst, "Cooper v. Aaron," in *Encyclopedia of the American Constitution*, Leonard Levy, et al., eds. (New York: Macmillan Publishing Company, 1986), 2:502.

7. Marbury v. Madison, 176.

8. John Hart Ely, *Democracy and Distrust: A Theory of Judicial Review* (Cambridge: Harvard University Press, 1980), 39.

9. A commentator on an earlier draft of this article disagreed that *Brown* was the first case explicitly to declare the irrelevance of the Constitution. That "honor," he declared, belonged to *Dred Scott*, the first "substantive due process case." In an argument redolent of Robert Bork's claims in *The Tempting of America* (New York: The Free Press, 1990), this commentator maintained that Taney manufactured a right that was nowhere to be found in the Constitution—the right to own slaves. Thus Taney "poured substance" into the due process clause of the Fifth Amendment, a provision that was intended only to protect procedure. Defining "substance" is properly a role for the legislature and the Court had usurped legislative power in an unconscionable act of judicial activism. The notion that the Constitution does not recognize the right to hold slaves is, of course, utterly ludicrous. The three-fifths clause and the fugitive slave clause, however much they may have been compromises with

constitutional principle, are nonetheless recognition of the right to property in slaves. Besides, if the Court had reached out to overrule the Missouri Compromise, it was merely ratifying what Congress had *already done* in the Kansas-Nebraska Act of 1854. Among a host of other considerations, the author of the Kansas-Nebraska Act, Stephen A. Douglas, stated repeatedly on the floor of the Senate that the constitutionality of the act was a matter to be determined by the Supreme Court. (*Congressional Globe*, 34th Cong., 1st Sess. 797, 1371-72 [1856]; See David M. Potter, *The Impending Crisis, 1848-1861* [New York: Harper and Row, 1976], 74, 116, 161, 271, 276, 285, 292, 294, 403, 410.) President Franklin Pierce in his message to Congress in December, 1855 had opined that the Missouri Compromise "restrictions were, in the estimation of many thoughtful men, null from the beginning, unauthorized by the Constitution ... and inconsistent with the equality of these States." And in his last message to Congress in December 1856, delivered while the *Dred Scott* decision was under deliberation by the Supreme Court, Pierce pronounced the Missouri Compromise law a "mere nullity" and a "monument of error and a beacon of warning to the legislature and the statesman." (*A Compilation of the Messages and Papers of the Presidents,* James D. Richardson, ed. [Washington, D.C.: Bureau of National Literature and Art, 1905], 5:348, 401.) Thus, if *Dred Scott* was an example of judicial activism, it was authorized *in advance* by the legislative branch and had the explicit approval of the executive branch! The notion of "substantive due process" was wholly unknown to Taney and his contemporaries. Indeed, Taney was adamant in his professed adherence to original intent jurisprudence: the Constitution, Taney wrote, "must be construed now as it was understood at the time of its adoption. It is not only the same in words, but the same in meaning ... and as long as it continues to exist in its present form, it speaks not only in the same words, but with the same meaning and intent with which it spoke when it came from the hands of its framers, and was voted on and adopted by the people of the United States" (Dred Scott v. Sandford, 60 U.S. [19 How.] 426 [1857]). In his desire to adhere to original intent, Taney was eminently correct; but his constitutional construction was utterly wrong. He was unable to uncover and articulate the original intent of the Constitution. But no one can doubt that his analysis—however mistaken—centered on the Constitution. As we will see below, *Brown*, on the other hand, explicitly rejects any reliance on the Constitution.

10. Karst, "Constitutional Equality and the Role of the Judiciary," in *The Promise of American Politics: Principles and Practice After 200 Years*, Robert Utley, ed. (Lanham, Md.: University Press of America, 1989), 211.

11. Robert L. Clinton, *Marbury v. Madison and Judicial Review* (Lawrence, Kan.: University Press of Kansas, 1989), 43-55; William E. Nelson, *Marbury v. Madison: The Origins and Legacy of Judicial Review* (Lawrence, Kan.: University Press of Kansas, 2000), 35-40; an excellent summary is Scott D. Gerber, "The Myth of *Marbury v. Madison* and the Origins of Judicial Review," in *Marbury v. Madison: Documents and Commentary*, Mark A. Graber and Michael Perhac, eds. (Washington, D.C.: Congressional Quarterly Press, 2002), 1-15. "There is no question that *Marbury* is a landmark case. However the case simply established, once and for all, a doctrine that has deep roots in early American constitutional theory and practice."

12. Marbury v. Madison, 177.

13. Ibid., 178. See Charles F. Hobson, *The Great Chief Justice: John Marshall and the Rule of Law* (Lawrence, Kan.: University Press of Kansas, 1996), 58: "The omission of citations to authorities was no doubt deliberate, for Marshall was surely acquainted with the so-called 'precedents' for judicial review. From his perspective these cases were not needed to establish the principle of judicial review, however useful they might be as illustrations of the principle. He firmly believed that judicial review was grounded in the very nature of American constitutionalism, if not confirmed by the text of the Constitution itself. A practice that was sanctioned by the highest authority did not require further support."

14. Hayburn's Case, 2 U.S. (2 Dall.) 409 (1792). See Charles G. Haines, *The American Doctrine of Judicial Supremacy* (Berkeley: University of California Press, 1932), 173-79.

15. William W. Crosskey, *Politics and the Constitution in the History of the United States* (Chicago: University of Chicago Press, 1953), 2:974-75.

16. Clinton, *Marbury v. Madison and Judicial Review*, 56, 55, 66-67, 76.

17. Leonard Levy, "Judicial Review, History, and Democracy," in *Judicial Review and the Supreme Court*, Leonard Levy, ed. (New York: Harper Torchbooks, 1967), 11.

18. Ibid., 10.

19. Edward S. Corwin, "The Establishment of Judicial Review," *Michigan Law Review* 9 (1910): 102, 108 (emphasis original); Corwin, "The Progress of Constitutional Theory Between the Declaration of Independence and the Meeting of the Philadelphia Convention," *American Historical Review* 30 (1925): 511, 513-14, 527, 534-36.

20. Alexander Hamilton, James Madison, John Jay, *The Federalist Papers*, Clinton Rossiter, ed. (New York: New American Library, 1961), No. 48, 309. All further references to *The Federalist Papers* will be in the text.

21. *The Records of the Federal Convention of 1787*, Max Farrand, ed. (New Haven: Yale University Press, 1966), 1:134.

22. Ibid., 2:27.

23. Ibid., 2:28; 1:164-65, 447.

24. Haines, *The American Doctrine of Judicial Supremacy,* 109-12; Crosskey, *Politics and the Constitution in the History of the United States,* 2:965-968; Clinton, *Marbury v. Madison and Judicial Review,* 51-53. Clinton uses *Trevett v. Weeden* as part of the evidence from state judiciaries that "the theory of judicial function proposed by the Founders and later expounded by Marshall and his Court was quite well-developed by the 1780s." But it is clear that Madison believed that lack of judicial independence made the Rhode Island court ineffective as a check on legislative power, regardless of how sound the arguments of the judges might have been in theory. What was lacking in Rhode Island—and in all the states—was a mechanism for enforcing the separation of powers in practice, a mechanism that required a truly independent judiciary possessing the power to declare laws of coordinate branches "null and void." See *The Records of the Federal Convention of 1787,* 2:93. Thus, as Madison indicates, the Rhode Island case was hardly a precedent for the independent judiciary that was contemplated in the Constitution of 1787.

25. *The Records of the Federal Convention of 1787,* 2:28.

26. Letter to Thomas Jefferson, Sept. 6, 1787, in *The Papers of James Madison,* Robert Rutland, et al., eds. (Chicago: University of Chicago Press, 1977), 10:163-64.

27. Letter to Thomas Jefferson, Oct. 24, 1787 in ibid., 10:209-11.

28. Letter to Thomas Jefferson, June 27, 1823, in *The Writings of James Madison,* Gaillard Hunt, ed. (New York: G. P. Putnam's Sons, 1900-10), 9:142. See Letter to Spencer Roane, June 29, 1821, in ibid., 9:65.

29. *The Debates in the Several State Conventions on the Adoption of the Federal Constitution,* Jonathan Elliot, ed. (Philadelphia: J. B. Lippincott Co., 1836), 3:654.

30. Cohens v. Virginia, 19 U.S. (6 Wheat.) 264, 381-82, 414 (1821).

31. One perceptive commentator argues that Marshall also "interpreted the contract clause in the spirit of Madison's negative on state laws and brought within its purview a larger class of state legislation than was contemplated by anyone at the time the Constitution was adopted ... [H]e believed ... that the contract clause, like the negative, would embrace not only past and present evils but also guard against unforeseen cases that might arise in consequence of state legislative ingenuity." Hobson, *The Great Chief Justice: John Marshall and the Rule of Law,* 78.

32. Marbury v. Madison, 180.

33. Hobson, *The Great Chief Justice: John Marshall and the Rule of Law,* 62.

34. *The Records of the Federal Convention of 1787,* 1:21.

35. Ibid., 2:79.

36. Ibid., 2:74.

37. Ibid.; 2:76 (Morris) and 1:254 (Wilson).

38. Ibid., 2:73 and 2:78 (Mason).

39. Ibid., 2:74.

40. Ibid., 2:75.

41. Ibid., 1:98.

42. Ibid., 1:97.

43. Ibid., 2:76-77.

44. Ibid., 2:430.

45. Ibid., 2:73.

46. *The Debates In the Several State Conventions On the Adoption of the Federal Constitution*, 2:196.

47. Ibid., 3:553.

48. Marbury v. Madison, 176.

49. Nelson, *Marbury v. Madison: The Origins and Legacy of Judicial Review*, 63.

50. Letter to Nicholas P. Trist, February 15, 1830, in *The Writings of James Madison*, 9:355; see Letter to Daniel Webster, March 15, 1833, in ibid., 6:605; "Sovereignty," in ibid., 9:570-71.

51. Harry V. Jaffa, *A New Birth of Freedom: Abraham Lincoln and the Coming of the Civil War* (Lanham, Md.: Rowman and Littlefield, 2000), 27.

52. Marbury v. Madison, 176.

53. Ibid.

54. See McCulloch v. Maryland, 17 U.S. (4 Wheat.) 316, 414-15 (1819).

55. Edward S. Corwin, *John Marshall and the Constitution* (New Haven: Yale University Press, 1920), 122.

56. Plato, *Laws* 968a-b.

57. Cohens v. Virginia, 380-81.

58. Ibid., 382.

59. Ibid., 384

60. Sturges v. Crowinshield, 17 U.S. (4 Wheat.) 122, 202 (1819). Trustees of Dartmouth College v. Woodward, 17 U.S. (4 Wheat.) 587, 645 (1819); Fletcher v. Peck, 10 U.S. (6 Cranch.) 87, 135 (1810). Hamilton wrote in *The Federalist*, that "there is not a syllable in the plan under consideration which *directly* empowers the national courts to construe the laws according to the spirit of the Constitution, or which gives them any greater latitude in this respect than may be claimed by the courts of every State. I admit, however, that the Constitution ought to be the standard of construction for the laws, and that wherever there is an evident opposition, the laws ought to give place to the Constitution. But this

doctrine is not deducible from any circumstance peculiar to the plan of the convention, but from the general theory of a limited Constitution" (No. 81, at 482 [emphasis original]). While there is nothing in the Constitution that "directly" empowers the Court to construe the Constitution according to its "spirit," it is authorized by the "general theory of a limited Constitution," i.e., *from its "spirit."*

61. "Fragment on the Constitution and the Union," in *The Collected Works of Abraham Lincoln,* Roy Basler, ed. (New Brunswick, N.J.: Rutgers University Press, 1953), 4:168-69.

62. Marbury v. Madison, 176.

63. *The Records of the Federal Convention of 1787,* 2:56.

64. For an extended account of the theory of the separation of powers, see Edward J. Erler, *The American Polity: Essays on the Theory and Practice of Constitutional Government* (New York: Crane Russak, 1991), 39-57.

65. Cohens v. Virginia, 264.

66. Marbury v. Madison, 170.

67. *Annals of Congress* (Gales and Seaton ed., 1834), 1:454.

68. Ibid., 1:458.

69. Marbury v. Madison, 170.

70. Nelson, *Marbury v. Madison: The Origins and Legacy of Judicial Review,* 59.

71. Robert K. Faulkner, *The Jurisprudence of John Marshall* (Princeton, N.J.: Princeton University Press, 1968), 201.

72. McCulloch v. Maryland, 423-24.

73. Marbury v. Madison, 163.

74. Ibid., 178.

75. Ibid., 177.

76. William W. Van Alystyne, "A Critical Guide to Marbury v. Madison," 1969 *Duke Law Journal* (1969): 32. This argument was also suggested by Edward S. Corwin, *The Doctrine of Judicial Review* (Princeton, N.J.: Princeton University Press, 1914), 4-5.

77. Marbury v. Madison, 174. David Currie argues in *The Constitution in the Supreme Court: The First Hundred Years 1789-1888* (Chicago: University of Chicago Press, 1985), 69, that "Marshall himself was to reject the implications of the *Marbury* reasoning in *Cohens v. Virginia,* where he declared that Congress could grant appellate jurisdiction in cases where the Constitution provided for original." I believe this assessment is mistaken. It is true that Marshall admitted that in "the reasoning of the court in support of [the *Marbury*] decision some expressions are used which go far beyond" what was necessary. Nevertheless, Marshall argued, there is

no inconsistency in the two decisions. "It is, we think, apparent, that to give this distributive clause the interpretation contended for, to give to its affirmative words a negative operation, in every possible case, would, in some instances, defeat the obvious intention of the article. Such an interpretation would not consist with those rules which, from time immemorial, have guided courts, in the construction of instruments brought under their consideration. It must, therefore, be discarded. Every part of the article must be taken into view, and that construction adopted which will consist with its words, and promote its general intention. The court may imply a negative from affirmative words, where the implication promotes, not where it defeats the intention" (*Cohens v. Virginia*, 393). In other words, whether general language is to be construed as exclusive or inclusive depends upon what constitutional principle is at issue and which reading will "preserve the true intent and meaning of the instrument" (Ibid.). In *Cohens*, reading the Article III language as exclusive—as *Marbury* did—would defeat the framers' intention that the Court be given "final construction" of the Constitution where a state court has ruled on a federal issue (Ibid., 173). Where a case should have been original to the Supreme Court, the Court can nevertheless still take jurisdiction in its appellate capacity when necessary to render a final judgment. The construction of constitutional language must always be governed by the ends of the Constitution, and this means, above all, its "fundamental principles." The argument that *Marbury* and *Cohens* were in conflict was also suggested by Corwin, *The Doctrine of Judicial Review*, 6.

78. Marbury v. Madison, 172.

79. Ibid.

80. U.S. v. Maurice, 26 F. Cas. 1211, 1213 (1823).

81. See Edward S. Corwin, *John Marshall and the Constitution*, 2-3.

82. Cohens v. Virginia, 387.

83. Ibid.

84. *The Collected Works of Abraham Lincoln*, 4:268.

85. Ibid., 2:401

86. Harry V. Jaffa, *Crisis of the House Divided: An Interpretation of the Lincoln-Douglas Debates* (Garden City, N.Y.: Doubleday and Co., 1959), 286.

87. Ibid., 285-86.

88. Ibid.

89. *The Collected Works of Abraham Lincoln*, 2:551; 3:80, 232, 242, 255.

90. "Speech of Stephen A. Douglas, Chicago, July 9, 1858," in *The Lincoln-Douglas Debates of 1858*, Robert W. Johannsen, ed. (New York: Oxford University Press, 1965), 31. See *The Collected Works of Abraham Lincoln*, 3:9, 54, 242, 259, 267, 287.

91. *The Collected Works of Abraham Lincoln*, 3:143.

92. Ibid., 3:255.

93. Daniel Farber, *Lincoln's Constitution* (Chicago: University of Chicago Press, 2003), 182, 183, 186; much the same point was made by Edward S. Corwin, "What Kind of Judicial Review Did the Framers Have in Mind?" in *Corwin's Constitution: Essays and Insights of Edward S. Corwin*, Kenneth Crews, ed. (New York: Greenwood Press, 1986), 84. This essay was first published in 1938.

94. *The Collected Works of Abraham Lincoln*, 2:467, 552-53; 3:29, 89, 225-26, 230-31, 232, 550; 4:151

95. Ibid., 3:230-31, 250, 421.

96. In re Archy, 9 Cal. 147 (1858).

97. Ibid., 162. See William E. Franklin, "The Archy Case: The California Supreme Court Refuses to Free a Slave," *Pacific Historical Review* 32 (1963): 137-154.

98. "Cooper Union Speech," in *The Collected Works of Abraham Lincoln*, 3:548; Paul Finkelman, *An Imperfect Union: Slavery, Federalism, and Comity* (Chapel Hill, N.C.: University of North Carolina Press, 1981), 316-338.

99. Lemmon v. The People, 20 N.Y. 562, 609, 611 (1860). "The [New York] Legislature had declared, in effect, that no person shall bring a slave into this State, even in the course of a journey between two slaveholding States, and that if he does, the slave shall be free. Our own citizens are of course bound by this regulation. If the owner of these is not in like manner bound it is because, in his quality of citizen of another State, he has rights superior to those of any citizen of New York ... and is entitled to have those laws enforced in the courts, notwithstanding the mandate of our own laws to the contrary." In disallowing the privileges and immunities claim the court argued that "the owner cannot lawfully do anything which our laws do not permit to be done by one of our own citizens, and as a citizen of this State cannot bring a slave within its limits except under the condition that he shall immediately become free, the owner of these slaves could not do it without involving himself in the same consequences."

100. *The Collected Works of Abraham Lincoln*, 3:548-49. See Lemmon v. The People, 20 N.Y. 562, 628 (1860). The Virginia slaveowner had claimed protection for his property under the privileges and immunities clause of Article IV. The New York Court of Appeals rejected this argument, noting that the relation of master and slave "exists, if at all under the laws of Virginia, and it is not claimed that there is any paramount obligation resting on this State to recognize and administer the laws of Virginia

within her territory, if they be contrary or repugnant to her policy or prejudicial to her interests."

101. Ibid. 2:467, 552-53; 3:29, 89, 225-26, 230-31, 232, 550; 4:151.

102. Ibid., 2:461, 492, 498, 514; 3:18, 92-93, 117, 180-81, 276, 307, 404.

103. Ibid., 3:527.

104. Dred Scott v. Sandford, 452.

105. See supra note 3.

106. *The Collected Works of Abraham Lincoln*, 2:249.

107. Jaffa, *A New Birth of Freedom: Abraham Lincoln and the Coming of the Civil War*, 8, 280-81, 416.

108. *The Collected Works of Abraham Lincoln*, 4:268. See "Speech at Chicago," December 10, 1856, 2:385: "Our government rests in public opinion. Whoever can change public opinion, can change the government, practically just so much. Public opinion, on any subject, always has a 'central idea,' from which all its minor thoughts radiate. That 'central idea' in our political public opinion, at the beginning was, and until recently has continued to be, 'the equality of men.'" See 2:405; 256, 281-82; 3:27, 312-13; 4:17.

109. Ibid., 2:269.

110. See Edward Erler, "From Subjects to Citizens: The Social Contract Origins of American Citizenship," in *The American Founding and the Social Compact*, Thomas G. West and Ronald J. Pestritto, eds. (Lanham, Md.: Lexington Books, 2003), 166.

111. The depth of Lincoln's philosophic statesmanship and the power of his philosophic rhetoric are indicated by a comparison of the rhetorical structure of the First and Second Inaugural. The First Inaugural begins with custom ("In compliance with a custom as old as the government itself ...") and ends with nature ("... the better angels of our nature."); the Second Inaugural begins with a "second coming" ("At this second appearing to take the oath ...") and ends with peace among nations ("... a lasting peace, among ourselves, and with all nations."). Thus the First Inaugural represents an appeal to reason whereas the Second represents an appeal to revelation. Harry Jaffa has argued—perfectly in the spirit of Lincoln—that the genius of the American founding is the recognition of the claims of both reason and revelation. The truth of the Declaration of Independence, Jaffa asserts, is "a truth no less of unassisted human reason than of divine revelation" (*Original Intent and the Framers of the Constitution: A Disputed Question* [Washington, D.C.: Regnery Gateway, 1994], 350; *New Birth of Freedom: Abraham Lincoln and the*

Coming of the Civil War, 122, 146, 403). It is obvious, however, that the "somber theology" of the Second Inaugural has none of the optimism of the First Inaugural. The two speeches represent a move from comedy, as it were, to tragedy.

112. Carl L. Becker, *The Declaration of Independence: A Study in the History of Political Ideas* (New York: Alfred A. Knopf, 1942 [originally published in 1922]), 279.

113. Ibid., 274.

114. Ibid., 277. See Jaffa, *New Birth of Freedom: Abraham Lincoln and the Coming of the Civil War*, 73-152. Jaffa provides a definitive critique of Becker.

115. Woodrow Wilson, *Constitutional Government*, in *The Papers of Woodrow Wilson*, Arthur S. Link, ed. (Princeton, N.J.: Princeton University Press, 1968), 18:71.

116. Ibid., 106.

117. Gitlow v. N.Y., 268 U.S. 652, 673 (1925) (Holmes, J., dissenting). John Marshall as a young man had studied assiduously Alexander Pope's *Essay on Man*, writing long passages in his copy book. Albert J. Beveridge, *The Life of John Marshall* (Boston: Houghton Mifflin Company, 1929), 1:44-45. Corwin perceptively captured the difference between the founding era and the Progressive era by noting that: "The *Essay on Man* filled, we may surmise, much the same place in the education of the first generation of American judges that Herbert Spencer's *Social Statics* filled in that of the judges of a later day." *John Marshall and the Constitution*, 28.

118. David Lowenthal, *Present Dangers: Rediscovering the First Amendment* (Dallas: Spence Publishing Co., 2002), 37.

119. Ibid., 35.

120. Madison, in his essay "Sovereignty" explained with mathematical precision the social contract origins of civil society and its relation to majority rule. "Whatever be the hypothesis of the origin of the *lex majoris partis*, it is evident that it operates as a plenary substitute of the will of the majority of the society for the will of the whole society; and that the sovereignty of the society as vested in and exercisable by the majority, may do anything that could be *rightfully* done by the unanimous concurrence of the members; the reserved rights of individuals (of conscience for example) in becoming parties to the original compact being beyond the legitimate reach of sovereignty, wherever vested or however viewed" (emphasis original). *The Writings of James Madison*, 9:570-71. Thus, for Madison, even "unanimous concurrence" is bound by what is "*rightful*" or intrinsically just. As a "plenary substitute" for the whole, the majority can also legitimately do only what is "rightful." It may not, any more

than unanimous consent, invade the rights of individuals or minorities. We note also that the Declaration specifies that consent authorizes only the "just powers" of government, not all powers.

121. Gertz v. Welch, 418 U.S. 323, 339 (1974); Barenblat v. U.S. 360 U.S. 109, 146 (1959); Hustler Magazine v. Falwell, 485 U.S. 46, 51 (1988); Waters v. Churchill, 511 U.S. 661, 672 (1994).

122. See Erler, *The American Polity: Essay on the Theory and Practice of Constitutional Government*, 4-17.

123. Nelson, *Marbury v. Madison: The Origins and Legacy of Judicial Review*, 120, 124. See Erler, "The Future of Civil Rights: Affirmative Action Redivivus," *Notre Dame Journal of Law, Ethics and Public Policy* 11 (1997): 33-40, 49-54 (1997) and Erler, "Sowing the Wind: Judicial Oligarchy and the Legacy of Brown v. Board of Education," *Harvard Journal of Law and Public Policy* 8 (1985): 399-426.

124. See Erler, "Discrete and Insular Minorities," *The Encyclopedia of the American Constitution*, 2:566-68 and Erler, "Judicial Legislation," in ibid., 3:1040-43.

125. Brown v. Board of Education, 347 U.S. 483, 492 (1954).

126. Ibid., 489.

127. Ibid.

128. See Erler, "Brown v. Board of Education at Fifty," *Claremont Review of Books* 4 (2004), 47-52.

129. Brown v. Board of Education, 494.

130. Ibid.

131. Plessy v. Ferguson, 163 U.S. 537, 551 (1896).

132. Grutter v. Bollinger, 539 U.S. 306, 364 (2003) (Justice Thomas dissenting).

133. Gina Holland, "Ginsburg: International Law Shaped Court Rulings," *Associated Press*, Aug, 2, 2004.

134. Grutter v. Bollinger, 539 U.S. 306, 344 (2003).

135. Atkins v. Virginia, 536 U.S. 304, 316 (2002).

136. Knight v. Florida, 528 U.S. 990, 996 (1999) cert. denied (Justice Souter dissenting from the denial of certiorari).

137. Lawrence v. Texas, 539 U.S. 558, 577 (2003).

138. Ibid., 598 (quoting Foster v. Florida, 537 U.S. 990).

139. Dred Scott v. Sandford, 60 U.S. (19 How.) 393 (1857), 407.

·⌣ Part II ⌣·

The Progressive Persuasion
in Practice and Theory

·ᴗChapter 7ᴗ·

Progressivism, Modern Political Science, and the Transformation of American Constitutionalism

John Marini *

American political science, as a social science discipline, recently cel-ebrated the one hundredth anniversary of its founding. It was born at the beginning of a century in which the philosophic study of politics, a considerably older endeavor, lost its authority. The new discipline of political science, which aspired to be the scientific study of politics, was the product of the marriage of the positive sciences and the mod-ern research university. That union inspired great expectations con-cerning the use of the scientific method as the means by which to solve the age-old problems that had plagued mankind (poverty, war, and social injustice). By the end of the nineteenth century, the pro-cess by which the old liberal arts college would be eclipsed by the newly established research university had already begun. The graduate university would become the new home of the social science disci-plines devoted to research on behalf of the rational, or administrative state. In the modern state the role of government and administration would be greatly expanded.

The old liberalism of the American founding had limited the power of government and preserved the rights of individuals by maintaining the distinction between government and civil society, or the public and private spheres. This distinction was to be replaced by the Hegelian concept of the rational State, which mandated the fusion of government and civil society into an organic whole. In what came to be understood as the new liberalism, government was no longer thought to be a danger to the rights of the individual. Rather, the power of government would be used on behalf of the liberty of the people. Government would free men of economic necessity thereby creating the possibility of genuine human freedom. Furthermore, the organic, or general will, not constitutionalism—or the dependence on reason—would provide legitimacy for the actions of government and its purposes. The enlightened class, the bureaucracy, whose interest would be synonymous with the public good—because it seeks only useful knowledge on behalf of the public—would provide the technical rationality to carry-out the general will. Its purpose would be to solve the problems that arise in civil society. Consequently, government would become increasingly dependent upon the expertise developed in the social sciences. The research university, which subsequently undercut the authority of the philosophic tradition within the old liberal arts college, would be allied with government through bureaucracy. It would establish the rational structures whereby organized intelligence, or knowledge derived from the scientific method, would begin the process of solving, progressively, the political, social, economic, and cultural problems of the nation. The university and bureaucracy would, of necessity, become the institutional heart of the administrative state. It is not surprising, therefore, that the founders of the social science disciplines had little regard for a constitutional regime in which the power of government was limited.

Although the discipline of political science, like the other social sciences, assumed the superiority of science to philosophy, its theoretical unity, its foundation, rested upon a philosophic conception of social justice implicit in the idea of the rational state. The most profound theoretical justification of the concept of the state is to be found in G. F. W. Hegel's *Philosophy of Right*. Although now largely ignored by the various disciplines, Hegel's influence on Progressivism, and the new social sciences, was enormous. Indeed, in the eyes of the founders of those disciplines, the theoretical ground of modern political and social science was not science—nor methodology—but the idea of the State. As a result, the moral foundation of progressive politics is presupposed in the acceptance of the rational, or evolutionary, character of History.[1] Indeed, political science, and the other social sciences, are justified and legitimized in their role as the applied sciences of the modern state, a role in which the scientific method plays an indispensable part. As both Hegel and Marx insisted, in the rational—or post-revolutionary—state, politics would become administration.

POLITICAL THEORY, THE STATE, AND MODERN POLITICAL SCIENCE

The social science disciplines, newly established at the turn of the twentieth century, grew out of the collapse of belief in the authority of traditional philosophy *and* religion.[2] The founders of the new sciences were confident that the philosophic or religious traditions could no longer provide guidance in contemporary political and social affairs; thus, the political thought of the American founding could be of no use to nineteenth century man. However, the earlier tradition of political thought could not be ignored. The theoretical foundation of the new disciplines rested upon a rejection of the philosophic authority upon which early American political thought was based. The founders of the new disciplines were thus united in their opposition to any doctrine of constitutionalism, or limited government. It was necessary, therefore, to discredit the natural right foundation of the social compact, for it had established the public philosophy of constitutional government. They based their rejection upon an understanding of the rationality of History, or evolution, as the ground of human progress. In short, they re-examined the earlier tradition, only for the purpose of discrediting it.

The American Founders had looked to ancient and modern political philosophy—and historical practice—in developing the political science that established constitutionalism. From Aristotle and Cicero to Locke and Montesquieu, political philosophy had attempted to transcend opinion about politics with knowledge derived from an understanding of nature. The discovery of man's nature made it possible to ascertain those permanent or timeless principles of justice, which established the ground of political right. The fundamental principles of political right, derived from natural right, were dependent upon man's capacity for reason, or "reflection and choice." But, from the point of view of political philosophy, the permanent human dilemmas, and those fundamental problems of politics from which conflict arises, could not be overcome. The quest for justice had provided only the elusive end.

The political theory of the American founding was greatly influenced by John Locke, who sought to preserve Christian morality and religion, but grounded the principles of politics, and the authority of government, in the laws of nature discernible by reason. Locke's social compact theory, built upon a doctrine of the natural rights of man, provided a framework for establishing a just, or non-tyrannical regime, in a world transformed by Christianity. The social contract required the subordination of government itself to the principles of natural right. Consequently, the protection of individual liberty and property becomes the fundamental purpose of government. This is so because private property itself originates in the diversity inherent in the faculties of men. As Madison noted, "the protection of the unequal faculties of men is the first object of government."[3] The exercise of those faculties results in the inequality which becomes manifest in civil society. The maintenance of a free society requires, therefore, that the power of government must be limited to the protection of rights. But, the legitimacy of a free society and of limited government is derived from a prior recognition of the inalienable rights of individuals. The theory of the natural rights of man becomes intelligible, and is made politically viable only after it becomes possible to understand the abstract principle of the natural equality of all men. With the triumph of Christianity, the belief in the fatherhood of *one* God had made it possible to contemplate a regime based upon recognition of the brotherhood or *equality* of all men.

The American Founders subsequently found a rational solution to what Leo Strauss called "the political question par excellence, of how to reconcile order which is not oppression with freedom which is not license."[4] They did so by establishing what they understood to be a regime of civil and religious liberty, one that limited the authority of government and the power of religion. Reason and revelation independently established the necessity of maintaining the conditions of moral virtue in civil society. Moreover, there was substantial agreement between philosophy and religion concerning the content of moral virtue. But the history of Christianity had shown the danger of attempting to combine governmental power and religious authority in the Church. It was necessary, therefore, to separate politics and religion, or government and civil society. To make the separation work in practice, there had to be a constitutional limit upon the power of government in civil society and the authority of the Church in politics. The rediscovery of a doctrine of natural right in modern political thought had enabled the American Founders to establish a social compact founded upon a doctrine of equal natural rights, or the principle of political equality. The American regime was dependent, therefore, upon a view of man and nature that was compatible with both ancient and modern conceptions of what John Adams called the "principles of nature and eternal reason."[5]

The founding fathers of the discipline of political science, unlike the American Founders, denied the permanence of any political or philosophic principles. In their view, the older American political tradition, which rested upon rational or eternal truths derived from philosophy or religion, had become an anachronism. They assumed that the Hegelian philosophy of History and Darwinian evolutionary theory had undercut the possibility of any such trans-historical truth. From that perspective, the tradition of natural rights, and the social compact itself, was meaningless in light of the changed circumstances of politics and economics in the nineteenth century. Although they rejected philosophic and religious authority, they embraced the authority of the new positive sciences without question. But, unlike the natural sciences, the social sciences were predicated upon the assumption that History, not nature, provided the ground of meaningful knowledge as regards politics and society. The most fully developed understanding of the meaning of History had been formulated in Hegel's idea of the state. Subsequently, this state theory was to provide the unifying concept of the discipline of political science at its very foundation. That concept, rested upon the discovery of the rational character of History. As such, it was meant to transcend the idea of nature as well as nature's God. Once accepted, it would replace the natural rights philosophy upon which the political science of the American Constitution was based.

PROGRESSIVISM, THE STATE, AND AMERICAN POLITICAL SCIENCE

In 1903, the American Political Science Association was established as an independent discipline. It adopted the progressive view of History and science. Charles Merriam, a young theorist of the new discipline, attempted to characterize the difference between Progressive political thought, and that of the American founding. At the time of the founding of the country, he noted, "the statesmen of the nation were familiar with the best products of the world's political experience and thought, as developed at that time: and they made free use of them in the formulation of their political philosophy and in the practical affairs of state." However, "these leaders were not attempting to work out a science of politics."[6] Such a science, which was not developed until the nineteenth century, would have required a comprehensive theory of social justice or a rational science of society and economics. That science was not yet available to the American Founders.

In America, up to the Civil War, Merriam observed, "there was little energy expended in the study of systematic politics, in comparison with the contemporary English and Continental developments in social science, economics and politics, where the rise of the science of society under the inspiration of Auguste Comte, and of Utopian and proletarian socialism, aroused general interest in social problems."[7] But, he noted, "in the last half of the nineteenth century, there appeared in the United States a group of political theorists differing from the earlier thinkers in respect to method and upon many important doctrines of political science. The new method was more systematic and scientific than that which preceded it, while the results reached showed a pronounced reaction from the individualistic philosophy of the early years of the century."[8] The new theorists accepted the European doctrines of social justice, and a science of society that required government to provide political solutions to social and economic problems. Their acceptance necessitated the rejection of the theoretical and institutional framework of a constitutionalism that separated government and civil society, politics and economics, and preserved the autonomy of the public and private spheres.

In addition, Merriam contended that new theories derived from the study of biology were of great importance in legitimizing progressive doctrines based on an understanding of man as a changing or historical being. He noted that "in the general development of political thought many striking changes were made during this period. Overshadowing all others were those caused by the discoveries of Darwin and the development of modern science. The Darwinian theory of evolution not only transformed biological study, but profoundly affected all forms of thought. The social sciences were no exception, and history, economics, ethics and political science, were all fundamentally altered by the new doctrine."[9] The Darwinian theory, however, served only to confirm in an empirical way the more abstract theoretical arguments that had been made by Rousseau and Hegel. By tracing the biological evolution of the various species, Darwin seemed to prove that in the natural world the lower moves to the higher involuntarily, without apparent design.[10] In the human world, it appeared to vindicate the view that if History is rational, the high (or perfection) will be achieved without, or in spite of, human choice. Indeed, the idea of progress is based on the assumption that History itself establishes the conditions which ensure the intellectual and moral advancement of mankind. However, the discipline of political science, although it accepted the legitimacy of Darwinian theory, had already established its theoretical foundations based primarily on the earlier German thought.

Merriam traced the origins of a new political science to Francis Lieber, who was born in Germany, and had begun his work in America in the 1820s. Lieber had attended the University of Berlin, where he had come under the influence of Johann Fichte and Hegel. John Gunnell, a leading modern scholar of the discipline, has suggested that "Lieber wished to identify the domain of political science with the state." In Lieber's view, "political science treats man in his most important earthly phase, the state is the institution which has to protect or to check all his endeavors, and, in turn reflects them."[11] In the 1830s, Lieber translated portions of a German encyclopedia and subsequently published an American version. "It was in the *Encyclopedia Americana*," Gunnell noted, "that the state, as the organizing concept of political inquiry, was first introduced in the United States."[12] In his thirteen-volume encyclopedia, Lieber observed, "as the idea of *politics* depends on that of the *state*, a definition of the latter will easily mark out the whole province of the political sciences ... This idea of the state is the basis of a class of sciences, and gives them a distinct character as belongs to the various classes of history, philosophy, theological, medica [medical] &c., sciences." For Lieber, the state is "the natural condition of man, because essential to the full development of his faculties." The form of government is "merely a means of obtaining the great objects of the state."[13] Lieber succeeded in establishing the systematic study

of politics upon the foundation of the state, and government, and its
institutions were to be subordinate to it. In addition, through his encyclopedia, he helped introduce German political thought and culture
into the newly created, or transformed, universities.

According to Charles Merriam, Lieber inspired a "long line of American political scientists, many of whom were trained in German
schools."[14] They included Theodore Woolsey, John W. Burgess, Arthur
L. Lowell, Woodrow Wilson, Frank J. Goodnow and W. W. Willoughby,
who differed in their approach to the study of politics, but were united
in their rejection of the political thought of the American founding.
Thus, the hostility of the first political scientists to the philosophic
doctrine of the natural rights of man, and the social contract, is apparent from the beginning. As Merriam noted, "Woolsey repudiated
the classical doctrine of 'natural rights,' declaring that rights implied
the coexistence of men. Historically the state arises out of custom and
usage ... The state 'is as truly natural as rights are, and as society is,'
and is the bond of both. It is the means for all the highest ends of man
and society." Furthermore, the power of the state "may reach 'as far
as the nature and needs of man reach, including intellectual and aesthetic wants of the individual, and the religious and moral nature of
its citizens.'"[15] The American Founders had separated politics and religion, state and society, to protect the freedom and autonomy of the
individual. They were aware, because they had studied the real past,
not an idealized past, that the unlimited power of government or religion led to tyranny. On the other hand, Woolsey was confident that
there was no danger in giving the state unlimited power. The
Progressives looked to the future.[16]

Woolsey's view of the American founding principles, like Lieber's
before him, was to become the standard opinion of the fathers of the
discipline of political science. For example, John W. Burgess, whose
"fundamental political philosophy was influenced by the ideas of Hegel,
followed the current political theory in repudiating the doctrines of
natural law and the social contract, declaring that they were wholly
contrary to our knowledge of the historical development of political
institutions."[17] It is true that the political theory of the American founding was revolutionary and was based upon abstract principles of political right, but the Founders' alleged failure to comprehend the
"historical development of political institutions," did not mean that

they had not learned from human nature and from human experience. Ironically, the history implicit in the Hegelian idea of the state is wholly abstract and is little dependent upon an understanding of the actual experience of man. It is not surprising that the Progressive intellectuals learned very little from the real past, and their disdain for it is made evident in their extravagant hopes for the future.

The new discipline was confident that the state could replace the social compact, the Constitution, and even the people themselves, as the source of sovereignty and legitimacy. Burgess insisted that "the state cannot be conceived without sovereignty, i.e., without unlimited power over its subjects; that is its very essence." Burgess, supremely confident of the justice of the state, went so far as to view the individual not as a citizen, but as a subject. He noted that "the original, absolute, unlimited, universal power over the individual subject, and all associations of subjects," was "the most fundamental and indispensable mark of statehood."[18] It is not surprising, therefore, as Charles Merriam insisted, "it was the idea of the State that supplanted the social contract as the ground of political right. The notion that political society and government are based upon a contract between independent individuals and that such a contract is the sole source of political obligation is regarded as no longer tenable."[19] The new theorists were convinced that tyranny, like natural right, was a thing of the past. Nonetheless, the new political scientists had not refuted the ideas of the American founding. They simply rejected them. They embraced, without question, the German critics of natural right who had established the doctrine of the modern rational state.

John Gunnell has observed that "by the time the major graduate programs in political science began to appear at institutions such as Columbia and Johns Hopkins in the 1880's, the theory of the state, as advanced by Lieber, Bluntschli, and Woolsey, constituted, both substantively and methodologically, a distinct and influential paradigm. And it would be further sedimented by the new generation of scholars who were trained in Germany and France and who were most influential in institutionalizing graduate education in political science during the last quarter of the century."[20] John W. Burgess, who followed in Francis Lieber's footsteps at Columbia, succeeded in creating the first autonomous department of political science in the United States. He would become the most influential of the first generation of political scientists. Burgess hoped to establish the new discipline as a profession and give it permanence within the new graduate school. He was persuaded that it would become the applied science of the modern rational state. Burgess insisted that "the national popular state alone furnishes the objective reality upon which political science can rest in the construction of a truly scientific political system."[21] As such, its authority would not be based upon partisanship, but on objective, or empirical, knowledge. As Gunnell noted, "progressive political scientists after the turn of the century would hold on to the idea of the state, because it offered an instrumentality for social control and change, and a substitute for politics."[22]

The new discipline would become an integral part of the emerging graduate university in the United States. Gunnell has observed that "the vision of political science that developed in the American university was one that united the field with history and combined civic education and leadership training with a general commitment to the scientific rationalization of society, and the goal was an articulation of government and university."[23] Indeed, as Gunnell noted, "the concern of political scientists for political reform during the Progressive Era reflected a deeper motivation—'they were in revolt against politics itself, full of a deep disgust at the dirt of politics that led to an aspiration for objectivity, dignity and the authority of science.'"[24] It is not surprising, therefore, that the Progressives and the discipline of political science embraced the Hegelian theory made practicable in the idea of the rational state: the view which systematized the progress of mind through historical science. Hegel, too, had insisted that the state must provide a haven for science because their goals are compatible: knowledge of "objective truth." Hegel noted, "the state is universal in form, a form whose essential principle is thought. This explains why it was in the state that freedom of thought and science had their origin ... Science too, therefore, has its place on the side of the state since it has one element, its form, in common with the state, and its aim is knowledge, knowledge of objective truth and rationality in terms of thought."[25] In the past, Hegel noted, science had been under the authority of the Church. Once it was established within the rational state, the university would become its institutional heart.

The progress of the natural and physical sciences had helped to establish the authority of science within society, and contributed to the growing prestige of the research university. It also led to great expectations concerning the use of science in political and social affairs. E. L. Godkin, founder of the *Nation* magazine, suggested that "the next great political revolution in the Western world" will give "scientific expression to the popular will, or in other words ... place men's relations in society where they never yet have been placed, under the control of trained human reason."[26] Indeed, as Leo Strauss subsequently observed, "the true public reason is the new political science, which judges in a universally valid, or objective, manner of what is to the interest of each, for it shows to everyone what means he must choose in order to attain his attainable ends, whatever those ends may be."[27] It is not accidental that the new political and social sciences would soon become more concerned with power, or control, than knowledge, or justice. Indeed, John Dewey was convinced that democracy, the most advanced form of government, would become superior to every other form of human organization, because it would require "a deliberate control of policies by the method of intelligence."[28] With the establishment of the method of intelligence within the discipline of political science, Charles Merriam was not far wrong in suggesting that "politics as the art of the traditional advances to politics as the science of constructive social control."[29]

The new discipline rested upon the view that progress of the mind and the method of science had made possible the ongoing transformation of man and society. Moreover, in terms of politics, society, and culture, an evolving consciousness of freedom established the moral foundation in each historical epoch. Thus, the discipline accepted the views of Immanuel Kant and Hegel, which established the ground of morality in will, not nature. As a result, it was not possible, thereafter, to apprehend the moral law by reason (as the Founders thought) apart from the willing of it. Morality and legitimacy, as well as the sovereignty of the people, are derivative of will. In addition, the discipline rejected the view that natural right, or natural law—now understood to be the laws of science or physics—could establish the moral foundation of politics and society. Thus, Woodrow Wilson objected to the theory of the American founding not because he denied that equality and liberty were fundamental principles in a democratic society. Rather, he was convinced that those principles were not derivative of natural law or natural right as understood by the framers.

Wilson believed that the political thought of the founding, which had limited the power of government and separated politics and society, was based upon a *misunderstanding* of man and nature.[30] He contended that the laws of politics are indeed dependent upon the laws of science, or History. The American Founders, however, based their political theories upon principles of the physical, or natural, universe.[31] But, Wilson insisted that the natural laws are descriptive only of the physical world, as Kant had shown. As a result, he maintained the view that political and social principles derived their authority from a different source. They are derivative of the laws of History and the science of organic life. He argued therefore, that "the government of the United States was constructed upon the Whig theory of political dynamics, which was an unconscious copy of the Newtonian theory of the universe. In our own day, whenever we discuss the structure or development of a thing, whether in nature or in society, we consciously follow Mr. Darwin; but before Mr. Darwin they followed Newton."[32] Thus, Wilson criticized *The Federalist Papers* because "they are full of the theory of checks and balances ... Politics is turned into mechanics under his touch. The theory of gravitation is supreme." However, Wilson believed that "the trouble with the theory is that government is not a machine but a living thing. It falls, not under the theory of the universe, but the theory of organic life. It is accountable to Darwin, not to Newton."[33]

In bringing government into conformity with the proper science, Wilson suggested that it was necessary to unify what the Founders had divided. "The object of constitutional government, is to bring the active, planning will of each part of the government into accord with the prevailing popular thought and need, and thus make it an impartial instrument of symmetrical national development; and to give to the operation of the government thus shaped under the influence of opinion and adjusted to the general interest both stability and an incorruptible efficiency." In unifying government on behalf of will, Wilson assumed that Darwinian science provided support for democratic government, as opposed to constitutional government.[34] It is not surprising, therefore, that any impediment to carrying out the will of the people is undemocratic. It is not the separation of powers (Newtonian), but the separation of politics and administration (Darwinian) which is compatible with the idea of progress in human affairs. Politics is the organic expression of the will (or spirit) of the people; administration is the technical, rational, means by which it is made adaptable and put into practice.

Wilson's view becomes intelligible in light of Hegel's doctrine of the rational, or administrative state. It was Hegel who established the theoretical foundation of progressive politics. In his view, the rational mind established itself through History and Will, thus denying the traditional view, that mind becomes intelligible by virtue of an understanding of nature through theoretical or metaphysical reason. Furthermore, in post-Hegelian thought, the scientific method, (or the technical rationality of the social sciences) replaced practical reason, or prudence, in determining the means to carry out that Will.

The new discipline of political science, would, of necessity, become dependent upon a method derived from the positive sciences. The scientific method presupposed the distinction between facts and values, or, the *is* and the *ought*. As an instrumental science, it would be concerned with means only, hence its preoccupation with method and efficiency. By separating means and ends, facts and values, political science was no longer required—or able—to understand politics in moral terms. Consequently, it lost sight of the original understanding of the concept of regime, and was incapable of making prudential judgments about the questions of justice and tyranny. It was not surprising therefore, that Progressive thinkers and politicians had so little fear of the abuse of power by government itself. In their view, once the people have established a democratic society, the power of government will be used only for the benefit of the people. In carrying out the will of the people, government must be a progressive force used for the benefit of society.

Nonetheless, the optimism inherent in progressive thought, rested upon the confident assumption, spelled out by Hegel, that the historical process is rational. Furthermore, History is completed, or at its end. The final principles of political and social life—freedom, equal rights, and democracy—had made their appearance on the world stage. This process was completed when Christianity, the universal religion, showed itself as having a rational foundation. Religion, too, as History revealed, was a projection of the human mind. Nonetheless, that very universal religion, when secularized, would provide the moral foundation of the rational state. Once established, the state itself would satisfy the need for religion. As Hegel insisted, "as high as mind stands above nature, so high does the state stand above physical life. Man must therefore venerate the state *as a secular deity*, and observe that if it is difficult to comprehend nature, it is infinitely harder to understand the state."[35] In short, in the rational state, principled quarrels over politics and religion would no longer exist. Politics would become a technical problem, or merely a matter of rational administration.

Thus the discipline of political science, though an instrumental science, was established upon a theoretical and normative foundation, which was developed in the concept of the rational state. It was the idea of the state, itself, which gave meaning to its existence and legitimacy to its method. It depended upon a philosophy of History— or progress—to determine the goal, which is social justice. As a result, political science could be established as an applied science of the rational state. Therefore, it could be emancipated from the endless and fruitless quarrels over values and politics. In establishing the technical and rational authority of the scientific method—the means by which to achieve social justice—the discipline would find its moral justification. In all of the new social science disciplines created to serve the state, the philosophical—the normative, or value—questions would become meaningless. The only useful, and hence genuine, or objective, (i.e. non-political) knowledge would be empirical knowledge. As a result, even the discipline of political science would not, and could not, question its own values; or its own theoretical presuppositions. The dependence upon the idea of the state is implicit, or presupposed.

Nonetheless, the concept of the state, which established the necessity and authority of the social science disciplines, was forgotten not long after they were established. It was not surprising, however, that political scientists would become ardent defenders of the modern state. Like other social scientists, they sought to advance the progressive agenda in political affairs. It was in the interest of the discipline itself to cultivate the expertise that would enable it to become an indispensable part of the administrative state. In order to establish itself as the new authority, the social sciences were forced to deny the meaningful character of the philosophic or religious traditions that had made constitutionalism possible.[36] At the same time, in accepting the theoretical foundations of progressive thought, the social science disciplines acquiesced in the view that the end of History had established the condition for understanding its rationality. In doing so, it assumed as Hegel had done, that man had the capacity to become fully wise or knowledgeable. Or, to put it another way, man had developed the method that could solve every human problem. Thus, recognition of the end of History already presupposed the end of philosophy as well.

PROGRESSIVISM AND ITS CRITICS: RECONSIDERING CONSTITUTIONALISM

The social sciences were established to facilitate, in a practical way, the theoretical and moral principles of progressive thought. They had great success in transforming, and subsequently dominating, the American university. The new sciences would provide the expertise to enable government, and the enlightened bureaucracy, to administer progress or change in the emerging administrative state. But, the modern state—its science and its politics—was not without its critics. Indeed, history itself played a decisive role in revealing the true character of the modern state. In the twentieth century, the new revolutionary states, in Russia, Germany, and Italy, were founded upon progressive doctrines, which embodied the will of charismatic leaders and the parties they created. They justified themselves in terms of historical or biological necessity. Nonetheless, they showed that the unlimited power of government, even in the hands of so-called progressive forces, had been capable of destroying millions of their own citizens. On the other hand, the constitutional democracies, products of the earlier tradition of political thought, had maintained stable and moderate governments that stood in opposition to the totalitarian dictatorships.

In the aftermath of the Second World War, important critics of progressive thought, who became critics of the social sciences as well, began to re-evaluate the foundations of constitutional government. Among the most important was Leo Strauss, a maverick political scientist, whose work gave new meaning to the understanding of constitutionalism and its relationship to natural right. He showed that the theoretical justification of Progressivism had been derived from an acceptance of the philosophy of History. The belief in the rationality and inevitability of the historical process had attained the status of scientific truth when united with the Darwinian biological theory of evolution. However, Strauss insisted that the rejection of the older philosophic tradition of natural right was itself a product of the new Hegelian theory and not historical necessity. Therefore, it was possible, and necessary, to reconsider the earlier tradition in which nature and natural right still retained its meaning. The new scholarship on natural right revealed the fundamental theoretical and practical distinctions that made it possible to differentiate constitutionalism from the modern rational state.

Strauss exposed the theoretical roots of historicism by taking seriously the philosophic tradition of political thought that preceded modernity. He did so by re-examining the theoretical ground of ancient and medieval political thought and its relationship to the religious tradition. The Enlightenment had succeeded in undermining the intellectual authority of religion, and its hostility to religion extended to the older philosophic tradition as well. In attempting to overcome religion, modern thought had obscured those theoretical elements within the rational philosophic tradition that constituted a common ground of human understanding. It was metaphysical reason, or natural right, which had provided continuity in ancient and early modern political thought. But, natural right had become obscured by the triumph of historical thought. It was only by taking the older traditions of philosophy and religion seriously that Strauss was able to draw a distinction among the variations in modern political thought.

Strauss made a distinction between what he called the first and second waves of modernity, which made it possible to reveal differences in the political practice of each. Progressive political thought was dependent upon the idea of the state that grew out of the second wave of modern political thought, which replaced nature with History. It originated in the attack on nature and reason by Jean Jacques Rousseau. That attack was fueled by contempt for the bourgeois virtues of individualism that had been fostered by the separation of politics and religion, which necessitated the separation of government and civil society. The modern doctrine of the state grew out of the theoretical attempt to transcend nature and religion by resolving the contradictions upon which constitutional thought had been based, and which required a limited government. The modern state would produce citizens who were committed to the common good, a product of the general will. It was Rousseau's attack on the liberalism of Hobbes and Locke that began the process of undermining the political doctrine of natural right and gave rise to the historical sense.

In Rousseau's political thought, and those theorists and practitioners who embraced it, the general will replaced the transcendent natural law as a standard of right.[37] It provided the means of reconciling law and nature, and the *is* and the *ought*, as well. Thus the general will established the foundation for the absolute sovereignty of the people, free of all restraints of reason and the moral law rooted in nature. In Hobbes and Locke, Strauss observed, "the fundamental right of man had retained its original status even within civil society: natural law remained the standard for positive law; there remained the possibility of appealing from positive law to natural law." Strauss argued that in Rousseau's view, civil society "must be so constructed as to make the appeal from positive to natural law utterly superfluous; a civil society properly constructed ... will automatically produce just positive law."[38] In Rousseau's *Social Contract*, the sovereign, through the general will, becomes the source of legitimacy. The appeal to nature is no longer necessary, or possible. The sovereign will becomes the source of morality.

Strauss has observed that "Rousseau's concept of the general will, which as such cannot err—which by merely being is what it ought to be—showed how the gulf between the is and the ought can be overcome."[39] Nonetheless, Strauss continued,

> strictly speaking, Rousseau showed this only under the condition that his doctrine of the general will, his political doctrine proper, is linked with his doctrine of the historical process, and this linking was the work of Rousseau's great successors, Kant and Hegel, rather than of Rousseau himself. According to this view, the rational or just society, the society characterized by the existence of a general will known to be the general will, i.e., the ideal, is necessarily actualized by the historical process without men's intending to actualize it. Why can the general will not err? Why is the general will necessarily good? The answer is: it is good because it is rational, and it is rational because it is general; it emerges through the generalization of the particular will, of the will which as such is not good.[40]

By replacing the limitations imposed by the old understanding of human nature, a product of reason, the modern state would be a triumph of will and method. It was this idea of the rational, or scientific, state, based upon a new understanding of social justice, which inspired the Progressive movement in politics. The new view of social justice— unlike philosophical, or metaphysical, justice—was an empirical phenomenon, in which success could be measured by the extent to which government is able to transform society. Indeed, a new science, statistics—the name is derived from the state— would measure the extent of that success in a wholly empirical way.

Leo Strauss traced the political crisis of the West to the abandonment of the idea of natural right. As we have seen, it was the doctrine of natural right that had provided the foundation for the political science, and the public philosophy, of constitutionalism. Nonetheless, Strauss was aware of the fact that "the seriousness of the need of natural right does not prove that the need can be satisfied." The reason for the difficulty was, as Strauss noted, "the problem of natural right is today a matter of recollection rather than of actual knowledge." He insisted, therefore, that we are "in need of historical studies in order to familiarize ourselves with the whole complexity of the issue."[41] We must become "students of the 'history of ideas.'" But, "contrary to a popular notion," he cautioned, "this will aggravate rather than remove the difficulty of impartial treatment."[42] In becoming, once again, students of the "history of ideas," it will become necessary to question the fundamental assertion of the political science of the modern state—that politics can be understood as an impartial, objective, or neutral science. In short, the method adopted by the discipline of political science itself would make the recovery of genuine knowledge of natural right all the more difficult. Strauss revealed the difficulty by alluding to a quotation from Lord Acton. "Few discoveries are more irritating than those which expose the pedigree of ideas. Sharp definitions and unsparing analysis would displace the veil beneath which society dissembles its divisions, would make political disputes too violent for compromise and political alliances too precarious for use, and would embitter politics with all the passions of social and religious strife."[43]

Strauss made it clear that the understanding of modern politics was no longer derived from practical observation of the conduct of political life itself.[44] In addition, modern political science had become wholly abstract or theoretical insofar as its primary concern had come to be empirical, or mathematical knowledge. It had separated itself from philosophy and had fallen under the authority of an ethically neutral science. In returning to Aristotelian political science, Strauss pointed the way back to a theoretical defense of reasonable or prudential politics.[45] However, Strauss was well aware that "prudence is always endangered by false doctrines about the whole of which man is a part; prudence is therefore always in need of defense against such opinions, and that defense is necessarily theoretical."[46] Nonetheless, he knew that theory, as such, cannot be "taken to be the basis of prudence." Rather, it is also "the fact that the sphere of prudence is, as it were, only *de jure* but not *de facto* wholly independent of theoretical science," which makes understandable, Strauss maintained, "the view underlying the new political science according to which no awareness inherent in practice, and in general no natural awareness, is genuine knowledge, or in other words only 'scientific' knowledge is genuine knowledge. This view," Strauss continued, "implies that there cannot be practical sciences proper, or that the distinction between practical and theoretical sciences must be replaced by the distinction between theoretical and applied sciences—applied sciences being sciences based on the theoretical sciences that precede the applied sciences in time and in order."[47] The political science discipline had aspired to become the applied science of the rational state. As a result, it was forced to reject the ordinary understanding of political life. In opposing the new political science, Strauss thought it necessary to reaffirm the dignity of the political by returning to a natural, or pre-scientific, understanding of the political. In doing so, prudence, and the political phenomena, could once again be seen for what they are.

Strauss' attempt to expose the foundations of modern historical thought led him to re-examine the distinction between theory and practice that had been undermined by modern philosophy itself. In doing so, he was forced to reconsider the relationship of philosophy and politics. The politicization of modern philosophy had undermined the autonomy of philosophy, which had been understood as the quest for knowledge of the eternal, or the whole. It had abandoned the distinction between the "conditions of understanding and its sources, between the conditions for the existence and the pursuit of philosophy (specific kinds of societies, etc.) on the one hand, and the sources of philosophical knowledge on the other."[48] The result was the corruption of philosophy and politics, theory and practice. Strauss showed that it had become more difficult to achieve moderate political practice precisely because political theory had abandoned reason at the point in which practice (or History) provided the ground for theory (i.e. had become rational).[49] The end of History, or the politicization of philosophy, culminated in the view that man had or would become fully knowledgeable. The fundamental problems of politics, morality, and religion, will have been resolved. In the future, the human problems would require a technical or scientific solution. However, the new political thought, which spawned the various attempts to create the rational state in the twentieth century, did not bring about the best regime. Rather, the political practice of those states showed the price that was to be paid by abandoning prudence.

The intellectual ascendancy of the philosophy of History, and with it the triumph of scientific methodology, resulted in the transformation of the traditional meaning as well as the language of politics. The discipline of political science, therefore, was unable to understand politics in terms of practical reason, or prudence. Hence morality, which is the choice of means, was no longer meaningful. History, or progress, necessarily moved in the right direction because, as Hegel insisted, the real is the rational, and the rational is real. Consequently, the ordinary understanding of politics in terms of human choice, of good and evil, had become meaningless. As a result, the customary vocabulary of politics—which goes back to Aristotle, who had developed the categories of regimes around the ideas of justice and tyranny—lost its capacity to elucidate political phenomena. As a result, partisan politics in the modern state came to be understood not in moral terms, but with reference to History. Modern liberalism was distinguished by being rationally progressive, while conservatism, characterized by its resistance to historical change, was considered to be politically reactionary.[50] From the point of view of History, the fully developed rational state is what it ought to be. Nonetheless, the twentieth century showed that tyranny was not a thing of the past.[51]

Post-Hegelian philosophy had obscured the distinction between theory and practice, and undermined prudence as the fundamental practical virtue of politics. Moreover, as Strauss showed, the social sciences, which accompanied the modern state, revealed themselves to be incapable of making sound—or reasonable—judgments about politics. They could not identify the most vicious regimes as tyrannies. The older understanding of politics, that was the foundation of the American regime, regarded justice and tyranny as permanent alternatives in human political affairs. The twentieth century had shown that the traditional view was not obsolete. Strauss, therefore, pointed to the failure of the discipline. He noted,

> tyranny is a danger coeval with political life. The analysis of tyranny is therefore as old as political science itself. The analysis of tyranny that was made by the first political scientists was so clear, so comprehensive, and so unforgettably expressed that it was remembered and understood by generations that did not have any direct experience of actual tyranny. On the other hand, when we were brought face to face with tyranny—with a kind of tyranny that surpassed the boldest imagination of the most powerful thinkers of the past—our political science failed to recognize it.[52]

The twentieth century proved to be a laboratory for the political theory that had become dominant in the century before. Consequently, it was not surprising that political science failed to recognize the tyranny of the modern state. It too was a product of the same political thought. Therefore, even after the fact, political science could not admit the connection between historicist political thought and the political practice that resulted from its acceptance. One thing did become clear, however: the fundamental opposition to tyranny, or totalitarianism, came from the liberal, or constitutional, regimes. Those regimes were a product of the political thought of the earlier tradition (however modified by progressive thought) of natural right. The older liberal tradition, insofar as it had resisted the most dangerous tendencies of progressive reform, had maintained moderate and non-tyrannical governments. They had preserved the autonomy and dignity of the individual. On the other hand, Hegelian, or progressive, thought had culminated in the triumph of unbridled will.

The dictatorships, the product of will to power, had justified the use of power on behalf of race or class, in the service of progress, or History. The result was the massacre of millions of fellow citizens and the devastation of the countries themselves. The progressive assumption that power of government would be used only for benevolent purposes was shattered. The legitimacy of the political thought that produced those regimes was brought into question. However, the social science disciplines, which remained the heart of the rational state, lost none of their legitimacy or authority. Indeed, the growing dependence upon the technical rationality of the sciences had opened up the prospect of a rational and universal state. As a result, Strauss noted, "we are now brought face to face with a tyranny which holds out the threat of becoming, thanks to 'the conquest of nature' and in particular human nature, what no earlier tyranny ever became: perpetual and universal."[53] Ironically, as the history of the last century made clear, the political and social sciences were unable to understand or provide a solution to the problem of tyranny. Indeed, they had become part of the problem.

CONCLUSION

The political theory of the American founding rested upon a philosophic doctrine in which the ancient understanding of the idea of nature, obscured by the political triumph of a universal religion, was made politically relevant once again in the modern doctrine of natural right. The rediscovery of natural right as a product of reason opened up the possibility of a new science of politics. That new science established the theoretical foundation of constitutional government. It recognized the essential liberty and equality of all men as the ground of the social compact, which necessitated a limited government as the best defense of individual freedom. Furthermore, the institutional arrangements of constitutionalism, with its separation of powers, were reflective of their understanding that tyranny is a problem coeval with political life. Limited government, therefore, is only a reflection of the reality that the "latent causes of factionalism"—self-interest and self-love—"are sown into the nature of man" and thus cannot be transcended. On the other hand, the politics of the rational state derived from a theory that denied the truth of the natural and permanent necessities that required limited government. Rather, it presupposed a governmental solution to every human problem. The unlimited power of the administrative state rested upon the expectation that science, or knowledge, combined with power, could transform—or transcend—human nature, and therefore Nature itself.

The forms of the Constitution still shape the character of contemporary politics. But the philosophy of government that sustains constitutionalism is only a memory. The only differences that are politically relevant for those who are active in politics revolve around the question of who in government should control and regulate the modern administrative state, and how should it be done. But, in a more profound sense, what lies at the heart of the political differences, is a philosophical disagreement concerning the meaning of justice, or what constitutes the good society. From the point of view of those animated by the desire for social justice implicit in the idea of the state, the American Constitution is indefensible. It stands in the way of a full-blown attempt to establish social justice, which would require a rational solution to the social, economic, and cultural problems that arise in modern society. The Constitution, on the other hand, had created a government of limited power, and structured the institutions of the national government in such a way as to protect the rights of individuals. It was the defense of civil and religious liberty, and not social justice, which established the ground of constitutionalism.

American constitutional government attempted to establish a just, or good, society that was in accordance with an understanding of man's nature. Consequently, Madison insisted that "justice is the end of government. It is the end of civil society. It ever has been and ever will be pursued until it be obtained, or until liberty be lost in the pursuit."[54] However, the American Founders, unlike the Progressives, would not have attempted to achieve the kind of social justice implicit in the idea of the rational state. Such an attempt required the transformation of society and man himself. To do so would have required the necessity of mandating social justice, or the virtuous society, by force. It would have meant the end of liberty and political justice as well. Furthermore, they were doubtful that it was humanly possible to do so. Rather, they thought it was sufficient to create the conditions necessary for a free society. The people themselves would determine the meaning of happiness, or the good life. For they had been witness to a time when another powerful authority, the Church, had utilized government to enforce the virtuous, or good life. The Church, in the name of religion, had justified its use of power as necessary for the attainment of the highest aspiration of man, the desire for immortality, which required salvation of the soul. Indeed, constitutionalism itself, with the separation of church and state, and the protection of the autonomy of civil society, had arisen out of the necessity to avert the tyranny of the Church. The establishment of constitutional government was the result of an attempt to find a reasonable solution to the politicization of religion. An all-powerful Church had corrupted politics—and religion—by empowering an elite, which relied upon knowledge that was beyond question, and therefore, precluded the possibility of debate and compromise. The knowledge, or scientific elite, which becomes the actual ruler of the rational state according to Max Weber, poses a similar threat.

The American Founders knew that the attempts to mandate the best society, even the city of God on earth, had not resulted in the good society. Rather, they had led to the tyranny of the established Church. In the modern state, there is no doubt that the power and authority of science, and social science, has grown dramatically, especially in the last century. In many ways, it has replaced the authority of both religion and philosophy. Moreover, the rational authority of the sciences has undercut the moral authority of tradition, the family, and religion. It has, thereby, undermined those institutions that have helped maintain the autonomy of civil society. Nonetheless, no political, or scientific elite has succeeded in establishing the rational state, or the good society. Rather, in those places where such an elite has attained absolute power, the result has been more likely to bring about the establishment of a new kind of despotism. Thus, prudence would seem to dictate, as the American Founders insisted, that in human affairs a regime of civil equality and religious liberty is the best that can be achieved. For that reason, separation of church and state, government and society, has been essential in preserving the autonomy of each, by limiting the power of both. In light of the experience of the last century, constitutional government has been shown to be the best defense against any form of despotism.

Endnotes

* The author would like to acknowledge the generous support of the Earhart Foundation in the research and writing of this article.

1. What is sometimes considered a distinctively American philosophy, pragmatism, rests upon the same theoretical foundation. In recognizing the importance of John Dewey's contribution to social thought, Charles Merriam noted, "pragmatism is a tentative philosophy of developing life. Its basis lies in the broad historical background of modern life, in the central place of evolution in the scheme of modern thought, in the social character of consciousness—in short, it bears many of the resemblances of the general theory of things adapted to a democratic era. In ethics its followers applied it to the evolutionary theory of morality, although they did not originate this point of view." Charles Merriam, *American Political Ideas: Studies in the Development of American Political Thought 1865-1917* (New York: The MacMillan Company, 1923), 424.

2. The crisis within the regime created by the abandonment of a public philosophy is more fully developed in John Marini, "Constitutionalism, the Public Philosophy, and Political Science," in *Public Philosophy and Political Science: Crisis and Reflection,* E. Robert Stathan, Jr., ed. (Lanham, Md.: Lexington Books, 2002), 187-204.

3. See Madison, Hamilton, Jay, *The Federalist Papers*, introduction and notes by Charles R. Kesler, Clinton Rossiter, ed. (New York: Mentor Books, 1999), 46.

4. Leo Strauss, *Persecution and the Art of Writing* (Glencoe, Ill., The Free Press, 1952), 37.

5. *Revolutionary Writings of John Adams,* C. Bradley Thompson, ed. (Indianapolis: Liberty Fund, 2000). Adams notes that these principles are of "Aristotle and Plato, of Livy and Cicero, and Sidney, Harrington, and Locke; the principles on which the whole government over us now stands." *Novanglus*, no. 1 (Fall 1774): 152.

6. Merriam, *American Political Ideas,* 370.

7. Ibid., 371.

8. Charles E. Merriam, *A History of American Political Theories* (New York: The MacMillan Company, 1903), 305.

9. Merriam, *American Political Ideas,* 371.

10. It is not surprising that Darwin's theory posed more of a problem for religion, than it did for philosophy. The philosophers had long before abandoned the view that man's humanity is understood in terms of his rationality. That rejection paved the way for the acceptance of man's

historicity. As a result, it had become impossible to understand man in terms of his nature. It was possible, therefore, to deny that there is such a thing as human nature. Religion, however, still understood man to be a creature of God. It was God, therefore, who established the ground of moral choice. By defining man in terms of the lower (his origins in the animal world), rather than the higher (God), Darwin's theory undermined belief in the authority that established the necessity, and justification, of moral choice.

11. John Gunnell, *The Descent of Political Theory* (Chicago: University of Chicago Press, 1993), 30.

12. Ibid., 27.

13. Ibid.

14. Merriam, *A History of American Political Theories*, 305.

15. Merriam, *American Political Ideas*, 378.

16. The unbounded expectation concerning the future is best expressed in Woodrow Wilson's view of progress. "Progress! Did you ever reflect that that word is almost a new one? No word comes more often or more naturally to the lips of modern man, as if the thing it stands for were almost synonymous with life itself, and yet men through many thousand years never talked or thought of progress. They thought in the other direction. Their stories of heroism and glory were tales of the past. The ancestor wore the heavier armor and carried the larger spear. 'There were giants in those days.' Now all that has altered. We think of the future, not the past, as the more glorious time in comparison with which the present is nothing." "What is Progress?" in Woodrow Wilson, *The New Freedom: A Call for the Emancipation of the Generous Energies of a People* (New York: Doubleday, Page and Company, 1913), 39.

17. Merriam, *American Political Ideas*, 379.

18. Ibid., 380

19. Merriam, *A History of American Political Theories*, 307, 312. Merriam rejected the understanding of liberty implicit in the doctrine of natural right because it limited the power of government. He noted that in the Founders' view, "liberty is, in short, the natural and inherent right of all men; government is the necessary limitation of this liberty." Furthermore, he rejected the Founders' view of equality and liberty as the ground of political right. In denying the natural right foundation of the American regime, Merriam embraced the racial theories of John C. Calhoun. "Calhoun and his school, as it has been shown," Merriam observed, "repudiated this idea, and maintained that liberty is not the natural right of all men, but only the reward of the races or individuals properly qualified for its possession." Although Merriam accepted the historicist view of

racial superiority, he does not condone slavery. Nonetheless, he defends the principle that legitimized slavery. In the end, he thinks Calhoun's theory is vindicated only after slavery has been ended. "The mistaken application of the idea had the effect of delaying recognition of the truth in what had been said until the controversy over slavery was at an end." With the end of slavery, it becomes possible to see the historical and scientific truth that only certain races are capable of self-government.

20. Gunnell, *The Descent of Political Theory*, 36.

21. John W. Burgess, *Political Science and Comparative Constitutional Law* (Boston: Ginn and Company, 1891), 58.

22. Gunnell, *Descent,* 58.

23. Ibid., 37.

24. Ibid., 23.

25. G. F. W. Hegel, *Philosophy of Right,* trans. T. M. Knox, (London: Oxford University Press, 1967), 172-173.

26. Cited in William Nelson, *The Roots of American Bureaucracy, 1830-1900* (Cambridge: Harvard University Press, 1982), 82.

27. Leo Strauss, "An Epilogue," in *Essays on the Scientific Study of Politics,* Herbert J. Storing, ed. (New York: Holt, Rinehart and Winston, 1962), 324.

28. Merriam, *American Political Ideas*, 425.

29. Cited in Gunnel, *The Descent of Political Theory*, 99.

30. Woodrow Wilson provides insight into the link between the new discipline of Political Science, and its use in the transformation of the politics of the American regime. Wilson, with a Ph.D. in Political Science from Johns Hopkins, attempted that transformation of American politics based upon a new political theory. He well understood that his adversary was the Constitution and the political science that had created it. In 1885, he noted that "those incomparable papers of the 'Federalist'... though they were written to influence only the voters of 1788, still, with a strange, persistent, longevity of power, shape the constitutional criticism of the present day, obscuring much of that development of constitutional practice which has since taken place. The Constitution in operation is manifestly a very different thing from the Constitution of the books." Wilson knew that the Constitution, interpreted in light of *The Federalist*, imposed limitations on the scope of government that were unrealistic and incapable of changing with the times. That is why Wilson insisted that "it is getting harder to run a constitution than to frame one." See "The Study of Administration." *Political Science Quarterly*, 2 (July 1887): 197-222.

31. Wilson is surely wrong in his assumption that the American Founders understood politics from a theoretical foundation provided by

Newtonian physics. The Founders would not have denied that Newton's theories are descriptive of the physical world. However, Madison, in *Federalist* No. 37, makes it very clear that political science is not dependent on theoretical physics, but upon metaphysical reason and prudence. He notes, "when we pass from the works of nature, in which all the delineations are perfectly accurate, and appear to be otherwise only from the imperfection of the eye which surveys them, to the institutions of man, in which the obscurity arises as well from the object itself as from the organ by which it is contemplated, we must perceive the necessity of moderating still further our expectations and hopes from the efforts of human sagacity." Even the institutional structure of the Constitution is not based upon an exact science, but on the dictates of prudence. Madison notes further, "experience has instructed us that no skill in the science of government has yet been able to discriminate and define, with sufficient certainty, its three great provinces—the legislative, executive, and judiciary.... Questions daily occur in the course of practice, which prove the obscurity which reigns in these subjects, and which puzzle the greatest adepts in political science." *The Federalist Papers*, No. 37, 196.

32. Woodrow Wilson, *Constitutional Government in the United States*, new introduction by Sidney A. Pearson, Jr. (New Brunswick, N.J.: Transaction Publishers, 2002 [originally published in 1908]), 54-55.

33. Ibid., 56.

34. It was already clear in the nineteenth century, that Darwinian theory was more likely to be used in defense of tyranny rather than in support of democratic equality and liberty. In the Civil War, the South's arguments in defense of slavery drew powerful support from evolutionary theories of race. In the twentieth century, the triumph of the will, on behalf of a master race, or a master class, produced despotic regimes that claimed to establish legitimacy based on laws of history and evolution.

35. Hegel, *Philosophy of Right*, 285 (emphasis added).

36. A more complete account of this problem is presented in my article, "Theology, Metaphysics, and Positivism: The Origins of the Social Sciences and the Transformation of the American University," in *Challenges to the American Founding: Slavery, Historicism, and Progressivism in the Nineteenth Century*, Ronald J. Pestritto and Thomas G. West, eds. (Lanham, Md.: Lexington Books, forthcoming).

37. In the political philosophy that underlies the concept of the modern state, the general (or universal) will is the source of right, which provides the ground of the legitimacy of the people's will. On the other hand, in a constitutional regime, majority will must be subordinate to

reason, and the laws of nature. Even though the will of the majority provides the basis for the legitimate use of power, it is not the source of right. It is for this reason that Thomas Jefferson would remind the people in his First Inaugural Address, that "though the will of the majority is in all cases to prevail, that will to be rightful must be reasonable." The Constitution prevents a majority from giving up its reason in the service of its will. Even the people themselves, although sovereign, said Jefferson, "are inherently independent of all but moral law."

38. Leo Strauss, *What is Political Philosophy?* (Glencoe: The Free Press, 1959), 51.

39. Leo Strauss, "The Three Waves of Modernity," in *An Introduction to Political Philosophy: Ten Essays by Leo Strauss*, Hilail Gildin, ed. (Detroit: Wayne State University Press, 1989), 91.

40. Ibid.

41. Leo Strauss, *Natural Right and History* (Chicago: University of Chicago Press, 1953), 7.

42. Ibid.

43. Ibid.

44. Strauss made it possible to understand the theory and practice of constitutional government once again. He made it clear that "it would not be difficult to show that liberal or constitutional democracy comes closer to what the classics demanded than any alternative that is viable in our age." He noted: "According to the classics, the best constitution is a contrivance of reason, i.e. of conscious activity or of planning on the part of an individual or a few individuals. It is in accordance with nature, or it is a natural order, since it fulfills to the highest degree the requirements of the perfection of human nature, or since its structure imitates the pattern of nature." Strauss' defense of constitutionalism was a defense of reason rooted in nature which required limited government. It presupposed rational expectations regarding the ends of politics and prudential judgment concerning the means. Moreover, he supplied the philosophic critique which made it possible to recover an understanding of the theoretical roots of rational or prudential politics, which had been undermined by the victory of historicism. He knew that the immoderate political practice of the twentieth century was a consequence of the utopian character of its political thought. In providing a defense of constitutionalism, and in laying bare the tyranny of the universal homogeneous state, Strauss provided the foundations for an analysis of modern life which could bring to light the deepest problems of modernity.

45. Strauss noted that "the Aristotelian distinction between theoretical and practical sciences implies that human action has principles of its

own which are known independently of theoretical science (physics and metaphysics) and therefore that the practical sciences do not depend on the theoretical sciences or are not derivative from them. The principles of action are the natural ends toward which man is by nature inclined and of which he has by nature some awareness. This awareness is the necessary condition for his seeking and finding appropriate means for his ends, or for his becoming practically wise or prudent. Practical science, in contradistinction to practical wisdom itself, sets forth coherently the principles of action and the general rules of prudence ('proverbial wisdom'). Practical science raises questions that within practical or political experience, or at any rate on the basis of such experience reveal themselves to be the most important questions and that are not stated, let alone answered, with sufficient clarity by practical wisdom itself. The sphere governed by prudence is then in principle self-sufficient or closed." "Epilogue," in *Essays on the Scientific Study of Politics*, 309.

46. Ibid.

47. Ibid., 310.

48. Leo Strauss, *On Tyranny*, Victor Gourevitch and Michael S. Roth, eds. (New York: The Free Press, 1991), 212.

49. Strauss observed that "the revolts against Hegelianism ... increased the confusion, since they destroyed, as far as in them lay, the very possibility of theory. 'Doctrinairism' and 'existentialism' appear to us as the two faulty extremes. While being opposed to each other, they agree with each other in the decisive respect—they agree in ignoring prudence, 'the god of this lower world.' Prudence and 'this lower world' cannot be seen properly without some knowledge of 'the higher world'—without genuine *theoria*." *Natural Right and History*, 320-21.

50. As Strauss noted, "the substitution of the distinction between progressive and reactionary for the distinction between good and bad is another aspect of the discovery of history." See, "Progress or Return?" in *The Rebirth of Classical Political Rationalism* (Chicago: University of Chicago Press, 1989), 239.

51. Strauss came to the realization that modern despotism must be understood in light of the modern science of politics, or the theory of the state itself. He was fully aware that, although tyranny was not a thing of the past, modern political science could not provide a satisfactory analysis of it. It is within the rational state that the corruption of modern political thought has been shown in the practice of its politics. The political practice of the rational state tended inexorably in the direction of what Tocqueville called a centralized administration. On the basis of Strauss'

analysis, it becomes clear that the centralized administrative state, which in principle leads to the universal and homogeneous state, also leads to the subsequent loss of man's freedom and humanity.

52. Strauss understood tyranny in the same way as the American Founders. Tyranny is a problem coeval with political life. Consequently, the realm of politics cannot be transcended. *On Tyranny*, 22-23.

53. Ibid., 127.

54. *The Federalist* No. 51, 340.

·⁀Chapter 8 ⌣·

Darwin's Public Policy:
Nineteenth Century Science and the Rise of the American Welfare State

John G. West

It is often claimed that Charles Darwin's theory of evolution supplied a powerful justification for limited government and laissez faire capitalism in late nineteenth century America. During the era of "robber barons," sweatshops, and corporate greed, capitalist defenders of limited government allegedly seized on Darwin's idea of natural selection as the perfect rationale for the do-nothing state.

Propagated by countless textbooks, this view of American history has become part of the received wisdom about the late 1800s and early 1900s. It is, however, more fiction than fact. Far from providing a defense of limited government, Darwinism during this period became one of the most powerful doctrines supporting the creation of a regulatory welfare state. First, Darwinism was employed to destroy the moral legitimacy of capitalism, opening the door to greater government regulation of the economy. Second, Darwinism was used to bolster the Progressives' attack on the limited government of America's Founders. Finally, Darwinism was invoked to justify coercive welfare policies that inserted the government into the most private decisions of family life.

1. USING DARWINISM TO DEBUNK THE LEGITIMACY OF CAPITALISM
Many educated people may find it hard to believe that Darwinism's primary influence in the nineteenth century was the subversion of

limited government rather than its defense. After all, history textbooks still routinely depict the late nineteenth century as the golden age of "Social Darwinism," the idea that the struggle for survival in nature justified cut-throat competition in the economy unhampered by any government regulation or efforts to improve the plight of the poor. In the words of one textbook, "Social Darwinists ... long claimed that since society operated like a jungle ... efforts to improve social conditions were misguided attempts to interfere with the 'natural' order."[1] "The new doctrine thus opposed poor relief, housing regulations, and public education and justified poverty and slums," adds another one.[2] Given the ideas of such "Social Darwinists," how can any sensible person assert that Darwinism was actually enlisted to *undermine* the legitimacy of capitalism?

To answer this question, we must examine how the popularly received view of Social Darwinism came to be adopted in the first place. Historian Richard Hofstadter bears much of the responsibility for solidifying the view that Social Darwinists were the preeminent defenders of capitalism during the Gilded Age. In his classic book *Social Darwinism in American Thought*, originally published in 1944, Hofstadter contended that "it was those who wished to defend the political status quo, above all the laissez-faire conservatives, who were first to pick up the instruments of social argument that were forged out of the Darwinian concepts."[3]

Preeminent among the Social Darwinists identified by Hofstadter were British social theorist Herbert Spencer and American sociologist William Graham Sumner. An evolutionist even before Darwin, Spencer was the one who actually coined the phrase "survival of the fittest," which Darwin later invoked as a description of natural selection.[4] Applying this doctrine to human society, Spencer argued that government aid to the poor was counterproductive because it interfered with the natural process of the elimination of the unfit. "The whole effort of nature is to get rid of such, to clear the world of them, and make room for better."[5] Yale Professor Sumner, whom Hofstadter called "the most vigorous and influential social Darwinist in America," propounded similar themes.[6] He argued that "millionaires are a product of natural selection," and said that "if we do not like the survival of the fittest, we have only one possible alternative, and that is the survival of the unfittest."

According to Hofstadter, America's business leaders enthusiastically embraced the ideology espoused by Spencer and Sumner. In support of this thesis, Hofstadter supplied a collection of seemingly irrefutable quotes from leading men of business who championed Darwinian capitalism. Railroad magnate James J. Hill declared that "the fortunes of railroad companies are determined by the law of the survival of the fittest." Oil baron John D. Rockefeller told a Sunday School group that "the growth of a large business is merely a survival of the fittest," comparing the salutary effects of economic competition to a wise gardener who prunes his roses. "The American Beauty rose can be produced in the splendor and fragrance which bring cheer to its beholder only by sacrificing the early buds which grow up around it," said Rockefeller. "This is not an evil tendency in business. It is merely the working-out of a law of nature and a law of God." Steel magnate Andrew Carnegie likewise proclaimed that Darwin's law of natural selection was essential to human society, no matter the hardships it may pose for specific individuals: "While the law may sometimes be hard for the individual, it is best for the race, because it insures the survival of the fittest in every department."[7]

Hofstadter's claim that Social Darwinism supplied the business community's justification for cut-throat competition in the economy eventually became the popularly received view of late nineteenth century capitalism. According to this interpretation, Darwinism's most pernicious social effect happened to be the powerful quasi-scientific rationalization it handed businessmen for old-fashioned greed and injustice. There was just one problem with Hofstadter's thesis: It was largely untrue.

Fifteen years after Hofstadter published his book, University of Wisconsin historian Irvin Wyllie urged fellow historians to re-evaluate Hofstadter's case for Social Darwinism in the business community. In an address offered at a meeting marking the centennial of *The Origin of Species*, Wyllie argued that the evidence for Darwinism's influence on the American business community during the Gilded Age was spotty, at best. To be sure, there were Darwinists in America who tried to apply Darwin's theory to society, but they "were for the most part scientists, social scientists, philosophers, clergymen, editors, and other educationally advantaged persons."[8] Because most businessmen at the time were not well-educated, it would have been strange to find many of them even knowledgeable about the ideas of Darwin and Spencer, let alone advocating those ideas.

Wyllie acknowledged that a few business leaders such as Carnegie did reflect the influence of Spencer and Darwin, but he argued that the most salient point was that there were so few examples among the business class.[9] Moreover, some of the examples that had been adduced by Hofstadter were either ambiguous or false. Pointing out an embarrassing misattribution by Hofstadter, Wyllie noted that it was not John D. Rockefeller who defended business as "a survival of the fittest," but John D. Rockefeller, Jr., the industrialist's son. "This sentiment, uttered by John D. Rockefeller, Jr. in 1902 at an address to the YMCA at his alma mater ... may prove that the university-trained son knew how to use Darwinian phraseology, but it does not prove that his Bible-reading father was a Spencerian in the Gilded Age."[10]

Nineteenth century American businessmen and economists did praise free enterprise, vigorous competition, and laissez faire. But these ideas did not originate with Darwin. Instead, they sprang from such classical economists as Adam Smith and Frederic Bastiat. Darwin was not only unnecessary for the defense of free enterprise and competition, his model conflicted with prevalent ideas about the morality of commerce. Most businessmen of the period would have found it thoroughly unpalatable to justify economic success as the product of an amoral struggle for survival in which only the strongest and most ruthless competitors can survive. Far from believing that commerce was amoral or harsh, nineteenth century American businessmen argued that business success was squarely based on moral virtue. According to Wyllie,

> anyone who examines the voluminous nineteenth-century literature of business success cannot fail to be impressed that businessmen who talked about success and failure took their texts from Christian moralists, not from Darwin and Spencer. In the race for wealth they attributed little influence to native intelligence, physical strength, or any other endowment of nature, and paramount influence to industry, frugality, and sobriety—simple moral virtues that any man could cultivate. They urged young men to seek the business way of life in the Bible, not in *The*

Descent of Man or *The Principles of Sociology.* The problem of success was not that of grinding down one's competitors, but of elevating one's self—and the two were not equivalent.[11]

Since business success was supposed to be based on "good character," one businessman's success did not have to be built on top of another businessman's failure. Instead, "opportunities for success, like opportunities for salvation, were limitless; heaven could receive as many as were worthy."[12]

At its core, the American resistance to invoking Darwinism as a rationale for laissez faire reflected a rejection of the pessimism at the heart of Darwin's theory, which had been inspired by the Reverend Thomas Malthus' dour *Essay on the Principle of Population* (1798).[13] By Darwin's own account, it was his reading of Malthus that stimulated him to develop his theory of natural selection, and in *The Origin of Species,* Darwin claimed that the "struggle for existence" of which he spoke was merely "the doctrine of Malthus applied with manifold force to the whole animal and vegetable kingdoms."[14] That statement was not quite right, because Malthus himself already indicated that his theory applied to the entire biological world, not just human beings.[15] But Darwin was correct to suggest that he emphasized the broader implications of Malthus' theory of population more than Malthus himself.

Malthus argued that men, animals, and plants all tend to reproduce more offspring than nature can support. The inevitable result of this overpopulation is widespread death until the population is reduced to a level that nature can support. Hence, plants and animals die off due to lack "of room and nourishment, which is common to animals and plants, and among animals by becoming the prey of others."[16] Human beings are similarly killed off by disease, famine, and vice. There is little that can be done to counteract this struggle for survival because it is grounded in the laws of nature. "The perpetual tendency in the race of man to increase beyond the means of subsistence is one of the general laws of animated nature which we can have no reason to expect will change."[17] Darwin adopted this struggle for existence articulated by Malthus as the foundation for his theory of evolution by natural selection. Darwin wrote that while reading Malthus, "it at once struck me that under these circumstances [of the

struggle for existence] favourable variations would tend to be preserved and unfavourable ones to be destroyed. The result of this would
be the formation of new species."[18]

Applied to the world of commerce, Malthusian theory presented
economics as a zero-sum game. Additional people almost inevitably
meant greater privation for many human beings. The more people
there are, the less food there will be to go around. The more laborers
there are, the lower the standard wage will be.[19] While Malthus noted
some exceptions to this rule, he suggested they were temporary. In
America, for example, "the reward of labour is at present ... liberal,"
but "it may be expected that in the progress of the population of
America, the labourers will in time be much less liberally rewarded."[20]
In the Malthusian view, economic progress for the few could only be
purchased at the price of misery for the many.

American defenders of capitalism during the latter 1800s explicitly repudiated the Malthusian view of economics, which meant that
they also had little desire to invoke Social Darwinism as a defense of
free enterprise. In 1879, for example, Harvard political economist
Francis Bowen inveighed against "Malthusianism, Darwinism, and
Pessimism" in the *North American Review*. Bowen generally supported
laissez faire, but he was anything but a Malthusian or a Social Darwinist. Contra Malthus, Bowen argued that "the bounties of nature
are practically inexhaustible."[21] Therefore starvation and misery among
human beings were not inevitable consequences of overpopulation
but the products of human ignorance, indolence, and self-indulgence.
"It is not the excess of population which causes the misery, but the
misery which causes the excess of population," he insisted.[22] Bowen
noted that "since 1850 ... English writers upon political economy have
generally ceased to advocate Malthusianism and its subsidiary doctrines," and observed how ironic it was that "in 1860, at the very time
when this gloomy doctrine of 'a battle for life' had nearly died out in
political economy ... it was revived in biology, and made the basis in
that science of a theory still more comprehensive and appalling than
that which had been founded upon it by Malthus."[23]

American businessman and economist Edward Atkinson likewise
denounced any attempt to wed economics to Malthus' theory of population or to David Ricardo's similarly pessimistic theory of rent. Regarding both theories as premised on a false "law of diminishing

returns," he also objected that they promoted the spurious view "that the struggle for life must inevitably become more difficult and more violent, and must inevitably fail."[24] In fact, capitalism allowed mankind to alleviate the struggle for existence by creating greater abundance for everyone according to Atkinson. Instead of being a destructive struggle for static resources, commerce in a free society could generate sufficient new resources to raise the standard of living for ever greater numbers of people:

> Through competition among capitalists, capital itself is every year more effective in production, and tends ever to increasing abundance. Under its working the commodities that have been the luxuries of one generation become the comforts of the next and the necessities of the third ... The plane of what constitutes a comfortable subsistence is constantly rising, and as the years go by greater and greater numbers attain this plane.[25]

Atkinson argued that capitalism's abundance was brought about chiefly by harnessing "the mental faculties of man" through new technologies.[26] Malthus' theory "finds as yet no warrant in the experience of men" in large part because "invention and discovery have yielded greater and greater abundance for each given portion of time devoted to the work of procuring subsistence."[27]

So far from promoting the destruction of the many on behalf of the success of the few, commerce could lead to progress for all. "In a free state, governed by just laws, the more the few increase in wealth the more the many gain in welfare."[28] And this increased wealth was generated not by ruthless and amoral competition but by mutual service, which in Atkinson's view lay at the heart of economics. "Commerce is an occupation in which men serve each other; it is an exchange in which both parties in the transaction gain something which they desire more than the thing they part with."[29] Atkinson's optimistic defense of free enterprise was the standard view adopted by businessmen during the Gilded Age. According to Irvin Wyllie, "because American businessmen operated in a land blessed with an abundance of resources they rejected the Malthusian idea that chances were so limited that one man's rise meant the fall of many others. Theirs was a more optimistic view, that every triumph opened the way for more."[30]

Thus, far from being defenders of the idea of Social Darwinism, the most articulate champions of free enterprise in America during the latter 1800s explicitly condemned the idea that Darwinism supported capitalism. The real champions of capitalism repudiated Darwinism because they rejected the Malthusian depiction of economics as a zero-sum game where the benefit of some must necessarily lead to the destruction of others. Instead, they viewed capitalism as an ever-expanding way of spreading benefits to all.

In reality, it was not capitalism's defenders but its detractors who most identified capitalism with Darwinian theory. Except for academics such as Spencer and Sumner, those who most often equated free enterprise with the law of the jungle were the *opponents* of laissez faire economics. According to historian Robert Bannister, "[n]ew Liberals and socialists asserted in almost a single voice that opponents of state activity wedded Darwinism to classical economics and thus traded illicitly on the prestige of the new biology."[31] A "Declaration of Principles" published by the Nationalist Club in 1889, for example, charged that "the principle of competition is simply the application of the brutal law of the survival of the strongest and most cunning."[32] Henry Demarest Lloyd wrote that "the 'survival of the fittest' theory ... is practically professed" by American businessmen.[33] And socialist writer Jack London observed that "the key-note to *laissez faire*" was "everybody for himself and devil take the hindmost ... It is the let-alone policy, the struggle for existence, which strengthens the strong, destroys the weak, and makes a finer and more capable breed of men."[34] Nor were popular polemicists the only ones promoting the new view of American capitalism. "Academic economists and sociologists ... added their authority to the developing stereotype," writes Bannister.[35] As a result, the primary use of Darwinism was not to justify capitalism, but to de-legitimize it. As Wyllie points out, "all the leading muckrakers sensed that there was no better way to discredit a businessman than to portray him as a renegade of the jungle."[36] Their purpose was to stigmatize capitalism as nothing but "survival of the fittest" in order to undermine its legitimacy and generate support for expanded government control over the economy. Accordingly, the label of "Darwinism" became one of the most potent rhetorical weapons in the arsenal of those who wanted to build a regulatory welfare state.

2. USING DARWINISM TO ATTACK
THE FOUNDERS' IDEA OF LIMITED GOVERNMENT

Challenging the legitimacy of capitalism was not the only way those who favored an expanded state used Darwinism to further their ends. Progressive era reformers also invoked Darwin's theory to make the case for the inevitability—indeed, the necessity—of change. According to the Progressives, nations and their economic systems are subject to evolution just as much as plants and animals; and like plants and animals, nations must adapt to new conditions or die. Governments must evolve in order to deal with new challenges.

The roots of the Progressive idea of social and political evolution were supplied not by Darwin but by Hegel and the political science of the German administrative state.[37] But Darwin was honored for showing that the truths preached by the political philosophers had been substantiated by biology. This faith in the necessity of social evolution underlay the Progressive movement's rejection of laissez faire capitalism. While laissez faire may have been required by the circumstances of a previous era, new social conditions called for new economic policies according to the Progressives, and therefore American government must evolve and grow in order to meet the demands of the new circumstances. In adopting their evolutionary view of government, the Progressive reformers had to discard the political theory of the American Founders just as much as they did the teachings of laissez faire capitalism. The Founders had claimed that government existed to secure certain unchanging natural rights. Because these rights did not change, neither did the purposes of the government. The Founders' conception of government was thus more stationary than evolutionary. But such a conception was tantamount to heresy in the new scientific view of the world.[38]

One of the most articulate spokesmen for the new view was a political scientist from New Jersey, who argued that "in our own day, whenever we discuss the structure or development of a thing ... we consciously or unconsciously follow Mr. Darwin."[39] That political scientist was Woodrow Wilson, then president of Princeton, soon to be Governor of New Jersey and eventually President of the United States. During the presidential election campaign of 1912, Wilson explicitly invoked Darwin to justify an evolutionary understanding of the U.S.

Constitution that would allow the federal government to dramatically expand its powers over the economy. According to Wilson, the problem with the original Constitution was that it embodied the Founders' "Newtonian" view that government was built on unchanging laws like "the law of gravitation." In truth, however, government "falls, not under the theory of the universe, but under the theory of organic life. It is accountable to Darwin, not to Newton. It is modified by its environment, necessitated by its tasks, shaped to its functions by the sheer pressure of life." Hence, "living political constitutions must be Darwinian in structure and in practice. Society is a living organism and must obey the laws of Life ... it must develop." According to Wilson, "all that progressives ask or desire is permission—in an era when 'development,' 'evolution,' is the scientific word—to interpret the Constitution according to the Darwinian principle." [40] The doctrine of the evolving Constitution articulated by Wilson and others opened the door to much greater regulation of business and the economy, eventually paving the way for the New Deal.

But once the door was opened to regulate the rich, there was no reason increased government powers should not also be used to regulate the poor. This set the stage for a new kind of Social Darwinism, one based not on laissez faire but on the idea that government should scientifically plan and regulate even the most intimate questions of family life.

3. USING DARWINISM TO PROMOTE COERCIVE WELFARE

During the same year presidential candidate Woodrow Wilson was campaigning for a Darwinian understanding of the Constitution, psychologist Henry Goddard was urging the nation to apply Darwinism to its social welfare policies as well. Goddard, who holds the dubious distinction of introducing the term "moron" into the English language,[41] was obsessed with how "feeble-minded" Americans were degrading their country's racial stock. One of the star witnesses for his resultant crusade was a girl he named Deborah Kallikak, who was prominently featured in his inflammatory 1912 volume *The Kallikak Family: A Study in Feeble-Mindedness.*

Born to an unmarried woman on welfare, Deborah Kallikak came from what Goddard believed was a long line of biological defectives. In an effort to prove that her feeble-mindedness was hereditary,

Goddard and fellow researchers at the Training School for Backward and Feeble-minded Children in New Jersey zealously tracked down Deborah's relatives and researched her ancestors in search of other defectives. According to Goddard, a field investigation of the area surrounding the "ancestral home" of Deborah's family "showed that the family had always been notorious for the number of defectives and delinquents it had produced." Indeed, the more Kallikak family members the investigators located, the more deficient the family's bloodline appeared to be. "The surprise and horror of it all was that no matter where we traced them, whether in the prosperous rural district, in the city slums ... or in the more remote mountain regions, or whether it was a question of the second or the sixth generation, an appalling amount of defectiveness was everywhere found."[42] Goddard eventually traced the family line all the way back to one Martin Kallikak, Sr., a soldier during the Revolutionary War whose affair with a tavern girl produced an illegitimate son. Of the 480 descendants to come from this son, Goddard claimed to have "conclusive proof" that 143 "were or are feeble-minded, while only forty-six have been found normal. The rest are unknown or doubtful."[43]

Goddard believed that members of the Kallikak family were especially dangerous to America's racial stock because on the surface many of them did not appear to be particularly deficient. "A large proportion of those who are considered feeble-minded in this study are persons who would not be recognized as such by the untrained observer," acknowledged Goddard.[44] Deborah herself was in this category. According to her teachers, Deborah Kallikak could "run an electric sewing machine, cook, and do practically everything about the house." While it might take her half an hour to memorize four lines, once she learned something, she retained it. She was "cheerful," "affectionate," and learned "a new occupation quickly." She also exhibited an independent spirit. "Active and restless," she was "inclined to be quarrelsome." At the same time, she was "fairly good-tempered."[45]

"The description ... is one that millions of parents might give of their own teenage daughters," notes a recent writer.[46] But in the eyes of Goddard there was nothing normal about Deborah. In fact, Goddard was convinced that this free-spirited young girl who was kind to animals, loved music, and "was bold towards strangers," was nothing less than a menace to the future of American civilization.

Goddard complained about "the unwillingness of ... [Deborah's] teachers to admit even to themselves that she is really feeble-minded,"[47] and he worried that this sort of refusal to face reality was common among teachers. Faced with a "high-grade" feeble-minded girl like Deborah who is "rather good-looking, bright in appearance, with many attractive ways, the teacher clings to the hope, indeed insists, that such a girl will come out all right. Our work with Deborah convinces us that such hopes are delusions."[48] Calling the family history of the Kallikaks a "ghastly story," Goddard went on to declare that "there are Kallikak families all about us. They are multiplying at twice the rate of the general population, and not until we recognize this fact ... will we begin to solve these social problems."[49]

Goddard invoked the story of Deborah Kallikak to prove that the underclass was produced more by bad heredity than bad environment, which led him to the conclusion that heredity rather than charity was the key to eliminating the underclass and its associated social ills. Goddard's conclusion was shared in the early 1900s by a growing number of scientists and policymakers in America who championed the cause of eugenics, which proposed producing better human beings through directed breeding. Charles Darwin's cousin Francis Galton is generally recognized as the founder of the modern eugenics movement. After researching the family connections of members of the British elite, Galton announced in articles and then in books that talent was largely hereditary.[50] Thus, if society wanted to guarantee its future improvement, it needed to pay attention to who were having the most babies at present. By the 1880s Galton had coined the actual term eugenics (adapted from a Greek root word meaning "good in birth"[51]), and he was urging efforts to improve the race through better breeding. "Positive eugenics" focused on encouraging those deemed the most fit to reproduce more, while "negative eugenics" focused on curtailing reproduction by those deemed unfit, including mental defectives and criminals. While Galton tended to stress the need for positive eugenics (in order to cultivate the geniuses needed for society to thrive and progress), he also favored negative eugenic measures and thought that those deemed unfit could be segregated in institutions where they would not be allowed to reproduce.[52]

Initially, eugenists were hampered by the scientific community's misunderstanding of heredity. In the nineteenth century, many scientists—including Darwin himself—believed that behaviors and characteristics acquired during a person's lifetime could be inherited by his children. As Mark Haller has pointed out, "as long as people believed in the inheritance of acquired characters, there was little need for eugenics; instead all efforts could be devoted to betterment of present health and education, with the assurance that the improvement would appear in the hereditary endowment of succeeding generations."[53] Galton rejected the heritability of acquired characteristics, but it was not until the early years of the twentieth century that this view became popular in the scientific community.[54] Once that happened, eugenists could claim with confidence that "nearly all forms of mental deficiency are incurable" and according to "most biologists ... acquired characters are not inherited."[55] This new view of unchangeable heredity made the rationale for eugenics much more powerful. If heredity could not be reformed by environment, the only way to eliminate biological defectives was to make sure they did not breed at all.

The eugenics agenda was promoted in the United States by a growing number of national organizations, including the American Breeders Association (established 1903), the Eugenics Records Office (established 1910), and the Race Betterment Foundation of Battle Creek, Michigan (established 1911).[56] The American Breeders Association (later the American Genetic Association) was organized at the instigation of the U.S. Secretary of Agriculture James Wilson and Assistant Secretary of Agriculture W. Hays.[57] Besides publishing an influential periodical eventually titled *The Journal of Heredity*, the Association helped create the Eugenics Records Office (ERO) in Cold Spring Harbor, New York. The goal of the ERO was to collect comprehensive eugenics information on "a large portion of the families of America," records which would be stored permanently in the group's fire-proof vaults and could be consulted by those who wanted to ensure that their prospective mates were eugenically fit.[58] Agriculture Secretary Wilson praised those "assembling the genetic data of thousands of families" for "making records of the very souls of our people, of the very life essence of our racial blood."[59]

The American eugenics movement was so well established by 1912 that it was drawing favorable notices in Europe, and in July of that year American eugenists had a starring role in the first International Eugenics Congress held in London.[60] At that event, Professor G. Ruggeri from Italy publicly recognized the American contribution to eugenics, declaring that "thanks to recent researches in the United States, it was now certain that the races of man acted in exactly the same way as the races of animals."[61]

The eugenics movement drew direct inspiration from Darwinian biology, although many today try to downplay the connection. When the ABC newsmagazine *20/20* did an expose of American eugenics in 2000, the report curiously sidestepped the intellectual origins of the eugenics crusade. "It was all a reflection of the culture at the time where people genuinely believed if mentally deficient people were sterilized most of society's problems would disappear," viewers were told.[62] But *why* did people find such a claim persuasive? What was the underlying logic for their belief? Viewers never learned. Incredibly, one scholar writing recently about eugenics not only failed to mention Darwinism, he instead traced the eugenists' beliefs back to "the biblical concept that 'like breeds like,' to which eugenics researchers provided a scientific gloss."[63] Yet it was society's violation of natural selection, not the Bible, that supplied the operating premise for the eugenists' ideology. The eugenists' underlying fear was the same as the one Charles Darwin had articulated in his book *The Descent of Man*: By saving the weak through medicine and charity, and by allowing defective classes to reproduce, civilized societies were counteracting the law of natural selection to the detriment of the human race.[64]

Time and again American eugenists lamented their country's sins against natural selection. According to former Governor of Illinois Frank Lowden, "in a state of nature" defective individuals "would long ago have disappeared from the face of the earth. Starvation, disease, and exposure, if they had been left to their own resources, would have eliminated them long ago. Man's interference with natural laws alone save them from perishing."[65] Edwin Conklin, Professor of Biology at Princeton University, observed that while nature may still kill off the worst defectives, "nevertheless a good many defectives survive in modern society and are capable of reproduction who would have perished in more primitive society before reaching maturity."[66] Such defectives survive "in the most highly civilized States" because they "are preserved by charity, and ... are allowed to reproduce ... thus natural selection, the great law of evolution and progress, is set at naught." For this reason some eugenists criticized efforts to reduce infant mortality by improving sanitation, hygiene, and prenatal care. According to these critics, such efforts merely postponed the deaths of many defective babies, and those defective babies who did survive long-term would drag the race down by perpetuating "another strain of weak heredity, which natural selection would have cut off ruthlessly in the interests of race betterment."[67] Hence, "from a strict biological viewpoint" efforts to reduce infant mortality by improving environmental influences were "often detrimental to the future of the race." H. E. Jordan of Virginia made the same point more generally: "What sanitary science and hygiene seek to accomplish by attention to external conditions alone largely defeats its own ends by counteracting the working of the principle of selection."[68]

Despite their law-of-the-jungle rhetoric, American eugenists did not advocate going back to the days when "war ... poverty, disease, and capital punishment did a fairly thorough if not a very beautiful piece of work before we began to civilize them away."[69] Instead, they argued that "some substitute has to be found for natural selection." That substitute was the directed selection of eugenics. Man had to take control of his own evolution by encouraging the "best" to breed more and discouraging the "worst" from breeding at all.

According to the eugenists, human beings were essentially no different than horses, dogs, or blackberries, and so the techniques perfected to breed animals and plants could easily be applied to men and women with just as much success. "Man is an organism—an animal," declared Charles Davenport, "and the laws of improvement of corn and of race horses hold true for him also."[70] "All life is conditioned by the same fundamental laws of nature," agreed H. E. Jordan. "It would seem, then, that the same methods that man now employs in producing a high quality breed of dogs, or birds, or cattle, or horses, he must apply to himself."[71] "If the human race is to be permanently improved in its inherited characteristics," wrote Princeton biologist Edward Conklin, "there is no doubt that it must be accomplished in the same way in which man has made improvements in the various races of domesticated animals and cultivated plants."[72] Since breeders of animals and plants are experts in heredity, the public should let them determine how humans should breed. According to inventor (and eugenist) Alexander Graham Bell, "all recognize the fact that the laws of heredity which apply to animals also apply to man; and that therefore the breeder of animals is fitted to guide public opinion on questions relating to human heredity."[73] Bell said that this represented "an opportunity for the members of the American Genetic Association.... Most of the disputed questions of human heredity can be settled by them, and their verdict will be acquiesced in by the general public."

The underlying assumption of the eugenists was a thoroughgoing biological reductionism. In their view, social problems like poverty and unemployment were rooted in man's biology rather than in his environment or his free choices. One eugenist described going into a prosperous town in Iowa and visiting families whose houses were "truly the dirtiest, most ill-smelling places I have ever seen." "Now honestly, my uplifting environmental friend," asked the eugenist, "what *can* you do for such people? They had plenty of money and ample opportunity. They went to picture shows, and their children attended, or rather were forced to attend, school ... But their poverty was pure biological poverty, inborn, ineradicable. Their real poverty was poor heredity." [74] If such biological defectives moved into the cities they would "fall naturally into the slums." Similarly, another eugenist proclaimed that "we know that some by no means small proportion of the unemployed were really destined to be unemployable from the first, as for instance by reason of hereditary disease. It were better for them and for us that they had never been born."[75] Those who objected to this view of man as a machine were told to stop standing in the way of scientific progress. "Science seeks to explain phenomena in terms of mechanism, and no other interpretation now brings entire satisfaction," argued Charles Davenport. "If human behavior can be brought under a mechanical law instead of being conceived of as controlled by demons or by a 'free' will ... why should we regret it?"[76]

Many eugenists acknowledged that environment played some role in social problems, but they insisted that heredity was more decisive. "An understanding of the facts of biology leads us to expect that heredity should be nearly all-powerful and the force of environment slight," proclaimed one essay in the *Journal of Heredity*.[77] "The number of social problems whose solution lies with genetics rather than with ordinary sociology is far greater than anyone except the eugenist realizes," claimed another article.[78] Because of the primacy of heredity, some eugenists even questioned the utility of universal education. Many students may be biologically unfit for education, they claimed. "The expensive 'special classes' of the public schools are filled with children a large part of whom are morons," reported the *Journal of Heredity*, which complained that "an attempt is made to educate" such students "when an examination of their ancestry would show that it is humanly impossible to educate them, in the way that their playmates are educated."[79]

Not all eugenists were quite so strident, and some endorsed the importance of "euthenics"—trying to improve human beings by improving social conditions. But even the more moderate eugenists maintained that eugenics was still required to make such social efforts fruitful. According to Paul Popenoe and Roswell Johnson, "eugenics is, in fact, a prerequisite of euthenics, for it is only the capable and altruistic man who can contribute to social progress; and such a man can only be produced through eugenics."[80] Accordingly, eugenists like Charles Davenport encouraged philanthropists to shift money from traditional charity to eugenics programs. "Vastly more effective than ten million dollars to 'Charity' would be ten million dollars to eugenics," declared Davenport.[81] "He who, by such a gift, should redeem mankind from vice, imbecility and suffering would be the world's wisest philanthropist."

If the fear of being swamped by biological defectives was a powerful motivator for eugenists, the hope of achieving biological perfection was equally inspiring. The eugenists' blind faith in modern science spawned a virulent utopianism. Dressed up in quasi-religious terminology, the eugenics faith promised to create heaven on earth through the magic of human breeding. This utopian vision had been a key part of the eugenics crusade from its inception. The originator of eugenics, Francis Galton, had promoted the goal of "gradually raising the present miserably low standard of the human race to one in which the Utopias in the dreamland of philanthropists may become practical possibilities."[82] American eugenists were no less optimistic about what could be accomplished. "The Garden of Eden is not in the past, it is in the future," promised Albert Wiggam.[83] A "rigidly applied eugenics" will eventually produce an "ideal state of human society!" seconded H. E. Jordan, adding that "thoroly [sic] healthy bodies could develop the highest ranges of mental capacity. There would be little suffering, weakness, sickness, crime, or vice."[84] These benefits of eugenics "may seem utopian.... But by all the signs of the times, this day is coming....

And it behooves us as intelligent, moral men and women to do our share.... to hasten the time of this life more abundant in this kingdom of heaven on the earth."[85] Maynard Metcalf similarly expressed "entire confidence that we shall in time almost banish physical, mental and moral invalidism, which today are most prominent characteristics of the human species."[86] Indeed, eugenics could rid human beings of original sin, allowing society to re-engineer human nature and "build a race that is physically sound, intellectually keen and strong and whose natural impulses are wholesome! Not a race of men who are decent because they are restrained from following their natural bent, but a race whose natural quality is wholesome, who need not so much to restrain as to develop themselves." Metcalf urged people to make eugenics their religion. "The people who make eugenics part of their religion and are loyal to its truth will have found ... the fountain of youth," [87] he declared. Eugenists seemed certain that once man took control of his own evolution, he could do an even better job than nature. "It has taken Mother Nature long, long ages to turn fierce greedy hairy ape-like beasts into such people as we are," wrote feminist eugenist Charlotte Perkins Gilman.[88] "It will take us but two or three close-linked generations to make human beings far more superior to us than we are to the apes." Sometimes the visions of future paradise were intermixed with explicit racism. According to the *American Breeders Magazine*, the "aryo-germans which all through history have proved to be carriers of culture and civilization can assure themselves of the continuance of their dominance in world affairs, and of the permanence and even brilliant expansion of the splendid civilization they have created, by scientifically directing their evolution."[89]

Some eugenists qualified their utopian rhetoric. Edward Conklin expressed doubts that mankind could ever create "a race of supermen," and Albert Wiggam stated that "the Eden of eugenics can never be attained."[90] But such reservations often seemed half-hearted at best. At the same time that Albert Wiggam conceded that "the Eden of eugenics can never be attained," he also urged people to pursue it as their goal, so that "the passion for it, the going toward it, the belief in it, the training and education of men for it, [will] constitute that 'new religion' of a better humanity which Galton said would 'sweep the world.'"[91] At the same time that Edward Conklin doubted man's ability to create "a race of supermen," he nonetheless insisted "there is no doubt that something may be gained by eliminating the worst human kinds from the possibility of reproduction, even though no great improvement in the human race can be expected as a result of such a feeble measure."[92] Herbert Walter acknowledged that giving society the power to decide who can bear children might be abused—in theory. "One needs only to recall the days of the Spanish Inquisition or of the Salem witchcraft persecution to realize what fearful blunders human judgment is capable of."[93] Nevertheless, Walter was sanguine that in an age of modern science nothing similar would recur. "It is unlikely that the world will ever see another great religious inquisition, or that in applying to man the newly found laws of heredity there will ever be undertaken an equally deplorable eugenic inquisition." James Wilson, Secretary of Agriculture under Theodore Roosevelt, probably typified the attitude of many eugenists. While admitting that the promise of eugenics "at first seems like an Utopian vision," he went on to assure people that its goals might be attainable after all. "Like world peace ... it may come, and may we not all ask ... Why should it not come? Must science stop in its beneficence with the plant and the animal? Is not man, after all, the architect of his own racial destiny?"[94]

Confident that modern biology had revealed to them how to breed a better race, eugenists set about turning their scientific ideas into action. A few months before the first International Eugenics Congress in 1912 a British eugenist aptly summarized the practical outlook of many eugenists around the world, including those in America. She observed that research had generated "fairly authoritative opinions about certain defects and the method of their transmission. The present necessity ... is to convert these opinions into social action and legislation."[95] American supporters of eugenics were already well on their way to achieving that goal.

Marriage laws represented the first wave of eugenics legislation in America. While states had long regulated who could marry, eugenists advocated strengthening legal standards to prevent the "feebleminded" and others with hereditary defects from marrying lest they spread their defective germ-plasm to the next generation. Connecticut enacted the first eugenic marriage law in 1896.[96] Several other states adopted similar laws soon after the turn of the century, "so that by 1914 more than half of the states had imposed new restrictions on the marriage of persons afflicted with mental defects."[97] Some of these new laws were difficult to enforce, but others enlisted medical profes-sionals as gatekeepers. In Wisconsin, for example, couples could only marry if they obtained a certificate from a doctor verifying that they were free from physical and mental defects and communicable dis-eases.[98] Because the new marriage restrictions typically sought to prevent the spread of venereal disease as well as hereditary defects, some eugenists frowned on them, believing that eugenics should not be confused with the effort to prevent communicable diseases.[99] But even if the marriage laws were not purely eugenic, eugenics was un-questionably one of their primary objectives.

Immigration policies were also targeted by some eugenists who believed that biological defectives from foreign countries contributed disproportionately to America's social-welfare problems. Eugenists were by no means the only advocates of immigration restrictions, of course, but their invocation of science provided a powerful new ratio-nale for the restrictions. Writing in 1913, eugenist Herbert Walter urged Americans to select new immigrants in the same way that they might select a new horse. Just as the "wise breeder" looks into the *pedigree* of his prospective stock" when "selecting horses for a stock-farm," wrote Walter, "it is to be hoped that the time will come when we, as a nation" will demand "knowledge of the germplasm" of "the foreign applicants who knock at our portals."[100] Walter proposed sending "trained inspectors" to the home countries of prospective immigrants so that they could "look up the ancestry of prospective applicants and ... stamp desirable ones with approval." After all, "the United States Department of Agriculture already has field agents scouring every land for desirable animals and plants to introduce into this country, as well as stringent laws to prevent the importation of dangerous weeds, para-sites, and organisms of various kinds. Is the inspection and supervi-sion of human blood less important?"

The eugenists' anti-immigration arguments attracted the atten-tion of members of Congress, and in 1920 the House of Representa-tives held hearings on the "Biological Aspects of Immigration" featur-ing testimony by Harry H. Laughlin of the Eugenics Records Office. "Our failure to sort immigrants on the basis of natural worth is a very serious national menace," Laughlin testified at the hearings before the House Committee on Immigration and Naturalization. "By setting up an eugenical standard for admission demanding a high natural excellence of all immigrants regardless of nationality and past opportunities, we can enhance and improve the national stamina and ability of future Americans."[101] Laughlin was subsequently appointed "Expert Eugenical Agent" of the Committee, and in that capacity he carried out research and advised Congress as it developed the new immigration law adopted in 1924.[102] That law sharply curtailed the number of immigrants allowed from southern and eastern Europe. It was hailed by some eugenists and criticized by others: Eugenists supporting the law saw it as an important "step forward" in applying—albeit crudely— the principles of selection to immigration, while eugenists opposing the law pointed out that the act effectively excluded specific racial groups rather than selecting the most eugenically fit immigrants from among all groups.[103] The *New York Times* sided with critics, arguing that "in every race the great mass is, eugenically speaking, so much deadweight or worse." Thus, the United States should implement an immigration law that would select only the top 10 percent "of all applicants, quite independent of geography."[104] In short, according to the *Times*, the new immigration law was not nearly eugenic enough.

Marriage laws and immigration restrictions, however, were only part of the eugenists' agenda to eradicate chronic poverty and associated social ills. Even more far-reaching was the effort to identify biological defectives throughout America so that they could be incarcerated and sterilized.

Indiana enacted the first compulsory sterilization law in 1907. The bill had been pushed by a doctor and superintendent at the Indiana Reformatory, and it mandated sterilization for "confirmed criminals, idiots, imbeciles, and rapists in state institutions when recommended by a board of experts."[105] After passage of the bill, Dr. Harry Sharp of the Indiana Reformatory declared that he was proud "that Indiana is the first State to enact such a law, and that the Indiana Reformatory is the pioneer in this work."[106] By the early 1930s, thirty states had enacted sterilization laws, "and in twenty-seven states the laws were still on the books, if not always enforced."[107] By 1931 more than 12,000 Americans had been sterilized under these laws, and the national sterilization rate jumped five-fold from the 1920s to the end of the 1930s, from two to four per hundred thousand to twenty per hundred thousand.[108] By 1958, more than 60,000 Americans had been sterilized.[109]

In a number of states sterilization became an important tool of government welfare policy. In Virginia, state authorities raided welfare families in rural mountain communities and took them to be sterilized at a state facility. A former county official later recalled that "everybody who was drawing welfare then was scared they were going to have it done on them.... They were hiding all through these mountains, and the sheriff and his men had to go up after them."[110] In Vermont, there were regular eugenic surveys to identify defectives among the poor and trace their bad heredity. The surveys eventually led to the adoption of a sterilization statute in the state.[111] The Abenaki Indians were especially impacted by the Vermont eugenics program. "Many members of Abenaki families who were investigated by the Eugenics Survey were also incarcerated in institutions and subsequently sterilized."[112] Similar efforts to identify and sterilize defectives were undertaken in Indiana by its Committee on Mental Defectives.[113] Despite such initiatives, many American eugenists wanted even more aggressive measures. When Nazi Germany enacted a comprehensive sterilization program of its own in the early 1930s, Dr. Joseph DeJarnette complained that "[t]he Germans are beating us at our own game."[114] Eventually the popularity of eugenics began to wane in the United States as the movement attracted increased opposition in the 1930s, and as revulsion against Nazi social policies set in.[115]

Eugenics is sometimes cited as an example of how politicians can hijack science for their own ideological ends, but this is misleading. Eugenics is more accurately described as an effort by *scientists* to hijack government social policy based on their presumed scientific expertise. Modern scientists may be loathe to admit it, but the leaders of the eugenics crusade were largely biologists and doctors, not politicians, and they pushed for eugenics because they thought it was fully justified by biological science. Nor were the scientists who advocated eugenics on the fringes of the scientific community, at least during the heyday of the movement. An indication of how "mainstream" eugenists were can be gleaned from high school and college biology textbooks, which for several decades openly advocated eugenics.[116]

Historically speaking, the eugenics movement is important because it was one of the first—and most powerful—efforts to use science to expand the power of the state over social welfare. Eugenists claimed that their superior scientific knowledge trumped the beliefs of non-scientists, and so they should be allowed to design a truly scientific welfare policy. Although this attempt to fuse science and social policy ultimately unraveled, it paved the way for a new generation of scientists and "social scientists" to make similar claims in the future.

DARWINISM'S CONTINUING LEGACY

Although the Gilded Age is over, Woodrow Wilson is dead, and eugenics has long since become a dirty word, Darwinism continues to cast its shadow on the modern welfare state. One example is the continued use by the left of the epithet "Social Darwinism" to upbraid anyone who favors a more limited government. A survey of American political discourse during the past two decades shows just how central "Social Darwinism" remains to the rhetoric of the left.

During the 1980s, columnist Molly Ivins sniped that Ronald Reagan's "mind is mired somewhere in the dawn of social Darwinism," while political analyst Kevin Phillips condemned Reagan for promoting a system of "economic Darwinism" in which "corporate raiders like T. Boone Pickens and Carl C. Icahn perform a social and economic service by weeding out the weak—like wolves in the forest."[117] *Los Angeles Times* editorial writer Ernest Conine likewise intoned that Reagan "brought with him a crew of ideologues who preached a doctrine of social and economic Darwinism—a dog-eat-dog, survival-of-the-fittest dogma that included little sympathy for victims of the revolutionary changes occurring in the U.S. economy."[118] During the presidential election campaign of 1984, Mario Cuomo proclaimed that "President Reagan told us from the beginning that he believed in a kind of social Darwinism, survival of the fittest," and Democratic presidential candidate Walter Mondale assured audiences that unlike his Republican opponent, he believed "in social decency, not Social Darwinism."[119]

During the 1990s, similar charges were leveled at Newt Gingrich and the Republican Congress. Columnist Robert Scheer attacked Gingrich's program of tax cuts and welfare reform as representing "a social Darwinism that holds that only the strong deserve to live."[120] Occidental College political science professor Roger Boesche equated the Republicans' ideas on welfare reform with the nineteenth century "social Darwinism" of William Graham Sumner, who believed (in Boesche's words) that "survival of the fittest and poverty for the least fit are simply laws of nature."[121] *The New Yorker's* Sidney Blumenthal charged that Republican policies were "rooted in traditions of no-nothing nativism and Social Darwinism."[122] And in what was supposed to be an objective news article, The *Los Angeles Times* described the California Libertarian Party's platform as "a synthesis of social Darwinism, individualism and laissez-faire economics."[123] (A party official retorted that in his view the Libertarian Party "clearly takes a position in opposition to contemporary social Darwinism."[124])

During the early years of the twenty-first century, the Social Darwinist label has remained a powerful rhetorical bludgeon for anyone wishing to criticize the problems of capitalism and limited government. Writing in 2001, former Clinton administration official Robert Reich dismissed the past policies of Britain's Margaret Thatcher as "Lady Thatcher's small-government Social Darwinism."[125] In *USA Today*, a columnist criticized China's moves toward greater economic freedom as "neo-liberal social Darwinism."[126] In the midst of the financial accounting scandals of 2002, Kevin Phillips resurrected his charge of Social Darwinism from the 1980s and applied it to the last two decades of American economic life: "The 1980's and 1990's have imitated the Gilded Age in intellectual excesses of market worship, laissez-faire and social Darwinism."[127]

These ritual invocations of Social Darwinism have strayed increasingly far from reality in recent years. For example, whatever the actual demerits of the Reagan administration's economic policies during the 1980s, Social Darwinism was not a particularly apt indictment of its failings. The economic Bible of the Reagan administration was not supplied by Herbert Spencer, but George Gilder, whose best seller *Wealth and Poverty* articulated a view of economics that was anything but Darwinian.[128] Indeed, in Gilder's view the driving force behind capitalism is not greed, but something close to altruism. "Capitalism begins with giving," wrote Gilder, and the products generated by capitalists "will succeed only to the extent that they are altruistic and spring from an understanding of the needs of others."[129] According to Gilder, capitalism not only leads to greater material plenty for everyone, but properly understood it cultivates the non-material virtues of faith, hope, and love.[130]

While Gilder's optimistic assessment of capitalism can be debated, it is difficult to equate it with Social Darwinism. It is just as incongruous to label Newt Gingrich a Social Darwinist. Gingrich could be abrasive as a politician, but his vision of a "conservative opportunity society" was not premised on a Darwinian struggle for existence in which only a handful of rich people prospered.[131] Instead, Gingrich preached economic growth as a method of empowering the poor, and welfare reform as a way of helping the poor gain dignity and self-sufficiency. The thinker most emblematic of this agenda was not William Graham Sumner but Marvin Olasky, whose book *The Tragedy of American Compassion* argued for rethinking welfare because welfare had failed to help the poor. In his book, Olasky explicitly condemned adopting a mentality of "Social Darwinism" toward the poor.[132] Olasky became the architect of George W. Bush's "compassionate conservatism," and Bush later picked up the anti-Social Darwinism theme. "We believe in social mobility, not social Darwinism," he declared at the University of Notre Dame in 2001.[133] Such protests notwithstanding, leftist critics will likely continue to decry "Social Darwinism" for the foreseeable future. It is far too powerful a rhetorical tool for them to give up.

While the left continues to cling to its straw man of "Social Darwinism," it remains even more passionately devoted to Woodrow Wilson's vision of the evolving Constitution, which has been enshrined at the heart of liberal jurisprudence for decades. Although debates about how to interpret the Constitution's text are typically the arcane stuff of lawyers and political theorists, they occasionally break out into the public arena, such as when presidential candidate Al Gore explicitly endorsed the evolving Constitution in 2000. In a debate with Bill Bradley, Gore promised he would seek Supreme Court justices "who understand that our Constitution is a living and breathing document" and who realize "that it was intended by our Founders to be interpreted in the light of the constantly evolving experience of the American people."[134]

Of course, the most dramatic fruit of evolutionary constitutionalism is the Supreme Court's decision in *Roe v. Wade*, which ignored both history and precedent to create a right of abortion by judicial fiat. But equally important have been the dozens of commerce clause and federalism cases in which the courts have dismantled the limited federal government set up by the Founders and replaced it with a

278 JOHN G. WEST

federal government of nearly unlimited powers over the economy and the states.

Compared with "Social Darwinism" and the evolving Constitution, eugenics might appear to be the Darwinian influence most irrelevant to the modern welfare state. Eugenics remains a tainted word, and in recent years a number of states have even issued apologies for their forced sterilization programs.[135] But while government-imposed eugenics may no longer be popular, the eugenists' underlying claim—that scientists should rule because of their scientific expertise—is more deeply ingrained than ever in the American political psyche. During the 1950s, C. S. Lewis warned that modern governments were heading toward what he called "technocracy," and he worried that politicians would "increasingly rely on the advice of scientists, till in the end the politicians proper become merely the scientists' puppets."[136] It is not difficult to see the fulfillment of Lewis' prophesy in modern America's maze of specialized agencies staffed by unelected experts who issue tens of thousands of pages of regulations each year that have the force of law but are never voted on by Congress.

In coming decades as the powers of science continue to grow apace with new discoveries in genetics, neuroscience, and computers, we would be well advised to remember Lewis' caution about the limits of science in politics: "Let scientists tell us about sciences. But government involves questions about the good for man, and justice, and what things are worth having at what price; and on these a scientific training gives a man's opinion no added value."[137]

Endnotes

1. John Mack Faragher and Mari Jo Buhle, et al., *Out of Many: A History of the American People* (Upper Saddle River, N.J.: Prentice Hall, 1997) 2, 654.

2. Carl N. Degler, Thomas C. Cochran, et al., *The Democratic Experience* (Glenview, Illinois: Scott, Foresman and Co., 1981), 53. For similar treatments of Social Darwinism see James Roark, Michael Johnson, et al., *The American Promise: A History of the United States* (Boston: Bedford Books,

1998), 710; Joseph Conlin, *The American Past, Part Two: A Survey of American History Since 1865* (San Diego: Harcourt Brace Jovanovich, 1990), 498; Mary Beth Norton, David M. Katzman, et al., *A People and a Nation: A History of the United States* (Boston: Houghton Mifflin Company, 1986), 490. Some textbooks have moderated their discussions of Social Darwinism. "It is not clear how seriously the business community took social Darwinism." Irwin Unger, *These United States: The Questions of Our Past, Volume II: Since 1865* (Englewood Cliffs, New Jersey: Prentice-Hall, 1992), 474; "Few men of practical affairs were directly influenced by Darwin's ideas." John A. Garraty and Robert A. McCaughey, *The American Nation: A History of the United States Since 1865, Volume Two* (New York: Harper and Row, 1983), 490; "Despite their seeming lack of regard for common people, many of the robber barons who had embraced Social Darwinism also supported the spirit of charity." Gary B. Nash, *American Odyssey: The United States in the Twentieth Century* (New York: Glencoe/McGraw-Hill, 1997), 210.

3. Richard Hofstadter, *Social Darwinism in American Thought* (Boston: The Beacon Press, 1955), 5.

4. Indeed, Darwin described "survival of the fittest" as "more accurate" than his own term of "natural selection"; see Charles Darwin, *The Origin of Species* (New York: Mentor Books/New American Library, 1958), 74.

5. Quoted in Hofstadter, *Social Darwinism*, 41.

6. Ibid., 51.

7. Ibid., 45.

8. Irvin G. Wyllie, "Social Darwinism and the Businessman," *Proceedings of the American Philosophical Society* 103, no. 5 (October 1959): 633.

9. Wyllie, "Social Darwinism," 632.

10. Ibid. Ironically, Rockefeller's talk did not even promote the view that was attributed to it. "The title of his talk had been 'Christianity in Business,' and ... he had entered a plea for more Christian virtue in the transaction of business." Ibid., 635.

11. Ibid., 634.

12. Ibid.

13. Thomas Robert Malthus, *First Essay on Population 1798* (London: Macmillan and Co. Ltd., 1926).

14. See Francis Darwin, ed., *The Autobiography of Charles Darwin and Selected Letters* (New York: Dover, 1958), 42-43; Darwin, *Origin*, 75.

15. Malthus, *First Essay*, 27.

16. Ibid.

17. Ibid., 346.

18. Darwin, *Autobiography*, 42-43.

19. Malthus, *First Essay*, 18-38.

20. Ibid., 131.

21. Francis Bowen, "Malthusianism, Darwinism, and Pessimism," *North American Review* 129 (1879): 452.

22. Ibid., 454.

23. Ibid., 455, 456.

24. Edward Atkinson, *The Industrial Progress of the Nation* (New York: Arno Press, 1973 [originally published by G.P. Putnam's Sons, 1889]), 156, 159.

25. Edward Atkinson, "The Unlearned Professions," *The Atlantic Monthly* 45, no. 272 (June 1880): 747.

26. Atkinson, *Industrial Progress*, 160.

27. Edward Atkinson, "Commercial Development," *Harper's* 51, no. 302 (July 1875): 267.

28. Atkinson, "The Unlearned Professions," 745.

29. Atkinson, "Commercial Development," 260. Also see the discussion in *The Industrial Progress of the Nation*, 383-388.

30. Wyllie, "Social Darwinism," 634.

31. Robert Bannister, *Social Darwinism: Science and Myth in Anglo-American Social Thought*, with a new preface (Philadelphia: Temple University Press, 1988), 114.

32. "A Declaration of Principles," adopted by the Nationalist Club in 1889, quoted in Arthur E. Moran, *Edward Bellamy* (New York: Columbia University Press, 1944), 262. See also Bannister, *Social Darwinism*, 124-125.

33. Henry Demarest Lloyd, *Wealth against Commonwealth* (New York: Harper and Brothers, 1898), 495.

34. Jack London, "The Class Struggle," in Jack London, *War of the Classes* (Oakland: Star Rover House, 1982), 18.

35. Bannister, *Social Darwinism*, 126.

36. Wyllie, "Social Darwinism," 635.

37. For a discussion of the impact of Germanic political science on America during the Progressive era, see Dennis John Mahoney, "A New Political Science for a World Made Wholly New: The Doctrine of Progress and the Emergence of American Political Science," (Ph.D. dissertation, Claremont Graduate School, 1984), especially 25-45. Mahoney discusses the evolutionary character of Hegelian political science on 33-35.

38. Ibid., 103-142.

39. Woodrow Wilson, *Constitutional Government*, in *The Papers of Woodrow Wilson*, Arthur S. Link, ed., vol. 18 (Princeton: Princeton University Press, 1974), 105.

40. Woodrow Wilson, *The New Freedom*, with an introduction and notes by William Leuchtenburg (Englewood Cliffs: Prentice-Hall, Inc., 1961), 41-42.

41. "Dr. Henry Goddard, Psychologist, Dies," *New York Times* (June 22, 1957), 15.

42. Henry Herbert Goddard, *The Kallikak Family: A Study in the Heredity of Feeble-Mindedness* (New York: Macmillan Company, 1925), 16.

43. Ibid., 18.

44. Ibid., 104.

45. Ibid., 7.

46. Michael W. Perry, ed. *The Pivot of Civilization in Historical Perspective* by Margaret Sanger (Seattle: Inkling Books, 2001), 80.

47. Ibid., 7.

48. Ibid., 11-12.

49. Ibid., 29, 71.

50. For more information on Francis Galton, see Mark Haller, *Eugenics: Hereditarian Attitudes in American Thought* (New Brunswick: Rutgers University Press, 1963), 8-20, and Daniel J. Kevles, *In the Name of Eugenics: Genetics and the Uses of Human Heredity* (Cambridge: Harvard University Press, 1995), 3-19.

51. Kevles, *Eugenics*, xiii.

52. Ibid., see also Haller, *Eugenics*, 17-18.

53. Haller, *Eugenics*, 11.

54. Ibid.

55. "Eugenic Legislation, A Review," *The Journal of Heredity* 6 (March 1915): 142.

56. "Eugenics Organizations," *Image Archive on the American Eugenics Movement*, http://www.eugenicsarchive.org; also see "Description of the American Breeders Association," (American Breeders Association, 1909), available as document 410 at the *Image Archive on the American Eugenics Movement*, http://www.eugenicsarchive.org (accessed August 15, 2003).

57. James Wilson, "Presidential Address," *American Breeders Magazine* 6, no. 1 (First Quarter, 1913): 53.

58. "Eugenics Seeks to Improve the Natural, the Physical, Mental and Temperamental Qualities of the Human Family," (Cold Spring Harbor, N.Y.: Eugenics Records Office, 1927), 1, available as document 248 at the *Image Archive on the American Eugenics Movement*,http://www.eugenicsarchive.org (accessed August 15, 2003).

59. James Wilson, "Presidential Address," 55.

60. "First Eugenics Congress," *New York Times* (July 25, 1912), 5.

61. "Our Work in Eugenics," *New York Times* (July 26, 1912), 4.

62. Transcript, "Breeding Better Citizens," ABC News 20/20 (airdate: March 22, 2000), http://www.abcnews.go.com (accessed March 25, 2000).

63. David Micklos, "None Without Hope: Buck vs. Bell at 75," http://www.dnalc.org/resources/buckvbell.html (accessed August 15, 2003).

64. Charles Darwin, *The Descent of Man*, vol. 1 (Princeton: Princeton University Press, 1981 [originally published in 1871]), 168-184. Although eugenics is sometimes regarded as a perversion of Darwinian biology, Charles Darwin himself praised the idea of eugenic restrictions on marriage in *The Descent of Man*, and his sons George and Leonard actively promoted the eugenics agenda, with Leonard becoming in time the president of the main eugenics group in Great Britain. For Darwin's endorsement of eugenics, see *Descent* (1871), 2:403. In both *Descent* and in his correspondence with Francis Galton, Darwin did worry about whether the eugenics crusade might be "utopian," but he nevertheless thought it was a worthy effort. See John Bowlby, *Darwin: A New Life* (New York: W.W. Norton, 1990), 415-416. On the eugenic efforts of sons George and Leonard, see Kevles, *Eugenics*, 60, and Adrian Desmond and James Moore, *Darwin: The Life of a Tormented Evolutionist* (New York: W. W. Norton, 1991), 610-611.

65. Frank Lowden, "Social Work in Government," *Proceedings of the National Conference of Social Work*, May 16-23, 1923 (Chicago: University of Chicago Press), 150-151.

66. Edwin Conklin, "Value of Negative Eugenics," *Journal of Heredity* 6, no. 12 (December 1915): 539-540.

67. Paul Popenoe and Roswell Johnson, "Eugenics and Euthenics" in Horatio Hackett Newman, *Evolution, Genetics and Eugenics* (Chicago: University of Chicago Press, 1932), 517-518.

68. H. E. Jordan, "Heredity as a Factor in the Improvement of Social Conditions," *American Breeders Magazine* 2, no. 4. (Fourth Quarter, 1911): 253.

69. "Eugenic Legislation: A Review," *Journal of Heredity*, 6, no. 3 (March 1915): 144.

70. Charles Davenport, *Heredity in Relation to Eugenics* (New York: Henry Holt and Co., 1911), 1.

71. Jordan, "Heredity as a Factor," 249.

72. Conklin, "Value of Negative Eugenics," 538.

73. Alexander Graham Bell, "How to Improve the Race," *Journal of Heredity* 6, no. 1 (January 1914): 2.

74. Albert Edward Wiggam, "Does Heredity or Environment Make Men?" in Newman, *Evolution*, 501-502.

75. Caleb Williams Saleeby, "The Promise of Race Culture," in Newman, *Evolution*, 536-537. Saleeby was British, but this excerpt from one of his books appeared in an American textbook.

76. Charles Davenport, letter to the editor, *New York Times* (July 8, 1913), 6. The letter appeared under the title "The Duty of Society: Its Members Must Be Eugenically Responsive or It Will Die."

77. "Nature or Nurture?" *Journal of Heredity* 6, no. 5 (May 1915): 228.

78. "Feeblemindedness: A Review by the Editor" *Journal of Heredity* 6, no. 1. (January 1915): 33.

79. Ibid.

80. Popenoe and Johnson, "Eugenics and Euthenics," 511.

81. Quoted in Haller, *Eugenics*, 65.

82. Quoted in Saleeby, "The Promise of Race Culture," 543.

83. Wiggam, "Does Heredity ... Make Men?" 505.

84. Jordan, "Heredity as a Factor," 253.

85. Ibid., 254.

86. Maynard Metcalf, "Evolution and Man," *Journal of Heredity* 7, no. 8 (August 1916): 360.

87. Ibid., 364.

88. Quoted in Perry, *Pivot of Civilization*, 129.

89. "Race Genetics Problems," *American Breeders Magazine* 2, no. 3 (Third Quarter, 1911): 232.

90. Conklin, "Value of Negative Eugenics," 539; Wiggam, "Does Heredity ... Make Men?" 506.

91. Wiggam, "Does Heredity ... Make Men?" 506.

92. Conklin, "Value of Negative Eugenics," 539.

93. Herbert Walter, "Human Conservation," in Newman, *Evolution*, 531.

94. Wilson, "Presidential Address," 56.

95. Quoted in "To Improve the Race," *New York Times* (March 24, 1912), C5.

96. Edward J. Larson, *Sex, Race, and Science: Eugenics in the Deep South* (Baltimore: Johns Hopkins University Press, 1995), 22.

97. Ibid.

98. W. C. Rucker, "More 'Eugenic Laws'," *Journal of Heredity* (May 1915): 225.

99. Ibid., 223-226.

100. Walter, "Human Conservation," 524.

101. "Statement of Harry H. Laughlin," *Biological Aspects of Immigration: Hearings before the Committee on Immigration and Naturalization, House of Representatives, Sixty-Sixth Congress, Second Session, April 16-17, 1920* (Washington, D.C.: Government Printing Office, 1921), available as document 1113

at the *Image Archive on the American Eugenics Movement*, http://www.eugenicsarchive.org (accessed August 15, 2003).

102. Kevles, *Eugenics*, 103.

103. See Roswell Johnson, "Eugenics and Immigration," *New York Times* (February 16, 1924); "1890 Census Urged as Immigrant Base," *New York Times* (January 7, 1924).

104. "Like-Minded or Well-Born," *New York Times* (February 10, 1924), E6.

105. Haller, *Eugenics*, 50.

106. Quoted in Haller, *Eugenics*, 50.

107. Ibid., 137.

108. Ibid., 141; Kevles, *Eugenics*, 116.

109. Haller, *Eugenics*, 141.

110. Quoted in Kevles, *Eugenics*, 116.

111. See Nancy L. Gallagher, *Breeding Better Vermonters: The Eugenics Project in the Green Mountain State* (Hanover: University Press of New England, 1999).

112. Ibid., 7.

113. Valerie Parker, "Breeding Better Citizens: A Hidden Chapter of American History," March 22, 2000, ABCNews.com, http://abcnews.go.com/onair/2020/2020_000322_eugenics_feature.html (accessed March 25, 2000).

114. Kevles, *Eugenics*, 116.

115. Haller, *Eugenics*, 7.

116. For treatments of eugenics in secondary school biology textbooks of the period, see Clifton Hodge and Jean Dawson, *Civic Biology* (Boston: Ginn and Company, 1918), 344-345; William Smallwood, Ida Reveley, and Guy Bailey, *New Biology* (Boston: Allyn and Bacon, 1924), 660-662; George William Hunter, *New Civic Biology* (New York: American Book Company, 1926), 251, 398-403. For a general summary of the coverage of eugenics in secondary school biology texts, see Gerald Skoog, "Topic of Evolution in Secondary School Biology Textbooks: 1900-1977," *Science Education* 63, no. 5 (1979): 628. Some textbooks during this period did not promote eugenics, or only did so indirectly. Alfred Kinsey's *An Introduction to Biology* (Philadelphia: J. B. Lippincott, 1926) had no discussion of eugenics per se, but it did recommend books advocating eugenics in a list of reference books supplied on 539-540. By the 1940s, discussions of eugenics were significantly diluted and focused more on environment than heredity. For an example of a later treatment of the topic, see Edwin Sanders, *Practical Biology* (New York: D. Van Nostrand Co, 1947), 431-437. For examples of college biology textbooks that

covered eugenics, see George William Hunter, Herbert Eugene Walter, and George William Hunter III, *Biology: The Study of Living Things* (New York: American Book Company, 1937), 638-642; Arthur Haupt, *Fundamentals of Biology* (New York: McGraw-Hill Book Company, 1928), 216-221; Leslie Kenoyer and Henry Goddard, *General Biology* (New York, Harper and Brothers, 1937), 533-539; William Martin Smallwood, *A Text-Book of Biology for Students in Medical, Technical and General Courses* (Philadelphia: Lea and Febiger, 1913), 257-259. Not every college textbook during this period jumped on the eugenics bandwagon. Waldo Shumway's *Textbook of General Biology* (New York: John Wiley and Sons, 1931) told students that "it would appear judicious to walk slowly in enacting [eugenics] legislation until our knowledge of biological laws is more precise," 317.

117. Molly Ivins, quoted in Deirdre Donahue, "What's the story on 'Story'? Great reading," *USA Today* (October 6, 1989), 4D; Kevin Phillips, "Bold Ideas Reduced to Movie Talk, Budget Debate Demands More," *Los Angeles Times* (February 9, 1986), 5-1.

118. Ernest Conine, "Milk of Human Kindness Hasn't Borne a GOP Label," *Los Angeles Times* (October 27, 1987), 2-7.

119. Mario Cuomo, quoted in William Schneider, "The Democrats in '88," *The Atlantic Monthly* (April 1987), online edition, http://www.theantlantic.com/politics/policamp/demo88.htm (accessed August 15, 2003); Walter Mondale, quoted in Steven Tipton, "Religion and the Moral Rhetoric of Presidential Politics," http://www.religion-online.org/cgi-bin/relsearchd.dll/showarticle?item_id = 1429 (accessed August 15, 2003).

120. Robert Scheer, "Taking Food From Mouths of Babes, Gingrich's tax cut proposals would just help government better serve the rich," *Los Angeles Times* (May 16, 1995), B-7.

121. Roger Boesche, "Homeless? Hungry? It's All Your Fault; The Gingrich era means class-based politics, 'Us' vs. 'Them' in a war on the poor," *Los Angeles Times* (December 1, 1994), B-7.

122. Sidney Blumenthal, "Conservative Win Means GOP Intraparty Brawl," *Los Angeles Times* (October 30, 1964), M-1.

123. "Decision '92, Special Voters' Guide to State and Local Elections: The Third Parties," *Los Angeles Times* (October 25, 1992), T-5.

124. John Vernon, letter to the editor, *Los Angeles Times* (October 31, 1992), B-7.

125. Robert Reich, "The Political Center, Straight Up; It's Bogus: Real Leaders Don't Take People Where They Already Are," *Washington Post* (June 17, 2001), B-1.

126. Richard Madsen, "China emulates some U.S. values—good and bad," *USA Today* (February 20, 2002), 13A.

127. Kevin Phillips, "The Cycles of Financial Scandal," *New York Times* (July 17, 2002), A19.

128. For the influence of Gilder's book on the incoming Reagan administration, see George Gilder, *Wealth and Poverty: A New Edition of the Classic* (San Francisco: ICS Press, 1993), xv.

129. George Gilder, *Wealth and Poverty* (New York: Basic Books, 1981), 21, 27. Gilder further expanded his argument about the connection between altruism and capitalism in the revised paperback edition of his book, for which he added 6,000 words to the chapter "The Returns of Giving." See *Wealth and Poverty: A New Edition*, xxii, 21-38.

130. Gilder, *Wealth and Poverty* (1981), 259-269.

131. For examples of Gingrich's approach toward the poor, see his articles "How kids can learn in the inner city" (*Washington Post*, September 25, 1995) and "What Good is Government and Can We Make It Better?" (*Newsweek*, April 10, 1995).

132. Marvin Olasky, *The Tragedy of American Compassion* (Washington, D.C.: Regnery Publishing, 1992). For Olasky's discussion of Social Darwinism, see 60-98.

133. Quoted in Mike Allen, "President Urges War on Poverty; At Notre Dame, Bush Touts Faith Plan," *Washington Post* (May 21, 2001), A1.

134. Democratic Party presidential debate between Al Gore and Bill Bradley, (*Los Angeles Times* Building, Los Angeles, Ca., March 1, 2000).

135. See Paul Feist, "Davis apologizes for state's sterilization program," *San Francisco Chronicle* (March 12, 2003).

136. C. S. Lewis, "Is Progress Possible? Willing Slaves of the Welfare State," in *God in the Dock: Essays on Theology and Ethics* (Grand Rapids, Mich.: Eerdmans, 1970), 314.

137. Ibid., 315.

·⁔Chapter 9⁐·

Zoning
and Progressive
Political Theory

Eric R. Claeys [1]

INTRODUCTION

Suppose an ordinary citizen were to ask a political theorist what "Progressivism" meant. The theorist might start by trying to explain seminal Progressive writings such as Woodrow Wilson's *Constitutional Government in the United States*[2] or Herbert Croly's *The Promise of American Life*.[3] To most citizens, however, the political principles in these works would probably sound like old and bland generalities. Strictly at the level of principle, Progressive political theory might not seem to have any relevance to contemporary American life.

The political theorist might succeed, however, if he tried to explain the same theory using Euclidean zoning as a case study. Whether or not an ordinary citizen would appreciate Progressive terms like "expertise," "community," or "economic security" in the abstract, he most certainly would if they were used to describe his local planning commission, the character of his neighborhood, and the property values of the houses on his block. Local land-use regulation illustrates how sharply Progressives' modern liberal conceptions of justice and the common good broke with the classical liberal notions of the American founding. And zoning illustrates just how thoroughly Progressive political institutions displaced the founding's institutions. American homeowners love zoning: more than 97 percent of American cities with populations of five thousand or more residents employ zoning.[4]

Euclidean zoning is a centralized, command-and-control style of land-use regulation. It aims to guide city development in advance consistent with a comprehensive city plan. It operates on the principle "a place for everything, and everything in its place." The zoning process relies heavily on land-use experts, both when a plan is drafted and when landowners petition for exceptions from that plan. Taken together, these features work to encourage uniformity and discourage change in land-use patterns.

This essay analyzes Euclidean zoning as a case study in Progressive political theory. It uses zoning for two purposes: one is to illustrate how key tenets of Progressive political theory have become part of American political practice; the other is to highlight the main theoretical and practical differences between American natural rights, natural law, and social compact theory and modern liberal political theory. Part I starts with the law. It shows how contemporary zoning pursues a substantive agenda sharply different from what we know about the agenda of nineteenth century land-use regulation. The earlier approach encouraged freedom; zoning encourages order, homogeneity, and security. Part II explains the Progressive case for that shift. Interpreting the writings of leading land-use lawyers and reformers during the Progressive era, Part II shows how each of the key features of zoning—commitments to majority rule and expert planners, a communitarian vision of property, and a faith that majorities will discover and enforce strong conceptions of the local general welfare—comports with key themes of Progressive political theory. Finally, Part III uses the debate over zoning to illustrate the tension between the founding and Progressive elements in the American political tradition.

I. Nineteenth Century Land-Use Regulation and Euclidean Zoning

To appreciate the distinctive features of Euclidean zoning, it is worth taking a look back at the system of land-use regulation such zoning displaced. While we do not know enough about nineteenth century legislative regulation, many American cities regulated land in ways that were much more narrowly targeted than zoning. Municipalities could regulate the height and building composition of buildings. They could abate moral nuisances and gunpowder houses, slaughterhouses, and other sources of serious pollution.[5] When certain neighborhoods "tipped" toward industrial, residential, or other uses, a city might define the boundaries of the ready-made "locality" and exclude non-conforming uses. In *Buchanan v. Warley*, a 1917 case invalidating a race-based zoning scheme enacted in Louisville, Kentucky, the United States Supreme Court described the broad outlines of police power land-use regulation as follows:

> Harmful occupations may be controlled and regulated. Legitimate business may also be regulated in the interest of the public. Certain uses of property may be confined to portions of the municipality other than the resident district.... because of the impairment of the health and comfort of the occupants.[6]

By modern standards, these regulations made it impossible to use zoning for many important and routine public purposes. Judge D. C. Westenhaver gave a sense of what was left out when he declared unconstitutional the zoning ordinance of Euclid, Ohio in *Ambler Realty Co. v. Village of Euclid*. While zoning might be used to set uniform aesthetic standards throughout a town, such standards did not count as property "regulations" because they extinguished valuable use and development rights. (That is not to say that cities could not impose aesthetic requirements, but it did mean they needed to compensate owners through eminent domain procedures). Zoning could not be used to segregate stand-alone single-family houses from row houses, and it probably could not have been used to segregate any form of housing from apartments absent a showing that the apartments were unusually noisy. Zoning could not be used to restrain the course of development of undeveloped property, at least not without making sure that the restraints provided owners "reciprocity of advantage" by making the development rights they retained more valuable than the development rights they lost.[7]

This conception of the police powers was narrow and extremely decentralized by modern standards. It presupposed that "private property" and "regulation" both protected a negative liberty. The law presumed that owners deserved to enjoy the greatest range of freedom available to use their properties for their own purposes. The law protected owners from pollution, vibrations, and other discrete and physical invasions of their use rights. At the same time, it generally refrained from enforcing uniformity requirements or pursuing aesthetic goals.

Both sides of this tradeoff followed from a conception of freedom based on the natural law-natural rights ideas evident in the Declaration of Independence and other founding era public documents. The law followed from a conception of freedom centered on the individual. It recognized in each owner a right to decide, free from outside interference, how he should use his own property for his own chosen ends. This presumption held unless the state or a neighbor could specifically show that an owner's land use diminished and therefore injured the equal zone of non-interference to which each neighbor was entitled. *Buchanan v. Warley* described this presumptive zone of freedom as "the free use, enjoyment, and disposal of a person's acquisitions without control or diminution save by the law of the land." This conception of freedom followed from conceptions of equal and natural rights out of founding era social compact theory. These principles still influenced property law in the early twentieth century; in *Euclid*, Judge Westenhaver cited and applied provisions of the Ohio Constitution declaring that "[a]ll men ... have certain inalienable rights, among which are those of enjoying and defending life and liberty, acquiring, possessing, and protecting property," and that "[p]rivate property shall ever be held inviolate."

So understood, property harnesses naturally-occurring human passions—especially self-love, acquisitiveness, and industriousness—in the pursuit of permanent human goods—especially self-preservation. As it applies to property, the natural law prescribes and the social compact protects "property" as a freedom to be left alone, to apply one's own peculiar passions and talents to use one's own property for one's own advancement.[8] This conception sacrifices order and homogeneity, because it expects that all are better off when owners may use their natural property rights to manifest their own particular talents and faculties for their own preferred purposes.

Euclidean zoning broke from this early conception of property rights and regulatory powers. One can see the differences simply by comparing the outlines of the nineteenth century system to the zoning scheme the Supreme Court upheld in the 1926 zoning decision *Euclid v. Ambler Realty Co.*, and also to the Standard State Zoning Enabling

Act (here, the "Standard Enabling Act"), which the United States Department of Commerce published in 1926 with substantial input from Progressive land-use planners.[9]

Above all else, Euclidean zoning centralizes community land use. It generates what Dennis Coyle calls a "hierarchical" system and culture of land-use regulation.[10] The Enabling Act requires development to be coordinated in "accordance with a comprehensive plan." Most municipalities do not draft a "comprehensive plan" before they establish their zoning districts, but they still pre-approve major development decisions through a centralized review process. As the Supreme Court described Euclid's zoning scheme, it was a "comprehensive zoning plan for regulating and restricting the location of trades, industries, apartment houses, two-family houses, single-family houses, etc., the lot area to be built upon, the size and height of buildings, etc."[11]

Euclidean zoning plans expanded the range of public interests that could legally justify a local scheme of land-use regulation. Zoning expanded the conception of the "public interest" or "general welfare" protected by the police powers. Some of the factors considered in the comprehensive city plan closely tracked the conceptions of individual rights and general welfare that prevailed in the nineteenth century. These factors included, for instance, how "to lessen congestion in the streets," and "to secure safety from fire." But the plans also were required to incorporate many other factors that were not part of the normal nineteenth century conception of the public interest. Comprehensive plans needed to consider how "to provide adequate light," and "to avoid undue concentration of population." Most far-reaching, comprehensive plans also had to consider how zoning would affect property values—by "conserving the value of buildings"—and aesthetic and community-character concerns—by "encouraging the most appropriate use of land throughout [the] municipality."[12] These objects give zoning a communitarian purpose; in Dennis Coyle's description, zoning replaced a "strong individualist tradition" with "order and predictability."[13]

Progressive zoning gave local land-use planners a larger complement of regulatory tools. The Standard Enabling Act recognized some regulatory powers that were unexceptional in the earlier view, like the power to regulate the size and composition of buildings. It vested in municipalities new powers, including the powers to regulate the percentage of a lot that could be developed, minimum open space requirements, and population density levels. The most powerful new tools, however, were the use districts—the "zones." The Standard Enabling Act took to a new level what *Buchanan* had recognized as the power to "confine certain uses of property" to neighborhoods "other than the resident district." Section 2 recognized a power to "divide the municipality into districts of such number, shape, and area as may be deemed best suited to carry out the purposes of this act."[14]

Euclidean zoning thus shifts a great deal of control over land-use decisions from individual owners to local majorities and expert land-use planners. Each local owner loses substantial freedom to control the use of his own parcel of land, but gains the opportunity to vote on how his neighbors ought to use *their* properties. Euclidean zoning transfers substantial administrative powers to local land-use experts who implement the majority's will in two stages: zoning commissions supervise and enforce the zones; and boards of adjustment or similar entities consider requests for special exceptions, variances, or other deviations from the zones.[15]

Euclidean zoning also transforms the substance of property rights. In the system that preceded it, most land uses were presumed legitimate unless specifically shown to be dangerous or unsuitable to the neighborhood. Euclidean zoning reversed both the presumption and the underlying conception of property. The comprehensive plan and the use districts build into zoning a presumption that any use that does not conform to the local use district is unsuitable unless specifically shown to be suitable. This is an extremely hard presumption to reverse. Euclidean zoning thus transforms the orientation of property rights. It transforms what used to be a negative liberty into a positive entitlement. After Euclidean zoning took over, land no longer entailed a zone of free use and non-interference. Instead, each zoned lot came with it a security—a legal guarantee that neighbors would use their lots consistently with tastes, standards, and economic goals set by the control group in the local community.

II. The Progressives' Case for Zoning

These features of zoning are all hallmarks of Progressive political theory—the centralization of land-use planning, the transformation of property rights, and the reliance on majority rule in the broad picture and on experts in the details. To be sure, not every advocate for zoning, then or now, traces the details of zoning back to a systematic political theory. Many proponents justify zoning in the same manner as James Metzenbaum after he litigated *Euclid* before the Court. In his view, zoning was inevitable: it was a response to "the increase in traffic, with the growing congestion, the ills attendant upon modern complexities and the daily growing intensity of civic life." This analysis of zoning is apolitical: It does "no more than apply the rules of good housekeeping to public affairs. It keeps the stove out of the parlor, the bookcase out of the pantry and the dinner table out of the bedroom."[16]

Progress

These arguments make zoning seem inevitable and innocuous, but in reality they presuppose important political claims—the claims latent in a political theory of Progress. In general, the reformers, planners, and lawyers who paved the way for zoning did not connect their specific and practical arguments for zoning to any comprehensive and fully-articulated political theory. Even so, these advocates obviously shared some political consensus, which covered topics like changed circumstances, rights and regulation, and the proper roles of local majorities and expert planners. That consensus accords strikingly with general principles of Progressive political theory. I will use general Progressive principles to interpret the writings of early twentieth century zoning advocates—the books and pamphlets written to persuade cities to adopt zoning, the legal treatises written after zoning codes survived constitutional challenges in the courts, and many speeches, colloquies, and papers by urban planners involved in the annual *National Conference on City Planning*, the trade guild for professional zoning advocates. These writings apply to the practical case of land-use regulation the theory of Progress as restated by leading Progressives like Woodrow Wilson.

As Wilson defined Progress, it was a faith in the future; "[t]he modern idea is to leave the past and press onward to something new." The Progressive future unfolded through a process of adaptation. "The laws of this country have not kept up with the change of economic circumstances in this country," Wilson asserted; and "they have not kept up with the change of political circumstances; and therefore we are not even where we were when we started." This adaptation is not something the people enter into voluntarily; it is a fundamental political reality. "I do not say we may or may not," Wilson maintained, "I say we must; there is no choice. If you do not fit your facts, the facts are not injured, the law is damaged; because the law ... is the expression of the facts in legal relationships."[17]

Progressive adaptation in politics thus follows Darwin's principles of evolution in biology. Like a Darwinian species, society is in constant evolution—constant "development and accommodation to environment"—and evolution always proceeds onward and forward. In Progressive political theory, however, the analogue to the Darwinian species is not the individual person but the society. Government, Wilson explained, falls "under the theory of organic life;" it is "modified by its environment, necessitated by its tasks, shaped to its functions by the sheer pressure of life." A government, however, cannot adapt effectively unless its citizens constitute a well-formed people. A people is well-formed if its leading opinions are rational, if, that is, the opinions are shaped not in haphazard fashion but from intelligent planning, by "a quick concert of thought, uttered by those who know how to guide both counsel and action." Such a people has mastered its selfish tendencies and redirected its energies toward the common good, like the readers of *The New Freedom*, which Wilson dedicated "to every man or woman who may derive from it ... the impulse of unselfish public service."[18]

Changed Circumstances

These concepts of Progress, adaptation, and community inspired the Progressives to critique a wide range of American institutions, including the law of land-use. That critique started with the notion of changed circumstances. The Progressives held that new times required a new set of land-use laws. American city life and living patterns had changed drastically between the end of the eighteenth century and the beginning of the twentieth. Lawyers who subscribed to the earlier natural law-natural rights view would readily agree that land-use law needed to change with the times, but only to regulate new conditions to conform to permanent principles. Progressive land-use reformers, however, concluded that new times required not only new laws but also new principles. Frederick Law Olmsted, Jr., a Harvard professor of architecture and the first president of the National Conference on City Planning, described the new point of view when he explained that the modern city is a "live, productive organism ... in a constant state of change and growth." "Just as new generations replace the old with individuals who differ from their predecessors to some extent in body and in mind," Olmsted reasoned, "so in such a city old buildings, old streets, old institutions must give way, more slowly but no less certainly, to new and different generations."[19]

As in many other areas of reform, the most immediate agent of Progress in land-use reform was the Industrial Revolution. As Justice George Sutherland restated the conventional Progressive wisdom in his opinion for the Court in *Euclid*: "Until recent years, urban life was comparatively simple; but, with the great increase and concentration of population, problems have developed, and constantly are developing, which require, and will continue to require, additional restrictions in respect of the use and occupation of private lands." This growth caused unforeseen and unprecedented economic problems. Olmsted identified "the need for additional equipment"—buildings and housing—whose production was encouraged so "indirectly and often so tardily as to cause serious hardship and economic loss." For engineer and Planning Conference Vice Chairman Nelson Lewis, the proper response was to identify "[t]he economic considerations which should control city planning ... namely, adaptation to probable or possible increase in demand and capacity to supply that demand."[20]

But many Progressives rejected Lewis' assumption that economic forces were the most powerful agents of Progress. These reformers thought that economic factors merely reflected deeper psychological, social, and political changes. Sharp economic growth, coupled with the closing of the American frontier, worked a profound change in the American collective consciousness. The country embraced a new psychology of scarcity. As historian Christine Boyer explains this change, the demise of the frontier swept in "the concept of limit and the change of sympathies it entailed. When Americans reached the end of westward expansion and were finally forced to turn inward upon themselves, it was with hostility and embarrassment that they observed their disfigured and inhuman cities."[21]

The same historical forces also created demand for a new form of municipality, the "suburb." Progressive housing reformer Carol

Aronovici expected that "Utopia [could be] realized in the suburbs." Suburbs represented the next wave of Progress as soon as the cities declined. Suburbs promised to prevent many of the atomizing tendencies of industrialization. As social reformer Annie Diggs explained, workers were entitled to "a righteous share of the benefits of civilization they help[ed] to create." The way to do so was to give each worker a quarter-acre and a lawn to return to at the end of the working day in the city factory. "The demoralization and deprivation consequent on congested centers of population," warned Diggs, "have at length taught the Garden City economist the essential sin of divorcing the children of men from their Mother Earth." And in return, robust suburbs would also redound to the benefit of the cities. Homeowners habituated to enjoy the benefits of garden living would, in Christine Boyer's description, "no more tolerate the slum and the tenement than they would the plagues that were prevalent a generation ago."[22]

The Progressives were both concerned and optimistic about the prospects of reforming land-use planning in their day. They were concerned because they thought cities in the United States were lagging behind the finest European cities like Paris and especially the best-planned German cities, which had all embraced zoning.[23] Even so, the Progressives were optimistic because they expected to surpass their French and German role models. European planners needed to reckon with centuries of archaic traditions; the Progressives were in the fortunate position of legislating on what they regarded as a blank slate. As Chicago reformer Walter Moody proclaimed: "We of America, starting in a new country, acting without restraint of custom or ancient law, see our own remarkable opportunities in city building, and, it may be generally stated, are working for harmony and beauty in the building of our cities."[24]

The Rise of the General Welfare

Thus, the Progressives needed to ask how best to exploit both the opportunity and the challenge that the forces of Progress had thrust upon them. They had a wide range of proposals, including city clean-up, property-value stabilization, beautification, and above all urban planning. To establish each of these proposals in practice, they needed to redefine what counted as a legally cognizable "public interest." They did so through the notion of the "general welfare." American constitutional law recognized that states and localities enjoyed an inherent police power to legislate for the public health, safety, and morals and what one zoning enthusiast called "that novel, broad, and sweeping ground, 'the general welfare.'" Lawrence Veiller, Secretary of the National Housing Association, read turn-of-the-century precedents to "open a door a crack, which may be opened very wide. How wide it may be opened few of us can tell."[25]

The Progressives understood the general welfare in strongly communitarian terms. They hoped to instill Americans with a sense of local community as an antidote against the destructive and atomizing tendencies of the Industrial Revolution. The Industrial Revolution upset city life by making cities bigger, dirtier, more unwieldy, and more chaotic than they had ever been before. It upset the life of the working man by subordinating him into a huge industrial organization and by severing the connection that used to exist between his work and home. The Progressives tried to correct these problems at both the national and the local levels. At the national level, Progressives like Woodrow Wilson and Herbert Croly expected the Constitution, and especially the Commerce Clause, to hasten the formation of a general American will strong enough to give Congress a basis to respond to industrial dislocation with new vigorous economic regulation.[26] Paradoxically, however, this national project could not succeed without more energetic local government. As Wilson explained,

> morals enforced by the judgment and choices of the central authority at Washington, do not and cannot create vital habits or methods of life unless sustained by local opinion and purpose ... and only communities capable of taking care of themselves will, taken together, constitute a nation capable of vital action and control.[27]

The early social reform land-use literature is riddled with this idea of formation. Walter Moody claimed that national patriotism was getting "a companion sentiment—devotion and patriotism, an outgrowth of modern conditions of life, [which] takes the form generally of a high and controlling pride in one's native city, or in the city in which one abides and has adopted as his home." James Metzenbaum regarded the single-family home as "the bulwark and stamina of this country ... one of the important factors in the sustaining of the American people and American ideals." Many Progressives were uneasy with the commercialism of modern life and nostalgic for the intense patriotism of antiquity. Moody, for one, hoped that

> [s]tudents of modern history, seeking to classify or set apart this devotion to the city by its people, and love of a city by its children, will find the feeling not only a new, unique and valuable tendency of the times, but also a revival, under modern conditions, of a patriotism as old as civilization itself.[28]

These conceptions of patriotism and ideals gave Progressive legislation a communitarian spirit. Moody, Metzenbaum, and Wilson were voicing themes that trace back to Jean-Jacques Rousseau. Rousseau's social contract promised to solve what he diagnosed as the fundamental problem in the human condition: that man is so free that he knows little better than to enslave himself out of fear of his freedom. The social contract promised to solve this problem because "the total alienation of each associate, together with all his rights, to the whole community" would free him to partake in the community's "unity, its common identity, its life, and its will." The Progressives' concept of community is quite similar, because many American Progressives received their educations in German universities influenced by Hegel's theories of history and the state, which in turn were influenced by Rousseau's thought.[29] The historical march of Progress steered man toward the social contract; Progressive communities and laws finished the job.

The Progressives had at least four ways to institute the strong local communities of which they were so enamored. First, cities needed to control overcrowding. New York reformer Benjamin Marsh saw density controls as a way to prevent high mortality rates and physical deterioration.[30] Chicago reformer George Hooker worried that housing for "the masses of the people are chiefly characterized by disorder," caused by "the activity of certain great and special interests" and "tendencies more or less personal to the people themselves."[31] In some cases, controlling overcrowding was a polite way of excluding "undesirable" residents like new immigrants and members of different races.[32]

Second, cities and suburbs alike were expected to zone to make themselves more presentable and more beautiful. John Nolen disparaged the tendency in nineteenth century law to keep land-use regulation out of aesthetic disputes. "Nothing can be valid," he said of most American cities, "that has this degree of sordid and self-satisfied ugliness. We were meant to live in beauty, to cherish it and to create it, and a civilization that functions in the hideous and uncouth is a civilization of the wrong shape." Thus, when Daniel Burnham staged the 1893 World's Fair in Chicago to show off the city's architecture, he sparked a "City Beautiful" movement seeking to adorn America's great cities with neo-classical monuments.[33] While the cities promised grandeur, the suburbs beckoned with pastoral, idyllic tranquility. Englishman Ebenezer Howard encouraged the move to the suburbs in his 1902 book, *Garden Cities of Tomorrow*, which promised to remedy London's overcrowding by providing workers with wholesome homes outside city limits. Frederick Law Olmsted, Sr., a renowned architect and city designer, embraced the suburban vision for America. "[T]he demands of suburban life" would "advance upon" the refinement "characteristic of town life," because it would secure "the peculiar advantage of the country, such as purity of air, umbrageousness, facilities for quiet out-of-door recreation and distance from the jar, noise, confusion, and bustle of commercial thoroughfares."[34]

Third, cities and especially suburbs were expected to use regulatory powers to stabilize the price of home values. It might seem strange to call a suburbanite "communitarian" for wanting to exclude new development to prop-up the price of his home. Nevertheless, Charles Cheney, a California planner, insisted that "[i]t is the object of zoning to remove uncertainty and to stabilize as much property as possible." Robert Whitten, a nationally-known academic influential in New York City and Cleveland zoning efforts, insisted that the case for stabilization was not economic but moral. Even though "haphazard development has resulted in enormous waste and destruction of property values," he argued, the waste "is not nearly as important as the social and civic loss."

> From a social and civic point of view, there is nothing more important than the maintenance of the morale of the neighborhood. As soon as the confidence of the home owner in the maintenance of the character of the neighborhood is broken down through the coming of the store or of the apartment, his civic pride and his economic interest in the permanent welfare of the

section declines. As the home owner is replaced by the renting class, there is a further decline of civic interest and the neighborhood that once took a live and intelligent interest in all matters affecting its welfare becomes absolutely dead.[35]

Finally—and above all else—municipalities were expected to plan. The Progressives loathed the absence of a comprehensive plan. Recall that Progressives liked to equate the local community to an organism. The various organs of the body politic needed to act in coordination with the intelligent design of the organic mind. Progressives measured the political health of the city by the extent to which citizens acted with a common purpose; a comprehensive prearranged city plan was proof that they were. Thus, Benjamin Marsh's book *An Introduction to City Planning* begins: "A city without a plan is like a ship without a rudder." As leading lawyer Frank Williams warned in an early treatise on zoning, "[f]or good or for ill, as soon as two roads of a given width cross at a given place and angle, and a building starts at the intersection, its life and growth, have been carelessly, perhaps irrevocably fixed."[36]

All of these communitarian ideals exerted tremendous pressure on earlier conceptions of the police power. Because Progressives measured a city's well-being by the extent to which it was planned in advance, they saw nineteenth century regulation as an invitation to anarchy. Newman Baker, a land-use lawyer and author of a prominent land-use treatise, insisted that zoning was a "necessary first step to prevent utter chaos in municipal life, coming after years of unregulated development." Others argued more subtly for reforming the earlier conception. For instance, in his introductory address to the first City Planning Conference, Frederick Law Olmsted defined the police power traditionally, in terms of the doctrine that "no one may be permitted so to build or otherwise conduct himself upon his own property as to cause unreasonable danger or annoyance to other people." He subtly moved, however, to define what is "unreasonable" in Progressive terms—with reference to "gradually shifting public opinion."[37]

The Decline of Individual Property Rights

In order for the "general welfare" to expand, something else needed to contract—the scope of owners' "private property" in the rights to control the use of their land. Owners could retain many incidents of ownership of land, but the law needed to transform some incidents to guarantee common goods like aesthetics, orderliness, stable neighborhoods, and stable property values. To be sure, the Progressives were not the only ones or the last ones to criticize the more individually centered conception of use rights, but strands of their critique remain influential today.

Before setting this critique forth, it is worth noting that Progressive views varied more about property than about other features of land-use regulation. One can see the extremes in the land-use context as well as in other contexts. Some Progressives respected the institution of private property. For instance, as eager as Benjamin Marsh was to introduce zoning into New York, he conceded that "any effort to restrict the uses of such land to the basis of a lower value or to reduce the earning capacity of the land would be regarded by the Courts as a confiscation of property." Other Progressives were not so sympathetic. Edward Bassett found it "unthinkable that the city must compensate all of the private owners if reasonable aesthetic restrictions are placed on their use of city land." Frederick Howe envied German cities because "[i]n Germany the city is as sovereign over the property within its limits as it is over the people." He particularly envied the power German cities enjoyed to finance development by condemning more land than they needed and then selling the excess improved land for a profit.[38]

Even with these extremes, it is still possible to trace out an understanding of property rights that is distinctly "Progressive." Mainline Progressives still respected property as a negative liberty at a high level of generality and for a few key incidents of ownership. For instance, in his introductory address to the first Conference on City Planning, Frederick Law Olmsted, Jr., insisted that zoning rules should "leave open the maximum scope for individual enterprise, initiative, and ingenuity that is compatible with adequate protection of public interests."[39] This respect for private property is one of the important features distinguishing Progressivism and subsequent iterations of modern American liberalism, from historicist political theories with stronger communizing tendencies, like socialism.[40]

Yet while Progressivism respected private property at a broad level of generality, it treated the institution rather differently at the margins, especially with respect to the questions that made zoning politically controversial. Olmsted's warning is telling: he respects property as a source of individual initiative, but only to the extent "that is compatible with adequate protection of public interests." Free individual initiative over property was no longer inherently a part of the public interest. It might be part of the public interest, but it also might be in derogation of the public interest. It is no accident, then, that during the early twentieth century Progressive jurists like Oliver Wendell Holmes and Louis Brandeis started reasoning about constitutional property in terms of balancing tests, as they did in the due process/takings case *Pennsylvania Coal Co. v. Mahon*. Similarly, Frank Williams insisted in his land-use treatise that state constitutional eminent domain powers and police powers differed not in substance but in degree.[41]

Interest balancing need not be inimical to an individualist conception of private property, but other features of Progressive theory were. The Progressives' interpretation of American history encouraged them to conceive of property more as a source of group security than as an extension of individual freedom. James Metzenbaum insisted zoning was necessary to protect the residential owner from "in a single day, being robbed of a very half of the value of the home and property." As Charles Cheney explained, civic "contentment depends also on municipal regulations for the protection of home neighborhoods." After all, workers hesitate to buy homes and become solid members of the middle class "for fear some one later would ruin their investment and home neighborhood by building an apartment, stable, laundry or public garage next door."[42]

Separately, many Progressives decided that individually-centered conceptions of property were too expensive and constraining. Edward Bassett, for one, toyed with the idea of instituting zoning under the power of eminent domain instead of the police power. Under eminent domain, whenever a city restrained a legitimate use of property, it would need to exact a public servitude or easement, pay the owner just compensation, and then finance the compensation by charging special assessments to local owners who stand to benefit the most. Bassett rejected this project as too expensive. "If this is done for all of the parcels of a great city, the work is enormous. When, however, the city comes to assess these awards upon the property benefited the task is ten times as great." Even then, "the city would be worse off than it was before. It would be crystallized." "[A]s every living organism grows and changes," he explained, "these easements would have to be changed from time to time by successive applications of condemnation." Far better, Bassett concluded, to re-conceive of "property" and its proper "regulation" and finance all these changes for free. "Regulation under the police power," he noted, "adapts itself easily to the growth and change of the municipality."[43]

Most important, Progressive political theory encourages subscribers to view private property as the expression of an unhealthy tendency to elevate low selfish interests over high community interests. Again, the Progressives measured a community's state of political "maturity" by the extent to which all of its members sacrificed individual interests to form a common consciousness. Within these horizons, private property threatens to atomize political life unless it is reformed toward common ends; it is the quintessential Hegelian "matter" threatening to drag down by the political equivalent of gravity the Hegelian political spirit.[44] This opposition is not as strong in Progressivism as it was in Rousseau and Hegel, but it is still quite apparent in Progressive era writings on land use. Edward Bassett complained that "[p]rivate property and personal rights have been more sedulously guarded than community requirements." His New York colleague Benjamin Marsh demanded for New York City a government energetic to a degree "equal to the effort and the zeal which is now expended in the futile task of trying to make amends for the exploitations by private citizens and the wanton disregard of the rights of the many." Newman Baker defended zoning as a necessary response to the realization that "[t]he laissez faire theory of government is no longer tenable."[45] Taken together, these various tendencies subordinated individually-centered free use rights and elevated new community-centered incidents of ownership.

The Rise of Experts and the Decline of Judicial Review

Finally, the Progressives elevated experts and deprecated judges. They did so because Progress transformed how they understood law. Because Progress imparted reason to politics, it diminished the role for the rule of law as traditionally understood, as government under specific rules of conduct that applied generally to all citizens. It replaced rule under law with administration by experts. As Dennis Coyle explains, the Progressives replaced law and politics with "correct organization," which they expected "to provide essential knowledge, such as what the public interest is and how it can be obtained."[46]

Walter Moody illustrated this point of view when he stressed that "Chicago must no longer be a creature of chance. There must no longer be planless building." Moody assumed that the citizens of Chicago *could* and *must* overcome chance. He assumed that the forces of Progress had resolved the really fundamental questions of urban development. Since the *ends* of city life were more or less fixed by Progress, the only really important questions in city politics became questions of *means*. The city no longer needed legislators to write regulations reflecting local opinion and judges to enforce them; architects, engineers, and land-use planners had the specialized know-how to implement the priorities that a public-spirited and Progressive community would be expected to pursue. Thus, planners could pursue open-ended and rationalistic normative goals like "efficiency" without concern that they were legislating about controversial and politically-charged topics. For instance, as Canadian planner Thomas Adams assumed, "[e]fficiency requires that all planning should have regard to the best economic use to which land can be put, to the provision of the soundest economic basis for industrial development, and to the social organization of life so as to conserve the skill and physique of the workers," all while "trying to secure amenity [and] provide social intercourse, pleasant home surroundings, protection of natural beauty, and creation of structural beauty."[47]

The Progressives' writings presuppose such a transformation of politics. The best-respected Progressives assumed that the most important problems in land-use planning were not political but scientific and technical. Nelson Lewis looked forward to the day when the city engineer would assume the role once played by the city founder. The engineer's eyes "have been so closely fixed upon the drawing board that he has seldom looked up to catch a vision of the great city that is to come, the complex organism known as the modern city with ... its capacity to debase or elevate its citizens." While planner George Ford acknowledged that "[i]t is practically a physical impossibility for one man, in one lifetime, to acquire an adequate and impartial appreciation of all the points of view" that go into city planning, he was confident one could create a "lastingly satisfactory" plan by "put[ting] the work in charge of *several* experts—one an engineer, one an architect, and one, perhaps, a social expert." For Frederick Law Olmsted, Jr., these expectations for planning were not hopes but imperatives. A scientific planner could not possibly leave alone the "free interplay of economic forces and social impulses," not when he could perceive "the complex interwoven web of cause and effect that binds them all together." No one, Olmsted exclaimed, would rest content with an unscientific view of planning "after the imagination ha[d] grasped the larger possibility of control."[48]

Progressives also trusted local land-use experts to be non-partisan. Since Progress had already taken most of the politics out of politics, land-use reformers believed, they could vest wide-ranging powers in experts. They did not need, or so they thought, to worry that the experts might offend local community opinions or misuse public power for private ends. Robert Whitten expected that a zoning commission would "devote itself unreservedly to that work. It will take a broad view of the scope of city planning. It will realize that it needs the assistance of city plan experts. It will have something of the missionary spirit in propagating the gospel of city planning." Leading administrative law and local government professor, Frank Goodnow, expected the same of the administrators who reported to the commission. In his view, "the trend of american [*sic*] administrative development is in the direction of adopting the continental principle" of central administrative control, independent of political oversight. Expertise and non-partisanship combined to give zoning respectability. In *Euclid*, the Supreme Court respected the findings of expert "commissions" that published "comprehensive reports," which "b[ore] every evidence of painstaking consideration."[49]

On the other hand, as social progress and expert planners rationalized land use, they reduced the scope of judicial review. Edward Bassett recognized that "every state has been built on a fundamental law, purposely made hard to change, assuring permanency to government and emphasizing private rights, but omitting even the mention of any rights or powers of urban communities." But he distinguished away this fundamental law on the ground that: "[g]reat cities had not appeared.... In later years great cities developed with new and unforeseen needs ... But between the strong guarantees of personal liberty on the one side and the emphasis of the constitution on state government on the other, a municipality constantly struggles for suitable instruments to work out its own salvation."[50]

Bassett and other lawyers thus developed legal theories to make the police power more organic and adaptable. Bassett insisted that "a written constitution should be construed with a recognition of the changing needs of society and especially the community needs of modern cities, because, unlike a statu[t]e, a constitution should be fundamental, simple and enduring and is framed with an intention to cover the changing relations that progress may develop." To resort to Newman Baker's analogy, since zoning "laws fall in the 'legal dark continent,' i.e., in that field bounded by the older idea of the police power on the one side and on the other by the 'due process clause,'" one could make zoning "perfectly legal" by "expand[ing] the police power and contract[ing] the 'due process clause.'" Baker reasoned, "[a]s conditions change, governmental functions change; and our constitution is being expanded constantly to cover our needs."[51]

Such fundamental changes subordinated the role of the courts. Since social progress was more fundamental than the principles expressed in state constitutions, courts had no principled basis to cite those constitutions as authority to prevent new forms of land-use regulation. Some Progressives thus expressed impatience with state and federal judges. For instance, lawyer Andrew Wright Crawford complained that American judges "needed education." "If we can get over this bogey of the constitution and if we can fully realize the essentials of what we want," he complained, "we can probably persuade the judges that acts to provide those essentials should be upheld as constitutional." Other Progressives were more circumspect. University of Chicago administrative law professor Ernst Freund thought all that was needed was "a liberal interpretation of the constitution by the courts."[52]

III. THE FOUNDERS' CRITIQUE

The Supreme Court gave the Constitution that liberal interpretation in *Euclid v. Ambler Realty*, when it upheld zoning against constitutional challenge by drawing on Progressive themes about changing land-use conditions, superior planning, and optimizing land use. Zoning has been a mainstay of American law ever since. For instance, two leading land-use scholars recently published a zoning article in the *Harvard Law Review* titled "*Euclid* Lives: The Survival of Progressive Jurisprudence."[53]

Of course, some elements of the original Progressive case for zoning have survived the test of time better than others. Modern scholars and public officials are not as quick as the Progressives were to trust experts, or to speak of the local community in Hegelian or Rousseauan terms. The opposition between the Progressives and the American Founders is much more muted now than it was a century ago. Zoning has probably become popular and familiar enough to acquire the same aura of respectability, tradition, and authority as the founding.

Nevertheless, Progressive ideas continue to shape the law and politics of local land-use regulation. Even if they do not appreciate these ideas' pedigree back to Hegel or Rousseau, modern lawyers generally understand *Euclid v. Ambler Realty* as what one property casebook calls a "generous endorsement of social engineering in the name of the public health, safety, and welfare."[54] Modern property law has a strong historicist streak. Supreme Court justices are fond of saying that takings law must be careful not to rely on "a static body of ... property law," and that "[t]he human condition is one of constant learning and evolution—both moral and practical. Legislatures implement that new learning; in doing so they must often revise the definition of property and the rights of property owners."[55] Contemporary land-use scholarship is more post-modern than progressive, but even so it is still preoccupied with community, change, and social formation. In his recent book *City Making*, for instance, Professor Gerald Frug critiques zoning depending on the extent to which it helps citizens to engage in the process of forming their "sel[ves] ... in relationship with others."[56]

As a result, zoning makes an excellent practical test case of the main issue in American political theory since the Civil War. Most contemporary citizens may not appreciate it, but the American founding's classical liberalism and the Progressives' modern liberalism aimed to produce two very different regimes and two very different character types for their citizens. This claim would probably strike most contemporary Americans as strange, especially as applied to contemporary zoning. But the strangeness testifies to how thoroughly the Progressives succeeded. The most zealous zoning advocates saw the issues in these stark, political terms. Walter Moody, for one, confidently proclaimed: "He who makes the city makes the world. After all, though men make cities, it is cities which make men."[57]

If Moody was right, we can judge Progressivism by judging the sorts of men that progressively-managed cities have been making for three generations. Let us use zoning to compare Progressive political theory against the natural law and social compact theory of the American founding.

The proper place to begin is to compare the land-use reformers' vision of human nature, justice, and politics against the Founders' vision of the same, as expressed in such works as *The Federalist*. The fundamental difference between the two political theories lies in how each understands the relation between human reason, passions, and opinion. In Progressivism, group opinion and human reason are tied closely together, if they are not inseparable. The highest form of human reason expresses itself in the people's political consciousness, their collective will; human passions drive the people toward that higher reason. In founding era political theory, by contrast, the passions are subject to reason or opinion, and individual reason should aspire to guide opinion, even if it does not always succeed in doing so in practice. According to *The Federalist*, "all governments rest on opinion," but not all opinions are reasonable. The object of political life is to reform political opinion to avoid the situation in which "[t]he *passions*, ... not the *reason*, of the public would sit in judgment," and instead attain the situation in which "the reason, alone, of the public, ... ought to control and regulate the government."[58]

There are two broad theoretical differences that stem from this distinction. First, *The Federalist* and similar sources understood the institution of property markedly different from the Progressives. In the Founders' theory of politics, property is and ought to be a manifestation not of order, conformity, or security, but of individual freedom. Human reason can discern that the most likely purpose of talents like industriousness and acquisitiveness is to give each individual the capability for self-preservation and self-advancement. Reason concludes that each owner is entitled to a measure of free initiative over his possessions, so he may apply his passions to fulfill those ends. Reason also recognizes that, as the condition of his freedom, each owner owes his neighbors a corresponding duty to respect this same freedom.

Therefore property ought to be understood as a zone of non-interference. If so, it follows that the object of regulating property is then what Publius called in *Federalist* 10 "[t]he protection of ... different and unequal faculties of acquiring property.[59] If this account is true, the Progressives erred when they claimed the property-related passions could be reordered to achieve goals like a close sense of community. From Publius' point of view, the Progressives aimed too high. Whether or not they intended it, they encouraged citizens to use the law and the state to gratify the low.

Separately, the Founders would have criticized the Progressives for underestimating the importance of the rule of law. *The Federalist* is pessimistic about both reason and opinion. "The reason of man is timid and cautious when left alone." Because a "connection subsists between his reason and his self-love," man's "opinions and the passions will have a reciprocal influence on each other." Reasonable people must thus anticipate and use "the strength of opinion" on citizens as a counterweight against the passions. They must discern the best possible opinions and then institute those opinions into their law and culture. By instituting the opinions in longstanding laws, *The Federalist* explained, "[t]he wisest and freest governments" acquire "stability;" mutable opinions, by contrast, diminish the people's "attachment and reverence" for the principles that make civilized life decent.[60] From this perspective, Progressivism expects too much when it assumes that community opinion reflects a collective rationality. Public officials and local majorities could be trusted if local opinions were that rational; since the opinions are not so rational, Progressivism unintentionally encourages tyrannical behavior by those officials and majorities.

Let us consider how this theoretical critique applies to the practice of zoning. First, from the perspective of Publius and the Founders, zoning restrains the free and equal use of property. It interferes with developers' right to convert undeveloped property to uses that are legitimate, even if they do not conform to the tastes and economic interests of current residents. They interfere even more strongly with the freedom of poorer and less popular residents. Even if these residents do not have property to begin with, they can acquire it and advance themselves as long as the law *regulates*—protects, orders, and encourages—a wide-open market for property and a general right to use land actively and productively for a wide range of personal goals. At least as bad, zoning corrupts local majorities. It encourages them to gratify their passions by using the law to strip the equal rights of minorities. Since no one likes to think he is acting tyrannically, zoning then encourages those majorities to adopt local opinions that justify these oppressive actions.

The closest point of contact between zoning and this critique of it comes in *Euclid v. Ambler Realty Co.*, specifically in the trial-court opinion of Judge D. C. Westenhaver. Judge Westenhaver held Euclid's zoning scheme to be an unconstitutional interference with the rights of private property. Westenhaver invoked United States Supreme Court "substantive due process" precedents protecting natural property rights from unwarranted state regulation. He also held that the same results were barred by the guarantees in the Ohio Constitution mentioned in Part I: "All men ... have certain inalienable rights, among which are those of enjoying and defending life and liberty, acquiring, possessing, and protecting property," and that "[p]rivate property shall ever be held inviolate."[61] Because Judge Westenhaver chose to follow precedents steeped in the natural law-natural rights framework, he delivered a trenchant critique of zoning.

Judge Westenhaver began by grounding his constitutionalism on a footing very different from the Progressives. He insisted that "[t]he courts never hesitate to look through the false pretense to the substance" of legislative property regulation when they conduct judicial review.[62] For Westenhaver, judicial review and constitutionalism were indispensable to the rule of law. Individual reason can apprehend the substance of political life well enough to lay down intelligible general rules of conduct. Wise statesmen could write those guarantees into the United States and Ohio Constitutions. Local majorities might choose to ignore or circumvent those guarantees for understandable, predictable, but still self-serving reasons. But the constitutional rules had enough intelligibility and meaning for a judge like Westenhaver to understand and apply. From the Progressives' viewpoint, he was enforcing his own will over the expressed preferences of local majorities and the informed views of experts. From his standpoint, these groups were free to act reasonably—by living up to the reason already codified in the Ohio and United States Constitutions.

The principles that justified judicial review for Westenhaver also justified a right to property grounded in individual freedom. He followed Supreme Court precedent holding that "[t]he right to property, as used in the Constitution" must include not only its ownership but also "'its control and use, and upon its use depends its value.'"[63] The Progressives grounded property in its value to shared societal goals; Westenhaver's constitutional precedents grounded it in control and use, manifestations of individual freedom.

Because Westenhaver saw property as a manifestation of individual freedom, he saw Euclid's zoning scheme not as a public good but as a massive restraint. He began by noting that the zoning ordinance stripped the Ambler Realty Company of the freedom to develop its undeveloped land in the manner of its choosing. "It is a futile suggestion that plaintiff's present and obvious loss from being deprived of the normal and legitimate use of its property," Westenhaver insisted, "would be compensated indirectly by benefits accruing to that land from the restrictions imposed by the ordinance on other land." He could also see, however, that the Ambler Realty Company was not the only local party whose freedom was threatened. "The plain truth," he said, "is that the true object of the ordinance in question is to place all the property in an undeveloped area of 16 square miles in a straitjacket."[64]

Having established that the zoning scheme restrained the free and ordinary use of property, Westenhaver then predicted how the residents of Euclid's voting majority would use that power. Here, he followed Publius: When a community severs the connection between the positive law and equal natural rights, the control group in that community will sooner or later co-opt the positive law to gratify its passions. In part, Euclid's voting majority had gratified its economic passions. It had legislated a wealth transfer. To protect their home values and to make the entire village conform to their opinions about community design, the members of the majority had stripped Ambler Realty and other development companies of the right to make productive uses of their properties. Westenhaver was confident that "the property values taken from plaintiff and other owners similarly situated will simply disappear, or at best be transferred.... So far as the plaintiff is concerned, it is a pure loss."[65]

Westenhaver also suspected that local majority voters had embraced zoning to gratify some of their more preening and overbearing social passions. By severing the connection between local property regulation and the protection of equal rights, he predicted, zoning encouraged local white English-speaking majorities to strip the property rights of blacks, members of other disfavored races, and immigrants. He noted that southern cities had adopted race-based zoning initiatives, which the Supreme Court declared invalid in *Buchanan v. Warley*.[66] "[N]o gift of second sight," he noted, "is required to foresee that if this Kentucky statute had been sustained, its provisions would have spread from city to city throughout the length and breadth of the land. And ... the next step in the exercise of this police power would be to apply similar restrictions for the purpose of segregating in like manner various groups of newly arrived immigrants."[67] Westenhaver also expected well-off majorities to use zoning "to classify the population and segregate them according to their income or situation in life."[68]

Throughout, Westenhaver intimated a relationship between constitutionalism and political life radically different from that envisioned by the Progressives. At one point, he warned:

> The power asserted is not merely sovereign, but is power unshackled by any constitutional limitation protecting life, liberty, and property from its despotic exercise....If police power meant what is claimed [by Euclid], all private property is now held subject to temporary and passing phases of public opinion, dominant for a day, in legislative or municipal assemblies.[69]

Note how Westenhaver spoke skeptically of opinion in terms of "temporary and passing phases." Opinion had a lower status for Westenhaver than it does in zoning or in Progressive political theory. Euclidean zoning encourages communities to use zoning laws to reinforce local community opinions about the public interest. That tendency makes sense if, as Progressive political theory suggests, local communities of common interest give local life its character and its nobility. In both zoning and Progressive political theory, the community's reason and its judgments are inseparable from its opinions, because in both cases the opinions *make* the reason and the judgments.

Judge Westenhaver, by contrast, expected such powers to encourage citizens to behave like a mob. Municipal opinion needed steadying and guidance, in the form of constitutional guarantees marking off the objects that local community life was supposed to secure. (If

Westenhaver had been a state legislator, he probably would have insisted on reinforcing those same constitutional principles through enabling legislation like the Standard Enabling Act.) Those guarantees would force and teach citizens that they enjoyed the power of regulating themselves locally on condition that they used this power to secure the rights of all local residents. If local citizens ceased to respect this bargain, they would instead follow what Westenhaver called "temporary and passing phases of opinion." Sooner or later, local opinion would become unstable, fickle, and unworthy of local respect. Citizens would then forget the conditions under which they enjoyed the right to govern themselves. They would support local legislators who promised to pass laws representing what Westenhaver called the "despotic exercise" of local legislative power, transferring use rights from minorities and outsiders to legislative majorities. Such majorities would become, in Westenhaver and *The Federalist*'s horizons, slaves to their passions.

To most contemporary land-use lawyers, Westenhaver's opinion seems either quaint or dangerously radical. And yet Westenhaver diagnosed and predicted the problems most commonly associated with modern zoning today. After *Euclid*, the most famous case in American zoning law is *Southern Burlington County NAACP v. Township of Mount Laurel* (1975). Mount Laurel, a suburb of Camden, New Jersey, adopted a series of zoning ordinances and practices that make Judge Westenhaver sound like a modern-day prophet. The town zoned only 1 percent of the township's land for retail, 29 percent for industry (virtually all light industry), and the remaining 70 percent for single-family, detached dwellings, with lot and floor square-footage requirements that effectively excluded low-income housing. Town officials then negotiated side-deals with developers to build alternate forms of housing for high-income newcomers like single professionals and rich retirees who might choose to rent a luxury apartment or purchase a condominium. While the town's zoning plan did not permit such dwellings, these residents contributed to the tax base and the general impression that Mount Laurel was an "upper crust" community. Hence Mount Laurel permitted an exception to its general rule for these welcomed inhabitants.

By contrast, Mount Laurel discouraged housing for low-income earners and large families. Again, the zoning plan made apartments illegal. When town officials negotiated exceptions, they put ceilings on the number of multi-bedroom apartments and forced developers to promise to cover tuition and other school expenses if the number of children in the town rose too high. Developers also subsidized an increase in the township's public sector by contributing large sums of money for educational facilities, a cultural center, and a library.[70]

Land-use lawyers all regard *Mount Laurel* as a poster child capturing all the worst tendencies of Euclidean zoning.[71] In the name of the noble and Progressive ideal of preserving a "suburban way of life," local residents kept local property values high and the local public expenditure base low. To do so, those residents stripped developers and nonconforming owners of the right to use their properties. The residential majority in Mount Laurel and others like it throughout the state choked up the supply of affordable housing for lower-income and minority-race New Jersey residents. While the lower-income families who wanted to move into Mount Laurel might not have "fit" happily in a cozy suburban single-family residential neighborhood, their intended land uses were legitimate, non-polluting, and productive.

All the while, the zoning scheme encouraged corruption and undermined the rule of law. The restrictive provisions served not as a legal standard but rather as an opening bargaining position. They forced developers to "deal" with locals, by paying local residents a high premium for undeveloped land, and with local officials and planners, by making public concessions to receive permission to develop.

Finally, when the New Jersey Supreme Court intervened to protect the interests of lower-income and minority-race residents, suburban residents reacted in terms Westenhaver probably would have described as "despotic." The Governor of New Jersey scored political points with suburbanites by equating *Mount Laurel* with communism. A local mayor did the same when he promised to go to jail rather than follow *Mount Laurel* as precedent.[72]

Yet while *Mount Laurel* represents everything that is wrong with zoning for so many land-use lawyers, hardly any of them appreciate how the problems they see in *Mount Laurel* follow logically from zoning's Progressive commitments. Ironically, the New Jersey Supreme Court lamented Mount Laurel's zoning scheme on Progressive grounds. It accused the city of trying "to keep down local taxes on *property* … without regard for non-fiscal considerations with respect to *People*."

More generally, the court complained that almost every city "acts solely in its own selfish and parochial interest and in effect builds a wall around itself to keep out those people or entities not adding favorably to the tax base."[73] But cities and residents behaved in such fashion in large part because they were encouraged to do so by Progressive insistence on close regulation, Progressive faith in local majorities and experts, and above all Progressive optimism about human nature and the possibilities of political community.

CONCLUSION

Roderick Hills, a professor of local government and constitutional law, has wondered whether "[c]ommunity building ... might be critically related to the building of walls." Hills poses this Hobson's choice to suggest that "the lovers of local government ... are going to have to make a tough choice between the direct political participation that local governments facilitate and the social inequality and parochialism that local governments also seem to promote."[74]

Hills shows how thoroughly Progressivism has penetrated the law of local government, and he unwittingly points to the most important question facing local government. If the Progressives were more or less right about human nature, local government is probably stuck on the horns of Hills' dilemma. On that hypothesis, local residents need the kind of social engineering Progressivism encourages before they can become "citizens" worthy of the name. At the same time, such social engineering only works well in close quarters. It probably encourages strong pressures to exclude the wider community. If Progressivism is substantially accurate, the best local land-use law can hope to accomplish is to accept zoning and to provide a few outlets to prevent its most exclusionary tendencies. Those tendencies are the price of fostering Progressive citizens and real communities.

Yet *Mount Laurel* is one of many examples suggesting that the Progressives may have been profoundly wrong about human nature. If this is the case, we must view contemporary local government with a certain sadness. There is no reason why local homeowners must build their conception of their social interests around the property values of their homes and the homogeneity of their neighborhoods. From what we know, several generations of Americans conceived of their interests in land-use in terms of the free exercise of their property rights. From their perspective, Hills' choice is a false choice. If Progressivism is misguided, Euclidean zoning encourages local homeowners to build their communities around the wrong commons. It is then this misstep that causes those communities to become so exclusionary and their residents so parochial. The character of Progressivism remains the fundamental question in contemporary local government law—as it does in many other areas of American law and politics today.

Endnotes

1. The author thanks the Claremont Institute's Center for Local Government for supporting his research and Matt Jagger for his research assistance.

2. Woodrow Wilson, *Constitutional Government in the United States* (Piscataway, N.J.: Transaction Press, 2002 [originally published in 1908]).

3. Herbert Croly, *The Promise of American Life* (Boston: Northeastern University Press, 1989 [originally published in 1909]).

4. Robert Ellickson, "Alternatives to Zoning: Covenants, Nuisance Rules, and Fines as Land Use Controls," *University of Chicago Law Review* 40 (1973): 681, 692. On homeowners' attachment to their homes, cf. William A. Fischel, *The Homevoter Hypothesis: How Home Values Influence Local Government Taxation, School Finance, and Land-Use Policies* (Cambridge: Harvard University Press, 2001).

5. The account presented in text is provisional because we still know comparatively little about some forms of nineteenth century American land-use regulation, especially municipal police power regulations, and because much of the evidence that we do have has been interpreted in sharply conflicting ways. One comprehensive survey comes from William J. Novak, *The People's Welfare: Law & Regulation in Nineteenth-Century America* (Chapel Hill: University of North Carolina Press, 1996), 51-82, 149-90.

6. Buchanan v. Warley, 245 U.S. 60, 74-75 (1917).

7. Ambler Realty Co. v. Village of Euclid, 297 F. 307, 313-16 (N.D. Ohio 1924), rev'd, 272 U.S. 365 (1926). For discussions of Westenhaver's opinion, see Seymour I. Toll, *Zoned American* (New York: Grossman

Publishers, 1969), 213-27; Eric R. Claeys, "Takings, Regulations, and Natural Rights," *Cornell Law Review* 88 (2003): 1549, 1628-633.

8. Buchanan v. Warley, 245 U.S., at 74; Ambler Realty Co. v. Village of Euclid, 297 F., 310 (quoting Ohio Const. art. I, secs. 1, 19).

9. Department of Commerce Advisory Committee on Zoning, *A Standard State Zoning Enabling Act: Under which Municipalities May Adopt Zoning Regulations* (1926).

10. Dennis J. Coyle, *Property Rights and the Constitution: Shaping Society through Land Use Regulation* (New York: State University of New York Press, 1993), 20.

11. *Standard Enabling Act*, § 3; see Village of Euclid v. Ambler Realty Co., 272 U.S. 365, 379-80 (1926). Cf. Charles M. Haar, "In Accordance with a Comprehensive Plan," *Harvard Law Review* 1154 (1955).

12. *Standard Enabling Act*,§§ 1, 3.

13. Coyle, *Property Rights and the Constitution*, 21.

14. *Standard Enabling Act*, § 3.

15. Ibid., §§ 6-7.

16. James Metzenbaum, *The Law of Zoning* (New York: Baker, 1930), 5-7. Metzenbaum's arguments closely follow the Supreme Court's justification for zoning in Village of Euclid v. Ambler Realty Co., 272 U.S. 365 (1926).

17. Woodrow Wilson, *The New Freedom: A Call for the Emancipation of the Generous Energies of a People* (New York: Doubleday, 1913), 33, 35, 42.

18. Wilson, *Constitutional Government in the United States*, 21, 27, 56; Wilson, *The New Freedom*, 45.

19. Frederick Law Olmsted, Jr., "Reply in Behalf of the City Planning Conference," *Proceedings of the Third National Conference on City Planning* (Philadelphia, May 15-17, 1911): 3, 5, 10.

20. Village of Euclid v. Ambler Realty Co., 272 U.S. 365, 386-87 (1926). Olmsted, *Third Conference Proceedings*, 5-6; Nelson P. Lewis, "The City Plan Defined by a Municipal Engineer," *Proceedings of the Seventh National Conference on City Planning* (1915): 1, 3.

21. M. Christine Boyer, *Dreaming the Rational City: The Myth of American City Planning* (Cambridge: MIT Press, 1983), 4.

22. Carol Aronovici, "Suburban Development," *Annals of the American Academy of Political and Social Science* (January 1914): 234, 248; Annie L. Diggs, "Garden City Movement," *Arena* 28, no. 6 (1902): 626, 631-32. Cf. Boyer, *Dreaming the Rational City*, 42; Frank T. Carlton, "Urban and Rural Life," *Popular Science Monthly* 68 (March 1906): 225, see generally 40-43.

23. See, e.g., Walter D. Moody, *Wacker's Manual of the Plan of Chicago: Municipal Economy. Especially Prepared for Study in the Schools of Chicago*

(Chicago: Chicago Plan Commission, Hotel Sherman, 1920), 20-38; Frederick C. Howe, "The Municipal Real Estate Policies of German Cities," *Proceedings of the Third National Conference on City Planning* (Philadelphia, Pennsylvania, May 15-17, 1911): 14; Edward M. Bassett, "A Survey of the Legal Status of a Specific City in Relation to City Planning," *Proceedings of the Fifth National Conference on City Planning* 58 (1913): 58-59; Frank B. Williams, "Some Aspects of City Planning Administration in Europe," *Proceedings of the Seventh National Conference on City Planning* (1915):144, 147-53.

24. Moody, *Wacker's Manual*, 39.

25. Lawrence Veiller, "Districting by Municipal Regulation," *Proceedings of the Ninth National Conference on City Planning* (1916): 147, 153.

26. See Eric R. Claeys, "The Living Commerce Clause: Federalism in Progressive Political Theory and the Commerce Clause After Lopez and Morrison," *William & Mary Bill of Rights Journal* 11 (2003): 403.

27. Wilson, *Constitutional Government*, 195.

28. Moody, *Wacker's Manual*, 5-6; Metzenbaum, *Law of Zoning*, 127.

29. Jean-Jacques Rousseau, *The Social Contract*, in *The Social Contract and the Discourses*, with an introduction by Alan Ryan, trans. G. D. H. Cole (New York: Alfred A. Knopf, Inc., 1993), 179, 191-92. For the Hegelian connection, cf. Thomas H. Logan, "The Americanization of German Zoning," *American Institution of Planning Journal* 42.5 (October 1976): 377.

30. See Benjamin Clarke Marsh, *An Introduction to City Planning: Democracy's Challenge to the American City* (New York: privately printed, 1909), 9-10.

31. George E. Hooker, "Congestion and Its Causes in Chicago," *Proceedings of the Second National Conference on City Planning and the Problems of Congestion* (Rochester, New York, May 2-4, 1912 (originally published in 1910): 42, 49.

32. Metzenbaum, *Law of Zoning*, 128 (arguing that excluding immigrants prevents overcrowding and reduces the drain on public services); Bruno Lasker, "The Atlanta Zoning Plan," *Survey* 48 (April 22, 1922): 114 (warning of racial exclusion). See generally Constance Perin, *Everything in Its Place: Social Order and Land Use in America* (Princeton: Princeton University Press, 1977).

33. John Nolen, "The Place of the Beautiful in the City Plan, Some Everyday Examples," *Proceedings of the Fourteenth National Conference on City Planning* (1922): 133, 138; Jesse Dukeminier and James E. Krier, *Property*, 5th ed. (New York: Aspen Publishers, 2002), 954-55.

34. Frederick Law Olmsted, "Riverside Illinois: A Planned Community near Chicago," in *Civilizing American Cities: A Selection of Frederick Law*

Olmsted's Writings on City Landscapes, S. B. Sutton, ed. (Cambridge: MIT Press, 1971), 292, 295; see Carlton, "Urban and Rural Life."

35. Charles H. Cheney, "Zoning in Practice," *Proceedings of the Eleventh National Conference on City Planning* (1919): 162; Robert Harvey Whitten, "Zoning and Living Conditions," *Thirteenth National Conference on City Planning* (1921): 22, 25.

36. Marsh, *Introduction to City Planning*, 5; Frank Backus Williams, *The Law of City Planning and Zoning* (New York: Macmillan, 1922), 3.

37. Newman F. Baker, *The Legal Aspects of Zoning* (Chicago: University of Chicago Press, 1927), 35; Olmsted, *Third Conference Proceedings*, 26.

38. Marsh, *Introduction to City Planning*, 21-22; Bassett, *Legal Status*, 59; Howe, "Municipal Real Estate," 14-15, 21.

39. Olmsted, *Third Conference Proceedings*, 27.

40. See Baker, *Legal Aspects*, 1; Coyle, *Property Rights*, 21-22.

41. Pennsylvania Coal Co. v. Mahon, 260 U.S. 393 (1922); Williams, *Law of City Planning*, 25.

42. Metzenbaum, *Law of Zoning*, 6; Cheney, "Zoning in Practice," 164.

43. Edward M. Bassett, "The Question Box," *Proceedings of the Fourteenth National Conference on City Planning* (1922): 159; Edward M. Bassett, *Zoning: The Laws, Administration, and Court Decisions During the First Twenty Years* (New York: Sage, 1940), 27.

44. See George Wilhelm Friedrich Hegel, *The Philosophy of History*, with an introduction by C. J. Friedrich, trans. J. Sibree, (Mineola, N.Y.: Dover Publications, 1956), 15, 21.

45. Bassett, "Legal Status," 46; Marsh, *Introduction to City Planning*, 27; Baker, *Legal Aspects*, 35.

46. Coyle, *Property Rights*, 23.

47. Moody, *Wacker's Manual*, 53; Thomas Adams, "The Development of the Plan," *Proceedings of the Ninth National Conference on City Planning* (1916): 141, 148.

48. Nelson P. Lewis, *Seventh Conference Proceedings*, 1, 11; George B. Ford, "The City Scientific," *Proceedings of the Fifth National Conference on City Planning* 58 (1913): 31-32 (emphasis added); Olmsted, *Third Conference Proceedings*, 17-18.

49. Robert H. Whitten, "The Constitution and Powers of a City Planning Authority," *Proceedings of the Seventh National Conference on City Planning* (1915): 138; Frank J. Goodnow, "Municipal Home Rule," *Political Science Quarterly* 21 (March 1906): 77, 89; Village of Euclid v. Ambler Realty Co., 272 U.S. 365, 394 (1926).

50. Bassett, "Legal Status," 47; Village of Euclid v. Ambler Realty Co., 272 U.S. 365, 394 (1926).

51. Bassett, "Legal Status," 53; Baker, *Legal Aspects*, 140-41.

52. "Discussion," *Fifth Conference Proceedings*, 62-64, 66.

53. Charles M. Haar and Michael Allan Wolf, "*Euclid* Lives: The Survival of Progressive Jurisprudence," *Harvard Law Review* 115 (2002): 2158.

54. Dukeminier and Krier, *Property*, 1010.

55. Lucas v. South Carolina Coastal Council, 505 U.S. 1003, 1035, 1069 (1992) (Justice Kennedy concurring and Justice Stevens dissenting).

56. Gerald E. Frug, *City Making: Building Communities Without Building Walls* (Princeton: Princeton University Press, 2001), 73.

57. Moody, *Wacker's Manual*, 2 (quotations omitted).

58. James Madison, *Federalist* 49, in *The Federalist Papers*, with an introduction and notes by Charles R. Kesler, Clinton Rossiter, ed. (New York: Mentor Books, 1999), 281-82, 285.

59. James Madison, *Federalist* No. 10, in *The Federalist Papers*, 45-46. Cf. Claeys, "Takings," 1568-69.

60. *Federalist* No. 10, 46; *Federalist* No. 49, 282, 283; James Madison, *Federalist* No. 62, in *The Federalist Papers*, 344, 350.

61. Ambler Realty Co. v. Village of Euclid, 297 F. 307, 310 (N.D. Ohio 1924), rev'd, 272 U.S. 365 (1926) (quoting Ohio Const. art. I, secs. 1, 19).

62. Ibid., 314.

63. Ibid., 313 (quoting Buchanan v. Warley, 245 U.S. 74 [1917]).

64. Ibid., 315-16.

65. Ibid.

66. 245 U.S. 60 (1917); see Ambler Realty Co. v. Village of Euclid, 297 F. at 312-13.

67. Ambler Realty Co., 297 F. at 313.

68. Ibid., 316.

69. Ibid., 313-14.

70. 336 A.2d 713, 720-23 (N.J. 1975), appeal dismissed & cert. denied, 423 U.S. 808 (1975).

71. See e.g., Dukeminier and Krier, *Property*, 1065-1091.

72. John M. Payne, "Rethinking Fair Share: The Judicial Enforcement of Affordable Housing Policies," *Real Estate Law Journal* 16 (1987): 20, 22.

73. Southern Burlington County NAACP v. Township of Mount Laurel, 336 A.2d, 723.

74. Roderick M. Hills, Jr., "Romancing the Town: Why We (Still) Need a Democratic Defense of City Power," *Harvard Law Review* 113 (2000): 2009, 2011-2012.

·⁓Chapter 10⁓·

Campaign Finance Reform: The Progressive Reconstruction of Free Speech

Tiffany R. Jones

Introduction

Anyone seeking to understand American politics today must realize that our politics is made up of an uneasy mixture of ideas, institutions and policies that were spawned by two fundamentally different philosophical schools of thought. While virtually all scholars acknowledge the significant role the Founders' understanding of Lockean social compact theory played in the formation of American politics in the revolutionary period and beyond, relatively few scholars are sensitive to the equally significant role nineteenth century German idealism played in the reformation of American politics in the late nineteenth and twentieth centuries. As a consequence, scholars seeking to explain the remarkable institutional and policy reforms of these periods typically point merely to the necessity of adjusting to industrialization. In so doing, they simply ignore the profound intellectual change gathering strength at the same time. As Eldon Eisenach has rightly observed:

> Even as this period witnessed "the most profound and rapid alterations in the material conditions of life that human society has ever experienced," it also underwent a comparable intellectual and even spiritual transformation. These transformations

soon began to carry over into the larger political world, destroying many of its intellectual and institutional foundations.[1]

The American intellectuals (and later politicians, journalists, and reformers) who were decisively influenced in their understanding of politics by the historical school became known as Progressives. Progressive intellectuals articulated a strikingly self-conscious and thoroughgoing critique of Lockean social compact theory—and thus of the founding principles. As part and parcel of this larger critique, they rejected the Founders' understanding of liberty as false in theory and inadequate in practice. In its place, they articulated a new positive understanding of liberty that required, among other things, an extensive "democratic restructuring" of the old understanding of liberty in order to achieve what they considered its true realization.

In what follows, then, we shall concentrate on the reconstruction of one particularly important aspect of individual liberty: the freedom of speech. As we shall see, the campaign finance reform movement—a movement recently culminating in the Supreme Court's approval of the highly restrictive regulatory regime established by the Bipartisan Campaign Reform Act of 2002—has, and continues to be, substantially animated by the Progressive critique of the Founders' understanding of liberty. In other words, the concern for equality that has long rallied reformers is nothing more than the application of the Progressive critique of the Founders' understanding of liberty and, more specifically, an attack on the traditional meaning of freedom of speech.

THE REQUIREMENTS OF EQUALITY

Although various concerns have animated the campaign finance reform movement over time, arguably no concern has been as influential as that of ensuring "political equality."

"From the very beginning," Robert Mutch observes, "arguments in favor of limits [on political contributions and expenditures]... were egalitarian."[2] Despite the fact that the Supreme Court explicitly rejected the claim that "political equality" constitutes a "compelling state interest" warranting regulation of freedom of speech in its 1976 decision of *Buckley v. Valeo*, this concern continues to dominate discussion of reform. Concern for equality, Bradley Smith notes, "continues to be heavily promoted in the academic literature and is a persistent theme in popular writing, as well."[3]

In a post-*Buckley* survey of the campaign finance literature, Charles Beitz observes that concern for political equality manifests itself in two distinctive ways in the literature.[4] First, many commentators bespeak a concern for "the equality of voter influence over election outcomes." Those who take this position hold that each voter ought to exert a relatively equal amount of influence in determining who—or what—wins an election. The fact that every adult citizen enjoys an equal vote in any given election is not enough, by itself, to ensure this equality. Where individuals and groups may freely contribute or otherwise expend money on behalf of a particular cause or candidate, the equality of influence of voters is upset by the additional influence exerted by those who have or can raise a significant amount of money. "[I]n a society based upon an equal ballot," as another advocate puts it, freedom of speech "gives wealthy individuals or groups massively unequal opportunities to influence the ballots of their fellow citizens."[5] Concern for equality in this regard, Beitz continues, leads to a concern for "proportional finance," i.e. the idea that "candidates [or causes] should enjoy financial support in proportion to the portion of the electorate that favors them, so that their chances of victory will be determined by their popularity rather than by distorting financial advantages." Those who seek to assure this sort of equality, accordingly, typically favor regulations imposing low contribution limits on individuals and Political Action Committees, and a ban on independent expenditures.[6]

Second, many commentators express concern for "financial equality for candidates, not voters." Where individuals and groups may freely contribute or expend money on campaigns, however, some candidates—namely those who have or can raise a lot of money (like incumbents)—have a significant fund-raising advantage. In order to offset such inequalities in funding, advocates of candidate equality tend to favor public subsidies.[7] Interestingly, despite the prominence of the latter concern in the literature, Beitz himself doubts that candidate equality bears any principled relation to voter equality. The "one-man, one-vote principle" justifying *voter* equality, he concludes, can hardly be invoked to justify *candidate* equality.[8] By focusing so literally on the "one-man, one-vote" principle, however, Beitz overlooks a broader conception of political equality many take to be implicit in the "one-man, one-vote" requirement and that ties both aspects of equality together. In this formulation, both voter equality and candidate equality are based on the implicit premise that the ability of individuals to participate (or speak) effectively in elections, either as supporters seeking to "influence the ballots of their fellow citizens," or as candidates running for office, *should not be contingent upon the financial resources at their disposal.* All individuals, in short, should have a roughly equal opportunity to influence politics beyond casting a vote. While a concern for equality in this sense echoes throughout our public discourse, and has been elaborated in one way or another by a number of leading legal commentators, no one has developed the nature of this concept as clearly as John Rawls.

In *Political Liberalism,* the follow-up and clarification of his well-known treatise *A Theory of Justice,* Rawls seeks to map out a system of campaign finance that a democratic form of government must implement to ensure popular control over government. His argument begins with the claim that a government that seeks merely to protect the equal rights of man (individually and negatively understood) cannot ensure popular control over government:

> Many have argued, particularly radical democrats and socialists, that while it may appear that citizens are effectively equal, the social and economic inequalities likely to arise if the basic structure includes the basic liberties and fair equality of opportunity are too large. Those with greater responsibility and wealth can control the course of legislation to their advantage.[9]

Despite couching this critique in indirect discourse, Rawls agrees with it. In his estimation, a government that protects the equal rights (or liberties) of men only *seems* to secure their equality. The reason for this is twofold: First, government protection of equal liberties will inevitably result in significant "social and economic inequalities." Second, government protection of equal liberties will also enable each citizen to use whatever resources he commands in elections; in so doing, Rawls suggests, such a government simply allows those with greater means—i.e. those with "greater responsibility and wealth"—to control the course of legislative action to their own advantage.

In light of this problem, Rawls seeks to devise a way of ensuring that all men, regardless of the resources at their disposal, will be able to control the course of government. His solution to this problem is a regulatory principle called the "fair value of political liberty." In explaining this principle, Rawls draws an instructive distinction between the "basic liberties" and the "worth of these liberties." The "basic liberties" comprise the "institutional rights and duties that entitle citizens to do various things, if they wish, and that forbid others to interfere." As such, the "basic liberties" amount to a "framework of legally protected paths and opportunities." In contrast, the "worth of these liberties" represents the actual "usefulness" of the "basic liberties" to a person in light of the fact that "ignorance and poverty, and the lack of material means generally, prevent people from exercising their rights and from taking advantage of these openings." Obviously, "the worth or usefulness, of liberty is not the same for everyone" because those who have "greater wealth or income" simply possess "greater means for achieving their ends." Given the varying "worth" of the "basic liberties," therefore, the "first step toward combining liberty and equality into one coherent notion" is to "combine the equal basic liberties with a principle for regulating certain primary goods viewed as all-purpose means for advancing our ends [politically]." Since the overall aim, once again, is to prevent those with greater means from subverting democratic government by controlling the development of policy for their own advantage, the regulatory principle Rawls seeks centers on political liberty; hence, its designation as the "fair value of political liberties."[10]

The regulatory principle Rawls refers to as the "fair value of political liberties" principle *is* the broader conception of equality that unites voter equality and candidate equality, those two variants of equality identified by Charles Beitz. That is, the "fair value of political liberties" principle holds that "the worth of the political liberties to all citizens, whatever their social or economic position, must be approximately equal, or at least sufficiently equal, in the sense that everyone has a fair opportunity to hold public office and to influence the outcome of political decisions." The "fair value of political liberties" principle thus hinges on a conception of equality requiring that all citizens must be able to exercise their freedoms to hold office and influence election outcomes to an approximately equal extent. In the area of campaign finance, as Rawls makes plain, achieving equality so understood would at least require "public financing of political campaigns and election expenditures, various limits on contributions and other regulations." At the minimum, then, ensuring the "fair value of political liberties" would require a two-prong government strategy. The first prong, which might be called the positive strategy, would require government to supply the funding needed to ensure that everyone, regardless of the financial means at their disposal, "has a fair opportunity to hold public office." This would be the purpose of "public financing of political campaigns and election expenditures." The second prong, which might be called the negative strategy, would require government to impose limits on the ability of those who have or can raise money in order to prevent them from using their superior means to exert greater influence over "the outcome of political decisions." This is the purpose of "contribution limits." A government guided by Rawls' "fair value of political liberties" principle, in short, would promote both voter and candidate equality.[11]

It is important to stress, as Rawls himself stresses, that the requirements of equality thus understood are fulfilled in important part by regulating individual liberty. Although the concern for equality does not require the complete abolition of individual liberty, the second strategy mentioned above does require imposing restrictions on the rights or liberties of some, but not others. This is not to say that the equality concern justifies the imposition of all regulations. To be legitimate, Rawls clarifies, government regulations "must not impose any undue burdens on the various political groups in society and must affect them all in an equitable manner." In saying government must treat groups "in an equitable manner," Rawls does not mean that government should protect individual rights equally by refraining from regulating freedom of speech altogether. On the contrary, he simply means that government can regulate or burden free speech *so long as* the regulation promotes his conception of equality—i.e. the principle of the "fair value of political liberties." For example, a regulation barring large contributions from private persons or corporations to candidates would not be an undue burden on wealthy persons and groups because

> [s]uch a prohibition may be necessary so that citizens similarly gifted and motivated have roughly an equal chance of influencing

the government's policy and of attaining positions of authority irrespective of their economic and social class. *It is precisely this equality which defines the fair value of political liberties.*[12]

Any regulation restricting the activity of those who have or can raise money in order to amplify the voice of those who lack similar resources, therefore, impose due, rather than "undue," burdens. Although such limits do nothing positively to promote the voice of those who lack resources, in preventing those with superior means from using them—and thereby exercising more influence than those lacking such means—these limits may be said to promote equality.

To conclude, Rawls' "fair value of political liberties" principle is predicated upon a conception of political equality which holds that all citizens (or at least "those similarly gifted and motivated") should "have roughly an equal chance of influencing the government's policy and of attaining positions of authority irrespective of" the economic and social resources at their disposal. To achieve this end, government must, among other things, regulate the freedoms of speech and press of some in ways that will help promote the approximate equality of all in their use. When equality is understood in this way, as more than one commentator has noted, its requirements are substantially at odds with the requirements of individual liberty.[13]

THE ORIGINAL UNDERSTANDING OF EQUALITY

While equality and liberty are concepts that have profoundly shaped American politics since the founding, the suggestion that their requirements are at odds or somehow contradictory is a relatively recent development. The main, not to say only, vehicle through which these concepts originally entered the American political vocabulary was Lockean social compact theory. In the *Second Treatise of Government,* Locke explains that a proper understanding of the original source and extent of "political power" requires an examination of the "state of nature," i.e. the "state all men are naturally in." In Locke's estimation, the first characteristic of man's natural state is "freedom"—a term he seems to use interchangeably with "liberty." All men are born into "a state of perfect freedom to order their actions and dispose of their possessions, and persons as they think fit, within the bounds of the law of nature, without asking leave, or depending upon the will of any other man." Except for the obligation to obey the limits imposed by the laws of nature (principally by refraining from violating the "perfect freedom" of others), all adult human beings are otherwise free to rule themselves. In other words, no individual is bound to obey the will of another but has, rather, a *right* to govern himself.

The second main characteristic of man's natural state is equality. In describing this characteristic, Locke suggests that man's natural liberty—i.e. his freedom to rule himself—is a consequence of his natural equality:

> A *state* also *of equality*, wherein all the power and jurisdiction is reciprocal, no one having more than another: *there being nothing more evident, than that Creatures of the same species and rank promiscuously born to all the same advantages of nature, and the use of the same faculties, should also be equal one amongst another without subordination or subjection,* unless the Lord and Master of them all, should by any manifest declaration of His will set one above another, and confer on him by an evident and clear appointment an undoubted right to dominion and sovereignty.[14]

In other words, by nature no man has a right to rule another without his consent. The apparent reason for this is that all men are created equal. Locke argues that a species whose members are "born to all the same advantages of nature, and the use of the same faculties, should also be equal one amongst another without subordination or subjection." Among a species of this kind there is no clear hierarchy of natural rulers and ruled; as a consequence, each member of the species is free to rule himself. Human beings, Locke implies, are of this type, and so every adult human being has the right to rule himself. Equality and liberty are thus correlative principles: because all men are born equal, they are born free. This is precisely the relation Jefferson had in mind when, in the Declaration of Independence, he wrote: "We hold these truths to be self evident, that all men are created equal, that they are endowed by their Creator with certain inalienable rights, that among these are life, liberty and the pursuit of happiness."

Without going into a comprehensive discussion of Lockean social compact theory, suffice it to say that the fundamental fact of natural human equality produces a theory of government in which government is formed to secure the natural liberty—which liberty divides up into particular natural rights—of its citizens. The purpose for which government is formed thus limits what government may rightfully do. Calling the natural liberty of men—i.e. their "lives, liberties, and estates"—by "the general name, property," Locke notes that "[t]he great and chief end ... of mens uniting into commonwealths, and putting themselves under government, is the preservation of their property."[15] Or, as the Declaration so simply and eloquently concludes: "that to secure these rights, governments are instituted among men, deriving their just powers from the consent of the governed." According to this theory, there are two main ways in which government satisfies the requirements of natural human equality: first, by obtaining the people's consent in the formation or constitution of government and, to some extent, in its on-going operation;[16] second, by limiting its actions to those that are necessary to secure every individual's ability to enjoy or exercise as much of his natural liberty as is consistent with the preservation of the "political society."[17] As originally understood, then, the requirements of *equality* were met in important part by protecting individual *liberties* equally.

The embrace of this theory of government in the American founding eventually culminated in the formation of republican governments on the state and national levels whose purpose it was to protect the inalienable rights of men. As Madison explained in a 1792 essay entitled "Property":

> Government is instituted to protect property of every sort; as well that which lies in the various rights of individuals, as that which the term particularly expresses. This being the end of government, that alone is a just government, which impartially secures to every man, whatever is his own.

Echoing Locke's expansive use of the term "property," Madison notes that governments are established to secure the individual's right to control those things that he has a "right" to including his "land, or merchandize, or money," "his religious opinions and the profession and practice dictated by them," "the safety and liberty of his person," "the free use of his faculties and free choice of the objects on which to employ them," as well as, importantly, "his opinions and the free communication of them."[18] On the national level, of course, the original plan of government issuing from the Constitutional Convention entrusted the protection of these rights to the extent of the country and the internal structure of the government. As it turned out, however, a Bill of Rights was soon added, thereby providing explicit protection for some of these rights including freedom of speech—a right Madison, in preparing his speech introducing a proposed bill of rights to the first Congress, referred to as among the "natural rights, retained" by the people.[19] Here, as before, government fulfills the requirements of the equality principle to the extent to which it protects the right of individuals to speak and write free from government interference *equally*.

THE PROGRESSIVE DEMOCRATIZATION OF INDIVIDUAL LIBERTY

As originally understood, then, the equality principle does not require government to ensure that every individual has the roughly equal ability to exercise his freedom of speech—or any of his other liberties for that matter. On the contrary, it merely requires government to protect every individual's right to speak freely by refraining from interfering with his speech.[20] The question thus naturally arises: when did the meaning of equality become so convoluted? The answer to this question, I submit, lies in the Progressive transformation of liberty.

In the aftermath of the 1912 election in which the Progressive Party candidate Teddy Roosevelt received more electoral votes than the incumbent Republican, President William Howard Taft, Progressive theorist and *New Republic* founder Herbert Croly declared that a momentous change was underway in American political life: "[T]he really salutary aspect of the present situation," he wrote, "is the awakening of American public opinion to the necessity of scrutinizing the national ideal and of working over the guiding principles of its associated life."[21] However new this change was among the general public, by 1912 it was already well-advanced among the intellectual elite of American society. Pregnant with far-reaching implications for virtually every aspect of American political life, this "working over" of the nation's guiding principles had been underway for at least the past sixty years. In a 1903 survey of the "recent tendencies" in American political thinking, Progressive reformer and preeminent political scientist Charles Merriam approvingly described this change: "In the last half of the nineteenth century," he observes, "there appeared in the United States a group of political theorists differing from the earlier thinkers in respect to method and upon many important doctrines of political science." Merriam traced the roots of this group to the arrival of nineteenth century German philosophy in the persons of Francis Lieber, a German political scientist who emigrated to America in 1827, and a long "line of American political scientists, many of whom were trained in German schools," including Theodore Woolsey, John W. Burgess, Arthur L. Lowell, Woodrow Wilson, Frank J. Goodnow and W. W. Willoughby.[22] As Merriam reports, the writings of these theorists contain a frank rejection of the founding principles:

> The individualistic ideas of the "natural right" school of political theory, indorsed in the Revolution, are discredited and repudiated. The notion that political society and government are based upon a contract between independent individuals and that such a contract is the sole source of political obligation, is regarded as no longer tenable.[23]

According to Merriam, the new theorists rejected the Founders' understanding of Lockean social compact theory for various reasons. Lieber, for example, condemned social compact theory on two grounds. First, misconstruing the meaning of Locke's description of the state of nature, Lieber argued that the state of nature had "no basis in fact." The state of nature is comprised wholly of "independent individuals," he argues, but such a state cannot exist because man's natural state is social, not solitary. Because this is the case, moreover, no artificial means for bringing him into society, like a contract, is needed. Second, conceiving social contract theory to be a general theory of state formation—which it is not—Lieber rejected it as an inadequate explanation. While some states might originate through consent (as is required by social compact theory) others form, and have formed, by force, fraud, and religion. For these reasons and others, the new theorists dismissed social contract theory as mistaken and initiated a profound change in the American conception of political life: "In the refusal to accept the contract theory as the basis for government," Merriam concludes, "practically all the political scientists of note agree." "The doctrines of natural law and natural rights," he adds, "have met a similar fate."[24]

As Merriam was fully aware, the Progressive rejection of Lockean social compact theory implied a profound reorganization of the

Founders' understanding of politics. In some cases, the new theory would simply nullify old requirements—such as the need for obtaining the people's consent before changing the form of the government. In other cases, however, the new theory would perpetuate the form but redefine the meaning of earlier concepts. Of particular importance for present purposes is the Progressive redefinition of liberty. As Merriam notes: "The modern school has formulated a new idea of liberty, widely different from that taught in the early years of the Republic." The "new idea of liberty" differed from the old in at least two fundamental respects. First, the new understanding of liberty was derived from a wholly different foundation than the old. Thus, whereas the Founders believed liberty inhered in every individual simply by virtue of being a human being, the Progressives divorced liberty from its foundation in man's nature. "It is of vital importance to notice," Merriam stresses,

> that liberty is not a natural right which belongs to every human being without regard to the state or society under which he lives. On the contrary, it is logically true and may be historically demonstrated that "the state is the source of individual liberty." It is the state that makes liberty possible, determines what its limits shall be, guarantees and protects it.

In the Progressive redefinition of liberty, then, liberty becomes a condition that the different races or nations gradually come to enjoy over the course of their historical development. So understood,

> [l]iberty is not a right equally enjoyed by all. It is dependent upon the degree of civilization reached by the given people, and increases as this advances. The idea that liberty is a natural right is abandoned, and the inseparable connection between political liberty and political capacity is emphasized.

Of the "various nations or races" of the world, Merriam concludes, the "Teutonic nations are particularly endowed with political capacity."[25]

In addition to having a different foundation, the Progressive conception of liberty also differed fundamentally from the Founders' in its content. In contrast to the Founders, as Eldon Eisenach observes, "[t]he alternative starting point for the Progressives was a conception of democratic citizenship informed by values of 'positive' rather than 'negative' liberty."[26] Whereas the Founders defined liberty as the totality of rights individuals possess by nature, the enjoyment of which ultimately consists in the absence of government interference, the Progressives defined liberty in terms of individual self-realization— i.e. as the ability to engage in the activities through which one's capacities or potential can be fulfilled. In one variation or another, this positive conception of liberty was widely repeated throughout Progressive writings. For example, economist Richard Ely defines "true liberty" as "the expression of the positive powers of the individual." Similarly, sociologist Charles Horton Cooley rejected the relevance of liberty understood as "the absence of constraint" in favor of liberty understood as the "opportunity for right development, for development in accordance with the progressive ideal of life that we have in conscience."[27] As John Dewey aptly summarized this change, under the influence of the historical school

> [t]he problem of achieving freedom was immeasurably widened and deepened. It did not now present itself as a conflict between government and the liberty of individuals in matters of conscience and economic action, but as a problem of establishing an entire social order, possessed of a spiritual authority that would nurture and direct the inner as well as the outer life of individuals.[28]

From the standpoint of the new positive understanding of liberty, the old negative understanding of liberty seems terribly inadequate: "The freedom of an agent who is merely released from direct external obstructions," as John Dewey and James Tufts put it, "is formal and empty." Although negative liberty—understood as "exemption from restraint and from interference with overt action"—is the necessary condition of man's true freedom, it is not the sufficient condition. In order to become truly free, individuals must be exempt from external constraints *and* possess "positive control of the resources necessary to carry purposes into effect" as well as the "mental equipment with the trained powers of initiative and reflection requisite for free preference and for circumspect and far-seeing desires."[29] As a consequence of this requirement, the individual's true or "effective freedom" (as Dewey and Tufts call it) is usually far smaller than his formal or legal freedom:

A particular individual at a given time is possessed of certain secured resources in execution and certain formed habits of desire and reflection. In so far, he is positively free. Legally, his sphere of activity may be very much wider. The laws ... would protect him in exercising claims and powers far beyond those he can actually put forth. He is exempt from interference in travel, in reading, in hearing music, in pursuing scientific research. But if he has neither material means nor mental cultivation to enjoy these legal possibilities, mere exemption means little or nothing.[30]

In view of this problem, the Progressive conception of liberty is wedded to a positive conception of state power. A government whose power is limited to securing the natural rights of man may be able to ensure that every individual has the same legal opportunities, but it cannot ensure that every individual will control the resources he needs to take advantage of his vast formal opportunities. As a consequence, the Progressives believed that government must extend its power in whatever ways are necessary to transform merely "formal" freedom into "effective" freedom. The fewer the people with "effective freedom," Dewey and Tufts explain, the greater the need for reform:

[I]t is the possession by the more favored individuals in society of an effectual freedom to do and to enjoy things with respect to which the masses have only a formal and legal freedom, that arouses a sense of inequity, and that stirs the social judgment and will to such reforms of law, of administration and economic conditions as will transform the empty freedom of the less favored individuals into constructive realities.[31]

While the realization of "effectual" or positive freedom may not require the perfect equalization of each individual's ability to exercise his legal freedoms, it certainly requires a significant step in that direction. To accomplish this objective, government must extend its powers in two main ways: through redistribution and regulation. In some cases, government must use public funds to supply "less-favored" individuals with the various resources they need to take advantage of their formal opportunities. In other cases, it must regulate or "restructure" the liberties of some in the old sense with an eye to promoting equality in each individual's relative ability to exercise his formal liberties. Although those who continued to think of liberty in the old sense would inevitably oppose all such efforts "on the ground that these efforts would effect an invasion of individual liberties and rights," Dewey and Tufts predict, such invasions would be nonetheless necessary for "making individual liberty a more extensive and *equitable* matter."[32]

THE PROGRESSIVE DEMOCRATIZATION OF FREE SPEECH

With this critique of the Founders' understanding of liberty in mind, it is clear that the conception of equality animating the debate over campaign finance is nothing more than the application of the Progressive critique of the old understanding of liberty generally, and to the freedom of speech specifically. Thus, as we saw earlier, Rawls' "fair value of political liberties" principle hinges upon a conception of political equality which requires that all citizens (or at least "those similarly gifted and motivated") should "have roughly an equal chance of influencing the government's policy and of attaining positions of authority irrespective of" the economic and social resources at their disposal. If this conception of equality is to be realized in practice, government must provide the funding needed to ensure that anyone, regardless of the financial means at their disposal, can actually exercise their formal political liberties, as well as regulate the liberty of those who have or can raise money to prevent them from exercising their rights more effectively than their less well-funded fellow citizens. The equality concern is thus nothing more than a concern for "effective liberty," i.e. a concern for ensuring that government takes whatever action is necessary to ensure that every citizen can exercise his legal opportunities to participate in politics more effectively.

Rawls is by no means alone in understanding equality as "effective liberty." This same basic logic is repeated by the most prominent advocates of equality and supplies the guiding principle of their interpretations of the First Amendment. As Bradley Smith points out, "[t]he long-accepted reading of the ... First Amendment, is that it protects 'negative rights'—that is, rights to be free from government action—and does not create 'positive rights'—that is, requirements that the government act."[33] As we saw earlier, the First Amendment was explicitly designed to reserve the individual natural right to communicate one's opinions free from the interference of the national government. The negative phrasing of the First Amendment confirms this view: "Congress shall make no law … abridging the freedom of speech, or of the press," etc. Nevertheless, the advocates of equality argue that the First Amendment's Free Speech Clause not only allows, but may actually even require, government action that promotes equality understood as "effective liberty."

Ronald Dworkin, Owen Fiss and Cass Sunstein are among the leading exponents of the First Amendment as interpreted in this Progressive light.[34] Dworkin, to begin, argues that the First Amendment was designed to implement a particular conception of democracy called "partnership democracy." (As we shall see, what distinguishes "partnership democracy" from a merely "majoritarian" conception of democracy is its dedication to the idea of political equality understood as "effective liberty.") In a "mature democracy," Dworkin notes, citizens play two main roles. First, they are "the judges of political contests whose verdicts, expressed in formal elections or in referenda or other forms of direct legislation, are normally decisive." Their "verdicts," in turn, comprise "public opinion." In addition to acting in their capacity as voters, "citizens are also … participants in the political contests they judge: they are candidates and supporters whose actions help, in different ways, to shape public opinion and to fix how the rest of the citizens vote." Whereas the "majoritarian" concept only requires equality in the first role, "partnership" democracy requires citizen equality in both: "The partnership conception recognizes both roles, because it supposes that in a true democracy citizens must play a part, as equal partners in a collective enterprise, in shaping as well as constituting the public's opinion."[35]

As a consequence of this requirement, the partnership conception is "damaged when some groups of citizens have no or only a sharply diminished opportunity to appeal for their convictions because they lack the funds to compete with rich and powerful donors." Where people lack the resources to make their political liberties effective, in other words, they cannot participate as equal partners in the second sense: "People cannot plausibly regard themselves as partners in an enterprise of self-government when they are effectively shut out from the political debate because they cannot afford a grotesquely high admission price."[36] Viewed in light of "partnership democracy," and the particular threats attending it, Dworkin concludes that the First Amendment "permits ceilings on campaign expenditures when these help repair significant citizen inequality in politics, provided the ceilings are set high enough so that they do not dampen criticism of government, and so that no new inequality is introduced by foreclosing unfamiliar parties or candidates."[37] The First Amendment, in other words, permits Congress to regulate the campaign spending of individuals or groups in order to ensure that those who have or can raise money cannot overwhelm the voices of those who lack comparable resources. Thus, while Dworkin does not actually use the term "effective liberty," the conception of equality at the heart of "partnership democracy" is plainly that.

Although Owen Fiss expressly denies employing an "effective liberty" justification, he actually elaborates an even more sweeping variation of this argument than Dworkin.[38] Fiss begins his analysis of the First Amendment by focusing on what he takes to be the purpose of the Free Speech Clause. That clause, he argues, serves a public, not an individual, purpose: "The purpose of free speech is not individual self-actualization, but rather the preservation of democracy, and the right of a people, to decide what kind of life it wishes to live." More precisely put, the purpose of the Free Speech Clause is to ensure a "rich public debate."[39] While Fiss concedes that First Amendment precedent and scholarly commentary have traditionally associated the realization of this goal with the protection of individual "autonomy"— i.e. with the limitation of the government's power to interfere with the individual's right to speak freely—he argues that this approach actually subverts the purpose of the First Amendment. Instead of ensuring a "rich public debate, autonomy simply results in "a debate that bears the imprint of those forces that dominate the social structure." In a capitalist society, he explains,

> the protection of autonomy will on the whole produce a public debate that is dominated by those who are economically powerful. The market—even one that operates smoothly and efficiently—does not assure that all relevant views will be heard, but only those that are advocated by the rich, by those who can borrow from others, or by those who can put together a product that will attract sufficient advertisers or subscribers to sustain the enterprise.[40]

As a consequence, while all citizens have an equal right to express their views, only those citizens with the means to do so are able to take advantage of this right.

In view of this problem, Fiss argues that we must change the way we have traditionally thought about the government and its relation to the First Amendment: "the state," he argues, "can enrich as much as it constricts public debate." In order to enrich the public debate, government must seek to correct all the various ways in which the unequal distribution of politically-valuable resources hampers the expression of "all the relevant views." In some cases, accordingly, this will require government to regulate the freedom of speech by restraining those with superior financial resources from using them. In the area of campaign finance, for example, Fiss calls for imposing limits on the expenditures of political actors "to make certain all views are heard." In other cases, government must provide subsidies to ensure the expression of "issues and perspectives otherwise likely to be ignored or slighted by institutions privately owned and constrained by the market." Recipients of subsidies would include institutions like public television and radio, public and private universities, public libraries and the public education system. Finally, in still other cases, government must guarantee speaker access to valuable forums for the expression of their views.

To ensure that private institutions possessing an unequal opportunity to influence public opinion—like the media—use their resources in a manner that enables "all the relevant views" to be heard, for instance, "the power of the media to decide what it broadcasts must be regulated." Similarly, in order to make certain that other private property owners cannot deny advocates a valuable forum for the expression of their views, Fiss endorses laws "requiring the owners of the new public arenas—like shopping centers—to allow access for political pamphleteers." Far from being a limitation on government power, the First Amendment thus requires constant correction of "the skew of the social structure" in whatever way the skew is manifested.[41] As Fiss concludes,

> to serve the ultimate purpose of the First Amendment we may sometimes find it necessary to "restrict the speech of some elements of our society in order to enhance the relative voice of others," and that unless the Court allows, and sometimes

even requires, the state to do so, we as a people will never be truly free.[42]

Whatever he chooses to call it, Fiss' interpretation of the First Amendment plainly employs a far-reaching elaboration of the "political equality" as "effective liberty" logic.

Like Dworkin and Fiss, Cass Sunstein also interprets the requirements of the First Amendment in a Progressive light. In his estimation, there are three compelling state interests that justify restrictions on the freedom of speech: government's need to guard against "corruption;" to promote "political equality;" and to "promote the goal of ensuring political deliberation and reason-giving."[43] Of these three, however, Sunstein gives leading place to the second interest. As he declares at the outset,

> there is no good reason to allow disparities in wealth to be translated into disparities in political power....*Government has a legitimate interest in ensuring not only that political liberties exist as a formal and technical matter, but also that those liberties have real value to the people who have them.* The achievement of political equality is an important constitutional goal.[44]

Like Dworkin and Fiss, then, Sunstein also plainly advances a "political equality" as an "effective liberty" justification for campaign finance reform.

In defending the legitimacy of the equality justification, Sunstein draws an instructive parallel between the Court's decision in *Buckley* and its "pre-New Deal" jurisprudence. In his estimation, the Court's treatment of the individual right to free speech in *Buckley* was a throwback to its *Lochner*-era treatment of the individual right to acquire property. In "rejecting the claim that controls on financial expenditures could be justified as a means of promoting political equality," he argues, "*Buckley* might well be seen as the modern-day analogue of the infamous and discredited case of *Lochner v. New York*, in which the Court invalidated maximum hour laws."[45] In this 1905 case, and many others like it prior to 1937, he explains, the Court was asked to consider the constitutionality of various Progressive laws designed to promote greater equality between employers and employees by imposing certain restrictions on the terms of the contract—e.g. a maximum hour workday, minimum wage, etc. In deciding these cases, the Court made the mistake of treating the "existing distributions of resources [between employers and employees] as if they were prepolitical and just." [46] More precisely put, in these cases the Court was guided in its construction of the Fourteenth Amendment's Due Process Clause by the Founders' understanding of natural rights and the proper role of government in securing them. Specifically, the *Lochner* Court began from the premise that all individuals (employers and employees alike) have a natural right to enter into contracts for the exchange of goods free from the interference of any other party. (This right, like all natural rights, is "prepolitical" in the sense that it inheres in the individual by nature and is not the creation of government.) Under this theory, as we have seen, government is formed for the express purpose of securing this and every other "prepolitical" right of man. Government thus fulfills its purpose by securing the right of the employer as well as the employee to enter into contracts freely. Beyond this, government should not concern itself with the resulting "distribution of resources." On the basis of this reasoning, accordingly, the Court struck down many of these laws on the grounds that they effected an "impermissible redistribution" of goods—i.e. that they sought to take something to which one person was entitled and give it to another who was not so entitled.[47]

Sunstein applauds the Court for finally abandoning this approach in the late 1930s. The key to this development was an emerging consensus in the legal community that "property rights were a function of law rather than nature, and ought not to be immunized from legal change." In rejecting the idea that the right to contract is a natural right, the Court opened these rights up to government regulation. Regulation would no longer "be banned in principle," he concludes, "but would be evaluated on the basis of the particular reasons brought forward on their behalf." As the Supreme Court characterized its new approach in *West Coast Hotel Company v. Parrish*, the case in which it formally overruled *Lochner*, "the community is not bound to provide what is in effect a subsidy for unconscionable employers."[48] In short, government is not bound to protect the rights of employers where they are able to exercise their rights to better effect than their employees.

"In its essential premises," Sunstein rightly observes, "*Buckley* is quite similar to the pre-1937 cases." In assessing the constitutionality of the 1974 Amendments to the Federal Election Campaign Act, the

Buckley Court rejected the argument that restrictions on the freedom of speech are justified by the state's interest in promoting "political equality." In making this point, he notes,

> the Court announced that "the concept that government may re-
> strict the speech of some elements of our society in order to en-
> hance the relative voice of others is wholly foreign to the First
> Amendment." It added that the "First Amendment's protection
> against governmental abridgement of free expression cannot prop-
> erly be made to depend on a person's financial ability to engage
> in public discussion."[49]

The Court thus rejected the "political equality" justification on the grounds that the First Amendment protects every individual's right to speak freely regardless of his relative ability to use that right. In so finding, the Court's decision was a throwback to the logic of its "pre-New Deal" jurisprudence: "Just as the due process clause once for-bade government 'interference' with the economic marketplace, so too the First Amendment now bans government 'interference' with the political marketplace, with the term 'marketplace' understood quite literally." Although it has been "a constitutional truism in the post-New Deal era" that economic "markets" [and hence property rights] are legitimately subject to democratic restructuring," the Court inex-plicably refused to apply the same logic to "political markets [and hence the First Amendment freedom of speech]." The reason for this, he implies, is that the Court continues to cling to the notion that the individual right to free speech is "prepolitical," and hence in need of being "immunized from legal change," when in fact it is no less a creation of law than property rights. "What is perhaps not sufficiently appreciated," he explains,

> but what is equally true, is that elections based on existing dis-
> tributions of wealth and entitlements also embody a regulatory
> system, made possible and constituted through law. Here as else-
> where [i.e. the economic marketplace], law defines property in-
> terests; it specifies who owns what, and who may do what with
> what is owned.[50]

Like the Progressives, then, Sunstein clearly rejects the idea that rights are "prepolitical." Because rights are merely a creation of law, there is no reason "as a matter of principle" for government to refrain from "restructuring" them for the sake of promoting greater equality in their exercise. If the Court consistently applied the logic accepted in the post-New Deal era, he thus concludes, it would endorse "democratic restructuring" of the right to free speech every bit as much as it endorses the "democratic restructuring" of property rights. Like Dworkin and Fiss, then, Sunstein plainly advances an equality-understood-as-effective liberty critique of the Court's interpretation of the First Amendment.

CONCLUSION

Those who write about the debate over campaign finance reform frequently characterize it as arising from the fundamental conflict between the requirements of equality and the requirements of liberty that is inherent in any democratic nation. They thus imply that this conflict inheres in the origins of the United States of America. As I have shown in this discussion, however, the conflict between the requirements of equality and liberty does not inhere in the founding principles. On the contrary, the understanding of equality that substantially animates the campaign finance reform movement is the product of the new understanding of liberty embraced by Progressives beginning in the second half of the nineteenth century. The conflict between the requirements of equality and liberty, accordingly, is more accurately understood as a conflict between the progressive understanding of liberty and the Founders' understanding of liberty. As Fiss rightly observes, "free speech [is] one strand—perhaps the only left—of a more general plea for limited government."[51]

Endnotes

1. Eldon Eisenach, *The Lost Promise of Progressivism* (Lawrence, Kan.: University Press of Kansas, 1994), 2.
2. Robert Mutch, *Campaigns, Congress and Courts: The Making of Federal Campaign Finance Law* (New York: Praeger, 1988), 53.

3. Bradley Smith, *Unfree Speech: The Folly of Campaign Finance Reform* (Princeton: Princeton University Press, 2001), 137-138.

4. Charles R. Beitz, "Political Finance in the United States: A Survey of Research," *Ethics* 95, no. 1 (October 1984).

5. David Adamany, "Money, Politics, and Democracy: A Review Essay," *American Political Science Review* 71, no. 1 (March 1977): 297. See also Adamany, *Financing Politics: Recent Wisconsin Elections* (Madison: University of Wisconsin Press, 1969), 13.

6. Beitz, "Political Finance in the United States: A Survey of Research," 141-142.

7. Ibid., 142. On the concern for candidate equality, see also Adamany, *Financing Politics*, 258; Peter Levine, *The New Progressive Era: Toward a Fair and Deliberative Democracy* (Lanham, Ma.: Rowman and Littlefield, 2000), 113-114; Herbert Alexander, *Financing Politics: Money, Elections, and Political Reform* (Washington, D.C.: Congressional Quarterly, 1992), 167; and Anthony Gierzynski, *Money Rules: Financing Elections in America* (Boulder: Westview Press, 2000), chapter 4.

8. Regarding candidate equality, Beitz notes that "one might wonder why equality in this sense should be accorded any moral weight. Certainly a straightforward application of the principle of equal participation will not make this interpretation plausible. Since that principle defines the rights of citizens as equal participants in political decision making [i.e. as voters], its application to candidates could only be derivative." In "Political Finance in the United States," 143.

9. John Rawls, *Political Liberalism* (New York: Columbia University Press, 1996), 325.

10. Ibid., 325-327.

11. Ibid., 324-326.

12. Ibid., 357-358 (emphasis added).

13. See, for example, Gierzynski, *Money Rules*, 14: "The basic or underlying conflict of campaign finance is one that pits two values of great importance to a democracy against each other. Those two values are political freedom and political equality....The freedom of individuals and groups to spend money on/in political campaigns detracts from equal political representation ... and gives financially advantaged interests an upper hand in the interest-group system." See also Richard Gephardt, as quoted in Nancy Gibbs, "The Wake-Up Call," *Time* 3 (February 1997): 22. "What we have is two important values in direct conflict: freedom of speech and our desire for healthy campaigns in a healthy democracy."

14. John Locke, *Second Treatise*, in *Two Treatises of Government*, Peter Laslett, ed. (Cambridge: Cambridge University Press, 1992), sec. 4, 269 (emphasis added).

15. Ibid., secs. 123-124, 350-351.

16. In a chapter entitled "Of the forms of a Common-wealth," Locke seems to argue that the principle of natural human equality does not require the formation of any particular form of government: "The majority, having ... upon men first uniting into Society, the whole power of the community, naturally in them, may imploy all that power in making laws for the community from time to time, and executing those laws by officers of their own appointing; and then the form of the government is a perfect democracy: Or else may put the power of making laws into the hands of a few select men, and their heirs or successors; and then it is an oligarchy: Or else into the hands of one man, and then it is a monarchy: If to him and his heirs, it is an hereditary monarchy: If to him only for life, but upon his death the power only of nominating a successor return to them; an elective monarchy. And so accordingly of these the community may make compounded and mixed forms of government, as they think good." Ibid., sec. 132. But note the requirement for ongoing consent at ibid., secs. 138,142.

17. On this point, see ibid., sec. 135.

18. James Madison, "Property," (March 27, 1792), in *The Papers of James Madison*, Robert A. Rutland, et al., eds. (Charlottesville: University Press of Virginia, 1983), 14:266.

19. As quoted in Thomas G. West, "Free Speech: The Founders' Approach," in *Liberty Under Law*, Kenneth L. Grasso and Cecilia Rodriguez Castillo, eds. (Lanham, Maryland: University Press of America, 1998), 158.

20. I am not suggesting that the equality principle requires government to refrain from interfering with every possible type of speech. Instead, I am merely suggesting it requires government to refrain from interfering with any speech that neither injures the rights of others nor endangers the preservation of the community.

21. Herbert Croly, *Progressive Democracy* (New York: Macmillan Company, 1915), 27.

22. For a detailed account of the profound influence of nineteenth century German historicism on American intellectuals in the nineteenth and early twentieth centuries, see John G. Gunnell, *The Descent of Political Theory: The Genealogy of an American Vocation* (Chicago: University of Chicago Press, 1993), especially chapters 1-2.

23. Charles E. Merriam, *A History of American Political Theories* (New York: Macmillan Company, 1903), 305-307.

24. Ibid., 305-309.

25. Ibid., 311-314.

26. Eisenach, *The Lost Promise of Progressivism*, 189.

27. As quoted in ibid., 189-190.

28. John Dewey, *Liberalism and Social Action* (Amherst, N.Y.: Prometheus Books, 2000 [originally published in 1935]), 39. Eisenach, *The Lost Promise*, 189-191, provides numerous other examples on the same point.

29. John Dewey and James Tufts, *Ethics* (New York: Henry Holt and Company, 1908), 437-438.

30. Ibid., 438-439.

31. Ibid., 439.

32. Ibid., 481 (emphasis added). Similarly, Walter Weyl, *The New Democracy: An Essay on Certain Political and Economic Tendencies in the United States* (New York: MacMillan Company, 1912), 161, declares that "the inner soul of our new democracy is not the unalienable rights, negatively and individualistically interpreted, but those same rights, 'life, liberty, and the pursuit of happiness,' extended and given a social interpretation."

33. Smith, *Unfree Speech*, 141.

34. See also J. Skelly Wright, "Money and the Pollution of Politics: Is the First Amendment an Obstacle to Political Equality?" *Columbia Law Review* 82 (May 1982): 1001-1020; Burt Neuborne, "Toward a Democracy-Centered Reading of the First Amendment," *Northwestern University Law Review* 93 (1999): 1055-1073.

35. Ronald Dworkin, "Free Speech and the Dimensions of Democracy," in *If Buckley Fell: A First Amendment Blueprint for Regulating Money in Politics*, E. Joshua Rosenkranz, ed. (New York: Century Foundation Press, 1999), 70-72. For an earlier, more concise version of the same argument see Ronald Dworkin, "The Curse of American Politics," *New York Review of Books* 17 (October 1996): 19-24.

36. Dworkin, "Free Speech and the Dimensions of Democracy," 78-79.

37. Ibid., 84. According to Dworkin, 86-95, neither the "text" nor First Amendment precedent provides any clear guidance as to the actual meaning of the First Amendment. As regards the former, Dworkin concedes that it could be read as "forbidding regulation of speech for any reason whatsoever," but argues insofar as it "permits regulation of speech to protect national security, or the peace and quiet of neighborhoods, then it also permits, just as a matter of the bound of language, regulation to protect or perfect democracy."

38. Owen M. Fiss, "Free Speech and Social Structure," *Iowa Law Review* 71 (1986): 1417.

39. Ibid., 1409-1410.

40. Ibid., 1412-1413.

41. Ibid., 1416, 1419.

42. Ibid., 1425; see also, 1411.

43. Cass Sunstein, "Political Equality and Unintended Consequences," *Columbia Law Review* 94 (May 1994): 1390-1394.

44. Ibid., 1390 (emphasis added); see also 1392.

45. Lochner v. New York, 198 U.S. 45 (1905).

46. Sunstein, "Political Equality," 1397.

47. Ibid., 1397-1398.

48. Ibid., 1398, citing West Coast Hotel Company v. Parrish, 300 U.S. 379, 399 (1937).

49. Ibid., 1398.

50. Ibid., 1398-1399.

51. Fiss, "Free Speech," 1414.

·⤳Chapter 11⤷·

Aimless Theorizing:
The Progressive Legacy
for Political Science

Larry Peterman

Don't tell me how it works in practice, my postmodern colleagues insist. How does it work in theory? —James McManus[1]

My "cutting edge" political scientist colleagues tell me that to appreciate our discipline today, I should start with Anthony Downs' *An
Economic Theory of Democracy.*[2] A quick comparison of the book and
our "leading" journals suggests that they are correct. Surprisingly, it
does not give my colleagues much pause, outside a muted chuckle or
two, that Downs, an economist, imports the methods of his discipline
into political science and gives them primacy. My colleagues are com-
fortable in accepting the fact that political science is now effectively
an artifact of economics and that they are captives of economics'
methodologies, especially its rational choice presumptions, formal
modeling procedures, and statistical techniques. Originally the queen
of the sciences, the architectonic science, political science cannot claim
any longer even to be first among equals in the social sciences.[3] By
the same token, once an essentially empirical discipline, political science in emulating economics has turned largely theoretical, replacing
its old interest in illuminating the politics we experience with the goal
of generating theories that can stand in for, or improve upon, ordinary
perception. Leo Strauss, writing less than half a century ago, could

say that the demand to proceed "empirically" strikes a more "sympathetic chord in every political scientist" than the demand to proceed "scientifically" and that "political science surely is not a mathematical discipline."[4] One doubts that he would still say that today.

Why and how we came to be where we are is a long story that needs no retelling here. But what warrants comment is political science's commitment to a virtually obsessive, theoretical end; surely this zealotry runs afoul of classical warnings about keeping one's urge to know or theorize within prudential bounds. We can set aside the issue of whether, from an Aristotelian perspective, politics is open to the kind of study characteristic of the other sciences. But reaching for abstract theories in the present manner, albeit in the name of science, can turn self-destructive and worse.[5] In the Aristotelian perspective, contemporary political science reflects a perverse and politically debilitating understanding of the proper relationship between the theoretical life and political life. The work of Downs is a prime example of this, but the tendency is also clear in his precursors. This preoccupation with the scientific end of political science and with abstractions is anticipated in Charles Merriam's Progressive political science. A founder of modern political science, Merriam implicitly devalues political life in a manner that contrasts with the approach of Aristotle, who anticipated the inhuman devotion to theorizing for its own sake in much of his work but especially in Book VII of his *Nicomachean Ethics*. This essay, then, contrasts contemporary, theoretical political science with the practical political science of Aristotle. Those who are seriously interested in politics must not readily surrender to the pleasures of theorizing.

To appreciate American political science today, one needs to recognize that it has always favored what we may call theoretical perfectionism and that its posture has always been problematic according to the original, Aristotelian version of political science. In what follows, we explore this theoretical perfectionism and its dangers, first by considering the political science of Charles Merriam, who was present "at the creation" of American political science, and of Anthony Downs, who speaks for the current situation, and, then, by considering Aristotle's rejoinder.

Initially, one may dispute that there exists intellectual continuity between Progressive political science and today's political science, especially given the contrast between the Progressives' political activism and the frequently noted silence and even timidity of today's professional political scientists. There is also clearly a difference between the Progressives' historicist underpinnings and the rationalist roots of those of a Downsian persuasion.[6] However, we shall see that both the older and newer schools of American political science obscure the Aristotelian line between increasing knowledge of politics and demanding that political science be joined to theoretical science. That is, the political knowledge both schools purvey is theoretically induced. In this sense, as Leo Strauss put it, what was propaganda in Machiavelli and promise in Hegel, "an epoch in which the truth will reign, if not in the minds of all men, at any rate in the institutions which mold them," reinforced by trust in universal enlightenment, becomes the framework for almost all of American political science.[7]

But does Aristotle, who after all explicitly chooses the truth over friendship, take a political stand against an uncompromising search for truth?[8] On that point, one confronts recent attempts to bridge the gap between Aristotle's advocacy of a contemplative and leisured life devoted to unveiling the truth and his regard for moral activity, on the one hand, and a lawfulness that transcends reason, on the other.[9] In approaching Aristotle one needs to be aware of a current tendency to soften his stance on the tension between politics and philosophy. To restore this tension, I resort to authority and follow the lead of two especially astute interpreters, Dante and Nietzsche, who carry forward the old idea that a too zealous pursuit of the truth can be suspect. In the *Inferno*, Dante calls our attention to the possibility of intellectual excess by containing his genius (*ingegno*) for the sake of virtue prior to his account of his meeting with Ulysses, who suffers in Hell for, among other things, putting his ardor (*ardore*) to know the world ahead of affection for his son, piety towards his father, and love for Penelope: In Dante's novel account, that *ardore* leads to the deaths of Ulysses and all his crew.[10] Nietzsche, in turn, gives us another version of the same idea, although not necessarily in the same spirit, by explicitly remarking upon classical restraint about excessively pursuing knowledge.

Whoever concerns himself with the Greeks should be ever mindful that an unrestrained thirst for knowledge for its own sake barbarizes men just as much as a hatred of knowledge. The Greeks themselves, possessed of an inherently insatiable thirst for knowledge, controlled it by their ideal need for and consideration of all the values of life.[11]

As Dante and Nietzsche have it, then, the thirst for knowledge can turn destructive, e.g., Dante's Ulysses or barbaric, e.g., Nietzsche's unrestrained.[12] For the origins of this lesson, current taste aside, we will revive Aristotle's teaching on restraint.

CHARLES MERRIAM AND THE PROGRESSIVES

Charles Merriam, as noted, is probably known more for his political activism than for his theorizing.[13] His first book, *A History of American Political Theories* (1903), however, demonstrates that his political science looks beyond the practical and ethical considerations of public life. *A History of American Political Theories* is an account of American political theories from colonial times through the Civil War with a concluding suggestion about where the country is headed. More than a descriptive account, it emphasizes the development of American theories over time, which it fits into a historical framework that Merriam owed to his German-trained professors at Columbia: Merriam dedicates the book to his major professor William Dunning, who had seen to it that the curriculum at Columbia was dominated by the arguments of Ranke, Hegel, and their successors.[14] Merriam does not, then, simply analyze "the characteristic types of political theory" that had dominated American life, he takes his argument to a higher level by "discuss[ing] these theories in their relation to the peculiar conditions under which they were developed [keeping] in sight the intimate connection between the philosophy and the facts that condition it." The idea is that "like all other political theory, American political ideas are of little importance aside from the great historical movements of which they are an organic part" and that political science is assigned the task of identifying why we stand where we do at any given moment.[15] This especially means that Merriam sets aside any thought that Americans have always adhered to, or ought to adhere to, the natural rights philosophy of their founding.[16] Although the "popular mind" might think of America in terms of contract theories that are part of the natural rights argument, educated Progressive minds know better. The "philosophic mind" correctly sees the nation in other terms, as "an organic product" and "the result of an evolutionary process." The Civil War, for example, rather than testing the limits of consent of the governed, unfolds the idea that "the United States, by virtue of a community of race, interests, and geographical location, *ought to be* and is a nation; and ought to be held together by force, if no other means would avail." In a Progressive variant of Machiavelli's "rule of iron," force is acceptable, and the appeal to consent overruled, to the theoretical end of aligning the nation and the historical moment. The "feeling," Merriam writes, of needing to be a nation underlay the "great national movement of 1861-1865," and was sufficient to support the call to arms and the bloodletting that held the Union together. Merriam hardly bothers to talk of slavery, let alone of equality, and is sympathetic to the most notorious American opponent of natural rights, John C. Calhoun. For Merriam, the nation, carrying with it "the idea of an ethnic and geographical unity, constituted without the consent of any one in particular," trumps the "people" understood as "a body formed by a contract between certain individuals."[17] The nation replaces "We, the people."[18] Consistent with the belief of modern political science that the tension between theory and practice can be dissolved, Merriam holds that "the tendency of the time is overwhelmingly national both in fact and in theory."[19]

The Progressives were conscious that to succeed as political scientists in these terms meant that they needed to align the objects of their study with what is essentially mysterious or abstract. Thus, in a 1923 report commissioned by the American Political Science Association, Merriam conceded that "the political scientist must be something of a utopian in his prophetic view," while remaining "something both of a statesman and a scientist in his practical methods." The prophetic posture then moves further forward as he outlined his vision. Here Merriam's prose echoes the scriptural cadences of another of his teachers, John Burgess, as he pictured a dreamlike "ultimate" state where pure reason is realized, nature mastered, and men are "emancipat[ed]" from "manual toil," a state where human destiny becomes a new kind of civilization and reason is perfected, and where the mistaken and malignant natural rights focus on the individual is overcome.[20] "[It is the] perfection of humanity, the civilization of the world; the perfect development of human reason and its attainment to universal command over individualism; the *apotheosis* of man."

For the Progressives, it follows, political science may look objective but in reality plays handmaid to an intellectual goal that is tyrannical in its control of the political agenda. The new political science, needing to close the gap between the abstract goal and where we presently stand, fastens on accumulating knowledge as the key to success. Political scientists are to be intellectual conductors on the line to the human "*apotheosis.*" For Merriam, this immediately means advocating "executive leadership" directed by "expert and technically qualified" administration.[21] Rather than thinking of statesmanship in terms of virtue and prudence on the old-fashioned model, he looked toward a cadre of knowledgeable political scientists taking charge. To that end, he admirably matched his behavior to his principles and became an extraordinary raiser of research funds and a generous distributor of them to colleagues and students.[22] As Barry Karl puts it, he sought to realize "the promise of the shared community of intellectuals" and, in Merriam's words, raise a "crop of wise men with good temper, balanced judgment, and good will toward men," who by skilled application of their knowledge would "introduce more intelligent and scientific technique into the study and practice of government."[23] Merriam's confidence in the power of intellect, in this respect, is impressive. As he saw it, his newly raised "political *savants*" might even have solved the slavery problem in some manner short of the "wasteful" struggle the nation had had to endure: the slavery problem that seems, according to Merriam, not to have played much of a part in the run-up to the Civil War is, curiously, the exemplary problem for the "*savants.*" Similarly, the right people following the scientific approach could assemble the facts necessary to handle the Ku Klux Klan problem.[24] In these respects, the scientific method would be put to political use.

Where earlier political science had faced the obstacles of "the lack of minute inquiry patiently carried out on a small scale, the absence of microscopic studies ... carried on in objective manner," the newer political science was freed to concern itself with minutiae. Later, some critics would regret this, but for Merriam the narrowing focus would pay dividends. Tellingly, his model is the success of entomologists in describing and studying ten thousand species of bees and ten thousand studies of wasps.[25] In the minutiae, that is, in the "widely different kinds of knowledge of the science of government," would be found the keys to "more intelligent control of the process of government."[26] Moreover, the process was well on its way already. "Religion and philosophy," he says, "have relatively declined in their hold upon the political mind, and ... science has greatly increased its sphere of influence—these are facts with which political research must reckon."[27]

With the last claim, Merriam releases political science from its pre-modern moral and political limitations, and opens the way to contemporary political science. He also, however, points to some problems that would dog the new science. Despite his seemingly hyperbolic enthusiasm about the possibilities opening to his followers—a posture also typical of his successors—there is a gap between his political vision and his political science. Merriam knew what he wanted. He favored such Progressive reforms as proportional representation, simplifying the amendment process, and increasing executive power.[28] As a political scientist, however, he encouraged a research agenda that never effectively reached these policy issues. Instead, his work described a "cycle of inquiry" that may be intriguing and challenging in its own right but is short on generating political proposals: "The political observer, reasoner, or experimenter who uses a scientific technique will be likely to find situations and relations quite unanticipated ... a fairyland of adventure to those who seemed only patient fools, half-tolerated under the cloak of magic, religion, and of science or 'education.'"[29]

There exists, in this respect, an internal contradiction in the political science of Merriam and his Progressive colleagues. Their interest in bettering society through an activist agenda needs to be set against the minutiae that they looked to confront and the "fairyland" of research that they sponsored. Between the two, their political science tended toward an infinite regress insofar as research that encouraged further research was more valued than research that encouraged political action. When Merriam speaks purely as a political scientist researcher, politics takes a back seat in favor of the propositions of historicist theory: "Fundamentally what is most urgently needed is not the solution of specific problems, however important they may be of themselves—and many are of vital significance—but in a still broader sense to realize that we are living in a world of adaptation with constant reconstruction in process."[30]

ANTHONY DOWNS

Political science moves even further in the direction of unalloyed intellectualism, abstractions, and heightened formalism under the influence of Anthony Downs. We are in the realm of rationalist economics rather than Progressivism's historicism. For Downs, government is an element in a universe of economic forces, and is to be understood in terms of stimulus-response mechanisms, that is, as a dependent variable answering to independent variables composed of economic forces: for Merriam, historical forces were the independent variables. In the new Downsian terms, it follows, we eschew empiricism save as it relates to determining the relationships of the variables. Empirical evidence, in other words, is of interest only as it applies to the hypotheses that political science generates. It is characteristic of the new political science that *An Economic Theory of Democracy* ends with twenty-five purportedly testable theoretical propositions—hypotheses, as it were—of which not one entails a concrete political proposal but all of which can generate further testable hypotheses.[31] For the new political scientist, theory begets theory.

The centerpiece of the new political science, in keeping with its economics source, is the model that makes the hypothesis concrete and testable. The underlying presumption of the model is that politicized versions of theorized economic actors will maximize their utility in choosing between alternatives, that is, they will be rational choosers. If we are sufficiently clever political scientists, in turn, we can test our models by tracing the activities of our rational choosers through data lifted from political sources or, at a further remove from reality, by conducting experiments. The hope is that, should the data prove the model statistically significant or should the model prove out experimentally, we may increase our ability to predict political behavior and events. This turns out, however, to happen very rarely, given, among other things, that the theoretical perfection of the model tends to be incommensurable with the material limitations of the data or the artificiality of the experiment.[32] Such disappointment, however, appears secondary to today's political scientists. The interest now is in the model as plaything, and in the clever ways we can test it.[33] Hence, contemporary political science proves more theoretical and is more politically removed than even Progressive political science. The new political science also adopts the posture of ethical neutrality of contemporary social science in general. Setting aside that a moral stance is implied by a system wherein actors *always* seek their personal advantage, rational choice is uninterested in the rightness or wrongness of a subject's end but only in how he gets there. What people are committed to or want takes precedence over what is reasonable or best for them, although the two may certainly be conflated.[34] Societal ends, in such terms, are the points where individual desires overlap, and "the central problem of political theory [becomes] ... how can social goals be developed from differing individual values.[35] To operate in the theoretical universe he presumes, Downs must pass on asking what morally makes for a good social goal. He may be more committed to individualism than Merriam, then, but not to the problem of what is suitable for an individual or, as Locke would have it, what the natural law might command. His political theory, in this respect, abandons the issues that dominate traditional political theory, whether of an ancient or modern variety. Rather than political theory and moral theory being essentially the same, political theory (in its new, abstract meaning) now replaces moral theory. The cost here is indicated, for example, by Downs' position on voting. Given that individual votes do not count for much in the normal scheme of things, the correct theoretical position is that a rational actor has little incentive to vote. In terms of utility it is better to sell one's vote, notwithstanding the potential impact upon the idea of consent of the governed. In Downsian theory's amoral *"hypothetical* world it is always more rational for a voter to sell his vote than to vote."[36]

Resistance to traditional ethics is also displayed in Downs' flight from ideology. Here, too, the sacrifice is for the sake of achieving a kind of certainty. Although Downs grants that uncertainty may sometimes be best for political health since it may "mask" political difficulties, it must be overcome to the degree possible to make our models satisfactory or convincing.[37] In other words, uncertainties that may be acceptable in practice are to be avoided in theory. Where such uncertainties arise, theory bypasses them by assigning them to the realm of ideology. We guarantee theoretical, or intellectual, success by excluding ideological issues, those involving questions of justice and injustice. Political science success, one might say, is inversely proportional to the prevalence of ideology.[38] Here, too, voting is a signpost to what rational choice entails. If a voter is too simple-minded not to have sold his vote, rational choice advises him to leave ideology at the door of the voting booth and vote his own course—the Downsian space—looking always for conditions of perfect information, the new political science's "ideal point." Such political information—not the formerly esteemed virtue of judgment—is the most valuable commodity for the new political science. The highly theoretical or intellectual world of models paradoxically prizes the most mundane type of information: Data sets and ways of manipulating data are subjects of intense attention. Differences in information, in this setting, are understood as the foundation for differences, or inequalities, in power.[39] Similarly, there seems unexamined agreement that problems today are more complex than they used to be, and they therefore call, in another nod to the Progressives, for knowledge above all else, which means the rule of experts or of those who possess theoretical political science.[40]

While bypassing some admirable features of *An Economic Theory of Democracy*, this brief sketch indicates the theoretically charged character of the political science Downs prompts. In addition to this theorizing, it shares certain of its ends with Progressive political science. The Progressives gave the highest priority to pursuing knowledge for the sake of bringing political practice to heel; contemporary political scientists push their models to higher and higher levels of sophistication and compile accordingly complex data sets for the sake of making politics predictable, which, if successful, would also bring practice to heel. Administrative, sub-political, or economic techniques would replace politics. Similarly, both Progressive and Downsian political science subordinates all other considerations to truth, another mark of their theoretical commitment. On this score, Leo Strauss described the "devotees" of the new political science as "filtered by something like an Hippocratic oath."[41] On the surface, of course, the Progressives and contemporary political scientists look dissimilar, the former inclined to involve themselves in the political hurly-burly, the latter tending to stand above, even to disdain, the battle.[42] But the apparent difference simply disguises the commonality. As political scientists *per se*, the Progressives were as devoted to hypothetical ends as their recent descendants, notwithstanding that as political practitioners, as previously mentioned, they hoped to reform American politics.

Contemporary political scientists have, in this respect, improved upon the Progressives in one way. They have largely done away with the clash between an appetite for confronting practical political problems and a taste for hypothetical abstractions. For most of today's political scientists, any appetite for practical politics has long since been beaten out of them by the time they leave graduate school.

ARISTOTLE

For Aristotle's counterpoint to what we have encountered in Merriam and Downs, we may start with his version of prudence, the intellectual virtue characteristic of rulers and, on that standard, most politically critical. For prudence serves the moral virtues, leading the way towards "practicable good(s)," as St. Thomas puts it.[43] We are prudent for the sake of justice or to fashion a just result, not the other way around, and the same holds true for the other moral virtues. In keeping with this, as political scientists we study justice and the just regime in order to realize them, not in order to score highly on some political science version of the SAT. Prudence and natural science are intellectual virtues that architectonic political science commands, although in the case of the philosopher, following Leo Strauss' argument, they "are intended.... as mere means towards his end": For Strauss, this entails that the moral virtues that prudence, especially, serves are a "kind of half-way house" between the two ends that distinguish men, that of the social life and that of the private contemplative life."[44]

The philosopher's idiosyncratic understanding of the intersection of moral virtue and intellectual virtue notwithstanding, however, Aristotle does not countenance the separation between moral and therefore political, and intellectual activity. To be good, he says, requires right order (*taxis*) and intellect (*nous*). "[T]o be good, a man must have been well educated and trained, and must afterward continue to live fittingly and not do anything base voluntarily or involuntarily, and this will be brought about *if men live according to a certain intellect and a right order that has force.*"[45] Intellectual activity, noetic activity of a "certain" kind, does not, then, excuse nor justify neglecting a life of moral and political order.[46] Cultivating the mind may be the mark of a philosopher, who is, at once, the happiest of men and most beloved by the gods, but even such a man must be conscious of the requirements of "right order."[47]

Regarding such requirements, Aristotle's main text is the *Politics*.[48] In regime terms, right order refers to a country's governmental arrangement. A particular constitution, a *politeia*, is the *taxis* of those who live in a *polis*. One compares regimes on the basis of their orders, and decides, on the same basis, where justice lies between them. Right order, then, has an ethical dimension.[49] Any law may provide for order, but only just laws make for good order.[50] Good order in the good person has the same bearing. It requires that reason control desires and that desires operate within the range allowed by moral virtue, which is why Aristotle says that right order must have force behind it. To be good, it is not enough to know what is right; one must be moved to *do* what one knows is right and avoid what is wrong. Where the intellect operates in a moral void or where passion of some sort is in charge, the result may be viciousness or unrestraint (incontinence). We will examine these qualities further below. For the moment, it is enough to say that without right order, the intellect (*nous*) cannot be expected to develop properly.[51] In this view, the tendency of contemporary political science to free the search for knowledge at all stages from political and moral constraints is potentially self-destructive. To the contrary, moral considerations, at the least, precede full intellectual maturity, which means they also precede full intellectual freedom. When we achieve such freedom, it may be possible to leave political considerations behind, but that is very difficult so long as we possess bodies and appetites—i.e., as long as we remain human.[52]

The relationship of our two natural ends in Aristotle, that to which philosophy is devoted and that to which moral activity is devoted, is hardly transparent, but one can say this about it: The philosopher may act morally for reasons or purposes the moral actor, the gentleman, will not appreciate, but this does not mean the philosopher can ignore the need for action in keeping with moral virtue. That the moral virtues are not dictated by reason or theoretical science does not mean that reasonable or theoretically oriented people can consider themselves independent of the moral virtues in their actions.[53] To lose sight of the actions for which morality calls, the urge to know notwithstanding, risks the self-destruction Dante assigns Ulysses or the barbarism Nietzsche foresaw.

Aristotle expands on this argument when he turns thematically to unrestraint (*akrasia*) in *Nicomachean Ethics* VII. Having completed consideration of the intellectual virtues in Book VI, he says he will begin anew in Book VII and turns to three conditions that people are to avoid: vice, unrestraint, and bestiality.[54] His emphasis from the outset, however, is on unrestraint. Strictly speaking, the word connotes doing what is wrong when one knows what is right, and the question it raises is how can a person who knows what one ought to do act contrarily.[55] The emphasis on unrestraint coupled with Book VII's new beginning suggests two things. First, there is a logical progression from Book VI to VII, that is, from the discussion in VI of the different ways in which a person, who through reason understands and behaves correctly, can nonetheless in Book VII consider flipping a coin. How can a person who has knowledge do something he knows to be wrong? How can he be unrestrained?[56] Considering where understanding or knowing fails or is overridden, in other words, recapitulates the various ways in which we know. What happens, we are led to ask, when the virtues extolled in Book VI fail, that is, when people with intellectual qualities we admire still act poorly? Book VII also looks forward, however, its subject eventually culminating in the discussion of philosophy in Book X. There we resolve the problem of unrestraint, of knowing what is right but acting wrong, by determining that living philosophically means always adhering to the right course. The discussion of unrestraint is thus surrounded by considerations of the intellectual virtues in Book VI and of philosophy in Book X, and the relation of knowing and doing may thereby be said to be at the center of Aristotle's discussion of the life of the mind.[57]

Turning to the specifics of Aristotle's discussion of unrestraint, how are we to explain knowing what is right but not doing it, something which is more often experienced than examined?[58] And, to extend the point and place it in the context of contemporary political science, how is it that as political scientists we can know the moral dimensions of things yet ignore them in our research, and how is it that our thirst for knowledge can overcome all other concerns? On these questions, Aristotle sometimes sounds very familiar. For example, his criticism in the *Politics* of Hippodamus—perhaps the first professional political scientist—for being overly concerned with clarity and technological progress brings Rousseau's criticism of his world to mind.

Consider as well Aristotle's recognition that some truths and kinds of knowledge can be bad (*phaulos*); knowledge does not always have a positive effect.[59] More important for our purposes, however, Aristotle retains a pre-modern flavor by standing for what we can call a kind of intellectual moderation. The argument for restraint originates in the familiar classical position that being virtuous is a product of virtuous activity. The logic here is circular—virtuous behavior begets virtue which begets virtuous behavior—but it is a mistake to think that virtue is something learned as, for example, mathematics is learned. People go wrong in thinking that studying and talking about virtue— literally, betaking themselves to *logos*—can replace practicing virtue. To fancy that one becomes good by practicing philosophic behavior, or, as St. Thomas glosses the relevant passages, by philosophizing is to forget that virtue does not spring from talking or thinking and that discussing theory cannot substitute for action where virtue is concerned.[60] Paradoxically, people who think philosophizing leads to virtue are not being properly philosophical about virtue. Those given to talking rather than doing, we are told, are like sick persons who listen carefully to what doctors say but fail to take their medicine. Diagnoses and prescriptions alone do not produce health. Adopting a philosophic pose regarding goodness, then, does not produce a healthy soul.[61] This warning, in turn, is not confined to the many or to those who are counterfeiting being philosophic. It also extends, as St. Thomas puts it, to those who genuinely think they are being philosophic. A devotion to *logos* or a life that is intellectually centered cannot, in this sense, be allowed to disguise failure to fulfill virtue's demands.[62]

The sense that people can misbehave when they pursue intellectual affairs to the exclusion of appropriate behavior is reinforced when Aristotle speaks of a few individuals popularly thought to be wise but lacking in prudence. The description, in particular, applies to Thales and Anaxagoras, of whom, according to Aristotle, people say that men may be wise *but not prudent*. Thales and Anaxagoras, as wise as they may be, seem unaware of their own well-being and, as important, uninterested in the human goods (*ta anthropina*).[63] This sets them apart from Pericles, who, Aristotle says a bit earlier, is deemed prudent because he can discern what is good for himself and for men at large.[64] Thales and Anaxagoras, then, may have been exceptional in their wisdom—people concede, Aristotle says, that their knowledge is rare, wondrous, difficult, and even daemonic—but they rank below Pericles where virtue is concerned.[65] St. Thomas bears this point home in his gloss when he reminds readers that Thales, to his own consternation, fell in a ditch while looking at the stars, and that Anaxagoras was negligent about civic affairs, exclaiming when challenged that, "I will have great concern for my country after I have explained the heavens."[66] Thales and Anaxagoras thus become vehicles for Aristotle's lesson that the philosophically and/or scientifically inclined run the danger of becoming politically aloof.

This problem lies just beneath the surface in the closing lines of Book VI and sets the stage for taking up unrestraint in Book VII. The subject at the end of Book VI is the relationship of prudence and wisdom, where Aristotle makes the point that prudence is not in authority over wisdom any more than medical science is in authority over health. Medical science can issue orders for the sake of health but not to health, the implication being that political science can govern for the sake of wisdom but not govern wisdom itself. One might as well say, Aristotle concludes, that political science governs the gods, because it orders everything in the *polis*.[67]

At the end of the thematic discussion of the intellectual virtues, therefore, Aristotle counterpoises political science/prudence and wisdom and equates the wise with divinities, an idea that he repeats later in the *Ethics* and that points to philosophy as being somehow superhuman.[68] But while this signals that the life of the mind is the highest kind of life imaginable, it also imparts the problem of the undependability of the intellectually gifted. The Greek gods, while powerful and worthy of respect, were notably fickle and untrustworthy, and certainly no models of prudence. By identifying philosophy with divinity, Aristotle forces the issue that surfaces in his comments on Thales and Anaxagoras. How much confidence can we have in the practicality of the speculatively minded or of others whose search for knowledge makes them politically disinterested or, just as bad, politically unstable? We leave Book VI, in this respect, asking whether Aristotle anticipates the concerns of Dante and Nietzsche and the style of our more driven modern social scientists by compelling us to ask whether an unmitigated thirsting after knowledge might interfere with prudence and inhibit attending to the practical and moral dimensions of life.

Such questions are the immediate setting for Aristotle's treatment of unrestraint and help explain his giving so much more attention to that than to restraint. The problem we confront by the end of Book VI is what happens when knowers go wrong, as in unrestraint, not how knowers withstand temptation, as in restraint. Strictly speaking, in Book VII Aristotle attributes unrestraint in most cases to passion (*pathos*), describing the unrestrained as being in the grip of the same pleasures that operate in the virtue of temperance and its vice, intemperance or profligacy.[69] In unrestraint, unlike intemperance, however, undue pleasure-taking does not necessarily connote viciousness, since the error is not one of habit, and the unrestrained, unlike the vicious, retain a sense of what is right. Unrestraint is a mistake, not a sign of vice.[70] Passion may overwhelm reason without perverting or erasing it and turning us vicious. This does not excuse the excess, but it tempers our reaction to it.[71]

The pleasures that apply to temperance and intemperance are not the only sources of unrestraint that Aristotle describes, and it is in these other cases that intellectual activity and unrestraint potentially converge. When he speaks of temperance and intemperance, Aristotle explicitly excludes from consideration the pleasures of the mind (*dianoia*), which include a love of learning (*philomatheia*).[72] It is not intemperate to give oneself over to the dianoetic pleasures or to submerge oneself in one's studies. By the same token, the moderate pursuit of such pleasure is not virtuous. Philosophic devotion to wisdom is not intemperance and men at large are not temperate because they do not care to pursue wisdom. When Aristotle discusses unrestraint, on the other hand, he does not exclude the pleasures of the mind. Indeed, they return through the back door, as it were, as he describes what he calls qualified unrestraint or unrestraint with additions (*prostithentes*). In such unrestraint, men are explicitly governed by the passions and pleasures that are not applicable to temperance and intemperance.[73] According to Aristotle's logic pleasures foreign to temperance and intemperance, which, according to his express exclusion would include the pleasures of the mind, are among the pleasures attractive to people who are qualifiedly unrestrained. Qualified unrestraint, then, resembles simple unrestraint, but it is devoted to uncommon pleasures, such as those of the mind, rather than common pleasures such as bodily ones.[74] Aristotle also indicates another way in which the unrestrained and the *dianoetic* pleasures can, at least upon occasion, be associated. As noted, he describes the pleasures that lead to qualified unrestraint as the unnecessary pleasures, that is, the pleasures desirable in themselves associated with living well. In this class, he specifically includes the pleasures that relate to wealth, gain, honor, and spirit (*thumos*).[75] Of these, spirit points most directly to the kind of unrestraint with which we are interested.[76] Spirit as a spur to qualified unrestraint represents a kind of overzealousness.[77] The question the term prompts, of course, is single-mindedness or zealotry to what purpose. Here, the most ready answer is that spirit is connected somehow with intellectual affairs and accompanies those especially given to the life of the mind.[78]

Plato, for example, couples the first mentions of philosophy and of spirit in *The Republic*: The philosophic puppies that are the models for the guardian defenders of the just city are spirited.[79] Combining spirit with a speculative or philosophic inclination, however, creates a problem, which is the source of spirit's connection to qualified unrestraint. Spirit and knowledge are, as such, morally neutral. We recall, for example, Aristotle's criticism of Thales and Anaxagoras and are also reminded of how Plato demonstrates for the benefit of Polemarchus that it is not knowledge or the willingness to use it that differentiates the thief from the policeman. Indeed, Seth Benardete connects all these dots and argues that spirit's neutrality is equivalent to the neutrality of the knowledge, or art, of which Socrates' thief and policeman dispose:[80] "*Thumos* [spirit] reproduces on the level of nature the argument Socrates developed with Polemarchus on the level of art. Art was neutral to kill or cure, steal or guard; and *thumos* is likewise neutral and indifferent."

Together, therefore, spirit and the thirst for knowledge have a mischievous potential that outdoes the threat of either alone. It is the uncommon quality of the spirited and intellectually gifted which threatens, which is not to say that the spirited and intellectually gifted cannot be a great boon to the community. However, to repeat, in combination the qualities are dangerous. Waller Newell, for instance, speaks of the possibility that an individual possessed of them may self-destruct if he lacks an internal gyroscope of some sort. As Newell puts it, spirit is a "sort of engine of the desires," one of "the winged horses whose energies can plunge *the charioteer of mind* into the abyss if he does not

direct them toward their proper ends."[81] This, of course, does not decide the issue of where the philosopher stands as regards checking a
spirited impulse to know that might raise political or ethical problems. That question remains opaque. Here, too, Newell is helpful, however, reminding us that from the Aristotelian point of view, as the
discussion of qualified unrestraint reveals, spirit in conjunction with
philosophy or the life devoted to knowing represents a persistent danger. As he says, "The equation of well-bred *thumos* with philosophizing remains a breathtaking leap" and is "a particularly apt example of
what Aristotle means when he criticizes the divine madness of
Platonism": Newell calls *thumos* "the ticking time bomb in the political
psychology of *The Republic.*"[82]

Aristotle's abbreviated discussion of qualified unrestraint, it follows, provides a route to the behaviors Dante and Nietzsche warn
about by way of the former's version of Ulysses and the latter's statement on the barbarism that accompanies "an unrestrained thirst for
knowledge." By the same token, we also recognize why we hesitate to
be as critical of such behavior as we are of viciousness. The urge to
know is natural and in most circumstances positive, and, therefore,
unrestraint driven by a spirited desire to know is forgivable in a way
that unrestraint driven by simple passion or desire is not.[83] On this
basis, we can honor Thales and Anaxagoras for their intellectual per-
sistence but, with Aristotle, at least circumspectly criticize them for
their neglect of the political arena. The urge to knowledge is to be
encouraged, but there are apparently limits. A measure of self-restraint may be required of all varieties of knowledge seekers, perhaps
even philosophers.[84] Noble and good things, Aristotle says, can be
pursued to excess.[85] To stand for a true principle is good, but to adhere to it beyond reason is obstinacy, which thereby may be seen as
another form of unrestraint.[86] In our theoretical lives, as elsewhere,
we conclude that prudence is required. It is indicative of where Aristotle
leaves us on the subject of unrestraint and restraint, therefore, that
the last subject he raises in discussing them is their relation to prudence. Prudence, he says, is incompatible with unrestraint. But cleverness, which does not distinguish between nobility and knavery, is
compatible with unrestraint; Aristotle adds that restraint and unrestraint are characteristics of atypical men. Prudence, it follows, is more
critical for the spirited than the ordinary run of men because there is

no guarantee that what can be known will not be put to knavish purposes by the clever.[87]

In keeping with his principle of going no farther than the subject matter allows, Aristotle does not specify the points at which the pursuit of good things, including knowledge, becomes excessive. A sense of his general direction in this regard, however, is conveyed by his use of the example of Neoptolemus in Sophocles' *Philoctetes*: the focus is on Neoptolemus' breaking of a resolution to which Odysseus had persuaded him. Aristotle mentions Neoptolemus twice. The first time he says that Neoptolemus showed unrestraint in terms of his commitment to Odysseus because it pained him to tell a lie, to which he adds that Neoptolemus' behavior in this respect was praiseworthy. The second time he says that Neoptolemus did not act out of a lack of self-restraint but out of his pleasure in speaking the truth, thereby leaving the impression that he does not think Neoptolemus was unrestrained.[88] Aristotle thereby delivers a mixed message through Neoptolemus. A desire not to lie and the pleasure in telling the truth, which underlay the same act, are simultaneously unrestrained and not unrestrained. This is a measure of Aristotle's moderation and the care he takes with advising us on things which provide satisfaction at the level of spirit and thought. What is praiseworthy, whether not lying or telling the truth, can be understood as unrestrained and the reverse. It is for us to decide where the one leaves off and the other begins, which means keeping in mind whether we are going too far in intellectual as in other matters. Intellectual affairs are not insulated against prudence, which may serve as our last words on why Dante prepares for his meeting with Odysseus by checking his genius for the sake of virtue.

CONCLUSION

Modern political science is oblivious to the issues Aristotle raises. Whether one looks to the Progressives or our contemporaries, the allure of theoretical goods induces a kind of blindness where political reality and prudence are concerned. This is particularly true of the most spirited, thereby the best, of the new political scientists. Scholars like Merriam and Downs are genuinely devoted to the search for knowledge about politics. In Aristotelian terms, however, they have traded away prudence for cleverness. This is more obvious today given the invitation to cleverness of our sophisticated tools, but it was true of the Progressives as well. It is cleverness that appeals to the fund dispensers in the research organizations Merriam initiated. But, more to the point, the political science elite upon which he pinned such great hopes is the expert political scientists of today, who have all the key attributes Merriam anticipates—knowledge, expertise, and ambition—save that the research they do aims at cleverness as the route to heightening professional status.

The dangers in this situation are fairly obvious. We conclude by mentioning two signals which modern political science cannot heed. The first is offered by the great medieval Muslim classicist Alfarabi, who describes a "vain philosopher" as one who learns the theoretical sciences "but without going any further and without being habituated to doing the acts considered virtuous by a certain religion or the generally accepted noble acts."[89] The actions of such a person, Alfarabi goes on, are an instance of "mutilated philosophy." Thus, Alfarabi adds the danger to philosophy, to the theoretical life itself, to the list of dangers from unrestraint. The second danger is attested to by Plato and Aristotle themselves. They say that unrestrained and tyrannical persons share the same melancholic temperaments.[90] It is here, at the junction between unrestraint and tyranny that the greatest danger of ignoring political and moral obligations looms. Even a salutary desire, like the desire to know, if carried to excess, may turn us into tyrants; just ask anyone who questions the methods requirements in our cutting-edge departments.

Endnotes

1. James McManus, *Positively First Street* (New York: Farrar, Straus and Giroux, 2003), 213.
2. Anthony Downs, *An Economic Theory of Democracy* (New York: Harper and Row, 1957).
3. Aristotle, *Nicomachean Ethics,* 1094a27. References to Aristotle will be to the Loeb editions.
4. Leo Strauss, "An Epilogue," in *Essays on the Scientific Study of Politics*, Herbert Storing, ed. (New York: Holt, Rinehart and Winston, 1962), 314.

This remains the best introduction to modern political science and to its difference from Aristotelian political science. See, too, Leo Strauss, *Natural Right and History* (Chicago: University of Chicago Press, 1953), chapter 2 and *passim*. For the history of American political science, see John Gunnell, *The Descent of Political Theory* (Chicago: University of Chicago Press, 1993). Placing economics before politics contrasts with Aristotle's subordinating the *oikia* or household and economics literally understood to the *polis* and politics. Aristotle, *Politics* 1252b9, 1252b28. The trend of professional political science is not uncontested in the discipline. Witness, for example, the resistance to the rational choice approach, the *perestroika* movement, and the serious debate among international relations specialists over United States foreign policy subsequent to September 11. See, e.g., Gregory Kasza, "Perestroika: For an Ecumenical Political Science." www.btinternet.com/ ~ pac_news/Perestroika.htm#_Perestroika:_For_An (accessed August 2, 2001); Donald Green and Ian Shapiro, *Pathologies of Rational Choice Theory* (New Haven: Yale University Press, 1994); Robert Lieber, "Rethinking America's Grand Strategy," *The Chronicle of Higher Education* 50, no. 39 (June 4, 2004): B6-B9.

5. Strauss, "An Epilogue," 327, excuses political science from being diabolic but indicts it for not knowing that it fiddles and that Rome burns. Machiavelli ends his *Discourses* by calling for political physicians, the modern scientists *par excellence*, and lauding decimation, the tool of tyrants. *Discourses on Livy*, trans. Harvey Mansfield and Nathan Tarcov (Chicago: University of Chicago Press, 1996), 3.49; 209-210.

6. Strauss, "An Epilogue," 312, playfully points to the idea of political science as a literal union of strange bedfellows, i.e., as an unprecedented but "judicious mating of dialectical materialism and psychoanalysis to be consummated on a bed supplied by logical positivism."

7. Leo Strauss, *Thoughts on Machiavelli* (Glencoe: The Free Press, 1958), 297-8, n. 221. See too Leo Strauss, *The City and Man* (Chicago: University of Chicago Press, 1964), 20-21, 37-8.

8. Aristotle, *Nicomachean Ethics*, 1096a11.

9. See, e.g., Mary Nichols, *Citizens and Statesmen: A Study of Aristotle's Politics* (Lanham, Md.: Rowman and Littlefield, 1992), 135.

10. Dante, *Inferno* canto 26, line 21, lines 90-120. See Larry Peterman, "Ulysses and Modernity," *Dante Studies* CXIII (1966).

11. Friedrich Nietzsche, *Philosophy in the Tragic Age of the Greeks*, trans. Marianne Cowan (Chicago: Henry Regnery Co., 1962), 30-31. Nietzsche's concern is not to shore up moral virtue so much as to warn that the search for knowledge can turn deadly by exposing our intellectual pretenses or what we today call our "belief system." See, e.g., Werner

Dannhauser, "Nietzsche," in *History of Political Philosophy*, Leo Strauss and Joseph Cropsey, eds. (Chicago: University of Chicago Press, 1963), 727; Strauss, *The City and Man*, 49.

12. The question remains, of course, whether the speculative life requires moral virtue as a building block, but that aside, the message of Dante and Nietzsche seems to be that where moral virtue counts, the quest for knowledge requires standards and controls that theorizing does not supply. Strauss, *The City and Man*, 26-27.

13. In addition to his being a founder and early president of the American Political Science Association, he was a member of the progressive wing of the Republican party—*LaFollette's Weekly* anointed him "the Woodrow Wilson of the West"—where he served on the Chicago City Council and ran for mayor.

14. Gunnell, *Descent*, 60. Dunning had himself written a three-volume general history of political theories. In the foreword to a new edition of Charles Edward Merriam's *New Aspects of Politics* (Chicago: University of Chicago Press, 1970 [originally published in 1925]), 10-11, Barry Karl uses the titles of Merriam's books to call attention to his move towards process oriented political science. Karl gets the title of the 1903 book wrong, however, referring to it as *Political Thought*. It was *Political Theories*, which in a small way suggests Merriam's commitment to historically-centered political theory rather than to idea-centered political philosophy. Gunnell, *Descent*, 87, calls the competing public and academic ends of Merriam's life an "inherited" problem.

15. Charles Edward Merriam, *A History of American Political Theories*, (New York: MacMillan, 1903), 8.

16. Ibid., 89-90.

17. Ibid., 297-304.

18. Merriam, *New Aspects of Politics*, 154. The Progressives are mostly joined on this point, and Merriam cites in *New Aspects of Politics*, 306-8, among others, John Burgess, Woodrow Wilson, and W. W. Willoughby in the argument. Burgess was another of his German-educated teachers at Columbia, Willoughby was an influential Johns Hopkins professor for whom philosophy was to guide political practice. Gunnel, *Descent*, 67.

19. Merriam, *New Aspects of Politics*, 316.

20. Ibid., 292; Merriam, *American Political Theories*, 318.

21. Cf. Aristotle, *Politics* 1277b25. Charles Edward Merriam, *American Political Ideas: Studies in the Development of American Political Thought, 1865-1917* (New York, 1923), 454. Barry Karl, in the foreword to Merriam's *New Aspects of Politics*, 16, argues against the idea that Merriam favored the rule of experts.

22. Merriam, *New Aspects of Politics*, 8, 22-23. Among other organizations, Merriam started the Social Science Research Council. In that more innocent time, Merriam thought these creations a "benefaction to the race ... [and] an incalculable service ... to humanity," ibid., 315.

23. Ibid., 26, 57, 248, 327.

24. Ibid., 249, 252.

25. Ibid., 208.

26. Merriam, *American Political Ideas*, 372-4, 329-430; Merriam, *New Aspects of Politics*, 48, 67-9, 101, 106, 195, 328-29. Merriam also anticipates the behavioral revolution in his enthusiasm for the development of psychological studies of politics, in *New Aspects of Politics*, 11-12, 100.

27. Merriam, *New Aspects of Politics*, 100.

28. Ibid., 251.

29. Ibid., 217.

30. Ibid., 241. Downs' work, in this respect, picks up the scientific as opposed to political end of Merriam's enterprise. In keeping with this, Downs has largely avoided, at least publicly, anything resembling partisan politics and retains a low political profile. A Senior Fellow at the Brookings Institution since 1977, he has served on commissions in both Democratic and Republican administrations and, most recently, has been working on transportation issues. On the other hand, his work retains a measure of practicality absent in the vast majority of those who have adopted his principles and methods. As Merriam may be said to have been torn between scientific abstraction and political partisanship, Downs may be said to be torn between theoretical perfectionism and practical influence.

31. Downs, *An Economic Theory*, 292, speaks of his models generating concrete economic recommendations, but there is little evidence of that in the book.

32. See Green and Shapiro, *Pathologies of Rational Choice Theory*.

33. Cutting-edge departments typically distinguish between modelers and statisticians, and both types are needed if a department hopes to be credible methodologically.

34. Here, Downs borrows from John C. Calhoun the notion of what he calls the *self-interest axiom*, the idea that individuals be considered so committed to their "own safety and happiness" that they are ready to "sacrifice the interests of others to [their] own" (*An Economic Theory*, 27, 37). Calhoun was the pre-Civil War intellectual leader of the pro-slavery forces, for whom the "interests" of the minority slave states would permit their veto of the decisions of the majority free states—even if the latter were anchored by the natural rights and equality of the Declaration of Independence. Downs' sympathy to Calhoun, combined with that of

Merriam, testifies to Harry Jaffa's contention that "we ... see in Calhoun the generation of the most powerful forces that today dominate the intellectual life, not only of the United States, but also of the Western world generally." Harry Jaffa, *A New Birth of Freedom* (Lanham, Md.: Rowman and Littlefield, 2000), 86.

35. Downs, *An Economic Theory*, 160.

36. Ibid., 190 (my emphasis). Downs is not insensitive to how this sounds, and recommends that "men must be taught to view such situations emotionally and morally instead of statistically." Apparently the science of rational choice is to be counteracted by rhetorically blinding people to their own advantage.

37. Ibid., 62, n. 11.

38. Scarce resources do not satisfactorily explain why some most ambitious political science departments have banished political theory.

39. Downs, *An Economic Theory*, 237. For genuinely rational voters, of course, there is little incentive to acquire information since their votes are to such little purpose. Ibid., 244-45.

40. Ibid., 230-33. It is a small step from these ideas to a justification of the administrative state.

41. Strauss, "Epilogue," 307.

42. See Jonathan Cohn, "Revenge of the Nerds," *The New Republic* (October 25, 1999).

43. *Commentary on Aristotle's Nicomachean Ethics*, vol. 2, trans. and ed. C. I. Litzinger (Chicago: Henry Regnery Co., 1964), 6.6.1193, 571.

44. Aristotle, *Politics*, 1277b25; Strauss, *City and Man*, 26-7.

45. Aristotle, *Politics*, 1180a15-20 (my emphasis); Aristotle *Metaphysics* 980a20.

46. *Nous* is one of the five intellectual virtues and is subordinate only to wisdom (*sophia*), which combines it and knowledge or science (*episteme*). Simply stated, *nous* apprehends the first principles, the immutable and primary things that we cannot reach through reason alone, and at the same time is the ultimate ruler of the desires. Aristotle, *Nicomachean Ethics* 1141a4 ff.; Aristotle, *Politics*, 1254b5. Without it, without the knowledge of first principles that constitutes our humanity, we would be reduced to bestiality. *Nous*, in this sense, is a necessary but insufficient condition of happiness, one of three soulful elements—the others are sensation (*aisthesis*) and desire (*orexis*)—required for attaining truth and promoting actions. In its own right, in turn, intellectual activity is judged good or bad in terms of truth and falsity. There is, however, another sense of intellectual good, that whereby it rules the desires. This is the good of the practical intellect, the "conformable" truth St. Thomas calls it, that

corresponds to rightly directed desire. *Nous* in the fully realized sense requires a correctly aligned soul in which both senses of the faculty operate.

47. Aristotle, *Nicomachean Ethics,* 1179a25-32, *Politics* 1334b14-289. We cannot here pursue the matter of the relationship of wisdom (*sophia*) and intellect (*nous*) that Aristotle handles in the sixth book of the *Nicomachean Ethics.*

48. *Taxis* occurs in the *Nicomachean Ethics* only in the passage cited. *Nous* in various forms occurs frequently. *Taxis,* in various forms, occurs about twenty-five times in the *Politics.*

49. Aristotle, *Politics,* 1253a37, 1271b40, 1273a20, 1274b37, 1278b8.

50. Ibid., 1326a29, 1287a31, cf. *Physics* 252a12.

51. Aristotle, *Politics* 1334b14.

52. Ibid., 1334b25. On the possibility of ascending from politics to a higher kind of life, consider Allan Bloom's interpretation of the Myth of Er, where he concludes that Plato's intention is that we understand "that there is no sin but ignorance." *The Republic of Plato,* (New York: Basic Books, 1991), 435-436.

53. Strauss, *City and Man,* 26-27.

54. Translating *akrasia* is a problem. The most common translation is "incontinence," but the word is somewhat archaic besides its physiological meaning, and some translators avoid it. Ross and Irwin stay with "incontinence," but Rackham uses "unrestraint;" Broadie and Rowe "lack of self-control;" and Sachs "lack of self-restraint." See the translations of the *Nicomachean Ethics* by Sarah Broadie and Christopher Rowe (Oxford: Oxford University Press, 2002); Terence Irwin, 2nd ed. (Indianapolis: Hackett Publishing, 2000); H. Rackham, 2nd ed. (Cambridge: Harvard University Press, 1962); W. D. Ross (Oxford: Oxford University Press, 1915); Joe Sachs (Newburyport, Ma.: Focus Publishing, R. Pullins Company, 2002).

55. Aristotle, *Nicomachean Ethics,* 1145a15, 34.

56. Ibid., 1138b22, 1145b21-23.

57. David Schaefer agrees that the discussion of unrestraint culminates in the discussion of philosophy, but argues that Aristotle essentially agrees with Plato that *akrasia* is impossible at any level. ("Wisdom and Morality: Aristotle's Account of *Akrasia,*" *Polity* 21, no. 2 [Winter, 1988]: 245-246.) See too, on the tie between unrestraint and philosophy, Aristide Tessitore, *Reading Aristotle's Ethics: Virtue, Rhetoric, and Political Philosophy* (Albany: State University of New York Press, 1996), 56-8, 62.

58. Since Aristotle explicitly diverges here from Socrates, for whom to know the right is to do it and *akrasia* does not exist, the question receives

abundant scholarly attention. Aristotle, *Nicomachean Ethics*, 1145b25; Plato *Protagoras* 352b. For Schaefer, "*Akrasia*," 223, n.6, the *akratic* person acts on opinion rather than knowledge, thereby exonerating Aristotle of the self-inflicted charge that he overrules Socrates. Tessitore, *Aristotle's Ethics*, 54, 57, disagrees, saying that "incontinence both exists and is intelligible." Terence Irwin, *Aristotle's First Principles* (Oxford: Clarendon, 1988), 43, 75-6, essentially takes the same line. I have dealt with the Plato-Aristotle divide elsewhere. See, for example, "The Public Philosophy and the Limits of Philosophy," in *Public Philosophy and Political Science*, Robert Statham, ed. (Lanham, Md.: Rowman and Littlefield, 2002), 80-86; "A Framework for Examining Aristotle on *Akrasia*" (paper delivered at the annual meeting of the Midwest Political Science Association, Chicago, April 3-6, 2003). At the risk of over-simplifying, most attempts to settle the differences between Plato and Aristotle may be said to adopt a version of the idea that for both unrestraint results from intellectual failure, that is, as Alfred Mele puts it, there must be a "deficiency in the agent's cognitive condition at the time of action" else there would not be unrestraint. "Aristotle on *Akrasia, Eudaimonia*, and the Psychology of Action," in *Aristotle's Ethics*, Nancy Sherman, ed. (Lanham, Md.: Rowman and Littlefield, 1993), 183. See, too, Richard Robinson, "Aristotle on *Akrasia*," in *Articles on Aristotle: 2*, Jonathan Barnes, Malcolm Schofield and Richard Sorabji, eds. (New York: St. Martin's Press, 1977), 84; Dennis McKerlie, "The Practical Syllogism and *Akrasia*," *Canadian Journal of Philosophy* 21, no. 3 (1991): 310, 312; James Walsh, *Aristotle's Conception of Moral Weakness* (New York: Columbia University Press, 1963), 2; Aristotle, *Nicomachean Ethics*, trans. Sarah Broadie and Christopher Rowe, 386; Steven Salkever, *Finding the Mean* (Princeton: Princeton University Press, 1990), 43.

     59. Aristotle, *Politics*, 1267b22-25, 1268b23-1269a29; Aristotle, *Nicomachean Ethics*, 1153b9. Aristotle criticizes Hippodamus for proposing that improvements in politics be encouraged in the same way as improvements in the arts and sciences, with honors and other rewards. The Hippodamian spirit, in this respect, is at home wherever breakthroughs are the most valued coin, as in the American Political Science Association and academic personnel committees. For Aristotle, however, the benefits of scientific advances, thus, of scientific truth, must be measured against possible losses when we change things and shake the habitual behavior, beliefs, and laws upon which the community rests. In large part, this caution becomes the basis of classicism's reputation for conservatism for it entails watching out that there be moral-political supervision of those who seek to advance knowledge. Leo Strauss, *Thoughts on Machiavelli*, 298-99; Leo Strauss, *City and Man*, 21-22. The community,

in a classical framework, cannot afford the openness that the arts and sciences encourage, which is one reason for the tension between those who speak for the community and those who speak for the arts and sciences. An instance of a modern version of the lesson is the following recent attribution to one of the founders of Sun Microsystems: "Good science ... is the discovery of truth. But science may not be good for us anymore if it yields a bad outcome. 'The Greeks knew better ... Oedipus was destroyed by truth.'" *New York Times Magazine*, 6 (June 2004): 36.

60. Aristotle, *Nicomachean Ethics*, 1105b12-13, 1177a18; St. Thomas Aquinas, *Commentary on Aristotle's Nicomachean Ethics*, vol. 2, 2.4.288.

61. Aristotle, *Nicomachean Ethics*, 1105 b13-18.

62. Jacob Klein, "Aristotle, An Introduction," in *Ancients and Moderns: Essays on the Tradition of Political Philosophy in Honor of Leo Strauss*, Joseph Cropsey, ed. (New York: Basic Books, 1964), 53.

63. Aristotle, *Nicomachean Ethics*, 1141b5.

64. Ibid., 1140b8.

65. Ibid., 1141b7; Tessitore, *Aristotle's Ethics*, 64.

66. *Commentary on the Ethics*, 6.6.1192, p. 571. In a similar, if less inflammatory, fashion, Aristotle in Book X again employs the example of Anaxagoras to illustrate the chasm between the many and those who do not value wealth or power, the difference being, to again utilize St. Thomas, that the many "are ignorant of intellectual goods, which are the real human goods according to which a man is happy." Aristotle, *Nicomachean Ethics*, 1179a13, St. Thomas Aquinas, *Commentary on the Ethics*, 10.13.2131, p. 924.

67. Aristotle, *Nicomachean Ethics*, 1145a2-12.

68. Ibid., 1179a31, 1164b2.

69. Ibid., 1145b13, 1145b31, 1146b22; Aristotle, *Eudemian Ethics*, 1223a37-b2; Tessitore, *Aristotle's Ethics*, 59; Irwin, *Ethics*, 76; Schaefer, "Wisdom and Morality: Aristotle's Account of *Akrasia*," 227, 236. Contemporary scholars mostly interpret this as meaning that in the unrestrained, passion nullifies knowledge, thus reducing what is known, rather than leave standing the point that passion is simply stronger than reason, which would allow for knowing to remain active even if it is overpowered. See, for example, Broadie and Rowe, *Nicomachean Ethics*, 387. The point in Aristotle's discussion that receives the most attention is his analysis of the practical syllogism, where he concludes that an unrestrained person may have universal knowledge, but fails as regards particulars.

70. Laurence Berns, "Spiritedness in Ethics and Politics: A Study in Aristotelian Psychology," *Interpretation* 12 (1984): 344, connects the *Ethics'*

position on unrestraint with its position on shame. As shame is not a virtue, so unrestraint is not a vice. See, too, Aristotle, *Nicomachean Ethics*, 1148a3, 1153a15.

71. Aristotle is relatively gentle on Thales and Anaxagoras, more gentle, for instance, than St. Thomas, and specifically equates Anaxagoras with Solon regarding their opinions on happiness. Aristotle, *Nicomachean Ethics*, 1179a9-17.

72. Ibid., 1117b29-32.

73. Ibid., 1147a33, 1148b13, 1149a21.

74. Think of the reformed drunkards addressed by Lincoln in his Temperance Speech, whom he playfully urged to follow a rule of *"mind, all conquering mind,"* to which Aristotle might add that such a course risks trading intemperance for unrestraint. Perhaps Aristotle, with his tongue as firmly in his cheek as Lincoln, also might have warned not to go overboard in pursuing "all conquering *mind.*" Abraham Lincoln, *The Collected Works of Abraham Lincoln*, Roy P. Basler, ed. (New Brunswick, N.J.: Rutgers University Press, 1953), I.279.

75. Aristotle, *Nicomachean Ethics*, 1147b34.

76. The most frequent translation of *thumos* is anger, a passion that contributes to unrestraint. It is not an adequate translation in all cases, however. For one thing, Aristotle employs *orgei* when he refers to anger elsewhere, for another, the unnecessary pleasures that apply in qualified unrestraint are desirable in themselves, which does not apply to anger, which carries an element of pain. Aristotle, *Nicomachean Ethics*, 1125b26-31, 1126a24; Aristotle, *Politics* 1312b33. Anger and spirit are connected, of course. The spirited are more prone to anger than those we think of as dispirited and it is allowable to say, perhaps, that the angry display spirit, but the spirited are not necessarily angry. See Aristotle, *Rhetoric*, 1387a20-1388b30; Aristotle, *Politics* 1334b23; Aristotle, *Nicomachean Ethics*, 1105b21, 1111a25-b4. The translators' choices reflect *thumos'* ambiguity: Rackham, anger and passion; Ross, anger; Irwin, emotion; Sachs, spiritedness; Broadie and Rowe, temper. On the mixing of anger and spirit, see, for a start, Carnes Lord, *Education and Culture in the Political Thought of Aristotle* (Ithaca, N.Y.: Cornell University Press, 1982), 161; Walsh, *Moral Weakness*, 35, 86; Tessitore, *Aristotle's Ethics*, 56; Berns, "Spiritedness," 345; Seth Benardete, *Socrates' Second Sailing* (Chicago: University of Chicago Press, 1989), 55-6; Barbara Koziak, *Retrieving Political Emotion* (State College, Pa.: Pennsylvania State University Press, 2000), 85.

77. Werner Dannhauser notes that Schleiermacher translates *thumos* as *eifer*, the German for zeal, and that for Nietzsche the quality is identified

with frenzy. "Spiritedness in *Thus Spoke Zarathustra*," in *Understanding the Political Spirit*, Catherine Zuckert, ed. (New Haven: Yale University Press, 1988), 181, 193. See, too, Waller R. Newell, *Ruling Passion: The Erotics of Statecraft in Platonic Political Philosophy* (Lanham, Md.: Rowman and Littlefield, 2000), 115.

78. Scholars go in opposite directions on the subject. For example, Arlene Saxonhouse builds on the Socratic image of the well-ordered soul and city to argue for *thumos* as the preserver of man-made rules, and thus something to be moderated or overcome if philosophy is to be free, "*Thymos*, Justice, and Moderation of Anger in the Story of Achilles," in Zuckert, *Understanding*, 30, 39-40. Mary Nichols, on the other hand, views it as in one sense united with philosophy and in another antagonistic to it. "Spiritedness and Philosophy in Plato's *Republic*," in Zuckert, *Understanding*, 48. The best source for the question is Newell's *Ruling Passion*.

79. Plato, *Republic*, 375a-e.

80. Benardete, *Second Sailing*, 56; Plato, *Republic*, 334a.

81. Newell, *Ruling Passion*, 103-104 (emphasis added). Compare Berns, "Spiritedness," 347.

82. Newell, *Ruling Passion*, 115, 156. See, too, Berns, "Spiritedness," 348.

83. Aristotle, *Nicomachean Ethics*, 1149b18.

84. Accepting that philosophy calls for an ascent from politics does not decide the question of how far the philosopher need go in the direction of evading politics and moral responsibility. On Platonic immoderation versus Aristotelian restraint, see, e.g., Allan Bloom, *Love and Friendship* (New York: Simon and Schuster, 1993), 537, 542; Newell, *Ruling Passion*, 160.

85. Aristotle, *Nicomachean Ethics*, 1148a23.

86. Ibid., 1151a29-b12.

87. Ibid., 1144a24, 1152a11-15, 25.

88. Ibid., 1146a19-22, 1151b17-22.

89. Alfarabi, "The Attainment of Happiness," In *Medieval Political Philosophy*, Ralph Lerner and Muhsin Mahdi, eds. (Ithaca, N.Y.: Cornell University Press, 1972 [originally published in 1963]), 80.

90. Plato, *Republic* 573b-c, Aristotle. *Nicomachean Ethics* 1152a28; Lord, *Education and Culture*, 163. See, too, note 5 above.

About the Editors
and Contributors

Paul Carrese is associate professor of political science at the United States Air Force Academy. He has been a Rhodes Scholar and held a post-doctoral fellowship in the Program on Constitutional Government, Harvard University. He is author of *The Cloaking of Power: Montesquieu, Blackstone, and the Rise of Judicial Activism*.

Eric R. Claeys is assistant professor at St. Louis University School of Law. A former clerk for Chief Justice William Rehnquist, he is author of monographs and scholarly articles on constitutional law. He is preparing a book on zoning and eminent domain.

Edward J. Erler is professor of political science at California State University at San Bernardino. He is author of *The American Polity* and has forthcoming a collection of essays on American politics. He is a senior fellow of the Claremont Institute.

Tiffany R. Jones is assistant professor of politics at the University of Dallas. She is preparing a book on the threats to the First Amendment in campaign finance reform. Her work emphasizes the hold of Progressivism on current political thought and practice.

John Marini is a senior fellow of the Claremont Institute and an associate professor of political science at the University of Nevada, Reno. He is co-editor of *The Imperial Congress: Crisis in the Separation of Powers* and author of *The Politics of Budget Control: Congress, the Presidency, and the Growth of* *the Administrative State*. From 1987-1988 he was a special assistant to Chairman Clarence Thomas of the U.S. Equal Employment Opportunity Commission.

Ken Masugi is Director of the Center for Local Government at the Claremont Institute. He is co-author, co-editor, or editor of seven books on American politics and political thought, including most recently *The California Republic*. His teaching positions have included the John M. Olin Distinguished Visiting Professorship at the United States Air Force Academy. From 1986-1990 he served as a special assistant to Chairman Clarence Thomas of the U.S. Equal Employment Opportunity Commission.

Will Morrisey is assistant professor of history and political science at Hillsdale College. His most recent books are *Self-Government, The American Theme: Presidents of the Founding and Civil War* and *Regime Change: What It Is, Why It Matters*. He is currently working on a study of self-government in the political thought of the presidents of the Progressive era.

Peter C. Myers is associate professor of political science at the University of Wisconsin, Eau Claire. He is author of *Our Only Star and Compass: Locke and the Struggle for Political Rationality*. He is writing a book on the thought and statesmanship of Frederick Douglass.

Larry Peterman is professor of political science at the University of California, Davis, and a senior fellow of the Claremont Institute. He has written extensively on Dante and on Machiavelli, among other major political theorists. Recently he has been studying family privacy in modern political thought.

John G. West is associate professor of political science at Seattle Pacific University and a senior fellow of the Discovery Institute, where he directs the program on religion and civic life. He is author of *The Politics of Revelation and Reason*.

Thomas G. West is professor of politics at the University of Dallas. A senior fellow of the Claremont Institute, he is author of *Vindicating the Founders* and *Plato's Apology of Socrates*. He is co-editor of *Shakespeare as Political Thinker* and most recently of *Challenges to the American Founding* and *The American Founding and the Social Compact*. He is co-translator and editor of *Four Texts on Socrates*.

Scot J. Zentner is professor of political science at California State University, San Bernardino. He has published extensively on the American party system and Progressivism. He is currently editing a collection of essays on Harry V. Jaffa's thought.

Index